Pentecostal and Charismatic Studies

For
Matthew and Samuel Kay
and for
Andrew and Miriam Dyer

Pentecostal and Charismatic Studies

A Reader

Edited by
William K. Kay
and
Anne E. Dyer

scm press

British Library Cataloguing in Publication data

A catalogue record for this book is available from the British Library

Bible extracts are from the Authorized Version of the Bible (the King James Bible), the rights of which are vested in the Crown, and are reproduced by permission of the Crown's Patentee, Cambridge University Press.

0 334 02940 6

First published in 2004 by SCM Press
9-17 St Albans Place, London N1 0NX

www.scm-canterburypress.co.uk

SCM Press is a division of
SCM-Canterbury Press Ltd

Typeset by Regent Typesetting, London
Printed and bound in Great Britain by
Biddles Ltd, www.biddles.co.uk

CONTENTS

PART 1   HISTORY

PART 2   THEOLOGY

PART 3   THEOLOGY IN PRACTICE

PART 4   ISSUES

Preface

Like many books, this one has complicated origins. Andrew Walls was at one time the external examiner for undergraduate degrees validated by the University of Sheffield, and then subsequently Wales, at Mattersey Hall, the Assemblies of God Bible College in Britain. During a feedback day to the faculty, Professor Walls called attention to the need for a reader in Pentecostal and charismatic texts.

Sometime later I was appointed to posts at two British universities, King's College London and the University of Wales, Bangor. I was appointed the first Director of the Centre for Pentecostal and Charismatic Studies in the Theology and Religious Studies Department at Bangor – a move that seems entirely to the credit of the department and especially to Professors Gareth Lloyd-Jones and Leslie Francis. A little later I noticed that three members of the theology department at King's College had produced a reader entitled *The Practice of Theology*. I telephoned Colin Gunton asking whether it would be sensible to contact SCM Press and propose a further reader that might fit into a series that had the King's College imprint on it. He warmed to the idea. So I made my proposal to SCM Press while, at the same time, wanting to unite the two aspects of my working life. My students at Bangor needed a reader to allow them to grapple with the complexities of the subject I taught them, and to stimulate their research. A little later, when the British Academy provided funding, Anne Dyer joined the work.

As we began the enormous task of collecting texts that might represent 100 years of Pentecostalism, it became clear that it would be impossible to do perfect justice to the vast phenomenon that is worldwide Pentecostalism today. We have taken editorial decisions that have been guided by attempts to present the variety of views within the Pentecostal movement while, at the same time, showing how these views have developed or diversified over time. Inevitably there are sections of the Pentecostal movement that we may have been deaf to and others that have been omitted for lack of space or because they are represented elsewhere by other equally good extracts. We apologize to those we have overlooked. Our intention, however, has been to allow readers of this book to grasp firsthand the *typical and representative* words of Pentecostals as writers, speakers and preachers, to appreciate their concerns and understand the imperatives that shaped their world. Indeed, if possible, we would like readers to grasp the religious experiences that transfigured them. Essentially, therefore, we want people to see the movement for what it is, with all its good and bad, and to throw aside prejudices and misconceptions, whether these stem from a theological position or from a secular humanistic perspective.

It is particularly the preached word that represents Pentecostalism, since the campaigns, crusades, church meetings, house meetings, conferences and cell groups all involve some form of preaching. So here, in this collection of texts, you will detect the voice of preachers. Yet from the 1960s onwards Pentecostalism found itself coexisting with the charismatic movement. Whether the charismatic movement sprang from the Pentecostal movement, or was generated spontaneously in much the same way as the Pentecostal movement itself, is a matter that is difficult to answer and may vary from country to country. In any event the charismatic movement and its subsequent waves of influence are also included within the compass of this collection of texts. Sometimes there is an argument between Pentecostals and charismatics, and at other times there is debate within sections of these different 'waves'. This helps create theological variety.

At a future conjunction of technology and opportunity, publishing may make a quantum leap forward. Books may come to incorporate video clips and snatches of audio so that the printed page will coexist and interact with visual and verbal records. Only such a multi-media collection would do justice to the energy and variety of the Pentecostal and charismatic movements. Meanwhile we ask you to read what is collected here remembering that much, but by no means all, of what is given in the following pages is derived from busy and worshipping lives; this is not a compendium of the thoughts of scholar bishops or cave-dwelling hermits.

Yet the texts have this in common: they were all originally written in English and, for this reason, stand for a certain kind of Pentecostal and charismatic life. We are conscious that Latin America and Asia are not heard as loudly as they should be and we hope that scholars from these countries will compile their own collections in due time.

In one respect this book is an historical record and in another it is an attempt to let the Pentecostal and charismatic movements explain themselves. We have an eye on the future and this is why the collection has been dedicated to the children of each of the editors' separate families. Also the editors have experienced slightly different aspects of the whole movement but both wish to pass on its complex and vigorous heritage to the next generation. Anne Dyer and her husband were on the mission field in Thailand for 12 years and had a more charismatic than classical Pentecostal background, and William Kay, within a classical Pentecostal tradition, helped train Pentecostal and charismatic ministers for 10 years, during the 1980s and 1990s.

We are grateful to the editors at SCM Press, Alex Wright, Anna Hardman and Mary Matthews, as well as to Jill Wallis, for the patience and support they have given us in the production of this book. Other debts of gratitude are recorded in the acknowledgements.

William K. Kay
Anne E. Dyer

February 2004

Acknowledgements

We gratefully acknowledge the financial support (SG 34643) of the British Academy in the preparation of this text.

We also gratefully acknowledge the assistance of the archivist, Dr D. Garrard, for the materials found within the Donald Gee Centre for Pentecostal and Charismatic Research at Mattersey Hall, Nottinghamshire.

Equally thanks are also due to Dr Dave Allen for his help in compiling the extracts used in the eschatology section and to Mrs Beryl Allen for making library resources available at Mattersley.

We also appreciated the support of colleagues at the Centre for Ministry Studies at the University of Wales, Bangor, and particularly the help of Revd Professor L. J. Francis and Dr Mandy Robbins.

Staff at the Flower Pentecostal Heritage Center, Springfield, Missouri, including Wayne Warner, Joyce Lee and Brett Pavia, were also unfailingly efficient and helpful.

Gratitude should also go to the editors' families for their patience while the editors scoured archives and spent hours deciding which of the many possible items in 100 years of Pentecostal/charismatic history and theology should be included.

Abbreviations

AG	Assemblies of God, USA
AoG	[British] Assemblies of God
ASV	American Standard Version
AV	Authorized Version
IPCH	International Pentecostal Church of Holiness
KJV	King James Version
NIV	New International Version
NJV	New Jerusalem Version
NKJV	New King James Version
RSV	Revised Standard Version
RV	Revised Version
UPUSA	United Presbyterian Church, USA

Introduction

The purpose of this book

Since about 1900 the Pentecostal and charismatic movements have renewed, reformed and expanded great sections of Christianity.[1] At the centre of these movements is an experience. It is an experience of the Holy Spirit similar to that enjoyed by members of the early Church on the day of Pentecost and described in the Bible in the book of Acts – at least that is what Pentecostals and charismatics, with good reason, claim. The experience issues in a variety of *charismata* or spiritual gifts, including speaking with other tongues or glossolalia. The experience results in congregations which, at their best, adopt flexible patterns of 'being church' and powerful forms of leadership. In terms of worship, they are participatory and spontaneous and often weave together music and extempore prayer into a rich and harmonious whole; they stand in the same relationship to liturgical forms of worship as jazz stands to classical music. For, while liturgies are orchestrated by great verbal composers like Thomas Cranmer or St John Chrysostom whose prayers and responses are kept in sacred order within unchanging texts, Pentecostal worship (though not always charismatic, see 3.8) is unpredictable and largely unwritten and yet, like jazz, has a distinct sound and shape.

The Pentecostal and charismatic movements began and continued in a flurry of activity. Pamphlets, tracts, magazine articles, paperback books and editorials were written to meet sudden needs.[2] Conferences were held, tapes and videos were circulated, and the theology of the movement was often worked out 'on the wing'. Unfortunately, the material relating to the early years of Pentecostalism is difficult to obtain. It is to be found in archives and out-of-print or discontinued journals so that any serious or dependable study of the movement has difficulty in assessing its formative years.

---

[1] There were certainly Pentecostal-type outpourings of the Spirit after 1886 on the North Carolina–Tennessee boundary among farming communities whose converts became part of the Church of God. See C. W. Conn (1977), *Like a Mighty Army: A History of the Church of God 1886–1976*, Cleveland, Tenn.: Pathway Press. See also extract 1.3.

[2] See for instance, M. J. Taylor (1994), 'Publish and Be Blessed: A Case Study in Early Pentecostal Publishing History, 1906–1926', unpublished PhD dissertation, University of Birmingham.

We have made the assumption that academic theologians may well wish to re-examine the genesis and characteristics of the Pentecostal–charismatic movement. We also anticipate that undergraduate programmes may wish to cover the Pentecostal–charismatic movement and be unable to lay their hands on primary documents. Our aim has been to provide such documents and we have grouped them together into sets with the intention of showing the breadth of views entertained by Pentecostals and charismatics and the development of those views over time. Most of the sets are introduced and given an editorial perspective. Sometimes, as in the case of healing, the full range of views was already embryonically present from the very beginning, and, over the years, preachers and writers enhanced aspects of it according to their own convictions. At other times there is a more clear succession of ideas as, for example, in missions. At others, there are preferences for one position among Pentecostals and preferences for other positions by charismatics, as in the dispute over 'initial evidence' for the baptism in the Holy Spirit.

There should be enough information here to make a contribution to courses dealing with *twentieth-century theology*. There is evidence both for the distinctive beliefs of Pentecostals about speaking with tongues and for the eschatological mindset and context in which they worked out those beliefs. On many themes there is evidence for the development of those beliefs over time. There is also evidence for the oral nature of Pentecostal and charismatic theology within the black churches and its connection with vibrant non-liturgical worship.

Equally there ought to be enough material in this book to contribute towards a course on *Pentecostal and charismatic history*. The story of the movements is short enough to be encompassed in an undergraduate course and interesting enough to capture the attention of theology students of all kinds. There is evidence within these pages for revivals, crusades, camp meetings, renewals, television broadcasts and international perspectives on the entire process. Just as students might study the Methodist revival, the Mennonites or the Oxford Movement as part of the church history course, so the Pentecostal movement of the twentieth and twenty-first centuries is ready for exploration.

For those interested in the *sociology of religion* there are non-theoretical extracts (Chapters 11–21) that show how the Pentecostal and charismatic movements responded to changes within western culture during the twentieth century. We gain insight into the Azusa Street revival where blacks and whites mingled in the poorer districts of booming Los Angeles; we see pacifism in the United States coexist with patriotism; we hear the thinking behind the leadership structures necessary for new churches; we see the confrontation between an increasingly secular western society and 'power evangelism'; we gain an impression of the scale of megachurch communities.

For those concerned with *religious education in schools* the extracts offer information about non-liturgical Christianity that could be arranged into doctrinal, experiential or ethical themes.[3] The extracts dealing with Azusa Street (2.2–3) or the Latter Rain (2.6; 3.3) give an insight into the subjective reality of religious experience while the selection from *The Cross and the Switchblade* (Chapter 16) shows how a belief in the Holy Spirit has been relevant to 'doing cold turkey' or breaking free from addiction to hard drugs without medication. These are matters of interest to teenage pupils.

Historical overview

In an overview of the Pentecostal and subsequent charismatic movements over the course of the twentieth century there are various agreed phases and landmarks even though the twists and turns of the narrative vary from country to country. Charles Fox Parham styled himself the 'projector' of the Apostolic Faith after the students at his Bible School in Topeka, Kansas, realized that speaking with other tongues was the sign of the baptism in the Holy Spirit (2.1). Though there may be questions about Parham's exact role in the formulation of what became a doctrine, there is no doubt that the Azusa Street revival (1906–9) is judged to be a crucial stimulus and example for subsequent Pentecostalism (2.2; 12.1). It took place on the west coast of the United States in Los Angeles and was accessible to Asia across the Pacific Ocean and by rail to the Midwest and the rest of North America.

In the decades immediately following – roughly 1910–30 – there was planting and building. New Pentecostal movements in South America and South Africa (with John G. Lake) as well as in Norway (with T. B. Barratt), Britain (with Alexander Boddy), Germany and the Netherlands (with Geritt Polman) came into being. Once the initial centre of teaching or revival had spread to a particular country, institutional and denominational structures, however loosely, began to be formed. There was often bickering between proto-denominations of a more or less serious nature within each country as they established themselves but, after a decade or so, the dust began to settle and the outlines of the new groupings could be clearly seen. This period of consolidation (2.4; 2.5) and expansion lasted at least until the 1940s. Global economic recession did not inhibit the growth of Pentecostalism and important evangelistic campaigns were held in many major western cities (4.4; 4.8).

---

[3] This is an approach to religious education originally outlined by Ninian Smart (1968), *Secular Education and the Logic of Religion*, London: Faber & Faber.

It is arguable that the Pentecostal movement began to show signs of tiring within the 1940s as the early exuberant and bold pioneers began to reach middle or old age. However, a better account might accept the sociological analysis that the early pioneers began to find themselves boxed in by the bureaucratic and administrative machinery they had created for the running of the congregations that had been brought into existence. The freedom and flexibility of the early years began to be trammelled by the constitutional guidelines.[4] In any event it is possible to describe the Latter Rain movement of 1948 as a renewal movement within Pentecostalism.[5] It reasserted the need for contemporary apostles and prophets who were not answerable to constitutional committees and it recalled the importance of direct and overwhelming spiritual experience (2.6). The breadth of its impact was limited because it eventually promoted an over-realized eschatology, but its momentum was later transferred to independent healing evangelists whose media profile helped to broadcast Pentecostalism during the 1950s and 1960s.[6]

It was in the 1960s that the Spirit was outpoured upon the mainline churches and denominations, whether Episcopal or Anglican, Roman Catholic, Baptist or Methodist, which created charismatic streams within them. The streams excited the grass-roots with spiritual refreshment rather than revival but, in most of these denominations, charismatic conferences, parishes or magazines grew up as did bishops or cardinals who fostered the exercise of charismatic gifts within their jurisdictions and who sang many of the same songs, read many of the same books and found affinity among themselves. By the mid-1960s the Full Gospel Business Men's Fellowship International, acting in more than 80 countries as a para-church organization, was functioning as an attractive disseminating network for charismatic testimonies and gifts.[7] They created an impact in Britain when they jetted in, hired rooms in the most expensive hotels, invited Christians to prayer breakfasts where powerful testimonies were given, prayed for guests to receive the baptism in the Spirit and, within a couple of days, left to do the same thing elsewhere.

The charismatic movement was distinct from the Pentecostal movement of the 1920s and 1930s in the sense that the existing ecclesiastical structures and terminologies of the mainline denominations were left intact.

---

[4] B. R. Wilson (1961), *Sects and Society*, London: Heinemann.

[5] A view taken by Richard M. Riss (1988), *A Survey of Twentieth Century Revival Movements in North America*, Peabody, Mass.: Hendrickson.

[6] The *Voice of Healing* magazine, published 1948–67, further popularized a spate of healing evangelism.

[7] The FGBMFI forbade anyone who was ordained being elected to office: this had the effect of ensuring that its leadership remained in lay hands.

Anglicans did not turn their bishops into apostles; Roman Catholics did not alter the functions of various parts of their hierarchy; Lutherans did not alter the initiation rites to their churches. In effect, the charismatic outpouring, after the early excitement, often turned into a spiritual renewal that was inward and personal rather than outward, institutional and evangelistic. In theological terms and broadly speaking, the charismatic movement at first accepted the Pentecostal emphasis on a sudden new post-conversion baptism with power for service that was associated with the exercise of charismatic gifts but then retrenched and began to assimilate language about the Holy Spirit to sacramental theologies so as to preserve the validity of initiation rites concerning children (7.2; 21.1).

Yet even this general description of the charismatic movement is an over-simplification because different denominations and different parts of different denominations reacted to preserve the impact of the outpoured Spirit in different ways. Moreover the impact of the charismatic movement within the United States, when coupled with burgeoning Christian broadcasting, helped to enlarge potential audiences and raise the profile of charismatic and Pentecostal Christianity in complicated new ways. Religious television expanded its audience base in a way that helped create a conservative voice in public affairs while at the same time, and paradoxically, helping to pioneer a new chat-show form of confessional television that was focused on individual needs.[8] By contrast television was much more closely controlled within Europe from 1960 to 1990 and only the emergence of cable and satellite technologies helped to free broadcasting from quasi-governmental control. Yet by the early 1990s it was beginning to be possible to integrate Christian broadcasting with the Internet revolution and with home access to the world wide web as well as with devices for producing digital materials on CD-ROM, DVD or MP3; the potential for the spreading of Christian teaching, music and evangelistic packages grew exponentially.

Within the western world in the 1970s and 1980s new congregations emerged drawing from both Pentecostal and charismatic heritages. These were churches that might have begun as independent Pentecostal congregations or have attracted personnel with charismatic backgrounds. In Britain they were first called House Churches and then New Churches. They combined elements of charismatic theology with Pentecostal experience, and some were large and soon set up their own magazines, Bible schools and broadcasting facilities. The point here is that there is a contrast between the 1960s when the charismatic movement was confined to the

---

[8] The format and tone of Jerry Springer and Oprah Winfrey is not dissimilar to that of Bakker's *Praise the Lord*.

diocesan and hierarchical structures of mainline denominations and the 1970s and 1980s when, bit by bit, parts of it were transformed into something new, independent and freestanding. They became, depending on how you looked at it, unnecessary competitors against the classical Pentecostal churches in the religious marketplace or flexible innovative networks ready to appeal to baby-boomers and generation-Xers alike.

The 1990s were characterized by what might be called the second renewal movement within the Pentecostal and charismatic scene. This was the 'Toronto blessing'. It spread rapidly from Toronto across the world and jumped boundaries by being found in the classical Pentecostal groups, within charismatic settings in mainline denominations and within New Churches (20.1; 20.2). This is not to say that the Toronto blessing was universally welcomed; indeed, it was condemned by non-Pentecostals and non-charismatics and by some Pentecostals and charismatics who saw it as a doctrineless or unbiblical saturation in a questionable but possibly harmless form of experience that had little to do with the New Testament.[9] Yet, because the Toronto blessing could be seen as the sign of a fresh revival that would reach beyond the walls of churches into the streets and into the heart of society, its importance was magnified. In some quarters Toronto was seen as being pregnant with hope for the rapid Christianization of a secularized world. In the event, Toronto died down by about 1997 and, while it may have loosened collars and structures, failed to deliver the promises its uncritical proponents proclaimed. Revival failed to arrive. The normal business of church life, evangelism and church-planting continued.

At this point, we must admit we have not attempted to give alternative conceptions of the development of the Pentecostal and charismatic movements. For instance Hwa, writing from a Singaporean perspective, argues that we should not see the movements in three waves – classical Pentecostal, then charismatic, then new churches – because this pattern only applies satisfactorily to western churches. Instead we should recognize that other configurations apply in Asia where the waves may be breaking *simultaneously* onto diverse populations some of whom share a supernaturalistic worldview and some of whom do not.[10] As editors, we do not question alternative readings of history but we need to say loud and clear that, for the purposes of the collection of texts in this book, we

---

[9] See the searching assessment, 'Ecstatic Spirituality and Entrepreneurial Revivalism: Reflections on the "Toronto Blessing"' by Rob Warner (2003), in A. Walker and K. Aune (eds), *On Revival: A Critical Examination*, Carlisle: Paternoster.

[10] Hwa Yung (2003), 'Endued with Power: the Pentecostal–charismatic Renewal and the Asian Church of the Twenty-first Century', *Asian Journal of Pentecostal Studies* 6.1, 63–82.

have been limited to works that are written in English. Naturally, English-language texts tend to be weighted towards the western hemisphere and its perspectives. We contend that it is impossible to write 'the view from everywhere' and that criticisms that we should be more Asio-centric or Afro-centric miss the point; Asio-centric or Afro-centric accounts would be open to the accusation of being eccentric in their own ways. Since editors are not omniscient, they must work within the languages and cultures with which they are familiar.

Orientation: Pentecostalism

Academic theology, the psychology of religion, the sociology of religion and cultural studies have rarely paid proper attention to the Pentecostal and charismatic movements. Early in the twentieth century the Pentecostal movement began in a humble (though not necessarily a quiet!) way at various places in the world. There had been stirrings within the Holiness Church in Tennessee at the end of the 1890s (1.3) and then, at the very start of the twentieth century, there were independent prayer and revival groups in Wales, Scotland and India.[11] Historical consensus, however, takes the Azusa Street revival in Los Angeles of 1907 as the crucial starting-point for Pentecostal expansion since it was from here that many of the main protagonists of Pentecostal life and experience first caught fire. It is true that the Welsh Revival of 1904–5 indicated heartfelt religious fervour, but the distinct marks of Pentecostalism, notably speaking with other tongues, are usually thought to have been absent from that revival even though the characteristically Pentecostal phrase 'baptism in the Spirit' was to be heard on the lips of Evan Roberts, the man at the centre of those events (1.2).[12]

The Azusa Street revival occurred in a converted livery stable in a poor district of Los Angeles, USA, and was, in its first phases, notable for the mixed-race congregation that grew up around the black preacher W. J. Seymour (2.2). The son of a freed slave, Seymour was in no doubt about the importance of speaking with other tongues and the value of the

---

[11] C. W. Conn (1977), *Like a Mighty Army: A History of the Church of God 1886–1976*, Cleveland, Tenn.: Pathway Press; G. Gee (1967), *Wind and Flame*, Nottingham: Assemblies of God Publishing House; D. Bundy (1992), 'Thomas B. Barratt and Byposten: An Early European Pentecostal Leader and his Periodical', in J. A. B. Jongeneel, C. van der Laan, P. N. van der Laan, M. Robinson and P. Staples (eds), *Pentecost, Mission and Ecumenism: Essays on Intercultural Theology*, Berlin: Peter Lang.

[12] B. P. Jones (1995), *An Instrument of Revival: The Complete Life of Evan Roberts 1878–1951*, South Plainfield, NJ: Bridge Publishing.

baptism in the Spirit in producing an end-time racially mixed church with evangelistic and missionary zeal. He was not a man to seek spiritual experience for its own sake and, when he *did* receive spiritual experience, he placed it firmly within a theological context derived from the Bible.[13] Most of the major Pentecostal denominations can trace themselves back one way or another to Azusa Street, and therefore to Seymour's influence, though many of their personnel came from earlier evangelical, holiness or revival groups with theological concerns of their own, and a significant proportion of them were missionaries.[14]

Some writers have seen the days before the First World War as an innocent and idyllic epoch.[15] The British Empire was at its height and this allowed the British missionaries to travel with the protection of a British passport and the comfort of a currency that was the strongest in the world. The telegraph, the train and iron steamships facilitated communication and travel, and at long last brought to an end the age of the horse and the stagecoach. By the close of the nineteenth century, Protestant missions had already gained success in Africa, India and China and established new congregations and, often, schools and hospitals. When the Pentecostal revival began, its impact spread rapidly in all directions: missionaries returned to the countries where they worked and, in the United States, and later in Europe, holiness and other independent groups realigned themselves into what became classical Pentecostal denominations.

Even so, the rapid growth and acceptance of Pentecostalism is astonishing. During the course of the remaining years of the twentieth century approximately 500 million people shared in the Pentecostal experience. It became another branch or brand or movement within the Church, rivalling the staid Roman Catholic and Protestant forms that had been built up over the preceding centuries.[16] Unlike communism, which also burst into the twentieth century at roughly the same time (the Russian Revolution occurred in 1917, only ten years after Azusa), Pentecostalism had no state funding, military police, propaganda apparatus, armies or other means of

---

[13] He learnt this aspect of his theology from Parham and took the message that tongues was the sign of the baptism in the Spirit from Topeka to Los Angeles.

[14] C. M. Robeck (2002), 'Azusa Street Revival', in S. Burgess and E. van der Maas (eds), *New International Dictionary of Pentecostal and Charismatic Movements*, 2nd edn., Grand Rapids, Mich.: Zondervan.

[15] B. Russell (1956), *Portraits from Memory*, London: George Allen & Unwin, p. 7, 'For those who are too young to remember the world before 1914, it must be difficult to imagine the contrast for a man of my age between childhood memories and the world of the present day.'

[16] D. B. Barrett and T. M. Johnson (1998), 'Annual statistical table on global mission: 1998', *International Bulletin* 22.1, 26, 27.

enforcing and spreading its message. So the story of the rise and spread of Pentecostalism is one of individual endeavour, church-planting and growth, and steady denominational building; it is not the story of armed insurrection, political chicanery and military coups. As Pentecostalism grew, its doctrine and its institutional infrastructure gradually diversified or, perhaps more accurately, its doctrine at first narrowed in the early unsettled days after its birth and then, when the first generation of Pentecostals had fought their battles and were contemplating retirement, reflected on itself and broadened in the second half of the century.[17] But the broadening does not mean all Pentecostals accepted variants on their tradition, only that several views might be found in each Pentecostal group when only one had previously been acceptable.

Within academic circles there has been discussion about whether the Pentecostal movement should be seen as a further phase of Protestant missionary expansion: from Asia to Europe in the first centuries of the common era, from Europe to the United States in the seventeenth century, and subsequently from the United States to the rest of the world.[18] Or, should the Pentecostal movement be seen as being essentially African in style and spirituality (following the example of Seymour), which has betrayed its origins by embracing western capitalism?[19] Worse, should Pentecostalism be seen as having forsaken its early testimony to the racial unity of the Spirit-filled church by splitting denominationally along racial lines?[20]

---

[17] Among the battles fought by the first generation of Pentecostals were those regarding the nature of the deity. After a sharp debate, the great majority of Pentecostals affirmed their faith in the Trinity, but a small minority asserted Oneness doctrine. See D. Barrett and T. Johnson (2002), 'Global Statistics', in S. Burgess and E. Van der Maas (eds), *New International Dictionary of Pentecostal and Charismatic Movements*, 2nd edn, Grand Rapids, Mich.: Zondervan. About 1 per cent of Pentecostals and charismatics worldwide follow Oneness doctrine; in the USA the percentages are higher. The texts selected here follow the main Trinitarian tradition. Pentecostal theology broadened in an ecumenical direction while at the same time accepting the validity of variant eschatologies and Christian initiations.

[18] As, in a complex way, might be argued from Mark Noll's analysis of the impact of the 1910 Edinburgh Missionary Conference. See M. A. Noll (1997), *Turning Points: Decisive Moments in the History of Christianity*, Leicester: InterVarsity Press.

[19] A view supported by aspects of Harvey Cox (1996), *Fire from Heaven*, London: Cassell, e.g. p. 101. The criticism of W. J. Hollenweger's (1997), *Pentecostalism: Origins and Developments Worldwide*, Peabody, Mass.: Hendrickson, in his chapters on 'the black oral root' of Pentecostalism, is more trenchant.

[20] A view argued by Iain MacRobert (1992), 'The Black Roots of Pentecostalism', in J. A. B. Jongeneel, C. van der Laan, P. N. van der Laan, M. Robinson and P. Staples (eds), *Pentecost, Mission and Ecumenism: Essays on Intercultural Theology*, Berlin: Peter Lang.

Certainly the Pentecostal denominations that emerged in the post-Azusa period were often fragmented on largely racial lines and it is to the credit of Charles H. Mason that the Church of God in Christ, among others, persisted in the struggle for interracialism.[21] Or, again, should Pentecostalism be seen as a world movement with no real point of origin and, where missionary work did burgeon into vast success, should the Pentecostalism of Latin America, parts of Africa or Asia, for example, be seen as a culturally adapted form owing as much, by the end of the twentieth century, to its indigenous roots as it ever did to the western church?[22] Or, in a synthesising proposal, should the Pentecostal movement be seen as an expression of primal spirituality – that is, a spirituality underlying the human condition itself – whose expression is contingent upon historical and cultural factors?[23] These are questions that, while they are certainly arresting, cannot be resolved without further detailed multi-national research. In the absence of this research we have taken the view that Pentecostalism's shape and feel should be seen as being crucially influenced by the revivalism and holiness disciplines of the beginning of the twentieth century in the United States simply because American preachers, American vitality and, by the end of the century, American money and technology, were so enormously influential: globalization is among other things the exporting of American culture.

These questions about the cultural baggage carried by the Pentecostal movement are in one sense unimportant. Pentecostals would argue that there is a transcendent revelation of God in Christ, confirmed by the Spirit, that is at the heart of Christianity. In other words that there is a clear and sharp distinction between the content of the gospel and its cultural accretions and clothing. Yet, the cultural baggage of Pentecostalism and, in a more attenuated way, of the (neo)charismatic movement is important

---

[21] See D. D. Daniels (2002), 'Charles Harrison Mason: The Interracial Impulse of Early Pentecostalism', in J. R. Goff and Grant Wacker (eds), *Portraits of a Generation*, Fayetteville: University of Arkansas Press, pp. 255–70.

[22] This is a line of argument that can be deduced from a reading of David D. Daniels (1999), '"Everybody Bids you Welcome": A Multicultural Approach to North American Pentecostalism', in M. W. Dempster, B. D. Klaus and D. Petersen (eds), *The Globalisation of Pentecostalism*, Carlisle: Regnum. Similarly the introduction to S. Burgess and E. van der Maas (eds), *New International Dictionary of Pentecostal and Charismatic Movements* (2nd edn), Grand Rapids, Mich.: Zondervan, p. xvii, points out that Pentecostal phenomena were known in Africa, England, Finland, Russia and India well before the twentieth century. See also Allan Anderson (2004), *An Introduction to Pentecostalism: Global Charismatic Christianity*, Cambridge: Cambridge University Press.

[23] Essentially, the thesis of Harvey Cox (1996), *Fire from Heaven*, London: Cassell.

when attempts at evaluation are made. What is central to these movements and what is peripheral? What is essential and what is accidental? The point we would wish to make is that nearly all religious forms and movements bring with them cultural additions. When the Hindu emigrates from India to Europe, the sari very often continues to be worn even though it is clothing unsuitable in the colder climate. When the orthodox Jew left the ghettos of central Europe and settled in Israel, he took with him a traditional black coat and fur-rimmed hat. As a result, in the heat of Jerusalem Orthodox Jews swelter in the summer weather. Even today during at least one of the liturgies of Russian Orthodoxy a movement is made by the priest to scare flies from the altar – and this movement is made even in countries and at times of the year when there are no flies to be seen. We conclude that the incorporation of cultural patterns into the stream of religion is a consequence of the nature of religion itself, as the examples from Judaism, Hinduism and Russian Orthodoxy show. This is because religion reproduces itself through religious communities, whether these are literal, cultural, academic or electronic.

We would argue that if American Pentecostals travel across the world and, in their spare time, play baseball or drink Coca-Cola, and their converts also learn to do this, this should be not a matter for criticism or derision. Similar criticisms were made of English missionaries in the nineteenth century who were said only to have taught their converts to play cricket – and such criticisms were only partly true and only true in the case of some missionaries. But culture and doctrine become more difficult to disentangle when one tries to analyse their impact on psychological dispositions or attitudes. Moreover, the difficulty is compounded when attitudes to political and economic freedom could be learnt from other sources than those provided by missionaries. The Philippines, for instance, were liberated after 1945 by American troops with the inevitable result that all things American, including its religion, were seen in a favourable light. An analogous commentary might be applied to South Korea. To connect Pentecostalism with capitalism is simplistic. There are individualistic and communitarian strands in Christianity as a whole, and the predominance of one over the other has little to do with capitalist drives.

There is a related complication for the Pentecostal movement about its linkage with contemporary culture. This concerns the impact of culture upon the nature of Pentecostalism itself. The crux of the matter can most easily be seen in relation to the televisual presentation of healing evangelism where the broadcasting medium has transformed the relationship between the evangelist and his or her congregation. Instead of a direct appeal by a sweaty evangelist who preaches with rolled up sleeves and a hoarse voice and who, at the end of the meeting, comes down from the platform to mingle with and lay hands on the congregation, we have a campaign that conforms itself to the parameters of the television studio. The evangelist is now in a suit, wearing television makeup, and the accompanying choir partakes of the production values of the entertainment programmes that precede and follow it on the broadcasting schedule. The evangelist has no direct physical contact with those who are prayed for and, though the preaching is beamed straight into the living room of the listeners, the electronic relationship is like that between a viewer and a celebrity rather than that between a congregant and a minister.

It is easy to feel that the original style of Pentecostalism is authentic and that the electronic version is inauthentic. This contrast occasionally comes through in the extracts selected within this book. The early extracts give an insight into the lives of determined and unrecognized pioneers of unquestionable sincerity. The later extracts may present a more institutional face. Although there is the truth in the contrast, it should not be assumed that more recent developments within the movements addressed in this book are necessarily a betrayal of original purity. It may be best to see the transformations within church structures that are occurring in these movements as being driven by complicated human needs and cultural forces. Opportunities to travel and to communicate have helped to give rise to the *megachurch*, and some of these are *cell churches*. Megachurches, especially in Korea or Latin America, use cells, or homegroups, to ensure that their members have close personal relationships in the surroundings of a home as well as the counterbalancing opportunity to belong to a large worshipping congregation where individual personalities are largely swallowed up. Although the cell provides personal relationships, however, this is not its primary purpose. It is intended to be a microcosm of the Church itself: to be a place of evangelism, discipleship, charismatic gifts and prayer, but particularly of evangelism (21.1).

Whether or not there is a cell structure in a megachurch, its huge size has the benefit of allowing it to provide a range of activities and resources for its members. There may be a school – a university even – broadcasting facilities, a sports hall, catering outlets, old people's homes, bookshops, recording studios, summer camps and affiliations with hotels and car rental businesses, that provide a complete social and intellectual environment for members while, at the same time, allowing the senior ministers to operate largely outside the constraints of denominational accountability. Statistics for American Assemblies of God show that, although only 1 per cent of its churches in the USA have more than 1,000 people, these churches, between them, account for more than 320,000 attenders, or 19 per cent of the total.[24]

---

[24] Assemblies of God, current facts, 2002. Order # 739086.

Instead of expecting members to battle against the general secular culture, megachurches have an opportunity to create their own Christianized microculture.

Continuation: the charismatic movement

The start of the charismatic movement is less complicated.[25] Again, there were stirrings in prayer and renewal groups in the previous decades but the eventual emergence of the fully-fledged charismatic movement is usually dated from the 1960s, an era of social change and freedom-loving individualism, in which the old mainline denominations found themselves facing a culture to which they were ill-adapted.[26] The charismatic movement is the spread of Pentecostal doctrine and experience – speaking in tongues, prophecy, healing, evangelism, house groups – to venerable ecclesiastical traditions for whom these were altogether unexpected phenomena. And there were surprises on both sides of the fence. The Pentecostals were surprised at the sudden embrace by mainline denominations of fresh spiritual experience. The charismatics were surprised to discover that the experiences they now enjoyed had been available for many years within Pentecostal settings. One can see the Pentecostal river as flooding over into new territory and creating new tributaries. Or, to use the biblical metaphor, new wine was being poured into old wine skins so that the old wine skins burst and changed shape. New religious forms, new styles of worship, new relationships between professional clergy and laity, new vision, new hope, new theologies of initiation and, inevitably, new problems followed.

So, while classical Pentecostals can be called 'the first wave', charismatics

---

[25] See P. D. Hocken (1984), 'Baptised in the Spirit: The Origins and Early Development of the Charismatic Movement in Great Britain', doctoral dissertation, University of Birmingham. This was published in at least two editions as *Streams of Renewal*, Carlisle: Paternoster. In one sense the origins of the charismatic movement *are* complicated because they are slightly different for each of the denominations that accepted charismata, but in another sense there were fewer struggles and less pain than there was with the birth of Pentecostalism.

[26] Hollenweger (1976) makes the point that the charismatic movement, in the sense of a non-Pentecostal denomination accepting charismatic phenomena, has existed since the formation of the Mulheim Association in 1910. Strictly speaking this is true. However, we have located the charismatic movement in the 1960s because of the sheer scale of the changes ushered in by the spiritual outpouring on the denominations in that decade. (W. J. Hollenweger (1976), 'Some Aspects of European Charismatics', in Russell P. Spittler (ed.), *Perspectives on the New Pentecostalism*, Grand Rapids, Mich.: Baker Book House, pp. 45–56.)

are the 'second wave'. The 'third wave',[27] coming in the early 1980s, comprised *both* men and women in the New Churches, people who broke free from their traditional denominations, Pentecostal or otherwise, to form new congregations, usually under the leadership of an apostolic figure *and* those involved in 'an increasing number of traditional evangelical churches and institutions [open] to the supernatural working of the Holy Spirit, even though they were not, nor did they wish to become, either Pentecostal or charismatic'.[28]

The New Churches emphasized personal relationships, the five ministry gifts found within Ephesians 4, and were normally unfettered by the remnants of any holiness code concerning clothing, drinking alcohol, television and other forms of adaptation to modern life (6.3; 6.5). They distinguish themselves from the classical Pentecostals by repudiating the constitutional basis and decision-making processes of committees which these denominations had adopted. In terms of numbers the New Church movement is a relatively small part of the 'third wave' but it has influence beyond its size to determine the agenda for the broad constituency to which both these groups belong. Indeed, so large has this constituency become that the *New International Dictionary of Pentecostal and Charismatic Movements* (pages xviif.) has broadened and relabelled third-wavers as 'neocharismatics' and included within this grouping Christian bodies with Pentecostal-like experiences with no traditional Pentecostal or charismatic denominational connections at all. So it is possible to classify the current position simply as comprising *Pentecostals* (denominational structures dating back to approximately the time of Azusa Street) and *neocharismatics* (everybody else with Pentecostal experience including those within main-line denominations, those within new churches and those in independent groups, for instance in Africa and China).

Although the diversity within the Pentecostal and neocharismatic movements is considerable, generalizations can be made about their attitude to that other worldwide trend within Christianity, the ecumenical movement. For many Pentecostals and neocharismatics the drive towards unity is slow, lumbering, probably boring, largely irrelevant and possibly sinister. For this reason, the relationship between the ecumenical movement, on the one hand, and the Pentecostal and neocharismatic movements, on the other, is complicated and underdeveloped. The complications arise from the diversity within both movements and the lack of development arises from the lack of enthusiasm among many

---

[27] A term coined by Peter Wagner in 1983.

[28] C. Peter Wagner in *Christian Life*, 1986, quoted by John Wimber in Kevin Springer (1987), *Riding the Third Wave*, Basingstoke: Marshall Pickering, p. 31.

Pentecostals and charismatics who can see no point in a form of doctrinal unity that slurs over the distinctives they hold dear. Indeed, the early Pentecostals and charismatics very often saw the 'unity of the Spirit' as being the 'true ecumenism' because it avoids the machinery of committees for its inception and implementation.

Note on the texts

All the texts have been prepared for publication on this basis: (a) the text should make sense as an independent unit of prose or poetry so that it can be read as it stands; (b) minor adjustments have been made to archaic or unusual spellings, the format of biblical references, capitalization of pronouns for God and unusual layout or punctuation so as to harmonize them; inclusive language (e.g. removing 'he' as a pronoun for God), however, has not been forced on any of the texts since this would be anachronistic and might change their meaning; (c) where abridgements have been made this is indicated by ellipses and in the heading; (d) where they have been given in this version biblical quotations have been retained in the words of the King James Bible; (e) occasionally references to forgotten individuals or events have been removed to allow for the free flow of sentences; (f) minor misprints or oddities of punctuation and grammar in the originals have been corrected; (g) extracts have been copied leaving their footnotes largely in their original formats.

PART 1
HISTORY

1 Precursors of Pentecostal and Charismatic History

Despite being considered unorthodox by prevailing denominationalists in the nineteenth century, Irving (1792–1834) daringly allowed the use of tongues in his meetings in 1830.

1.1 Gordon Strachan, *The Pentecostal Theology of Edward Irving,* London: Darton, Longman & Todd, 1973, pp. 70–2

Summer 1830

During the summer, Irving continued to receive information from those involved. 'Eye and ear witnesses, men of reputation, elders of the church' who he knew in the area of Port Glasgow and the Gareloch kept him posted as he endeavoured to leave no 'stone unturned in order to come at the truth'.[1] There was plenty of information to be passed on because manifestations continued to be in evidence at prayer meetings in the Macdonalds' house and at large gatherings in Helensburgh at which Mary Campbell wrote in tongues and prophesied.[2] These activities produced something of a national sensation and much literature began to be published about them. Large crowds gathered from all over the country. One of the Macdonald sisters wrote on 18 May, 'Ever since Margaret was raised and the gift of tongues given, the house has been filled every day with people from all parts of England, Scotland and Ireland.'[3] In Helensburgh it was recorded that Mary Campbell had attracted 'merchants, divinity students, writers to the Signet, advocates' and that 'gentlemen who rank high in society come from Edinburgh'.[4] It was an issue of spiritual importance and all felt called upon to decide for themselves whether or not these

---

[1] Edward Irving, 'Facts Connected with Recent Manifestations of Spiritual Gifts', *Frasers Magazine*, January 1832, pp. 755–6.

[2] W. Hanna, ed., *Letters of Thomas Erskine, of Linlathan*, 2nd edn, 1878, p. 132.

[3] Robert Norton MD, *Memoirs of James and George Macdonald of Port-Glasgow*, 1840, p. 125.

[4] Revd A. Robertson, *A Vindication of the Religion of the Land*, p. 311.

gifts were genuine. Many came to the conclusion that they were preten-
tious counterfeits but many more did not. The Revd Robert Story who was
the parish minister at Roseneath and who knew the Campbell family
intimately, went to visit Mary especially to judge for himself.[5] After doing
so he wrote to the Revd Dr Thomas Chalmers, Professor of Divinity at
Edinburgh, who was eager for a first-hand opinion, 'I am persuaded you
will be prepared to conclude that these things are of God and not of men.'[6]
. . .

When he returned he discovered that 'Mr Henderson and Dr Thompson
are fully convinced of the reality of the hand of God in the west country
work, and so is Mr Cardale.'[7] Mr Cardale gave a very favourable report on
all they had seen and heard. It was published in the December issue of *The
Morning Watch*. After describing the manner and matter of the gifts, which
he witnessed in operation and the lives of the gifted, he gave a testimony
to both:

> These persons, while uttering the unknown sounds, as also while speak-
> ing in the Spirit in their own language, have every appearance of being
> under supernatural direction. The manner and voice are (speaking
> generally) different from what they are at other times, and on ordinary
> occasions. This difference does not consist merely in the peculiar
> solemnity and fervour of manner (which they possess), but their whole
> deportment gives an impression, not to be conveyed in words, that their
> organs are made use of by supernatural power. In addition to the
> outward appearances, their own declarations, as the declarations of
> honest, pious, and sober individuals, may with propriety be taken in
> evidence. They declare that their organs of speech are made use of by the
> Spirit of God; and that they utter that which is given to them, and not the
> expressions of their own conceptions, or their own intention. But I had
> numerous opportunities of observing a variety of facts fully confirma-
> tory of this . . .
>
> In addition to what I have already stated, I have only to add my most
> decided testimony, that so far as three weeks' constant communication,
> and the information of those in the neighbourhood, can enable me to
> judge (and I conceive that the opportunity I enjoyed enabled me to form
> a correct judgement), the individuals thus gifted are persons living in
> close communion with God, and in love towards Him, and towards all
> men; abounding in faith and joy and peace; having an abhorrence of sin,

---

[5] Mrs M. O. W. Oliphant, *The Life of Edward Irving*, 1862, 5th edn, p. 290.

[6] R. H. Story, *Memoir of the Life of Rev Robert Story*, pp. 209–11.

[7] Mrs M. O. W. Oliphant, *The Life of Edward Irving*, p. 304.

and a thirst for holiness, with an abasement of self and yet with a hope full of immortality, such as I never witnessed elsewhere, and which I find nowhere recorded but in the history of the early church: and just as they are fervent in spirit, so are they diligent in the performance of all the relative duties of life. They are totally devoid of anything like fanaticism or enthusiasm; but, on the contrary, are persons of great simplicity of character, and of sound common sense. They have no fanciful theology of their own: they make no pretensions to deep knowledge: they are the very opposite of sectarians, both in conduct and principle: they do not assume to be teachers: they are not deeply read; but they seek to be taught of God, in the perusal of, and meditation on, his revealed word, and to 'live quiet and peaceable lives in all godliness and honesty'.[8]

Shortly after Mr Cardale and his party returned to London, the lay theologian Thomas Erskine of Linlathen arrived in Port Glasgow to assess the movement. He stayed for six weeks in the Macdonalds' house and took part in the daily prayer meetings, witnessing many spiritual manifestations. He had visited them briefly before as early as May and had declared himself to be 'more overpowered by the love, and assurance, and unity seen in their prayers and conversations than by the works'.[9] He now expressed his opinions of what he had experienced in a tract *On the Gifts of the Spirit* which he published before the end of the year. His findings were favourable:

Whilst I see nothing in Scripture against the reappearance or rather continuance of miraculous gifts in the Church, but a great deal for it, I must further say that I see a great deal of internal evidence in the West Country to prove their genuine miraculous character, especially in the speaking with tongues . . . After witnessing what I have witnessed, I cannot think of any person decidedly condemning them as impostors, without a feeling of great alarm. It is certainly not a thing to be lightly or rashly believed, but neither is it a thing to be lightly or rashly rejected. I believe that it is of God.

Permission sought.

---

[8] *Morning Watch* 2 (December 1830). John B. Cardale 'On the Extraordinary Manifestations in Port Glasgow'.

[9] W. Hanna, *Letters of Thomas Erskine*, p. 133.

News of these events went around the world stirring up Christians hungry for God. Though providing no definitive evidence of speaking in tongues, the Welsh Revival is often considered a catalyst to the Pentecostal Movement.

1.2   The Welsh Revival

On 12 November 1904, the *Western Mail* reported:

I felt that this was no ordinary gathering. Instead of the set order of proceedings to which we are accustomed at the orthodox religious service, everything here was left to the spontaneous impulse of the moment. The preacher [Evan Roberts], too, did not remain in his usual seat. For the most part he walked up and down the aisles, open Bible in one hand, exhorting one, encouraging another, and kneeling with a third to implore a blessing from the Throne of God. A young woman rose to give out a hymn, which was sung with deep earnestness. While it was being sung several people dropped down in their seats as if they had been struck, and commenced crying for pardon. Then from another part of the chapel could be heard the resonant voice of a young man reading a portion of scripture . . . Finally, Mr Roberts announced the holding of future meetings, and at 4.25 o'clock the gathering dispersed.

But even at this hour the people did not make their way home. When I left to walk back to Lannelly I left dozens of them about the road still discussing what is now the chief subject in their lives.

On 3 January 1905, *The Times* (p. 12) reported:

Presently a young man pushed his way through the crowd and, kneeling in the rostrum, began a fervent prayer of penitence and for pardon. Once again, in the midst of his prayer, the whole congregation breaks forth into a hymn, repeated with amazing fervour and vigour eight times. A man confesses his past – he has been a drunkard, he has been a Sabbath-breaker, he had known nothing of a Saviour, but now something has entered his heart and he feels a new power within him compelling him to speak. While he is speaking the people give vent to their feelings in a hymn of thanksgiving, repeated as before again and again. Thus the hours creep on. It is long past midnight. Now here, now there, someone rises to make his confession and lays bare his record before the people or falls upon his knees where he is and in loud and fervent tones prays for forgiveness.

An early claimant to becoming 'Pentecostal' comes from this church's history as follows. A. J. Tomlinson (1865–1943) tells the story of the emergence of the Church of God, which is now one of the main worldwide Pentecostal groups.

1.3 A. J. Tomlinson, '*Brief History of the Church that is Now Recognized as the Church of God*',
in A. J. Tomlinson, *The Last Great Conflict*, Cleveland, Tenn.: Press of Walter E. Rodgers, 1913, p. 184, abridged
http://www.churchofgod.cc/heritage/HistoryTomlinson.PDF

About the year 1884, a spirit of dissatisfaction and unrest began to work in the mind of a licensed minister of the Missionary Baptist church by the name of Richard G. Spurling, then living in Monroe County, Tennessee. The dissatisfaction arose because of certain traditions and creeds which were burdensome and exceedingly binding on the members. . . .

After two years or more of careful searching, praying and weeping, and pleading with his church for reform to no avail, he, with others, began to arrange for an independent meeting for a conference and a more careful consideration of religious matters.

The result of the prayers and research on the part of Mr Spurling and his companions proved three things to their entire satisfaction. . . .

After having taken plenty of time for consideration, the time and place for the meetings was arranged and announced. That day is worthy of remembrance. Thursday, 19 August 1886. . . .

The small company of humble, faithful, conscientious pilgrims met at Barney Creek meeting house, Monroe County, Tennessee. After prayer, a strong discourse was delivered by Richard G. Spurling, emphasizing the need of a reformation. The arguments were full of force and proved effective, and were endorsed by the hearers, so that when the time came for action there was free and earnest response.

The proposition and obligation was simple. We give it below: 'As many Christians as are here present that are desirous to be free from all men made creeds and traditions, and are willing to take the New Testament, or law of Christ, for your only rule of faith and practice; giving each other equal rights and privilege to read and interpret for yourselves as your conscience may dictate, and are willing to set together as the Church of God to transact business at the same, come forward.'

. . .

An invitation was then given for the reception of members, and they received Richard G. Spurling, who was then a licensed minister. The church chose him as their pastor, and had him ordained the next month, 26 September 1886.

The little church grew very slowly. Few cared anything about the infant organization.

. . .

In the year 1896 three men, who lived in the same county and locality, became much enthused religiously, and were powerfully wrought on by the Spirit of God. These men, whose names were William Martin, Joe M. Tipton and Milton McNabb, went over into Cherokee county, North Carolina, and commenced a meeting at the Shearer schoolhouse. They preached a clean gospel, and urged the people to seek and obtain sanctification subsequent to justification. They prayed, fasted and wept before the Lord until a great revival was the result. People became interested, and were stirred for miles around. Quite a large number professed salvation and sanctification through the blood of Christ. The Baptist and Methodist churches became antagonistic to the wonderful revival that was spreading, and about thirty were excluded from the Baptist church at one time because they professed to live a holy life, which the church denounced as heresy.

After the close of the series of meetings, and the three evangelists were gone, the people commenced a Sunday school, and regular prayer meetings were conducted, usually by William F. Bryant, a leading man of the community. The people earnestly sought God, and the interest increased until unexpectedly, like a cloud from a clear sky, the Holy Ghost began to fall on the honest, humble, sincere seekers after God. While the meetings were in progress one after another fell under the power of God, and soon quite a number were speaking in other tongues as the Spirit gave them utterance. The influence and excitement then spread like wildfire, and people came for many miles to investigate, hear and see the manifestations of the presence of God.

. . .

The power of healing was soon realized, and a number of miraculous cases of healings were wrought by the power of God. The people knew but little about the Bible, but they prayed, and shouted and exhorted until hundreds of hard sinners were converted. The influence grew and spread until it extended into three or four adjoining counties. Persecutions arose, and four or five houses were burned where these earnest, humble people met for worship.

. . . It is estimated that more than one hundred persons really received the baptism with the Holy Ghost and spoke in tongues as the evidence during the revival.

It was not until 15 May 1902 that any plan for government was adopted. On that day a number of humble people met at the home of Mr Bryant, Cherokee county, NC, and under the instructions and supervision of Mr Spurling, an organization was effected. While this was a continuation of the same organization that was started sixteen years before, yet it was not given the same name, as it was in a different locality. It was called 'The Holiness Church at Camp Creek', in Cherokee county, NC. One of the officers, W. F. Bryant, was set forth by the church and ordained, which made the church permanent. R. G. Spurling was chosen pastor, and they continued their meetings; . . .

In was in June 1903 that the work revived and took upon it a new impetus. . . .

The first Assembly of the churches of God was held on 26 and 27 January 1906, at the home of J. D. Murphy, Cherokee county, NC, about one-half mile from the school house where the great revival had broken out ten years before. Twenty-one members were in attendance as representatives from the different churches.

. . . The Second Annual Assembly was held at Union Grove, a meeting house in the country, ten miles from Cleveland, Tennessee . . . with a view to coming fully to the Bible standard and plan for the Bible church.

At a session held at 8.30 on Friday morning, 11 January, 1907, the name 'Church of God' was adopted, with the addition of the name of the place or locality where it existed. . . .

Following is nearly the common form of explanation and obligation:

As Jesus Christ is the sole founder and originator of His Church, and still retains the position as head and only lawgiver, all who connect themselves with His Church will be expected to obey His laws and government, walking in the light as He is in the light, thus giving fellowship to each other and the assurance of the blood cleansing from all sin (1 John 1.7).

The applicants for membership are expected to accept the teaching of repentance, water baptism (by immersion), sanctification subsequent to conversion, the baptism with the Holy Ghost on the sanctified life evidenced by the speaking in tongues as the Spirit gives utterance, the Lord's Supper, feet washing, eternal punishment for the wicked and eternal life for the righteous, divine healing, tithing and offerings, and the second pre-millennial coming of the Lord. Applicants must sever their connection with churches and lodges, if not already free from them. . . .

2 History of Pentecostal and Charismatic Movements

Charles Fox Parham (1873–1929) records his initial encounter with Pentecostal tongues.

2.1   Charles F. Parham, 'The Latter Rain', *Apostolic Faith*, December 1950–January 1951, pp. 3 and 15, abridged

We opened the Bible School at Topeka, Kansas, in October 1900. To which we invited all ministers and Christians who were willing to forsake all, sell what they had, give it away, and enter the school for study and prayer, where all of us together might trust God for food, fuel, rent and clothing. The purpose of this school was to fit men and women to go to the ends of the earth to preach 'This Gospel of the Kingdom' (Matt. 24.14) as a witness to all the world before the end of the age.

Our purpose in this Bible School was not to learn these things in our heads only but have each thing in the Scriptures wrought out in our hearts. And that every command that Jesus Christ gave should be literally obeyed. . . .

. . .

In December of 1900 we had had our examination upon the subject of repentance, conversion, consecration, sanctification, healing, and the soon coming of the Lord. We had reached in our studies a problem. What about Chapter 2 of Acts? I had felt for years that any missionary going to the foreign field should preach in the language of the natives. That if God had ever equipped His ministers in that way He could do it today. That if Balaam's mule could stop in the middle of the road and give the first preacher that went out for money a 'bawling out' in Arabic that anybody today ought to be able to preach in any language of the world if they had horse sense enough to let God use their tongue and throat. But still I believed our experience should tally exactly with the Bible, . . . Having heard so many different religious bodies claim different proofs as the evidence of their having the Pentecostal baptism, I set the students at work studying out diligently what was the Bible evidence of the baptism of the

Holy Ghost, that we might go before the world with something that was indisputable because it tallied absolutely with the Word.

Leaving the school for three days at this task, I went to Kansas City for three days services. I returned to the School on the morning preceding Watch Night services in the year 1900.

At about 10 o'clock in the morning I rang the bell calling all the students into the Chapel to get their report on the matter in hand. To my astonishment they all had the same story, that while different things occurred when the Pentecostal blessing fell, that the indisputable proof on each occasion was, that they spake with other tongues. About 75 people beside the school, which consisted of 40 students, had gathered for the Watch Night service. A mighty spiritual power filled the entire school.

Sister Agnes N. Ozman (now LaBerge) asked that hands might be laid upon her to receive the Holy Spirit as she hoped to go to foreign fields. At first I refused not having the experience myself. Then being further pressed to do it humbly in the name of Jesus, I laid my hand upon her head and prayed. I had scarcely repeated three dozen sentences when a glory fell upon her, a halo seemed to surround her head and face, and she began speaking in the Chinese language, and was unable to speak English for three days. When she tried to write in English to tell us of her experience she wrote the Chinese, copies of which we still have in newspapers printed at that time.

Seeing this marvellous manifestation of the restoration of Pentecostal power, we removed the beds from a dormitory on the upper floor, and there for two nights and three days we continued as a school to wait upon God. We felt that God was no respecter of persons and what He had so graciously poured out upon one, He would upon all.

Those three days of tarrying were wonderful days of blessings. We all got past any begging or pleading, we knew the blessing was ours with ever swelling tides of praise and thanksgiving and worship, interspersed with singing we waited for the coming of the Holy Spirit.

On the night of 3 January, I preached at the Free Methodist Church in the City of Topeka telling them what had already happened, and that I expected upon returning the entire school to be baptized in the Holy Spirit. On returning to the school with one of the students, we ascended to the second floor, and passing down along the corridor in the upper room, heard most wonderful sounds. The door was slightly ajar, the room was lit with only coal oil lamps. As I pushed open the door I found the room was filled with a sheen of white light above the brightness of the lamps.

Twelve ministers, who were in the school of different denominations, were filled with the Holy Spirit and spoke with other tongues. Some were sitting, some still kneeling, others standing with hands upraised. There was no violent physical manifestation, though some trembled under the power of the glory that filled them.

Sister Stanley, an elderly lady, came across the room as I entered, telling me that just before I entered tongues of fire were sitting above their heads.

When I beheld the evidence of the restoration of Pentecostal power, my heart was melted in gratitude to God for what my eyes had seen. For years I had suffered terrible persecutions for preaching holiness and healing and the soon coming of the Lord. I fell to my knees behind a table unnoticed by those upon whom the power of Pentecost had fallen to pour out my heart to God in thanksgiving. All at once they began to sing, 'Jesus Lover of My Soul' in at least six different languages, carrying the different parts with a more angelic voice than I had ever listened to in all my life.

After praising God for some time, I asked Him for the same blessing. He distinctly made it clear to me that He raised me up and trained me to declare this mighty truth to the world, and if I was willing to stand for it, with all the persecutions, hardships, trials, slander, scandal that it would entail, He would give me the blessing. And I said 'Lord I will, if You will just give me this blessing.' Right then there came a slight twist in my throat, a glory fell over me and I began to worship God in the Swedish tongue, which later changed to other languages and continued so until the morning.

Just a word: After preaching this for all these years with all the persecutions I have been permitted to go through with, misunderstanding and the treatment of false brethren, yet knowing all that this blessing would bring to me, if I had the time and was back there again I'd take the same way.

No sooner was this miraculous restoration of Pentecostal power noised abroad, than we were besieged with reporters from Topeka papers. Kansas City, St Louis and many other cities sent reporters who brought with them professors of languages, foreigners, Government interpreters, and they gave the work the most crucial test. One Government interpreter claimed to have heard twenty Chinese dialects distinctly spoken in one night. All agree that the students of the college were speaking in the languages of the world, and that with proper accent and intonation. There was no chattering, jabbering, or stuttering. Each one spoke clearly and distinctly in a foreign tongue, with earnestness, intensity and God-given unction. The propriety and decency of the conduct of each member of the Bible School won the warmest comment from many visitors.

Our first public appearance after others had received the baptism of the Holy Spirit was in Kansas City, in the Academy of Music, about 21 January. The Kansas City papers loudly announced our coming. Two columns appeared in the *Kansas City Journal*, with large headlines on the front page. These headlines, being the largest on the front page, attracted the attention of the newsboys, and they not knowing a Pentecost from a holocaust ran wildly up and down the street crying their papers, Pentecost, Pentecost, read all about the Pentecost.

I have on record the sermon preached on this occasion. The first upon the baptism of the Holy Ghost in all modern Pentecostal Apostolic Full Gospel movements. Also on file all that the papers had to say about these things in those days. Through great trials and persecutions we conducted the Bible school in the city of Topeka itself, then on in Kansas City.

'That the trial of your faith, being much more precious than of gold that perisheth, though it be tried with fire, might be found unto praise and honor and glory at the appearance of Jesus Christ' (1 Peter 1.7).

Before moving to the world-renowned Azusa Street mission, William J. Seymour (1870–1922), a black man, trained by Charles Parham in Houston, Texas, boldly declared his definition of the Baptism in the Spirit even before he had received it. He relates the events.

2.2   W. J. Seymour, in *Apostolic Faith*, September 1906, p. 1

It was the divine call that brought me from Houston, Texas, to Los Angeles. The Lord put it in the heart of one of the saints in Los Angeles to write to me that she felt the Lord would have me come over here and do a work, and I came, for I felt it was the leading of the Lord. The Lord sent the means, and I came to take charge of a mission on Santa Fe Street, and one night they locked the door against me, and afterwards got Bro. Roberts, the president of the Holiness Association, to come down and settle the doctrine of the Baptism with the Holy Ghost, that it was simply sanctification. He came down and a good many holiness preachers with him, and they stated that sanctification was the baptism with the Holy Ghost. But yet they did not have the evidence of the second chapter of Acts, for when the disciples were all filled with the Holy Ghost, they spoke in tongues as the Spirit gave utterance. After the president heard me speak of what the true baptism of the Holy Ghost was, he said he wanted it too, and told me when I had received it to let him know. So I received it and let him know. The beginning of the Pentecost started in a cottage prayer meeting at 214 Bonnie Brae.

A participant in all things Pentecostal in its early days in Los Angeles, Bartleman gives an account of his experiences from diaries and memories.

2.3   F. Bartlemann, *Azusa Street*,
Plainfield, NJ: Bridge Publishing, 1925, ch. 3, abridged

. . . Thursday, 19 April [1906], while sitting in the noon meeting at Peniel Hall, 227 South Main Street, the floor suddenly began to move with us. A most ugly sensation ran through the room. We sat in awe. Many people ran into the middle of the street, looking up anxiously at the buildings, fearing they were about to fall. It was an earnest time. I went home and after a season of prayer was impressed of the Lord to go to the meeting which had been removed from Bonnie Brae Street to 312 Azusa Street. Here they had rented an old frame building, formerly a Methodist church, in the center of the city, now a long time out of use for meetings. It had become a receptacle for old lumber, plaster, etc. They had cleared space enough in the surrounding dirt and debris to lay some planks on top of empty nail kegs, with seats enough for possibly thirty people, if I remember rightly. These were arranged in a square, facing one another. . . .

We finally reached 'Azusa' and found about a dozen saints there, some white, some colored. Brother Seymour was there, in charge. . . . the fire could not be smothered. Strong saints were gathered together to the help of the Lord. Gradually the tide arose in victory. But from a small beginning, a very little flame.

I gave a message at my first meeting at 'Azusa'. Two of the saints spoke in 'tongues'. Much blessing seemed to attend the utterance. It was soon noised abroad that God was working at 'Azusa'. All classes began to flock to the meetings. Many were curious and unbelieving, but others were hungry for God. The newspapers began to ridicule and abuse the meetings, thus giving us much free advertising. This brought the crowds. . . . Even spiritualists and hypnotists came to investigate, and to try their influence. Then all the religious sore-heads and crooks and cranks came, seeking a place in the work. We had the most to fear from these. But this is always the danger to every new work. They have no place elsewhere. This condition cast a fear over many which was hard to overcome. It hindered the Spirit much. . . .

. . . I found the earthquake had opened many hearts. . . . There was much persecution, especially from the press. They wrote us up shamefully, but this only drew the crowds. Some gave the work six months to live. Soon the meetings were running day and night. The place was packed out nightly. The whole building, upstairs and down, had now been cleared and put into use. There were far more white people than colored coming. The 'color line' was washed away in the blood. . . . Great emphasis was placed on the 'blood', for cleansing, etc. A high standard was held up for a clean life. . . . Divine love was wonderfully manifest in the meetings. They would not even allow an unkind word said against their opposers, or the churches. The message was the love of God. It was a sort of 'first love' of the early church returned. The 'baptism' as we received it in the beginning did not allow us to think, speak, or hear evil of any man. . . .

On the wall of the tarrying room was hung a placard with the words, 'No talking above a whisper'. We knew nothing of 'jazzing' them through at that time. The Spirit wrought very deeply. An unquiet spirit or a thoughtless talker, was immediately reproved by the Spirit. We were on 'holy ground'. This atmosphere was unbearable to the carnal spirit. . . .

Friday, 15 June, at 'Azusa', the Spirit dropped the 'heavenly chorus' into my soul. I found myself suddenly joining the rest who had received this supernatural 'gift'. It was a spontaneous manifestation and rapture no earthly tongue can describe. In the beginning this manifestation was wonderfully pure and powerful. We feared to try to reproduce it, as with the 'tongues' also. Now many seemingly have no hesitation in imitating all the 'gifts'. They have largely lost their power and influence because of this. No one could understand this 'gift of song' but those who had it. It was indeed a 'new song' in the Spirit. When I first heard it in the meetings a great hunger entered my soul to receive it. I felt it would exactly express my pent-up feelings. I had not yet spoken in 'tongues'. But the 'new song' captured me. It was a gift from God of high order, and appeared among us soon after the 'Azusa' work began. No one had preached it. The Lord had sovereignly bestowed it, with the outpouring of the 'residue of oil', the 'Latter Rain' baptism of the Spirit. It was exercised, as the Spirit moved the possessors, either in solo fashion, or by the company. It was sometimes without words, other times in 'tongues'. The effect was wonderful on the people. It brought a heavenly atmosphere, as though the angels them-selves were present and joining with us. And possibly they were. It seemed to still criticism and opposition, and was hard for even wicked men to gainsay or ridicule.

Some have condemned this 'new song', without words. But was not sound given before language? And is there not intelligence without language also? Who composed the first song? Must we necessarily follow some man's composition, before us, always? We are too much worship-pers of tradition. The speaking in 'tongues' is not according to man's wisdom or understanding. Then why not a 'gift of song'? It is certainly a rebuke to the 'jazzy' religious songs of our day. And possibly it was given for that purpose. Yet some of the old hymns are very good to sing, also. We need not despise or treat lightly of them. Some one has said that every fresh revival brings in its own hymnology. And this one surely did.

In the beginning in 'Azusa' we had no musical instruments. In fact we felt no need of them. There was no place for them in our worship. All was spontaneous. We did not even sing from hymn books. All the old well known hymns were sung from memory, quickened by the Spirit of God. 'The Comforter Has Come' was the one most sung. . . . Brother Seymour was recognized as the nominal leader in charge. . . .

Brother Seymour generally sat behind two empty shoe boxes, one on top of the other. He usually kept his head inside the top one during the meeting, in prayer. There was no pride there. The services ran almost continuously. Seeking souls could be found under the power almost any hour, night and day. The place was never closed nor empty. The people came to meet God. He was always there. Hence a continuous meeting. The meeting did not depend on the human leader. God's presence became more and more wonderful. In that old building, with its low rafters and bare floors, God took strong men and women to pieces, and put them together again, for His glory. It was a tremendous overhauling process. Pride and self-assertion, self-importance and self-esteem, could not survive there. The religious ego preached its own funeral sermon quickly.

No subjects or sermons were announced ahead of time, and no special speakers for such an hour. No one knew what might be coming, what God would do. All was spontaneous, ordered of the Spirit. We wanted to hear from God, through whoever he might speak. We had no 'respect of persons'. The rich and educated were the same as the poor and ignorant, and found a much harder death to die. We only recognized God. All were equal. No flesh might glory in His presence. He could not use the self-opinionated. Those were Holy Ghost meetings, led of the Lord. It had to start in poor surroundings, to keep out the selfish, human element. All came down in humility together, at His feet. They all looked alike, and had all things in common in that sense at least. The rafters were low, the tall must come down. By the time they got to 'Azusa' they were humbled, ready for the blessing. The fodder was thus placed for the lambs, not for giraffes. All could reach it.

. . .

Some one might be speaking. Suddenly the Spirit would fall upon the congregation God himself would give the altar call. Men would fall all over the house, like the slain in battle, or rush for the altar en masse, to seek God. The scene often resembled a forest of fallen trees. Such a scene cannot be imitated. I never heard an altar call given in those early days.

God himself would call them. And the preacher knew when to quit. When He spoke all obeyed. It seemed a fearful thing to hinder or grieve the Spirit. The whole place was steeped in prayer. God was in His holy temple. It was for man to keep silent. The shekinah glory rested there. In fact some claim to have seen the glory by night over the building. I do not doubt it. I have stopped more than once within two blocks of the place and prayed for strength before I dared go on. The presence of the Lord was so real.

❦

A. A. Boddy was used to order as an Anglican; hence he sought to hold his conventions in check against more extreme possibilities, as illustrated in this extract from the newspaper Confidence *that he edited for pentecostically minded people.*

2.4   A. A. Boddy, 'Whitsun Convention Sunderland',
Confidence, May 1910, p. 120, abridged

THE THIRD INTERNATIONAL CONVENTION

WHITSUNTIDE MAY 14–20 1910

All Saints' Parish Hall, Fulwell Road, Sunderland.

. . . Our Convention is for the teaching of Full Salvation, the New Birth, Sanctification, the Baptism of the Holy Ghost with the Signs ('Tongues'), Fruit, and Gifts, Divine Life for Spirit, Soul, and Body, Health and Healing in our Lord Jesus Christ, and the soon coming of the Lord.

We are expecting also at these preliminary meetings our Brother D. Awrey (USA). He is being much used in Germany. Also our Brothers Mr Mundell (Croydon), Mr Sandwith (Bracknell, Beds.), Mr Mogridge (Lytham), Mr Myerscough (Preston), Mr W. Andreus (South Wales), Baroness van Brasch (Russia), Mrs Beruldsen (Edinburgh), Mr Groves (India), Mr Reid and Mr J. Welsh (Carlisle).

   . . .

Admission to Meetings. With the exception of the Leaders' Meetings, the Meetings are mostly open this year. They are not for discussion. Compliance with the ruling of the Chairman is a condition of admission. The Convener reserves the right to exclude any whom he considers might be a hindrance to the meetings.

Tickets for the Leaders' Meetings from the Secretaries or Stewards. These must be signed by the Bearer, and are not transferable.

Used by permission of the Donald Gee Centre, Mattersey Hall, Mattersey, UK.

Typical of gatherings in the nineteenth century, Pentecostals also held camp meetings of various kinds in the twentieth century.

2.5   Guy Shields, *Camp-Meeting Special*, Amarillo, Tex.: Nebraska District Council, 1933, pp. 10–14, abridged

As we pull into the camp ground, which is shaded by a large grove of beautiful trees, carpeted with blue grass, surrounded by large fields of corn and alfalfa, there is at first a little feeling of disappointment to find that the camp is so far from a city, but as we drive down through the main street of the 20-acre grove of trees, all beautifully marked off with streets and avenues, we were soon overjoyed to see the tents that were up. After greeting the district Superintendent, we were ready for the opening of the service. My first text was: 'The Church Built on a Rock'. The altar was filled with people hungry for more of God. Three received the Holy Ghost baptism. And so the camp meeting was on.

The number of campers increased each day. Brother White had to make arrangements for more tents. The campers increased until the tents numbered 195 and several house cars and trucks on top of that. The estimation of the people camping is from 700 to 900 throughout the camp meeting. The tide was rising higher and higher each service, and many more of the pastors came in each day. By Monday night they were most all there. I preached morning and night, and various other preachers spoke in afternoon and early morning. People were surely getting through in every morning service. Many were being slain under the power, at one time I counted 22 lying under the mighty power, being filled with the Holy Ghost and power. At various times it seemed that the power just came like sheets of rain and great shouts of praise would sweep over the whole congregation. At one altar service we will never forget Revd Glen Read shouting and leaping for joy. The night we prayed for the sick I witnessed the presence of God I believe more than ever I ever did in my life. We anointed 153 and many were greatly blessed and healed. A number fell under the hand of the Lord.

. . .

Good meals were served in the cook shack as well as many cooked at private tents. A view of all the tents would make you think of the tents of

Israel. One of the most spiritual and inspiring parts of the meeting was dear old colored Bro. Evans of Colorado with his old guitar and he sang most every service. Other great singers were there all along and were enjoyed by all, but somehow he just seemed to lift everyone as he sang. We were very appreciative of the song he dedicated to us 'Stand by Me,' but his big hit was 'Every time I feel the Spirit move I'll pray'.

> Upon the mountain
> When my God spoke,
> Out of His mouth came
> Fire and smoke
> I looked around me
> It looked so fine
> I asked my Lord, if all was mine,
>
> *Chorus*:
> Every time I feel the Spirit
> Moving in my heart I will pray,
> Every time I feel the Spirit,
> Moving in my heart I will pray.

The events recounted here illustrate the hunger for a renewal of Pentecostal power that started at the Bible School at Sharon, Canada after 1945.

2.6   George R. Hawtin, Latter Rain Movement, 'Letter to Wayne Warner', Flower Pentecostal Heritage Center, Springfield, Mo., 65802, 15 December 1987

Thus, as the days passed by, classes became almost forgotten and the hours absorbed in prayer, fasting and repentance. Many students continued fasting for two or three weeks and one student, I understand, fasted for forty days. This was a phenomenal thing since the majority of these people were young people ranging in age from about eighteen years to perhaps twenty-five. Until this time there had been no particular manifestation of anything supernatural, but only the great and burning desire to SEEK THE FACE OF THE LORD.

At last came the wonderful morning of 12 February 1948. The day began with morning devotion as usual, but when we knelt for prayer as our custom was each morning, there came an overwhelming sense that some thing from heaven was about to occur. My description of it would be that a great awe possessed us all. It was not the fear of being afraid, but that sort of godly fear and reverence that one would experience if suddenly he found himself in the presence of an angel – the sort of fear that would make one remove his shoes from his feet, for the place was holy ground. On this occasion several students, overcome by the Spirit, had fallen prostrate on the classroom floor, and at last one, a married lady, perhaps the oldest person in the class, began to prophesy as she lay prostrate beneath the power of God. Her words were very brief and, as I was principal of the school, I mistakenly thought she was addressing me when she said by the Spirit, 'Brother Hawtin, if you will do what the Lord is telling you to do, the Lord will reveal Himself.' I did not know of any thing that the Spirit had asked me to do and had forgotten for the moment that my brother Ernest was present. To my surprise and great joy he arose, trembling, from where he was kneeling and began to prophesy to the kneeling students. His anointed prophecy continued for what seemed to be about fifteen minutes and, while it is not possible to remember it all, many words of instruction were given as to how our lives should be ordered before God. At this I opened my eyes to see a young man standing with his shoes off and his head bowed, listening devoutly to the word of the Lord.

After much warning and solemn exhortation the prophecy given by my brother continued in this manner – that none of us should write letters to friends or relatives to explain what the Lord was about to do, because they would not understand. And it is true that those who did try found they were completely misunderstood. Then in my brother's prophecy came the great truth of what was immediately in store in these words: 'I will restore *at this time to My church the nine gifts of the Holy Spirit and they will be restored by prophecy with the laying on of hands of the presbytery. I will indicate from TIME TO TIME certain ones who are ready to receive* the gifts of My Spirit.' These words were immediately followed by the calling out of a name. The sister who had first spoken, still lying prostrate, called out the name of the student who had fasted forty days. I must admit that none of us knew what to do next, but in an effort to obey the Spirit my brother called him forward and a prophecy concerning his life was given and a gift was promised to him. We then with some trepidation laid our hands on him to impart to him that which the Lord had spoken. This was done with fear and reverence and with great concern, as we had never walked this way before.

I am afraid my words would be fruitless should I endeavour to describe the majesty, the glory, the power and the reverence of those awesome moments. Only those who were there could grasp them. Heavenly things just cannot be described in human words. Only those who were in the upper room at Pentecost know what went on there. We today are as help-less as was Ezekiel when in chapter one of his book he did his best to describe by many likenesses the glory of the Lord which he saw. Perhaps because we were all filled with some apprehension concerning the way the Lord was leading us, the class was dismissed that time might be given to search the word of God whether or not these things were so. Such was the fear of the Lord, the awe and the reverence, that we felt unable to speak of the things that had happened.

PART 2
THEOLOGY

3 Pentecostal Eschatology

W. K. Kay, Introduction

During the latter part of the nineteenth century and in the early years of the last century, the period when the Pentecostal movement was beginning to see the light of day, dispensationalism's distinctive eschatological teachings (two-stage Second Advent, belief in a literal millennium, future central role of a re-established and re-gathered Israel) were very much in vogue among the vast majority of evangelicals in both the USA and the British Isles. Unsurprisingly, given their roots, the majority of Pentecostals adopted these teachings and, in some instances, incorporated them into their doctrinal formulations – the exception being that, whereas the dispensationalists and their successors the fundamentalists saw the miraculous primitive charisms as being restricted to the Apostolic Age, these 'new kids on the block' insisted either that the charisms had never been withdrawn or that they were being spectacularly restored in their own day.

Though traceable back to J. N. Darby (1800–82), whose visits to the USA inspired the influential Niagara Conferences of 1883 to 1897, it was *The Scofield Reference Bible*, first published in 1909 but going through many subsequent editions, that was the major source of the dispensational views that have dominated Pentecostalism for most of its history. Though not all Pentecostals hold to the view that the Church will be raptured or removed prior to the Great Tribulation – Darby's teaching and the prevailing view of the Niagara and other late nineteenth-century Bible conferences – the vast majority still do so, the horrors of the Great Tribulation being deemed incompatible with the Church's much anticipated 'Blessed Hope'.

These largely dispensationalist views, however, have had a limited appeal to the Neo-Pentecostals – Roman Catholics, Anglicans and Baptists, etc. – who, though adopting 'Pentecostal' doctrine and practices in other areas, have generally speaking retained the traditional eschatologies of their respective traditions. It goes almost without saying that Roman Catholics, albeit Spirit-filled, have had no sympathy with the dispensationalist identification of Romanism with the fearsome beast warring on God's people (Revelation 13.7) or 'Mystery Babylon, the Mother of Harlots' who is 'drunk with the blood of the saints' (17.5f.).

The excerpts that follow reflect these variations in the views of

Pentecostals and their charismatic cousins and heirs, beginning in the early nineteenth century with Edward Irving (1792–1834), 'the forerunner of the Pentecostal movement', and continuing in a series of commentaries and articles that lay out variations in the basic Second Adventist position.

The eschatological scheme accepted by Pentecostals implied that the course of future events was pre-ordained. This was the case whether the events were arranged in an order that anticipated the Church would suffer tribulation or escape it by the first stage of the Second Advent, the *parousia* or rapture. Psychologically, the issue turned on whether spiritual and economic conditions would get better and better or worse and worse. Those who expected a rapture might well anticipate a darkening world situation; those who considered the millennium only to be a symbolic era might anticipate an upward and bright path as the gospel, preached to every nation, spread its light ever more widely. Belief in a rapture, especially after the outpouring of the Holy Spirit at the beginning of the twentieth century, was often an incentive to evangelism and sacrificial missionary work. This sense that the world was on the brink of its final phase, that the 'birth pangs of a new age' were being felt, is evident in several of the excerpts in this section.

The Evangelical Anglican priest Alexander Boddy (1854–1930), a staunch 'Keswick' man and one of 'Lightfoot's lambs', soon emerged as the leader of the embryonic British Pentecostal movement. He founded and edited Britain's first Pentecostal journal, *Confidence*, organized the annual Sunderland Whitsun Conventions and, along with Cecil Polhill – he was a member of the Cambridge Seven – set up the Pentecostal Missionary Union for the support and promotion of Spirit-filled missionaries. The excerpt (3.1) shows Boddy's sense of urgency in the face of the events of his day.

The timeline created by eschatology was often illustrated by charts showing the order of events. One of the especially Pentecostal features of these charts was to be found in the equation of the new outpouring of the Holy Spirit in the twentieth century with the 'latter rain'. The rainfall in Israel is divided into a 'former rain' that occurs when the crops are planted and a 'latter rain' that falls just before the harvest (Deuteronomy 11.14). The latter rain swells the grain and fruit and increases the yield at the end of the agricultural year. Here the identification of the Holy Spirit with the latter rain indicates that a period of abundant spiritual harvest is forthcoming before the end of the age. It gives a wider eschatological purpose to the phenomena of speaking with tongues and the charismaticization of the Church. The two short excerpts (3.2 and 3.3), both taken from *Confidence*, one by Elizabeth Sisson about whom not much is known and the other by the leading Dutch Pentecostal Gerrit Polman (1868–1932), show how such expectations were woven into Pentecostal discourse.

In excerpt 3.4 we hear the dramatic voice of Aimee Semple McPherson (1890–1944), who shook off the grief of young widowhood to become one of America's most colourful, flamboyant, controversial and effective evangelists. Her histrionic sermons, preached before thousands in the huge Angelus Temple, Los Angeles, brought Hollywood to the pulpit. Aimee preached the uncompromising message of '*Now* is the time to seek the Lord' and the grim prospect of everlasting conscious punishment for the unregenerate.

Excerpts 3.5 and 3.6 centre on the debate over the millennium. Pentecostals were prone to defend it, whereas charismatics were more prone to be amillennialists and to bring with this a confidence about the future that could verge on triumphalism. David Allen taught several generations of students training for ministry within British Assemblies of God, while J. Rodman Williams, also working within an educational context, comes from a charismatic Presbyterian background.

During the 1960s and 1970s *The Late Great Planet Earth* by Hal Lindsay caused many to look again at eschatology. One result of looking at the world's condition came in Dave Wilkerson's *Vision* of which we give an excerpt (3.7).

Peter Hocken (3.8), speaking as a Catholic charismatic priest who was Secretary of the Society for Pentecostal Studies, is able to show how the gift of the Holy Spirit made him personally, and by extension can make other Christians, aware of the future orientation of the Church – of its biblical hopes, its ultimate place in a divine plan, and of the eventual reconciliation of Jews and Gentiles.

What is notable about all these excerpts is the way the often personal and private experience of speaking with other tongues becomes linked with a larger public theology concerning the destiny of the Church and the world. For Pentecostals and charismatics, eschatology was more than a theoretical framework or a philosophical conception of history: it was a spur to action and a way of aligning oneself with God's plans in a century when the old cultural and religious landmarks were being violently uprooted.

Sensitive to international change and unrest, A. A. Boddy (1854–1930) linked these changes, as well as the outpouring of the Holy Spirit, with an expectation of the second coming of Christ. The excerpt shows how early Pentecostalism was born in an anticipation of the end of the age.

3.1   A Report of the Address at the Sunderland Convention by the Revd A. A. Boddy,
Tuesday Night, 2 June, *Confidence*, June 1914, pp. 116–17

The coming of the Lord

The Revd A. A. Boddy remarked that, since the news of the outpouring of the Holy Spirit some time about the year 1906, when they heard of the wonderful way in which the Lord was baptizing people with the Holy Ghost with the sign following, there had been a marvellous quickening of interest in the soon coming of the Lord Jesus. Those of us in Pentecostal circles who had been privileged to see what was going on in different parts of the world – in America, in France, in Germany, and other parts – had been impressed with the fact that there is a general impression that the Lord was soon coming and everything seemed to point to the idea that something was going to happen. Look at the unrest in the different departments of life, see what unrest exists in the industrial world, think of the uprising in many parts of the world – in China, in Turkey, and in other parts – such a state of things extending all over the world. Think of the wonderful discoveries and the terrible disasters, the earthquakes, shipwrecks, everything showing that we are living in a time when everything is hurrying on and heading up to a great climax. We believe the meaning of it is that the end of this age, the Pentecostal age, is drawing near. The devil is trying as never before with awful temptations and possessions, and this Pentecostal outpouring of the Holy Ghost is also pointing to a close of the dispensation, while the messages given by the Holy Spirit in all parts of the world have been: 'Maranatha, Maranatha, Jesus is coming soon.' This was not because people wanted to hear such a message, but because God prophesied it through them.

While some are listening to this word, there are a good many who will not pay any attention to it; the world is deaf to it. But there is a certain class of people, and they are generally called Pentecostal people, throughout England, Scotland, in Germany, in Canada, in America, and other parts of the world, who are always ready to listen to any message about the coming of the Lord, because they believe it is a fact. Pentecostal people right round the world are looking as a body for the soon coming of our blessed Lord.

Therefore, it is right that among the subjects to be considered by such a gathering should be 'The Present Time in the Light of the Coming of the Lord'. We want not only to know about it in our heads; it is very important we should know all the reasons and circumstances which point to the Lord's coming. We want you all to be convinced of the truth. We want that all fear should be taken away, and that men and women should so love the Lord that they should love His appearing also, that they should be so filled with the Holy Ghost that the coming of the Lord should be a joy and not a terror, and that we should all feel, if He should come while we are holding this Convention, we should all say: 'Even so, come, Lord Jesus.' Some people said, 'Lord, don't come in my time; come a little after, if You will,' He is waiting for people who are ready to say: 'Come, Lord Jesus, come quickly.' He is waiting for people who are living near Him and have faith that He will come according to His promise, waiting on God day by day and walking with Him as Enoch, who represents the old dispensation, a sample of people who will be multiplied at the close of the Pentecostal dispensation, and who, because they are walking with God, will not be found. Enoch had this testimony that he pleased God, and by faith he was translated and taken from this earth just as he was, his body being glorified, as was our Lord's.

That is what will take place in many cases. There is no occasion to put on our best clothes to wait for the Lord; He wants us to be working and watching. In the meantime, we thank God for the glorious news that the Lord is coming soon.

Used by permission of the Donald Gee Centre, Mattersey Hall, Mattersey, UK.

A report of the contribution by G. R. Polman, Dutch Pentecostal leader, on speaking in tongues as indicative of a 'the last days'.

3.2   G. R. Polman, 'The Place of Tongues in the Pentecostal Movement', *Confidence*, August 1911, pp. 176–7

The great sign we want in connection with this Baptism in the Holy Ghost is love, so that if we do differ in our views it should not hurt our feelings. Whatever they say about me never troubles me; I love them even more. I thank God He is pouring out His Spirit upon us, and when the love of God is shed abroad in our hearts we are here gathered together in the love of God. In the second chapter of the Acts of the Apostles they saw that the disciples were all filled with the Holy Ghost, and began to speak with other tongues. Our hearts are open this morning, and I believe that God will teach us, and bring us more and more together – one heart and one soul. As dear Pastor Boddy had been reading, on the Day of Pentecost they were all filled with the Holy Ghost, and began to speak with other tongues as the Spirit gave them utterance. I believe this would not be a 'Pentecostal Movement' if there was no place for the Tongues. And because it is, as we believe, a Pentecostal Movement, so there was a place for this wonderful experience.

In Acts 2, fourth verse, we have the birth of the Church of God. It was born on the Day of Pentecost. The Holy Spirit created then a new Temple in which God must be glorified, in which God must be praised. There was present a body of disciples who followed the Lamb everywhere He went. Those 120 disciples were together, and then was born the Church of God, in which, during the dispensation of the Holy Spirit, He should glorify Himself; and the birth of the Church of God was proclaimed by speaking and singing in tongues, and in languages they never before had spoken.

God's signs

When God created a world the morning stars sang together, and the sons of God shouted for joy. When the Son of God was born and the Word became flesh, angels sang to the glory of God.

The birth of Jesus was announced by a heavenly song, and so it was when God created the Church of God, it was announced by glorifying God with tongues, with hymns, proclaiming the wonderful works of God. So we see that in every new thing brought about by God He was glorified in a marvellous way. And how glorious it is when this Baptism in the Holy Spirit in Pentecostal power comes down into our hearts, and He also is glorified by the Holy Spirit through the finished work of Jesus within us. As I have believed from the beginning, I believe today, that the Pentecostal Baptism has its Pentecostal evidence, namely, the speaking in tongues. We believe that God is moving on to the end quickly, that we are living in the last days, and that we are living even in the last hour. God works in cycles, and as was the beginning of the last dispensation, so will be the end. At the end of the present cycle we are touching the beginning. James speaks of the husbandman who is patiently waiting for the early and the latter rain in view of the Coming of the Lord Jesus. So we say while the outpouring of the Holy Spirit at Pentecost was the early rain, we are having now at the end of the outpouring, this 'Latter Rain'. At the early rain there was speaking in tongues. How are we to know that we are now receiving the Latter Rain? Because we see the same manifestation – speaking in tongues.

Used by permission of the Donald Gee Centre, Mattersey Hall, Mattersey, UK.

The presumption that the outpouring of the Holy Spirit corresponded to the eschatologically significant 'latter rain' was implicit in Pentecostal thinking and preaching.

3.3   Elizabeth Sisson, 'Want any Help?'
Confidence, October–December 1921, p. 52

. . . the prophet in the book of Joel (2.23), says that the former rain of that hour was but a 'moderate' exhibition of His grace provided for His church. 'I will cause to come down for you the former and the latter rain.'

Looking into the Palestine climate, which was the parable then in the mouth of God, we see it means treble or fourfold the measure of the Spirit's power given in the Apostolic Age. For such was the latter rains compared with the light, early rains. Then considering Zechariah 10.1, we find God dating a command *in the time* when latter rains were thus falling, to pray for torrential showers, over and above and upon all this treble or fourfold latter rain, 'lightning', clouds and showers.

Oh, those tropical tempests! I call to mind some I have witnessed in India. A neighbouring missionary, living in the same compound (yard), ran to our house on a minute errand, when a sudden clap of thunder and flash of lightning out of a clear sky arrested her returning footsteps. Then the instant darkness and pouring rain held her twenty minutes, when out came the sun and all was over. But the whole face of nature was changed. A monster tree uprooted lay in the path between the two houses, and the mighty power of the storm spoke volumes everywhere. So suddenly can God arise and fell the opposing force of the enemy, and put His seal upon His work.

When, several years ago, a Texas mob closed in upon F. F. Bosworth and knocked him down, two jumped with their brutal iron heels upon his back till it was a jellied mass of broken fibres, with two ribs and a wrist broken. As he fell into unconsciousness the last words he heard them utter with fearful oaths were, 'He'll never preach again.' Within two months *both had passed into eternity;* and Fred Bosworth! Well, he preaches some today, doesn't he?

I feel we have not yet sensed *what is* calling on God for 'rain in the time of latter rain'. God quicken our expectations! God cause us to 'possess our possessions'! God turn the flame of the Holy Ghost upon that whole Adamic nature of ours, till the 'beast' shall burn to a wisp in His presence, and spiritualized we shall 'see light in His light', and come forth as did Jesus after His forty days in the wilderness, a perfect, an uninterrupted union of the human with the Divine. 'He that seeth Me, seeth the Father.'

Used by permission of the Donald Gee Centre, Mattersey Hall, Mattersey, UK.

The dramatic preaching style of the flamboyant Aimee Semple McPherson (1890–1944) is caught in this extract. Clearly the world looked very different in the 1920s.

3.4   Aimee Semple McPherson, 'Premillennial Signal Towers', from 'The Bridal Call Foursquare', delivered at Angelus Temple, 24 August 1924, abridged

Our Newspapers have been carrying strange headlines recently! Strange phenomena, peculiar signs and signals, supposedly from the planet Mars, have been picked up by Government Signal Towers and Radio Stations in New York, Canada, England and Australia.

Scientists startled the world by declaring their belief that Mars, now in close proximity to the earth, is endeavouring to communicate with us. They state that the signals were of unearthly nature that they were given in a code undecipherable to man, and yet that they were of a precise and mechanical origin.

'Ta-da-da-Da-da-da-da!' came the signals from the sky. Where were they coming from? Millions asked the question.

The origin of these signals I know not, whether they came from Mars (which I doubt), or whether they originated from some static condition of the air (which is more probable).

But this I do know – strange flashes and signals are being received by the Church of Christ today from the Signal Towers of Heaven. These signals come in code. Only the believer has the key. To all others these dots and dashes from Heaven's Signal Towers are meaningless and uninterpretable.

'Why, Sister McPherson, what do you mean? What are you getting at? Signal Towers! Where–what–why–when?'

Heaven's Signal Towers speak by the Word of God, by the witness of the Spirit, and by prophecy fulfilled. The Signal Towers of the Church speak to Heaven by way of prayer, obedience, watchfulness, and relay the message, which she receives to the world by means of preaching, exhortation and warning.

Oh, I love the Old Time Religion! I love the old time power! What we need today is a great movement back to God, back to the Bible, back to the faith of our fathers, back to the Old Time Religion.

'Many shall come saying, I am the Christ.' This is another sign which we have lived to see fulfilled. But, be not deceived –

'If they shall say unto you, Behold, he is in the desert; go not forth: behold, he is in the secret chambers; believe it not. For as the lightning cometh out of the east and shineth even unto the west, so shall also the coming of the Son of Man be.'

'Nation shall rise against nation, kingdom against kingdom.'

Here again we have lived to see the World War, the most bloody carnage that was ever known to mortal man. Yet, 'tis but a shadow of the great tribulation that is to come.

'There shall be blood, and fire, and vapors of smoke.'

Blood! They fought knee-deep in it in the trenches.

Fire! For the first time in the history of the world, men fought each other during the late war with curtains and barrages of liquid fire. Vapours of smoke! For the first time in the history of the world, men fought each other with smoke, vapours, poisonous gases, and curtained in the ships at sea and the ships in the air behind smoked screens.

'There shall be plagues and pestilences.' The epidemic of influenza was one of these, coming from no one knows where and disappearing as quickly once its mission was accomplished, yet laying low more thousands than the war. The foot and mouth disease which recently afflicted the cattle here in our own California is another sample. To the world at large these things are but a series of annoyances, but to the Christian they are flashes and living codes from Heaven's Signal Tower.

'Ta-da-da- -da-da! When the fig tree putteth forth her leaf, you shall know that the summer is nigh.' We of today have lived to see that which our forefathers prophesied would some day come to pass – the birth and rise of the Zionist Movement, the unseating of the unspeakable Turk from his stronghold in Palestine, the opening of Palestinian Gates to the Jewish people, the blossoming of the desert which refused to yield its fruitage unto alien hands, the founding of Jewish colonies, and a great 'back to Palestine' movement among the Jewish people.

We have lived to see the Jewish fig tree put forth its leaves of science, education, finance, wealth and power. We have held our breath with wonder as the Scriptures were fulfilled when General Allenby with his troops took the Holy City. The narrow streets resounded with the tread of military heels. The allies advanced! The Turks retreated! The Union Jack was hoisted and waved on the breeze! Yet, not one drop of blood was shed – not one brick was dislodged from another as God fulfilled His Sacred Writ, and the impossible was accomplished!

'Ta-da-da- -da-da!' Premillennial Signal Towers spake loudly that day, saying, 'Behold, the Lord is near – He is even at the doors. Know, oh church, that the cup of the Gentiles is almost full – the Christ is coming back.'

Wake up, wake up, wake up! Work for the night is coming when man's work is done! Work now. Roll up your sleeves and go at it! Stop preaching mere politics! Stop cooking up oyster suppers and fixing strawberry festivals! Stop putting on bridge parties and trivial things! Stop showing moving pictures on Sunday night when you should be preaching the Gospel and getting people saved! Stop fighting other preachers and lifting up the sword to pierce the heart of other ministers! Whether we see eye to eye with them or not, the time is at hand – let us stop squabbling and fighting over little doctrinal differences. Let us stop fighting each other. Let us join hands, join hearts, voices and forces, and turn to fight the enemy – modernism, higher criticism, agnosticism and worldliness.

In fundamentals – unity! In non-essentials – liberty! In all things charity!'

We are relay stations for Christ. Let us speed the message out and away till it leaps the sea and girdles the globe, and all men hear the cry – 'Behold, the Christ is coming! He is even at the door!'

Used by permission of ICFG Communications, PO Box 26902, Los Angeles, CA 90026, USA.

Debates continue on millennialism; this is an abridgement of David Allen's summary of its history.

3.5   David Allen, 'The Millennium: An Embarrassment or a Fundamental of the Faith?'
Paper delivered at the European Pentecostal Theological Association Conference, Brussels, 16 April 1987, abridged

Traditionally, classic Pentecostals have been Premillennialist in eschatology. In recent years, however, the traditional doctrine has been called into question. In the British Assemblies of God this is reflected in the fact that there are some who would like to see the reference to the *'Premillennial Second Advent'* deleted from the 'Fundamental Truths'. They are probably a small minority; and a number of them only wish to amend the tenet in question because they feel it is contentious, and because they believe that it is the Return of Christ that is fundamental and not the sequence or scheme of eschatological events. Nevertheless, this does seem to indicate that some reappraisal of the traditional doctrine is now needed.

A number of factors have created this uncertainty regarding the doctrine of the Premillennial Second Advent. Firstly, several publications have assailed it in recent years. W. J. Grier's book *The Momentous Event*, though first published as long ago as 1945, has been reprinted several times in Britain.[1] In 1971 appeared Iain Murray's *The Puritan Hope*,[2] and soon after Dave MacPherson brought out *The Unbelievable Pre-Trib Origin* and *The Late Great Pre-Trib Rapture*.[3]

Murray and MacPherson both trace the Premillennial doctrine back to Edward Irving[4] and his circle and claim that it has no firm biblical foundation. Murray argues that because Premillennialism puts so much in the future, and such great emphasis on an unprecedented ingathering of souls after the Rapture, it has thereby been responsible for a slackening-off of missionary endeavour as compared with the nineteenth century. This argument seems very unconvincing. Pentecostals, the largest body of

---

[1] Banner of Truth Trust.

[2] Banner of Truth Trust.

[3] These two titles were combined, in revised form, as *The Incredible Cover-up*, Logos International, 1975.

[4] The opinion of both these writers regarding Edward Irving is not based on any objective and fair-minded assessment. They simply swallow the oft-repeated and baseless verdict of his unsympathetic and uncomprehending contemporaries, as does Arnold Dallimore's Banner of Truth biography (1983).

Premillennialists amongst evangelicals, have been conspicuously active in missionary outreach since the very beginning. . . .

Another factor leading to uncertainty in regard to the Premillennial Second Advent is the emergence of new and virile groups who, whilst sharing with classic or traditional Pentecostals emphasis on the baptism and gifts of the Spirit, stress that Christ reigns here and now and that the Church should 'possess the land' (and the world) here and now. The fact that these new 'Restoration' groups have attracted disgruntled Pentecostals into their ranks – and also experienced significant growth – has prompted questions. In putting such emphasis on the conversion of Israel after the Rapture, and in contrasting present difficulties and discouragements with future glory, have we, in fact, not been as positive as we ought to have been? And if these new groups, who either reject or, at least, play down what to us have been long-cherished millennial hopes, are nevertheless experiencing arguably greater growth and blessing than we are, does that not suggest that we have been mistaken in our doctrine and wrong in our emphasis? Finally, does it really matter whether we have a correct scheme of eschatology or not, as long as Christ's kingdom continues to expand and flourish in the contemporary world?

. . .

A fresh look at the Scriptures

One of our pastors recently said: 'Christ is not going to reign any more in the future than he does now.' This was not said from the pulpit but in private conversation. Another, and younger colleague in the ministry, expressed to me his opinion that the doctrine of the literal Millennium was an embarrassment – a leftover from the pioneering days that needed quietly putting to rest. These views probably reflect the thinking of a significant and articulate *minority* in British Assemblies of God but, as we said at the outset, some reappraisal is called for, particularly in the form of a fresh look at the Scriptures and a thinking through what many of us have taken for granted for as long as we can remember.

At this point, just to reassure you, and not try your patience too much, let me say that I have no intention of producing yet another ingenious chart of end-time events, or of going through the traditional doctrine point-by-point, seal-by-seal or trumpet-by-trumpet!

The excited disciples, hanging on every word of their Risen Lord, ask him in Acts 1.6, 'Lord, are you at this time going to restore the kingdom to Israel?' (NIV). At this point, had the promises to historic Israel been, because of their unbelief, transferred to the Church as the New Israel, in the form of spiritual benefits, as some would have us understand, or had the ancient prophetic Scriptures all along referred to a spiritual fulfilment in and through the Church, then Jesus has a golden opportunity and, indeed, a solemn duty, to tell them so. But he did no such thing. He did not round on them and say, 'Forget such ancient, nationalistic, chiliastic nonsense!' He said – and I paraphrase – 'The Father has not seen fit to disclose when that will take place. Now get filled with the Spirit and start planting the Kingdom in men's hearts!'

When Jesus was being interrogated by Pilate, the Roman Procurator asked him if he were King of the Jews. Jesus acknowledged that he was indeed a king, but explained, 'My kingdom is not of this world. If it were, my servants would fight to prevent my arrest . . . But now my kingdom is from another place' (John 18.36). These words have been taken by a number of commentators to mean that the Kingdom Jesus came to set up was purely spiritual, God's rule in the hearts of men. What Jesus was saying was, in fact, that his Kingdom was not, like others, to be set up by force of arms or *coup d'état* but by the power of God. His words certainly do not rule out a temporal and terrestrial kingdom; and Acts 1.7 strongly suggests that Jesus anticipated such a kingdom being set up at some time in the future. Pilate's determination not to alter the superscription or charge set up over the cross of Jesus is surely of great significance also. The dignified bearing, modesty and nobility of Christ, when under interrogation, had convinced the Roman that here was no charlatan or rabble-rouser but the King of the Jews, as he himself had acknowledged.

The fact is that the Kingdom Jesus came to set up has *two* major aspects . . . To do justice to all the data of Scripture does demand that we have a double emphasis in our preaching and teaching: the Kingdom exists now and, thank God, is growing; but it will take a crisis and a Divine Intervention in history once again before it is manifested.

Used by permission of the author, David Allen, Mattersey Hall, Mattersey, UK.

Though most Pentecostals of the twentieth century believed that Christ would literally rule in millennial glory on earth after his return, charismatics interpreted the crucial biblical passages differently. Christ rules now and there are only two ages: the present age and the age to come. There is no intermediate millennial period.

3.6   J. Rodman Williams, *Renewal Theology*, vol. 3: *The Millennium*, Grand Rapids, Michigan: Zondervan, 1988, pp. 428–31, abridged

That this reigning refers to the present is further attested by earlier statements in Revelation. In the opening chapter John joyously speaks about Jesus: 'To him who loves us and has freed US from our sins by his blood and made us a kingdom, priests to his God and Father, to him be glory and dominion for ever and ever. Amen' (vv. 5–6). He *'made us* a kingdom,' which means that all who have been freed from sins *are* also a kingdom, hence they reign as kings[1] even now. John is not so much saying that we are in His kingdom (however true that is) but that we *are* a kingdom.[2] Thus, we reign in life–now. Later in this chapter John declares, 'I, John, your brother . . . share with you in Jesus the tribulation and the kingdom and the patient endurance' (v. 9). This is not the kingdom to come but the present situation of his and of all saints – victoriously reigning over every earthly trial and tribulation with patient endurance.

Note also the imagery of 'priests'. We have not only been 'made . . . a kingdom' but we have also been made priests – to His God and Father. Hence, as believers we are presently both a kingdom (or kings, reigning) and Priests to God. Now we turn again to Revelation 20 and observe that 'they' are also called priests: 'They shall be priests of God and of Christ, and they shall reign with him a thousand years' (v. 6). It seems unmistakable, therefore, that both kingdom-reigning and priesthood refer in both Revelation 1 and 20 to the present victorious lives of all who have been freed by Christ from their sins. It is not a fact of the future, but a present joyous reality.

One further scripture relating to kingdom and priests and their victorious reigning is found in Revelation 5. In heaven a 'new song' is sung to the Lamb: 'Worthy art thou to take the book, and to open the seals thereof for thou wast slain, and didst purchase unto God with thy blood men of every

---

[1] The KJV reads, 'made us kings'. Although 'kingdom' (basileian) is a more literal rendering of the text, the KJV well conveys the idea of reigning as 'kings'.

[2] The Kingdom, in this context, is not so much realm as it is reign.

tribe, and tongue, and people, and nation, and madest them to be unto our God a kingdom and priests; and they reign upon [or "over"[3]] the earth' (vv. 9–10 ASV[4]). In accordance with Revelation 1.5–6 (which as noted, likewise speaks of salvation by the blood of Christ and being 'made a kingdom, priests . . .'), this reigning refers to the present. Reigning over the earth therefore signifies the victorious reign of believers 'in life' over everything that formerly held them captive. It is – in the language of Paul – to be 'in all these things . . . more than conquerors' (Rom. 8.37).

One further matter: The reign of the saints with Christ is said to be for a thousand years. How are we to understand the figure of a thousand? Does this refer to a literal calendar period? In light of the symbolic use of figures in the Book of Revelation,[5] it is more likely to express a complete but indeterminate period of time.[6] Indeed, the reference to a thousand years in regard to the reign of the saints sets it apart from the age to come when 'they shall reign for ever and ever' (Rev. 22.5), and places it within the limits of the present age. Hence, the thousand years specifies the period of reigning with Christ between His first coming and His final advent – that is, the gospel age. Upon Christ's return the thousand years will be complete, and the eternal reign begun.

---

[3] The more likely translation (as in Weymouth). The Greek preposition *epi* can mean 'upon' or 'over'; however, in a similar passage that also relates to reigning – 'and the woman whom thou sawest is the great city, which reigneth over [*epi*] the kings of earth' (Rev. 17.18 ASV) – the only possible translation is 'over' (all translations). Also cf. Luke 1.33: 'He will reign over [*epi*] the house of Jacob forever.' And Luke 19.14: 'We do not want this man to reign over [*epi*] us.' 'Upon' would make no sense. Bauer, *Greek–English Lexicon of the New Testament and Other Early Christian Literature* translates *epi* as 'over' in Revelation 5.10.

[4] In regard to the ASV translation 'they reign' we must recognize as Mounce says, 'textual evidence is rather equally divided between 'they reign' (ASV) and 'they shall reign' (RSV)' (*The Book of Revelation*, New International Commentaries of the New Testament, p. 149). My preference is the ASV rendering because it points more clearly to the reign as being present. However, the translation 'shall reign' (most commentaries) does not necessarily call for future reign any more than the 'will live' of John 5 . . . points to a future situation.

[5] See, e.g., [Williams'] previous discussion of 3½ years (also 42 months or 1,260 days). Recall also the 144,000 'sealed' in the time of the 'great tribulation'.

[6] Ladd speaks of the 'symbolic use of numbers in Revelation'. Then he adds, 'A thousand equals the third power of ten – and ideal time. While we need not take it literally, "the thousand years" does appear to represent a real period of time, however long or short it may be' (*A Commentary on the Revelation of John*, p. 262). This is what Hoekema speaks of as 'indeterminate length'. In a statement similar to Ladd's, he writes, 'Since the number ten signifies completeness, and since a thousand is ten to the third power, we may think of the expression "a thousand years" as standing for a complete period, a very long period of indeterminate length' (*The Bible and the Future*, p. 227).

The thousand-year period – or 'the Millennium' – is therefore a *present* reality. It cannot be placed in a future time prior to the eternal kingdom. The Bible is silent regarding an interim age; it speaks only of the present age and the age to come. The teaching of Jesus is unmistakable in this matter;[7] likewise Paul[8] and other New Testament writers give scant reason[9] for any other view. The Old Testament has many beautiful pictures of a coming messianic age, but it is very difficult – if not impossible – to discover a future earthly millennial period.[10] Indeed, the whole idea of such a future earthly reign seems out of harmony with the rest of Scripture.

---

[7] It is interesting that Ladd, who affirms a future millennium, writes, 'I can find no trace of the idea of either an interim earthly kingdom or of a millennium in the Gospels' (Robert G. Clouse, (ed.), *The Meaning of the Millennium: Four Views*, p. 38).

[8] In regard to Paul, Ladd states, 'There is, however, one passage in Paul which may refer to an interim kingdom if not millennium. In 1 Corinthians 15.23–6 Paul pictures the triumph of Christ's kingdom as being accomplished in several stages' (p. 9). The stages are Christ's resurrection, the resurrection of believers, and after that the end. In addition, says Ladd, there is 'an unidentified interval . . . between Christ's resurrection and his Parousia; and a second undefined interval . . . between Parousia and the *telos* when Christ completes the subjugation of his enemies' (p. 39). Ladd's delineation of an interval between the Parousia and the *telos* (end), however, is hardly Paul's teaching. The subjugation of Christ's enemies climaxes at the Parousia, not afterward. When Paul says, 'For he must reign until he has put all enemies under his feet.' This is better understood as referring not to a future reign but to a present reign that will end *at* His Parousia with the final subjection (on this see particularly G. Vos, *The Pauline Eschatology*, pp. 244–6). It is significant that Mounce, also a premillennialist, writes that 'the attempt to attribute to Paul a belief in the millennium on the basis of 1 Cor. 15.20–8 is unconvincing' (*The Book of Revelation*, NICNT, p. 357, n.15).

[9] Revelation 20 is the only conceivable possibility! However, as Richardson says, 'If verses four, five and six had been omitted from this chapter no one would ever have dreamed of a literal thousand years of Christ's reign on earth; of his setting up a temporal kingdom and inaugurating a millennial reign as an earthly monarch' (*The Revelation of Jesus Christ*, p. 157). Both the very limited evidence and the even more serious disharmony with other scriptures makes highly questionable a future millennium.

[10] According to the Old Testament, there is surely an age to come, but it is essentially undifferentiated. Indeed there is depicted only one coming of the Messiah, and His reign will by no means be for a thousand years but forever. Some of the earthly images of the coming messianic reign are frequently viewed as referring to a limited reign, but this is quite unwarranted. The reason for such a view, incidentally, is not hard to find. Since the Messiah did not literally reign on earth in His first coming, nor will this happen in the eternal kingdom, there must be then a limited period in between when Old Testament pictures and promises

But when the thousand years is viewed as a present reality, all Scripture fits together in its basic portrayal of two ages (not three): the present age and the age yet to come.

When it is also realized that Revelation 20.4–6 does not call for a future millennium, but emphasizes, along with Revelation 1 and 5, the present reign of the saints with Christ, then everything falls in place. Moreover, such an understanding highlights the victory that saints down through the years, even to the present day, have in Christ. They have sat on thrones – hence reigned – and by their lives the world has been judged. Many have been martyred, but this has not prevented them from living and reigning with Christ. Indeed, whatever the persecution, the saints have not bowed before the beast or received its mark on forehead or hand. They have reigned victoriously. Death has meant nothing, for they have already known the 'first resurrection' from spiritual death; hence over them the 'second death' – eternal death – has utterly no power. What a blessing to share in the resurrection to life, and thereby to become 'priests' of God and of Christ and to reign with Him throughout the thousand years!

Used by permission of Zondervan Publishers, 5300 Patterson Avenue SE, Grand Rapids, MI 49530, USA.

This vision caused a stir when it was published. It should be contrasted with the optimism about the Second Coming of Christ.

3.7   David Wilkerson, *The Vision*, Old Tappan, New Jersey: Spire Books, 1974, pp. 31, 32, 91, 92, abridged

Drastic weather changes

Drastic weather changes are breaking records around the world. Some experts believe it is caused by volcanic ash from the eruptions in Iceland

---

must be fulfilled. Thus the Millennium as such a period seems to be the solution. However, the Old Testament in no instance has such a limited prospect in view. It is far better to understand the Old Testament messianic blessings as fulfilled both in the church age and in the age to come. This includes both spiritual and material blessings. In regard to the latter (which the Old Testament often mentions), it is better to view many of them as fulfilled eternally in the 'the new heaven' and the 'new earth' of Revelation 21–22 rather than in a limited thousand-year period.

now being carried by the jet stream in the troposphere. I personally believe that much of the drastic weather we are seeing throughout the world today can be explained up to this point by science.

In past centuries the world has witnessed devastating major earthquakes, killer heat waves, horrible floods, and all kinds of bizarre changes in the weather. All things have always returned to normal.

In my vision, I have seen very little that is supernatural about the drastic weather changes we have experienced up to this time. But I also see very clearly divine intervention about to happen throughout the world. This world had best prepare for weather changes that cannot be explained by any other word but 'supernatural'. The world is about to witness the beginnings of great sorrows brought about by history's most drastic weather changes, earthquakes, floods, terrible calamities – far surpassing anything ever yet witnessed.

Earthquakes coming to the United States

The United States is going to experience, in the not-too-distant future, the most tragic earthquake in its history. One day soon this nation will be reeling under the impact of the biggest news story of modern times. It will be coverage of the biggest, most disastrous earthquake in history.

It will cause widespread panic and fear. Without a doubt, it will become one of the most completely reported earthquakes ever. Television networks will suspend all programming and carry all-day coverage.

Another earthquake, possibly in Japan, may precede the one that I see coming here. There is not the slightest doubt in my mind about this forthcoming massive earthquake on our continent . . .

Awakening behind the Iron and Bamboo Curtains

While the free nations experience a wave of real persecution, the Iron and Bamboo countries will experience a short period of spiritual awakening. Those who have lived under terrible religious persecution will enjoy a limited period of freedom. God's Holy Spirit will split the Iron and Bamboo Curtains and will seek out and find hungry hearts in Russia, China, and Eastern Europe.

God has promised to pour His Spirit out upon all flesh, and that includes the peoples behind the Iron and Bamboo Curtains.

God is bringing to pass a temporary truce between the East and the West for the express purpose of getting the gospel into these Communist countries. Japanese and Korean Christians alone can be used of God to reach thousands in China. Christians in West Germany can reach those in East

Germany. The path to Russia is through Finland. A tremendous move of the Holy Spirit in Finland can and will spill over into Russia.

Ironically, while the doors are beginning to close on this side of the Curtains, the doors will begin to open on the other side. And, after a short period of freedom and spiritual awakening among many, the doors will suddenly close, and the persecution madness will begin with intensity and engulf all those nations.

⚓⚓

A Catholic priest and scholar, Peter Hocken (b. 1932) explains here how the Baptism of the Spirit made a difference to his understanding of eschatology.

3.8   Peter Hocken, 'The Holy Spirit Makes the Church More Eschatological', in P. Hocken, *Blazing the Trail*, Guildford, Surrey: Eagle Publishing, 1994, abridged

Restoring the hope of the Church

Before my involvement in charismatic renewal, the second coming of Jesus was something I believed in, but never thought about. Consequently I never preached about it, even in Advent. It was an 'external' truth that did not touch my inner life. I thought of people who got excited about the last days as fanatical and weird. At best, eschatology was a theological topic that could be interesting, as long as it avoided all fundamentalism and naivety.

This indifference to the second coming of Jesus began to melt when I received a deep renewal in my faith through charismatic renewal. . . . So as I began to turn my gaze more towards God's future, I found the Holy Spirit bringing alive the 'blessed hope, the appearing of the glory of our great God and Saviour Jesus Christ' (Titus 2.13).

In fact, the gift of the Holy Spirit will always sow the blessed hope. The gift of the Spirit is the gift of the risen Lord. He is pouring out that which he has received totally into his humanity. 'Being therefore exalted at the right hand of God, and having received from the Father the promise of the Holy Spirit, he has poured out this which you see and hear' (Acts 2.33). The glorification of Jesus in his resurrection–ascension represents the total penetration of his humanity by the Holy Spirit. The Spirit penetrates and fills every part and dimension of the body of Jesus. When we receive the Holy Spirit into ourselves, we receive the seed and the promise of our own glorification. What Jesus now is as glorified man, we also shall be.

. . .

The gift of the Holy Spirit as first fruits

Perhaps the key that opened up the whole area of the second coming was the discovery of St Paul's teaching on the gift of the Holy Spirit as *aparche* (first fruits) and as *arrabon* (deposit). In the charismatic movement, with its accent on an experiential reception of the Spirit, the emphasis was all on receiving the Holy Spirit. It was easy to assume that receiving the Holy Spirit meant receiving everything now. It was then a wonderful corrective to receive light from these passages about first fruits and deposit. These passages both convey the greatness of the present gift of the Holy Spirit, and the vastness of what is to come that is heralded by the present gift. . . .

Renewal and the Parousia

The basic link between the experience of spiritual renewal and the awakening of hope for the second coming of Jesus lies in the gift of the Holy Spirit. As we welcome the gift of the Spirit in this life, we experience a desire for the fullness of the gift of the Spirit in the resurrection. This longing and desire can only be awoken by the Holy Spirit. 'Come' is the cry of the Spirit and of the Bride (Rev. 22.17); it is the cry that the Spirit teaches to the Bride.

The Spirit awakens this hope in the individual Christian and in the Church. As this hope is awakened, the Christian discovers that this longing for the Parousia and the Kingdom is mentioned as frequently as any other doctrine in the New Testament. We become aware how this hope suffuses the Catholic liturgy. It is found in acclamations after the consecration,[1] in Eucharistic Prayer no. 3 in the Commemoration,[2] in the *Libera nos* after the Our Father.[3] And of course it is found in countless prayers during the season of Advent . . .

. . . Here I want simply to draw attention to the more striking statements in the Catechism concerning the second coming. The first occurs in the

---

[1] e.g. 'Christ has died. Christ has risen. Christ will come again.' 'Dying you destroyed our death, rising you restored our life. Lord Jesus, come in glory.' 'When we eat this bread and drink this cup, we proclaim your death, Lord Jesus, until you come in glory.'

[2] 'ready to greet him when he comes again'.

[3] 'as we wait in joyful hope for the coming of our Saviour, Jesus Christ'.

context of the teaching of the Creed that 'He will come again to judge the living and the dead' within a section headed 'The glorious advent of Christ, the hope of Israel'. Here we find a long paragraph on the relationship between Israel's recognition of the Messiah and the second coming of Jesus, that would seem to be the first time that an official teaching of the Catholic Church has addressed this link. 'The glorious Messiah's coming is suspended at every moment of history until his recognition by "all Israel". . . . The "full inclusion" of the Jews in the Messiah's salvation, in the wake of "the full number of the Gentiles," will enable the People of God to achieve "the measure of the stature of the fulness of Christ," in which "God may be all in all"' (para. 674).[4]

The next two citations speak strongly of the Holy Spirit's role in the preparation of the age to come, and they come in the general sections on the sacraments and the liturgy before the treatment of each sacrament. 'The Holy Spirit's transforming power in the liturgy hastens the coming of the kingdom and the consummation of the mystery of salvation. While we wait in hope he causes us really to anticipate the fullness of communion with the Holy Trinity' (para. 1107). This belongs to the nature of the liturgy that is inspired and permeated by the Holy Spirit of God. The sacramental signs – the baptismal bath, the eucharistic banquet, the anointing with oil for healing – all symbolize and prepare for the glory of the age to come. Thus the celebration of the liturgy will continue until the dawn of that age: 'The Church celebrates the mystery of her Lord 'until he comes' when God will be 'everything to everyone. Since the apostolic age the liturgy has been drawn towards its goal by the Spirit's groaning in the Church: *Marana tha!'* (para. 1130).

The last citation comes from the final section of the Catechism's teaching on the Eucharist, which is entitled 'The Eucharist: Pledge of the Glory to Come'. Here the Catechism[5] applies the general teaching on the sacraments preparing for the age to come specifically to the Eucharist: 'the Eucharist is also an anticipation of the heavenly glory' (para. 1402). 'Whenever the Church celebrates the Eucharist she remembers this promise and turns her gaze "to him who is to come". In her prayer she calls for his coming: *"Marana tha!"*. "Come, Lord Jesus!" "May your grace come and this world pass away!"' (para. 1403). . . . the Catechism sees a particular significance to the recitation of the Lord's prayer and the petition 'Thy kingdom come' within the context of the Eucharist.

---

[4] The passages cited bring together Paul's teaching in Rom. 11.12, 25–6; Eph. 4.13; and 1 Cor. 15.28.

[5] These references come from the *Catechism of the Catholic Church*, published in 1994.

These passages from the Catechism bring out the dynamic faith of the Church in the second coming. They bring out the role of the Holy Spirit in producing a dynamic towards the Parousia, a hope in the Church, and a longing of the Church. They focus on the liturgical expression of this hope and this longing. It is not simply the hope and the longing of individual believers, but the hope and the longing of the whole Church, the Church on earth, the Church in 'Final Purification' and the Church triumphant in glory. . . .

As the Holy Spirit makes the Church more eschatological, the Spirit is restoring the fullness of the New Testament hope. This hope is of total salvation, the deliverance of all creation from its bondage to decay, the establishment of the new heavens and the new earth, our resurrection in glorified spiritual bodies, in which there will be total communion with all the saints and angels in the perfect harmony and eternal life of the Most Holy Trinity.

Used by permission of M. Conway mike@biblealive.demon.co.uk

4 Healing

W. K. Kay, Introduction

Nowhere is the essentially restorationist impetus of Pentecostal and charismatic theology more markedly shown than in the area of healing. The belief that the presence and power of God may be apprehended within the contemporary world and, indeed, that the God of canonical Scripture is essentially interventionist leads to an almost dualistic mentality when healing and sickness are juxtaposed. The mentality is 'almost dualistic' because Pentecostals have been insistent in their teaching that no illness is beyond the capacity of God to heal. It is not a battle between health and sickness, or between God and the devil, fought out on equal terms, since Christ's person and work embody divine victory. Yet, when the horrible reality of illness is closely contemplated – and Pentecostal preachers frequently came face-to-face with inoperable and apparently hopelessly tragic cases of human suffering in evangelistic meetings – the struggle between good and evil was starkly evident.

Pentecostals founded their theology on Scripture but they modified their healing doctrine in the light of experience. The readings in this section illustrate several criss-crossing themes. Among them is a tendency over time for a sharp antagonism between divine healing and medicine to be transformed into an irenic partnership that, in the case of Oral Roberts, was expressed by the building of a university into which this philosophy was institutionally implanted. There is also a tendency for an emphasis on faith as the great human weapon against illness to be upgraded or downplayed depending on other aspects of the writer's theology. To upgrade faith is to risk condemning the unhealed for their own illnesses and, worse, to make them feel guilty that they even asked for prayer. To downplay faith is to risk pushing healing back behind a barrier of divine inscrutability. Healing becomes conditional upon God's mysterious will, and human beings cannot do very much to find what this will is or to make it happen. Faith, within the evangelical tradition where Pentecostals and charismatics largely identified themselves, was integral to salvation. Faith was essential to Christianity, but was the faith that healed the same as the faith that saved?

Pentecostals and charismatics wrestled with the answer to this enquiry and to two others. First, how should Isaiah 53 be understood? Did Christ on the cross carry our illnesses in the same way as he carried our sins? The varying answers to these questions were all employed vigorously and more or less explicitly by Pentecostal preachers against the power of the devil, of Satan, the thief who comes to 'steal, kill and destroy' (John 10.10). Second, how should people today understand the charismatic gifts, including 'gifts of healings' described especially in 1 Corinthians 12 and 14 but also found elsewhere in the New Testament? Third and more generally, how should the healthy life and healing ministry of Christ be exemplified by the Church and within the bodies of individual Christians?

Pentecostals prepared the ground for answers by establishing that miracles of healing could indeed take place in the modern (and post-modern) world and, in doing this, they fought on two fronts. They argued vigorously, though often by assertion rather than by detailed rebuttal, against the worldview that presumed modern science had killed off the possibility of miracle. They believed instinctively in a God who controlled the universe and they did so at a time when Newtonian mechanics were on the wane. They also, especially at the start of the twentieth century, argued against a dispensationalist understanding of Scripture that denied miracles could occur in any era of church history apart from the very first.

Many of these themes and issues are seen in the writings of Alexander Boddy, the Anglican clergyman who founded the magazine *Confidence* (1908–26), that served to advertise Pentecostalism and stabilize its doctrinal implications. Boddy (4.1) constructed a theology of healing that primarily focused on identification with Christ. In Boddy's account Christ becomes 'the representative human life' who lived in such close communion with God as to be free of disease. The Christian is to follow this pattern and, accepting Christ as the 'indwelling Divine Life', to live without illness.[1] A Christian who tried to put this into practice could not be guaranteed a sickness-free existence and, when illness threatened, Boddy recommended an overcoming-by-faith approach that would have been applauded by a swathe of Pentecostals and charismatics sixty years later.

Yet Boddy's attempt to base his doctrine on the breadth of Scripture led him also to recognize the role of the charismata operating through the eldership of a local church.

Smith Wigglesworth (4.2), noted as an uneducated plumber who became an international preacher, was reputed to be a man of one message: 'only believe'. But an examination of his sermons shows a richer understanding. His notion of union with Christ, of the manifestation of divine life within the Christian, was fully, vividly and even mystically expressed to the

---

[1] 'Health in Christ', *Confidence*, August 1910.

extent that the distinction between healing as a result of Christ working within the believer and healing as a result of the manifestation of the Holy Spirit became blurred.[2] In Wigglesworth there is an apprehension of the vastness of God's love and an aggressive anger against disease, which he attributed directly to the devil.

Harold Horton (4.3), perhaps reacting against his Methodist origins, argued for the completely supernatural character of spiritual gifts.[3] He was insistent that they are quite unrelated to natural gifts. His polemic is partly directed at a liberal Christian 'explaining away' of the New Testament miracles and partly at an attitude that identified Christian ministry entirely with the work of an educated elite. At the time when he wrote, Pentecostals were largely ill-educated – most of them left school at the age of 14 – and almost none had the advantages of graduate or postgraduate training. By insisting that spiritual gifts are supernatural he was able to argue that they are available, through the grace of God, to any Christian. In this sense his argument implies a democratization of the Church.

George Jeffreys (4.4) took the dispensational issues seriously enough to construct a theology of healing on the basis of three great dispensations.[4] The dispensation of the Father occurs in the Old Testament, and healing here is as a result of the activity of the Father. The dispensation of the Son occurs in the ministry of Christ himself who heals directly by virtue of his divine power. The dispensation of the Spirit occurs in the church age after the day of Pentecost. All healing is predicated on Christ's 'healing and redeeming work' since in earlier dispensations people looked forward to it and in the present dispensation people may look back to it. Jeffreys constructs a careful scheme making parallel Adam and Christ. What Adam lost as a result of sin, Christ gained as a result of righteousness. The benefits of Christ's death are distributed between time and eternity. Those that are available in time may be enjoyed in the church age with a result that people with faith in Christ may find perfect healing. This analysis depends, as does most Pentecostal thinking about healing, on the view that ultimately sickness is only in the world as a consequence of human sin. In Jeffreys' scheme, as the reading shows, what is lost at the fall and what is gained by Christ are precisely balanced.

Of the healing evangelists who based their theology on the atonement none did so with greater care or attention to detail than the veteran F. F. Bosworth (4.5), one of the delegates to the first American Assemblies of God General Councils in Arkansas in 1914. His studies, according to the

---

[2] 'Filled with God', August 1922, Liardon edn, pp. 143f.
[3] *Gifts of the Spirit*, pp. 26–7, 107,108.
[4] *Healing Rays*, 1932, chs 6–8.

foreword of the book from which this extract is taken, became 'a textbook in church bible classes, bible schools, and seminars'.

Yet, C. L. Parker (4.6), a lecturer at the British Assemblies of God Bible College in the 1930s and the 1960s, would have profoundly disagreed with Bosworth. Whereas Bosworth took Christ's atonement to be a single undifferentiated concept, Parker distinguished between its reconciliatory and its expiatory aspects. Sickness has no moral or sin-like characteristics and so does not require expiatory atonement. Reconciliation with God, however, is the source of a great range of blessings, and these include physical benefits. To treat the removal of sickness in the same way as the removal of sin was mistaken. Healing belonged primarily in the context of evangelism or in the James 5 ministrations of church elders. Where the Holy Spirit operated to bring 'gifts of healings' to a sick person, this could not be predicted by a human formula.

Divergence in Pentecostal and charismatic theology of healing is also found in the contrast between T. L. Osborn (4.7) and Kathryn Kuhlman (4.8), both of whom were healing evangelists. Osborn's conception of faith led him to set it in opposition to sense experience so that the battle for healing was often one between what appeared to be the case on the basis of sense experience and what was actually the case according to faith in scriptural promises. He thought 'revelation faith' was a higher form of knowledge than other kinds. Another way of putting this was that sense-based knowledge derived from the wrong kind of faith. Effectively, Osborn began to rethink what faith means by moving its semantic range beyond Christian tradition into the secular world. This enlargement was taken further by the Faith and Prosperity movement stemming from the 1970s.

Kathryn Kuhlman's theology of healing was worked out in the practical arena (sometimes literally an arena) where, as a healing evangelist, she ministered. Like other Pentecostals she was a preacher and her theology was shaped by events in and after public evangelistic meetings. She saw remarkable miracles and came to appreciate that healings took place by contact with the presence of God, the Holy Spirit. Unlike earlier Pentecostals, she rejected the inflation of claims about faith itself as a natural power or as a key to miraculous and divine intervention. Her insight was to simplify the conjunction of conditions under which healing might take place. In her writing and preaching there is little emphasis on faith or on the theology of the atonement – though she preserved an evangelical position on these matters. Rather, drawing on a profound Trinitarian understanding, she believed that the love of God was verified when the abundant presence of the Holy Spirit demonstrated on the ill and infirm the power that raised Christ from the dead.

The complex and partially integrated doctrine of healing held at the start of the twentieth century showed signs of breaking apart in the post-World War II period as one or other element within the doctrine was elevated above others. John Wimber's (4.10) unification of an approach to healing was founded in his wholistic comprehension of tripartite (body, soul and spirit) human beings. Perfect health occurred when all the parts were in harmony because malfunctions within one part might have adverse effects on the others. In his stress on the healing presence of God the Holy Spirit, he was like Kuhlman, and he also, like her, saw gifts of healing(s) as being informed by other charismata. In a large auditorium, it was possible for the preacher to receive a 'word of knowledge' about the nature of illnesses suffered by individuals in a congregation and, by calling these out, to inspire them to be open to the Holy Spirit in ways that led to healing. More broadly, in Wimber's thinking, healing became paradigmatic of salvation; in a sense to be saved *was* to be healed, for everyone was thought to be harmed by sin whether they knew it or not. Healing, in contrast to its dispensational conception by Jeffreys, was a manifestation not only of the Holy Spirit's work but of the *whole* triune God's embrace of dysfunctional tripartite human beings.

To such wholistic perspectives Oral Roberts (4.9) would have given assent.[5] In the course of a lengthy ministry he made the transition from an old-time 'sawdust trail tent preacher' to a renowned televangelist and United Methodist with sufficient fund-raising capacity to build a university in Tulsa that contained both a prayer tower and a medical school. His underlying belief was simple: God is the Source of all good things, and health is one of these good things. If health comes through medical or biblical means, then no theological contradiction has been perpetrated.

---

[5] A holistic doctrine of healing was also found in the ministry of Francis MacNutt, a priest involved in the Catholic Charismatic Renewal. See F. MacNutt (1977), *The Power to Heal*, Notre Dame, Indiana: Ave Maria Press. It is also found in the writings of Agnes Sanford and her work on 'inner healing'.

Boddy's expository sermon embryonically includes many of the themes that would later be developed by twentieth-century Pentecostals and charismatics

4.1   A. A. Boddy, 'Health in Christ', *Confidence*, March 1910, pp. 175–9 (original footnotes), abridged

Our Lord is a 'Saviour' because He SAVES. Now when we read in the Acts of the Apostles (16.30), 'Believe on the Lord Jesus Christ and thou shalt be saved,' we must not forget what this glorious word 'saved' can include if we do not limit our faith in Him who is the Life.

The Word 'Saved' is rightly translated 'made whole' in St Luke 8.48 – 'Thy faith hath made thee whole,' and in the preceding chapter at the 50th verse, exactly the same sentence is translated, 'Thy faith hath saved thee.' The Greek verb 'save' (sozo) is rendered 'make whole' in about eleven passages in the New Testament.[1]

Surely men are quite as much justified in saying 'Believe on the Lord Jesus Christ and thou shalt be made whole' as in reading in the authorized version 'Believe on the Lord Jesus Christ and thou shalt be saved.' It is all of Grace.

If any man is truly 'born from above' he has a new life, a new nature, and that is Christ's nature. The Divine Christ became human, but He lived His life on earth in such unbroken communion with His Father in heaven that disease had no power to lay hold on Him.

For the time He emptied Himself (Phil 2.7). His was, I believe, the representative human life lived under our conditions. He accepted conditionally the Holy Ghost as *we* may accept Him to be the indwelling Divine Life. He was tempted and really tempted in all points like as we are, but without sin and without disease. He touched the fever-stricken and the leper, but he did not receive fever or leprosy.

Disease came into this world with sin, and both followed the yielding to Satan's temptation to unbelief. The Divine Nature died in our first parents with the FALL (Gen. 2.17), and their fallen, tainted, sin-stricken, disease-stricken nature has been handed down to us.

Christ our Saviour came to undo the Fall (and its consequences) in those who join themselves by continuous and persevering faith to Him in whom they were crucified. 'They that are Christ's have crucified (at Calvary) the flesh (the fallen nature) with its affections and lusts' (Gal. 5.24).

---

[1] See Grimm and Thayer's *Lexicon of the Greek New Testament*.

On the Cross He bare our sins, and on the Cross He also bare our sicknesses.

'Surely He hath borne our sicknesses and carried our sorrows' is the true rendering of Isaiah 53.4 (Revised Version, margin). With His stripes we are healed (verse 5).

'We died' (in Him) – there was the end of our old nature, 'We died, and our life is hid with Christ in God' (Col. 3.3).[2]

If we believe this with our whole heart, despite the desperate attempts of our great enemy to overthrow our faith – if we believe thus on the Lord Jesus Christ we shall be saved – we shall be made whole and be kept whole.

We are pointed to the noble army of brave doctors and devoted nurses, to the wonderful advance of medical science, and are asked if this is not a 'good' gift of God, and we gratefully acknowledge it is, while we believe that there is a higher way (a 'perfect' gift) for those who know they are in Christ, and know that He can SAVE to the uttermost.

We are asked whether sickness is not often used of God to make men and women think, and whether suffering does not bring out the finer qualities in a man.

We acknowledge that God does permit trouble and the approach of death to draw some to turn to Himself, but not always.

Sickness as a rule is considered, even by religious people, as so little a blessing that *every effort is made to get rid of it* as soon as possible or to counteract its influence. If it is really 'the Will of God', how dare they attempt by any means to get rid of it?

Disease is the inheritance of a fallen race. Our sinning first parents could only hand on to posterity that which was left to them. Disease is not by any means the index of the sin of the diseased persons. The Lord rebuked the questioner who said, 'Lord, did this man sin or his parents, that he was born blind.'

. . .

Christian Science, etc.

The so-called Christian Science says that all pain and disease is unreal – you are to believe you have not got it and it will go. It ignores the existence and power of Satan, and the work of the Atonement.[3] Whatever wonderful cures and changes of temper are worked among its disciples, I believe that

---

[2] See the writer's *Identification, or the Secret of Life and Power.*

[3] See the writer's little booklet on *Christian Science: A Soul Danger.*

greater works can he wrought by a simple trust in Christ's power. If as much trust is placed in God's Word (The Bible) as some place in the text-book of Christian Science, then that Word, which is quick and powerful, will produce its true results. Satan so counterfeits the works of Christ, and so mixes up truth and error, that he succeeds in confusing believers and getting unbelievers to dwell on the counterfeits, and reject the Reality. Christian Science means a loss of the true Christ who saved us by His Death on the Cross.

Imagine now that a very bad cold is coming on. The old symptoms tell us that it will go through the inevitable stages unless something unusual happens. But you know now that *Christ is your life*. You know that you are a new creature in Christ Jesus. You know that your old nature is dead, and that your life is hid with Christ in God. You know that in Christ there is no disease and you are His member, bone of His bone and flesh of His flesh. You are sure that this cold is not the will of God. It can in no way bring glory to Him, whereas deliverance from it will be a help to others and may induce them to trust Him also. You recognize that this cold is from Satan. Nay, that it is a counterfeit from the 'father of lies'. You are every whit whole in Christ. Saved (made whole), body, soul and spirit.

Then though you may be made by the enemy to sneeze, or cough, though from a physical point of view the bystander would say, perhaps, 'What a dreadful cold you have got,' you hold on to the truth that you are whole because you are in Jesus Christ, and you show your belief by *really* 'praising God' for Victory. As you do this unflinchingly you will find that Satan has to go. Perhaps instantaneously, perhaps gradually, the whole thing vanishes, and the unbelievers around will say, 'It is really strange how such an one gets rid of cold.' Satan is beaten!

I have only instanced cold because, as I have been writing, the above has been my own experience. Headache, cancer, paralysis, diabetes, pain in childbirth, rheumatism, have given way alike as the member of the Living Christ has rejected Satan's 'lies' in the very real (apparently) form of these troubles. . . .

'Faith-Healing'

So far we have thought of Divine Health in Christ, He who for His members has undone the Fall and its consequences. We have thought of the possibilities of direct and personal contact with Him Who is the Life.

But there are 'Gifts of Healing' given to some by the Holy Spirit (1 Cor. 12.9). The Lord said (Mark 16.18), 'These signs shall follow them that believe: they shall lay hands on the sick and they shall recover.'

So in James 5.14–16, we read: 'Is any sick among you? Let him call the elders of the Church; and let them pray over him, anointing him with oil in the name of the Lord: and the prayer of faith shall SAVE the sick, and the Lord shall raise him up; and if he have committed sins they shall be forgiven him. Confess your faults, one to another, and pray for one another, that ye may be healed.'

We thank God that in these latter days there are, here and there in the Christian Church, Elders, both men and women, to whom the Lord has given these gifts of healing, channels of the quickening Spirit.

WARNING – no one should give up the doctor or medicine unless fully convinced that the Lord not only can, but *has* healed. Giving up taking medicine, or dismissing the painstaking, skilful doctor, does not necessarily shew perfect trust in Christ. You may ask God to bless the medicine and the skill of the doctor, and trust to that, but this is altogether different from trusting Christ for His Spiritual Health. It is the way, however, for *you* until you are sure of the better way.

'Trophimus have I left at Miletum sick,' wrote St Paul (2 Tim. 4.20), and modern questioners say, 'Why?' Probably because he had not at that time faith to be divinely healed. Our Lord Himself could not heal where there was not the right faith. But when we see the very large number of cases of Divine Healing recorded in the Acts as compared with this one instance where the time for the healing did not seem to have come, let us choose to stand with those who accepted Divine Health. The Lord says to us, 'Believest thou that I am able to do this?' As to Paul's 'stake in the flesh', surely we have not like him been in spiritual danger through 'the abundant revelations', nor for that reason needed the messenger of Satan to buffet us. And we are not absolutely certain yet what that 'messenger of Satan', that 'thorn in the flesh', was.

Some in the present day have brought discredit upon the wonderful truth of 'Divine Life for the Body' by their pretensions or egotism. But the truth remains. Christ has redeemed us from all the curse of the Fall if we will accept this redemption and stand fast. It is for ever a fight of 'faith'. We are not waging warfare with flesh and blood, but with the demons, with Christ's personal enemy and his host.

Therefore let us think but little of human instruments, or human failures. If there was not a single case of healing in our own times, or within your own experience, yet we ought to believe that Christ has borne our sicknesses (Isa. 53.4, RV, marginal note).

If case after case *seems* utterly to fail, yet His Word is everlastingly true, and His own people should be glad to trust Him for their bodies as for their souls.

These attacks from the enemy must, however, cause heart-searchings as to whether we have opened any door by which he could come in. Are we really wholly surrendered to Christ? Is there one little sin or one great sin still yielded to? A quaint saying I once heard was, 'The Devil is God's fencing master.' His attacks are to show where there is a weak place in the armour and to teach us to repair it quickly.

No one can trust the Lord for Divine Health, or maintain that position if indulging secretly in ever so small an act of disobedience.

'Search me, O God, and try my heart. Look well if there be any way of wickedness in me, and lead me in the way everlasting.'

Used by permission of the Donald Gee Centre, Mattersey Hall, Mattersey, UK

Wigglesworth's sermon incidentally recounts remarkable miracles, but it also shows how he sees healing as stemming from a continuous relationship with Christ through the Holy Spirit.

4.2   Smith Wigglesworth, 'Filled with God' (Hebrews 2, August 1922), in R. Liardon (ed.), *Smith Wigglesworth: The Complete Collection of His Life Teachings*, Tulsa, Oklahoma: Albury, 1996, pp. 143–6 (edited punctuation)

I want to read to you, in the beginning, the second chapter of Hebrews. Now, this, like every other Scripture, is all very important for us. You could scarcely, at the beginning, pick any special Scripture out of this we have read, it is all so full of truth, it means so much to us, and we must understand that God, in these times, wants to bring us into perfect life, that we need never, under any circumstances, go outside of His Word for anything.

Some people only come with a very small thought concerning God's fullness, and a lot of people are satisfied with a thimbleful, and you can just imagine God saying, 'Oh, if they only knew how much they could take away!' Other people come with a larger vessel, and they go away satisfied, but you can feel how much God is longing for us to have such a desire for more, such a longing as only God Himself can satisfy. I suppose you women would have a good idea of what I mean from the illustration of a screaming child being taken about from one to another, but never satisfied till it gets to the bosom of its mother. You will find that there is no peace, no help, no source of strength, no power, no life, nothing can satisfy the cry of the child of God but the Word of God. God has a special way of satisfying the cry of His children. He is waiting to open to us the windows of heaven until He has so moved in the depths of our hearts that everything unlike Himself has been destroyed. There need be no one in this place go away dry, dry. God wants you to be filled. My brother, my sister, God wants you today to be like a watered garden, filled with the fragrance of His own heavenly joy, till you know at last you have touched immensity. The Son of God came for no other purpose than to lift and lift, and mould and fuse and remould, until we are just after His mind.

I know that the dry ground can have floods, and may God save me from ever wanting anything less than a flood. I will not stoop for small things when I have such a big God. Through the blood of Christ's atonement we may have riches and riches. We need the warming atmosphere of the Spirit's power to bring us closer and closer until nothing but God can satisfy, and then we may have some idea of what God has left after we have taken all that we can. It is only like a sparrow taking a drink of the ocean and then looking around and saying, 'What a vast ocean! What a lot more I could have taken if I had only had room.'

You may have sometimes things you can use, and not know it. Don't you know that you could be dying of thirst right in a river of plenty? There was once a vessel in the mouth of the Amazon River. They thought they were still in the ocean, and they were dying of thirst, some of them nearly mad. They saw a ship and asked if they would give them some water, for some of them were dying of thirst, and they replied, 'Dip your bucket right over; you are in the mouth of the river.' There are any amount of people today in the midst of a great river of life, but they are dying of thirst, because they do not dip down and take it. Dear brother, you may have the Word, but you need an awakened spirit. The Word is not alive until it is moved upon by the Spirit of God, and in the right sense it becomes Spirit and life when it is touched by His hand alone.

Oh, beloved, there is a stream that maketh glad the city of God. There is a stream of life that makes everything move. There is a touch of divine life and likeness through the Word of God that comes nowhere else. There is a death which has no life in it; and there is a death-likeness with Christ which is full of life.

Oh, beloved, there is no such thing as an end to God's beginnings. But we must be in it; we must know it. It is not a touch; it is not a breath; it is the Almighty God; it is a Person; it is the Holy One dwelling in the temple not made with hands. Oh, beloved, He touches and it is done. He is the same

God over all, rich unto all who call upon Him. Pentecost is the last thing that God has to touch the earth with. The baptism is the last thing. If you do not get this you are living in a weak and impoverished condition which is no good to yourself or anybody else. May God move us on to a place where there is no measure to this fullness that He wants to give us. God exalted Jesus and gave Him a name above every name. You notice that everything has been put under Him.

It is about eight years since I was in Oakland and in that time I have seen thousands and thousands healed by the power of God. Last year in Sweden, the last five months of the year, we had over 7,000 people saved by the power of God. The tide is rolling in; let us see to it today that we get right out into the tide, for it will bear you. The bosom of God's love is the centre of all things. Get your eyes off yourself; lift them up high and see the Lord, for in the Lord there is everlasting strength. If you went to see a doctor, the more you told him the more he would know, but when you come to Doctor Jesus, He knows all from the beginning, and He never gives you the wrong medicine. I went to see one today, and someone said, 'Here is a person who has been poisoned through and through by a doctor giving him the wrong medicine.' Jesus sends His healing power and brings His restoring grace, and so there is nothing to fear. The only thing that is wrong is your wrong conception of the mightiness of His redemption.

He was wounded that He might be touched with a feeling of your infirmities. He took your flesh and laid it upon the cross that He might destroy '. . . him that had the power of death, that is, the devil; And deliver them who through fear of death were all their lifetime subject to bondage' (Heb. 2.14, 15). You will find that almost all the ailments that you are heir to come on satanic lines, and they must be dealt with as satanic; they must be cast out. Do not listen to what Satan says to you, for the devil is a liar from the beginning. If people would only listen to the truth of God they would find out they were over the devil, over all satanic forces; they would realize that every evil spirit was subject to them; they would find out that they were always in the place of triumph, and they would 'reign in life' by King Jesus.

Never live in a less place than where God has called you to, and He has called you up on high to live with Him. God has designed that everything shall be subject to man. Through Christ He has given you power over all the power of the enemy. He has wrought out your eternal redemption.

I was finishing a meeting one day in Switzerland. And when we had finished the meeting and had ministered to all the sick, we went out to see some people. Two boys came to us and said that there was a blind man present at the meeting this afternoon, who had heard all the words of the preacher, and said he was surprised that he had not been prayed for. They went on to say this blind man had heard so much that he would not leave that place until he could see. I said, 'This is positively unique. God will do something today for that man.'

We got to the place. This blind man said he never had seen; he was born blind, but because of the Word preached in the afternoon he was not going home until he could see. If ever I have joy it is when I have a lot of people who will not be satisfied until they get all they have come for. With great joy I anointed him that day and laid hands on his eyes, and then immediately God opened his eyes. It was very strange how he acted. There were some electric lights. First he counted them; then he counted us. Oh, the ecstatic pleasure that every moment was created in that man because of his sight! It made us all feel like weeping and dancing and shouting. Then he pulled out his watch, and said that for years he had been feeling the watch for the time, by the raised figures, but now he could look at it and tell us the time. Then, looking as if he was awakened from some deep sleep, or some long, strange dream, he awakened to the fact that he had never seen the face of his father and mother, and he went to the door and rushed out. At night he was the first in the meeting. All the people knew him as the blind man, and I had to give him a long time to talk about his new sight.

Beloved, I wonder how much you want to take away today. You could not carry it if it was substance, but there is something about the grace and the power and the blessings of God that can be carried, no matter how big they are. Oh, what a Saviour; what a place we are in, by grace, that He may come in to commune with us. He is willing to say to every heart, 'Peace, be still,' and to every weak body 'Be strong.'

Are you going halfway; or are you going right to the end? Be not today deceived by Satan, but believe God.

Used by permission Roberts Liardon Ministries, PO Box 30710, Laguna Hills, CA 92654, USA. www.robertsliardon.org, email: info@robertsliardon.org Copyright 2003.

Horton's eloquent account of spiritual gifts is at pains to emphasize their supernatural nature and to minimize natural gifts and talents. Horton's teaching is said to have come from Howard Carter, one of the British Pentecostals imprisoned for conscientious objection in the 1914–18 war.

4.3   H. Horton, *The Gifts of the Spirit*,
Luton: Redemption Tidings Bookroom, 1934, pp. 106–18
(slightly abridged; original capitalization and italicization)

We now come to the second great group of Spiritual Gifts. The three Gifts of Power. Among these, Healings is the most widely distributed. From which we gather it is the least of the Gifts in its own group. . . .

First we must notice the important plurality in its title. It is not the Gift of Healing. It is the Gifts of Healings. Three times in this twelfth chapter [1 Corinthians] it is mentioned (vv. 28, 30) and each time in the original the two nouns are in the plural. This plurality is seen only in verse 28 in our rendering. It is the only Gift of the nine which is in itself a series. Each of the others is a Gift. This is 'Gifts'. But for the sake of keeping it clear from the other eight we will still refer to 'it' when convenient as 'a Gift' as though like the remainder it were in the singular.

These Gifts are for the supernatural healing of diseases and infirmities without natural means of any sort. They are the miraculous manifestation of the Spirit for the banishment of all human ills whether organic, functional or nervous; acute or chronic. Whatever difficulty writers have discovered in defining other Gifts of the Spirit, this particular Gift is understood by all. The Lord Jesus Himself forced it into prominence by the innumerable deliverances he wrought by it in His public ministry and in the authority He gave His disciples to accomplish the same beneficent works through the same endowment.

. . . The command to 'heal the sick' stands in the van of the royal Commission he gave them, that their divine words might be confirmed as they preached by miraculous signs and wonders (Matt. 10.8). This is the Gift that more than any lifted common fishermen and artisans into prominence in the early Christian Church while the envious professionals were wilting under the exposure of their failure, in the light of these non-professional triumphs.

And once again, as in all the other Gifts, we must emphasize the entirely supernatural character of the Gift. For these Gifts of Healings are commonly confused with a high degree of medical or surgical or manipulative or scientific ability. These are all of the natural man. They do not occur in the Scriptures at all, except as they are superseded in Christ. Healings through these Gifts are wrought by the power of Christ through the Spirit, by ignorant believers with no knowledge of physiology, diseases, symptoms, drugs or surgery. True, Luke the beloved physician was among the Lord's disciples. So was John the beloved fisherman. As the one became a spiritual fisher and supernatural healer, so the other became a supernatural healer and spiritual fisher. It is entirely dishonest to suggest as some writers do that Paul took Luke with him on his journeys as a safeguard, in case his miraculous Gifts failed! Those who know God's miraculous ways in the Scriptures look upon such a statement as an impossible travesty of the truth. For all God's Miracle-Gifts work only according to *faith.* Means, such as Luke's supposititious medicine chest, are the very opposite of faith. Unbelief, in short. The Gifts of the Spirit do not work *with* means but without them. The sin in Abraham that delayed the birth of Isaac until it was put away was the 'means' he provided as a resort in case the miracle of the promise failed to work. While Hagar was behind the door, so to speak, as an aid to God in the fulfilment of his promise, that promise could not possibly be fulfilled. The miracle eventually transpired, not through other expedients nor partial means, but through *faith* alone. When Luke the physician followed Jesus he no longer used medicines and media; he healed like the other disciples (if he healed at all) by the laying on of hands and anointing with oil. When Paul and Luke, and others, arrived at the island of Melita and found people desperately sick, it was not Luke the physician with his medicine chest who healed them, but Paul the tent-maker by the laying on of hands and the working of these mighty Gifts.

While we hope we should be among the last to speak disparagingly of hospitals, or of doctors and nurses who give so unsparingly of their time and efforts for the alleviation of human suffering, yet we must most emphatically state that modern medicine is not the legitimate fulfilment of Jesus' command to 'heal the sick'. Rather is it the negation, the neglect, if not the positive denial of it. And this is equally true of genuinely born-again 'Christian doctors'. The only 'Christian physicians' acknowledged in the Scriptures are those ordinary believers who heal miraculously through these Gifts, or equally miraculously through the laying on of hands or anointing with oil. The supposition that the Lord Jesus heals today through Harley Street is no more Scriptural than the claim that He saves through Oxford. Medicine and surgery is the world's way. God's way, the only way revealed in the Word, is healing by supernatural divine power. These two ways are entirely opposed. True, many real Christians resort to the way of the unbeliever, but that does not alter the fact that it is the way of the unbeliever. Divine healing is the only healing authorized by the

Scriptures. Medical healing is not, as some people declare, 'God's second best'. It is entirely of the educated world. God has no second best.

In an ultimate sense, of course, all healing is of God. But then in this ultimate sense all sickness is likewise of God, and all everything else, except sin. 'I kill and I make alive; I wound, and I heal' is Jehovah's declaration (Deut. 32.39). 'In faithfulness hast thou afflicted me,' admits the Psalmist.

No thinking person can really believe that poisonous drugs and cruel scalpels have anything to do with *divine* healing. To put it quite reasonably, with no shadow of intended offence, surely medicine at its best is merely a development of the world's ever-changing and ever-futile attempts to wipe out disease. As this generation laughs at the methods of the last, surely a wise man can see that the next generation will laugh (if the Lord tarry) at the methods of today. Is it not obvious that the Lord God has His hand on the world? And is it not possible that He Himself wonders at human attempts to rid the world of disease in order that ungodly men might be at ease in ignoring Him and mocking at His blessed Son and his merciful salvation? And is the world really more healthy today after all men's efforts than it was when our grandparents lived? Is it not just that as one disease begins to relax its mortifying hold another more terrible most relentlessly adjusts its grasp?

The Lord still has compassion on the sick. He still has a way of deliverance from the power of the enemy. It is still the way revealed in His Word. The sick will do well to seek it out and bring their diseases to Him as the distressed their maladies of old. It is a safe way; a painless way; a free way and a holy way. Because it is HIS way.

The Gifts may operate by a touch or a word: in the latter case distance is no object (Ps. 107.20; Matt. 8.8).

1. In exceptional cases healings may result from the operation of the Gifts *without* a word or a touch, by the very presence of the One possessed of them, as Peter, whose very shadow streamed forth like a mighty overflow of divine unction, sweeping all diseases before it (Acts 5.15); or from fabrics or garments which have been in contact with those possessed of the Gifts, as Paul at Ephesus (Acts 19.12). What a gracious provision is this transmission of healing power for those at a distance from assemblies of believers!

2. Healing by anointing with oil (James 5.14) is not through the operation of these Gifts, but in response to obedience and in answer to believing prayer. In James it is elders who are to anoint. In Mark 6.13 Jesus' disciples also healed through anointing with oil. There is no authority for promiscuous anointing by men and women generally. But elders will not forget that their pastor is not only an elder with them, but that he is the presiding elder. This simple fact seems sometimes to be overlooked.

3. The laying on of hands as in Mark 16.18 is not limited to those possessing the Gifts of Healings. It is an act of faith for any 'believer' as the context shows; for on the promise contained in it the Lord will graciously heal in response to living faith. The only condition here is 'believing' (verse 17). . . .

Faith is positively necessary in the operation of these – or indeed any of the Gifts. It may be (1) substitutionary faith where the sick one is too feeble to believe for himself (Mark 2.5); or (2) the faith of the sufferer alone (Matt. 9.22); or (3) the faith of the minister alone in special circumstances such as coma or unconsciousness (Matt. 9.25); or (4) the combined faith of sufferer and minister (Matt. 9.28, 29). This last seems to be the most usual. But those who claim to possess the Gifts of Healings must personally shoulder the burden of faith and blame themselves, not the sufferer, for failure or only partial success. It is of course different with anointing and prayer and laying on of hands. Faith is the indispensable requisite in healings.

And from what has already been said it is clear that the Gifts do not work indiscriminately at the will of the possessor. Not every blind man or deaf man or sick man can be healed at will by the Gifts. Bethesda's porches were filled with sick folk, all believers in divine healing, for they were all waiting for a heavenly miracle. And the Minister on this occasion was One supremely gifted with the power of the Spirit. Yet only one was actually healed. The one who actually got into touch with Jesus' living power. *All who really got into vital touch with the Lord*, however, were healed, not only on this occasion, but on every other occasion. It is not possible to state dogmatically why, among those who are prayed for today, some are healed and some are not. And certainly here is no room to discuss so large a problem. But here is a man who, it is quite certain, will never be healed, though he travel round all the assemblies and seek the ministrations of those most mightily endowed with divine power. He is desperately sick, and no doubt he has a Bible and believes. Ask him his name. It is Gehazi! His sickness shall cling to him so long as there is breath in his mortal body. For the Lord has decreed it. For we must remember that on the obverse side of divine healing is divine sickness (2 Kings 5.27). . . .

. . . Let us seek the face of the Lord for Gifts and mightier Gifts and use them as He instructs, to make straight crooked little children, to set at ease tortured men and women and to turn the awful groans of the constant sufferer into shouts of joy and praise to our lovely delivering Jesus!

Used by permission of Assemblies of God Publishing, Nottingham, UK.

This symmetrical diagram shows how George Jeffreys related the work of Christ to the fall of Adam. It schematically represents the theology behind his preaching on healing.

4.4   G. Jeffreys, *Healing Rays*, Worthing: H. E. Walter Ltd, 1985 (first published 1932), pp. 32–3

Original Condition and results of First Adam's disobedience as described in the Word of God	| | ——— | | | |	Present and ultimate benefits of Last Adam's obedience definitely promised in the Word of God

Original condition	Present condition confirmed by experience	Present benefits confirmed by experience	Future benefits
No sin	Sin	Deliverance from sin	–
No death	Death	–	Death destroyed
No bondage in the animal kingdom	Bondage in the animal kingdom	–	Animals delivered
No cure on the earth	Curse resting on the earth	–	Curse removed
No mortality	Mortality	–	Immortality
No bodily sickness	Bodily sickness	Bodily healing	–

The atoning and redeeming work of Christ on the cross is the sovereign remedy for all the evil results of the first Adam's disobedience. The future benefits of the last Adam's death on the cross include the destruction of the last enemy, which is death, the deliverance of the animal kingdom from the bondage of corruption, the removal of the curse that rests upon the earth, and the superseding of mortality by immortality. The present benefits of His atoning and redeeming work include deliverance from sin and healing for the mortal body. Before Calvary saints of God looked forward to the cross, and claimed in their day the benefits of salvation and healing. Saints after Calvary look backward to the cross, and claim the present benefits of salvation of healing. Saints of all ages will ultimately participate in the joy of seeing every evil effect of the first Adam's disobedience completely done away with, all because the last Adam became obedient unto death, even the death of the cross.

Used by permission of Elim Foursquare Gospel Alliance, PO Box 38, Cheltenham, Gloucestershire GL50 3HN, UK.

Bosworth locates healing firmly in Christ's atonement.

4.5   F. F. Bosworth, *Christ the Healer*,
Old Tappan, New Jersey: Fleming H. Revel Company, 1924,
(abridged from the edition in 1973, pp. 24–31)

He carried our pains

Before quoting from this chapter [Isaiah 53], may I state that the Hebrew words *choli* and *makob* have been incorrectly translated 'griefs' and 'sorrows'. All who have taken the time to examine the original text have found, what is everywhere acknowledged, that these two words mean, respectively, 'sicknesses' and 'pains', everywhere else throughout the Old Testament. This word, *choli* is interpreted 'disease' and 'sickness' in Deuteronomy 7.15; 28.61; 1 Kings 17.17; 2 Kings 1.2; 8.8; 2 Chronicles 16.12; 21.15; and other texts. The word *makob* is rendered 'pain' in Job 14.22; 33.19, etc. Therefore the prophet is saying, in this 4th verse, 'Surely He hath borne our sicknesses and carried our pains.' The reader is referred to any standard Commentary for additional testimony on this point; but there is no better commentary than Matthew 8.16, 17.

An inspired commentary

That Isaiah 53.4 cannot refer to disease of the soul, and that neither of the words translated 'sickness' and 'pain' have any reference to spiritual matters but to bodily sickness alone, is proven by Matthew 8.16, 17 – '. . . and He cast out the spirits with His word, and healed all that were sick; that it might be fulfilled which was spoken by Esaias, the Prophet, saying, Himself took our infirmities, and bare our sicknesses'. This is an inspired commentary on this 4th verse of Isaiah 53, plainly declaring that the prophet refers to bodily ailments, and therefore the word 'sickness', *choli*, must be read literally in Isaiah. The same Holy Spirit who inspired this verse quotes it in Matthew as the explanation of the universal application by Christ of His power to heal the body. To take any other view is equal to accusing the Holy Spirit of making a mistake in quoting His own prediction.

The cross a perfect remedy for the whole man

'Jesus went to the cross, spirit, soul and body, to redeem man, spirit, soul and body. Therefore, the Cross is the centre of the plan of salvation for man, spirit, soul and body.' Every form of sickness and disease known to man was included, and many of them even mentioned particularly, in the 'curse of the law' (Deut. 28.15–62, and other scriptures). Now, in Galatians 3.13, we have the positive statement that 'Christ hath redeemed us from the curse of the law, being made a curse for us, for it is written, Cursed is every one that hangeth on the tree.' What plainer declaration could we have than that Christ, Who was born under the law to redeem us, bore its curse, and therefore did redeem us from all sickness and disease. Here it is stated that it was on the cross that Jesus redeemed us from the law's curse. In other words, He redeemed us from the following diseases, specified in Deuteronomy, 'consumption' (tuberculosis), 'fever', 'inflamation', 'the botch of Egypt', 'emerods', 'scab', 'itch', 'madness' (insanity), 'blindness', 'plagues', 'all the diseases of Egypt', 'also every sickness and every plague which is not written in the book of this law'. This would include cancer, influenza, mumps, measles and every other modern disease. If Christ redeemed us from the curse of the law, and sickness is included in the curse, surely He redeemed us from sickness.

Used as public domain material with thanks for that information to Baker Book House Company, PO Box 6287, Grand Rapids, Michigan 495166287, USA.

Parker, once a lecturer at the British Assemblies of God Bible College, argues that healing cannot be in the atonement since only sin needs to be atoned for.

4.6   C. L. Parker, 'Gifts of Healing',
Redemption Tidings, 2 December 1960, pp. 5, 6, 3

It is clear from Genesis 2.9; 3.22–4; Ezekiel 47.7–12; and Revelations 22.2 that bodily sickness is not natural for humanity, which was to be, and again will be, kept in health through eating of the Tree of Life. Had Adam been allowed to continue eating of this tree he would in spite of his sin have lived forever. Death and sickness then are not the inevitable results of *sin*, but spring from the loss of the Tree of Life, which was the necessary food of men. The loss of these trees has resulted in the slow but steady deterioration of the human body until the present expectation of life is about 70 years, and sickness from time to time is almost universal. Hence the problem of Divine Healing is urgent, since the best efforts of doctors and surgeons are so often fruitless: and the Bible is full of instances of this Divine Healing from Exodus 15.25–6 to Acts 28.8–9.

In the actual practice of Divine Healing however many difficulties arise, and much disappointment is met, so that it is fair to say that as a whole our Pentecostal Movement is greatly perplexed to find an explanation for the situation, and it is increasingly normal for us to go to doctors and surgeons when we are ill, simply because our prayers are apparently not answered, and we are forced to do something about it. Before then coming to consider the spiritual Gifts of Healings, it may be wise to attempt to understand the whole subject.

Is healing in the Atonement?

This question is often asked and opinions about it differ. In attempting to find an answer it is necessary first to consider a matter of translation. The word for 'atonement' in Romans 5.11 is in every other case translated 'reconciliation', Romans 11.15; 2 Cor. 5.18–23, and that was the meaning of the word, at-one-ment, when the 1611 translation (AV) was made. Later on the word 'atonement' took on instead the totally different meaning of expiation or reparation, which it still has, cf. English Dictionary. Now sin does need expiation and the Lord's death was to make reparation for the sin of the world and make the law honourable and establish it by the death of those who broke it, Romans 3.31, Isaiah 42.21. On the other hand sickness is not an offence against the Law of God, and does not therefore need any expiation, but is simply a human misfortune due to the loss of the Tree of Life in Eden, and it falls upon men without any regard to their character. Cf. Psalm 73.1–15; Job 2.1–8; 1 Timothy 5.23; James 5.15.

In the At-one-ment then, or reconciliation, is included not only healing but all the myriad blessings that come to men through our Lord's sacrifice for sin. 'He that spared not His own Son but delivered Him up for us all, how shall He not with Him also freely give us all things?' (Romans 8.32). But the 'atonement' in its later meaning of expiation for sin did not include men's sicknesses, for they were not sinful nor abhorrent to God's righteousness, and did not call for the death of a Saviour. Christ had to suffer for sin, but not for sickness. Yet, having purged our sins and so reconciled us to God, he also brought us physical healing as one of the 'all things' of Romans 8.32.

Furthermore it seems clear from the Hebrew of Isaiah 53.2–4 where the mistranslated 'sorrow and grief' of the Authorized Version were correctly translated in Matt. 8.17 by 'infirmities and sicknesses' (cf. RV), that our Lord Himself not only had no comeliness, nor any beauty, but also was a 'man of infirmity and acquainted with sickness'. 'For we have not an High Priest which cannot be touched with the feeling of our *infirmities* (the same word as in Matt. 8.17), but was in all points tempted as we are, yet without sin' (Hebrews 4.15). This part of His experience we are told brought upon Him the rejection of His contemporaries who longed for a warrior Prince such as David to lead them against the Romans, and had not time for one who lacked beauty and strength and tasted the sickness common to man. It is sin and sin alone which requires an atonement; sickness does not.

Finally in Isaiah 53.5 and 1 Peter 2.24 the Hebrew and Greek words mistranslated 'stripes' are in both cases singular and not plural, and the Revised Version and margin render 'bruise', which refers to His death on the Cross, not to His scourging by the soldiers. The Greek and Hebrew words for 'healing' are also often translated 'salvation' so that Isaiah 53.5 and 1 Peter 2.24 can quite rightly be translated 'by whose bruise we were saved', and in 1 Peter 2.24 there is no reference to healing but only to Calvary.

In conclusion, then, in my opinion, physical healing like every other blessing from God is in the At-one-ment or reconciliation, but not in the Atonement or expiation for sin. For sickness is not morally wrong and does not call for the sentence of death as sin does, nor did it need any kind of expiation by Christ.

Three methods of healing

To continue then in our consideration of Divine Healing, it would seem that in the Bible it falls under three heads: (1) The healing of unbelievers through evangelists in order to confirm the Divine nature of their message, and convince their hearers that God is a God of love (Mark 16.15–20). (2) The routine healing of members of the Church of God through the prayer of the elders and the anointing with oil. This is a matter of corporate Church Life, when the determined prayers of the whole church may be needed, and where sins, if any, may need to be confessed (James 5.14–18). (3) 'The Gifts of Healings' given by the Lord to one of His servants to hand on to anyone whom He may desire to heal for some purpose of His own. Each separate healing is a separate gift and there is no such thing as a 'gift' of being able to heal everybody at will. It is not a 'gift of healing', but 'gifts of healings'.

Typical cases of these gifts are to be found (a) in the Old Testament, 2 Kings 5.8, where Elisha had Naaman's healing in his hand, though there were many lepers in Israel for whom he could do nothing! (Luke 4.27), and Isaiah received the gift of Hezekiah's healing just after he had told him that he was going to die! (2 Kings 20.4–5), and (b) in the New Testament when Ananias was sent to Saul, much against his will, to heal one whom he regarded as an enemy, as Elisha did Naaman (Acts 9.12–17). And Peter had in his hand the healing of the cripple whom Jesus must have passed by hundreds of times without healing him! 'Such as I *have*, give I thee,' he said (Acts 3.6).

Like any other gift, these gifts have not only to be given, but also received! Hezekiah after being told by God that he was to die was unable to receive Isaiah's 'gift of a healing' until his faith had been raised by the wonderful miracle of Kings 20.8–11. Naaman had a similar difficulty in receiving Elisha's gift (2 Kings 5.10–14). Saul had been warned by the Lord that a man called Ananias was coming with his healing (Acts 9.12), and Ananias left his house with Saul's healing in his hand but without any desire to help Saul, the enemy of God's people!

There is then a double act of faith in the operation of these particular gifts. The one has to receive the gift from God, and the sick person has to receive it from the one sent to hand it on. It is possible then in this way to receive a gift of a healing for either oneself or somebody else. In either case faith is the channel of reception as in all God's dealings with man.

Finally then whereas the healings which follow the preaching of the Gospel, or which come to church members through the prayer of the elders, do not require those who pray the prayer of faith to be baptized in the Holy Ghost – simple faith in the word of God is sufficient – these 'gifts of healings' can only come to those in whom the Holy Spirit dwells and so is able to communicate His special will. The Spirit is of course 'with' all believers but is only 'in' those who have received Him into their bodies in the Baptism of the Spirit.

To sum up then, the Lord has made His will clear for universal healing of the body as He has for universal salvation of the soul; for those as yet unsaved the preaching of the Gospel accompanied by the healing of the body (he healed them *all*, Matt. 12.15); for those who are members of His Church the prayer of the elders accompanied by anointing with oil; for special cases, e.g. those who have never heard the Gospel, or those who like Saul of Tarsus could not call for the elders of the Church, Gifts of Healings taken by a son of God filled with the Holy Ghost. Salvation of the soul and healing of the body are freely given to all upon one condition only, Faith, 'If thou canst believe all things are possible to him that believeth.' There is no instance in the Bible of our Lord refusing either salvation or healing to anyone who was able to accept: and delay is not denial.

Used by permission of Assemblies of God Publishing, Nottingham, UK.

T. L. Osborn, one of the twentieth century's great healing evangelists, argues that faith may well imply believing against the evidence of our natural senses, a position developed by other independent Pentecostals like Kenneth Hagin.

4.7   T. L. Osborn, *Healing the Sick*, Oklahoma: T. L. Osborn Evangelistic Association, 1951–92, 1992 edn, pp. 83–4

Faith and our five senses

While God's word alone creates faith, if we only related experiences, we would appeal to the natural senses. Your natural senses have nothing to do with faith and true faith must ignore them. If you walk by faith, you cannot walk by sight. If you are to consider the Word of God as true, then you cannot always consider the evidences of your senses as true.

Feeling, smelling, tasting, hearing, and seeing are the senses by which the natural person is directed. The word of God and faith are the two factors by which the spiritual person is directed.

The natural person walks by the senses, but the spiritual person walks by faith in the word of God (2 Cor. 5.7).

Sight and feeling belong to the natural person.

Faith and obedience belong to the supernatural person.

Every Christian is a supernatural person.

It seems unreasonable to some people not to believe the natural senses. They have accepted them as conclusive evidence for so long that it is difficult for them to realize that there is other evidence besides that of the five natural senses.

People have been taught that the final court of appeal is the natural senses. 'Seeing is believing,' they say. They have based their lives on that premise and have failed to take into account the higher source of knowledge. This higher knowledge is revelation faith, which comes through the word of God and through prayer. The Word of God should be the final court of appeal for the Christian – the super-person.

Often when Christians are told that they are to walk by faith not by sight, and to disregard the evidence of the physical senses, they think this is unreasonable. 'Do you mean to say,' they ask, 'that I cannot depend on what I see? I could never accept such an absurdity. When I hold a book in my hand, I see it and feel it and can smell printer's ink on its pages. If I drop it, I can hear it fall. Do you mean to tell me that the book is not real and that it is not here?' No. We do not mean that.

We may accept the evidence of our senses as true in natural things; but in spiritual things when this evidence contradicts God's word then we ignore our physical senses and believe what the word of God says.

What witnesses to our healing?

I have often wondered why people who think it's absurd to believe that God's word is true if their senses testify to the contrary, have faith in a contagious disease to which their child has been exposed. They believe that their child will manifest the symptoms of the disease in a certain number of days because a child, sick with the disease, was in their class at school.

They have no physical evidence that their child will have this disease. They are expecting it purely by faith – faith in Satan's disease. Without feeling it, they believe it – they have faith in it.

The child has no apparent symptoms of the disease. It is as well as ever, but they believe it will have the disease in a few days. Why do they believe that?

They have what we call 'faith' – faith in the disease. They believe the disease has begun its work, in spite of the fact that they cannot see, feel, smell, taste, or hear anything of it with their senses. That is faith.

The only fault here is that this is faith in the wrong thing, but it certainly is faith.

They trust in diseases completely and with unquestioned confidence, yet they may feel we are being unreasonable when we lay hands on them and tell them, 'Your sickness will leave. It must, because God has said it will go. He said, "You shall recover", so nothing can stop it.'

Seeing Not Believing

Many say, 'Seeing is believing,' yet they believe in the power of disease, they see its effects. According to the word of God, believing is seeing.

Others say, 'I will never believe it until I see it.'

I reply, 'You will never see it until you believe it.'

As soon as you believe it, God delights to let you see it, since faith is the evidence of things not seen (Heb. 11.1). Faith brings the unseen things into being and makes the unfelt things real to the senses.

It pleases God when you look only at His word. It pleases Him when you base your faith on His promise. By this kind of faith, people of God obtained a good report from Him (Heb. 11.2), and you will, too. Faith in God's word is always pleasing to Him.

When Jesus was here in human form, He recognized the evidence of the senses, but He never allowed Himself to be dominated by them. The senses were His servants; He lived above them.

He pronounced the blind man healed and the leper cleansed, when apparently they were still blind and still leprous. He called the things that were not as though they were – and they came to pass.

Jesus cursed a fig tree one day, and its roots died. But its death was not evidenced until the next day when it was seen to have died from the roots – not from the visible branches down, but from the invisible roots up (Mark 11.20).

Sense knowledge is deceptive

Our senses relate to the natural person in the natural world; but in obtaining blessings from the spiritual world, faith relates to the spiritual person.

We may accept the evidence of our senses as long as it does not contradict the word of God. However, when God's word differs from our senses, we are to ignore the evidence of our senses and act on the word. When we do this, the Father honours His word and makes it good in our lives.

We are always safe when we believe God, no matter how convincing the evidences of our senses may be. What God says is always true. Let God be true, but every person a liar (Rom. 3.4).

Sense knowledge is a deception when it does not agree with the word of God. When we are walking by faith, we delight to cast aside the senses and enjoy the Father's already-provided blessings.

Used by permission of T. L. Osborn Ministries, Osborn International, Box 10, Tulsa, Oklahoma 74102, USA. www.osborn.org/

The only female evangelist in this group takes a much gentler view of healing than those who say that it is in the atonement or that it depends on a faith which may contradict sense experience.

4.8   K. Kuhlman, *I Believe in Miracles*,
London: Oliphants, 1963, pp. 196–200

Too often I had seen pathetically sick people dragging their tired, weakened bodies home from a healing service, having been told that they were not healed simply because of their own lack of faith. My heart ached for these people, as I knew how they struggled, day after day, trying desperately to obtain *more* faith, taking out that which they had, and trying to analyse it, in a hopeless effort to discover its deficiency which was presumably keeping them from the healing power of God. And I knew the inevitability of their defeat, because they were unwittingly looking at themselves, rather than to God.

But what *was* the answer? Again and again I was to ask myself the question: why were some healed and others not? Was there no balm in Gilead?

Was faith something that one could manufacture, or work up in oneself? Was it something that could be obtained through one's own goodness or moral status? Was it something that could be procured in exchange for serving the Lord, or through benevolence? I knew God could not lie, for He had promised; I knew in my own heart that there *was* healing, for I had seen the evidence from those who had been healed. It was real, and it was genuine, but *what was the key?*

I could not see the hand of God in man's superfluity of zeal and I saw the harm that was being done in attributing everything to 'lack of faith' on the part of the individual who had not received his healing. Inside myself, I was crushed: my heart told me that God could do anything; my mind told me that through ignorance and lack of spiritual knowledge, there were those who were bringing a reproach on something that was sacred and wonderful and accessible to all. No preacher had to tell me that the Power of God was real and that God knew no such thing as a MIRACLE as such, for I was assured of these facts as I read the Word of God. The Word was there, the promise had been given: there was surely no changing of God's Mind, and certainly no cancelling of the promises!

I think that no one has ever wanted Truth more avidly than I – nor sought it harder.

I remember well the evening when I walked from under a big tent where a Divine Healing service was being conducted. The looks of despair and disappointment on the faces I had seen, when told that only their lack of faith was keeping them from God, was to haunt me for weeks.

Was this, then, the God of all mercy and great compassion? I remember that night how, with tears streaming down my face, I looked up and cried: 'They have taken away my Lord and I know not where they have laid Him.' And I remember going to my room and sobbing out my heart to God – praying for light on the Truth.

Fortunately I had learned a valuable spiritual lesson early in my ministry – one which was to come to my aid now: I had learned that the only way to get the truth is to come in sincerity and absolute honesty of heart and mind, and let the Lord Himself give one the blessed revelations of His Word, and *through* the Word, make His Presence real and His Truth known.

At no time in my search did I profess to wear the robe of infallibility. I did not seek as a dogmatist, nor as one with a closed mind, but only as one who was daily learning, willing to be guided by the Holy Spirit, and longing to be taught of the Father – as one who was hungry for deeper spiritual knowledge, not from man but from *God*.

I waited expectantly for the answer, and it came.

One night during a series of services that I was conducting, a very fine Christian lady arose from where she was sitting in the audience and said, 'Please – before you begin your sermon, may I give a word of testimony regarding something that happened last evening while you were preaching?'

I nodded, and quickly recalled what I had said the night before. There had not been anything unusual about the sermon: it had been a very simple message regarding the Person of the Holy Spirit. I clearly recalled the sum and substance of the message:

God the Father is seated on His Throne, and is the Giver of every good and perfect gift. At His right Hand is His Son, through Whom we receive salvation and healing for our bodies, and in Whom every need of our lives is met. The Holy Spirit is the only member of the Trinity Who is here on earth and working in conjunction with the Father and the Son. He is here to do anything and everything for us that Jesus would do, were He here in Person.

I listened now, as the little woman spoke: 'As you were preaching on the Holy Ghost,' she said, 'telling us that in Him lay the Resurrection power, I felt the Power of God flow through my body. Although not a word had been spoken regarding the healing of the sick, I knew instantly and definitely that my body had been healed. So sure was I of this, that I went to the doctor today and had my healing verified.'

The Holy Spirit, then, *was the answer:* an answer so profound that no human being can fathom the full extent of its depths and power, and yet so simple that most folk miss it!

I understood that night why there was no need for a healing line; no healing virtue in a card or a personality; no necessity for wild exhortations 'to have faith'.

That was the beginning of this healing ministry which God has given to me; strange to some because of the fact that hundreds have been healed just sitting quietly in the audience, without any demonstration whatsoever, and even without admonition. This is because the Presence of the Holy Spirit has been in such abundance that by His Presence alone, sick bodies are healed, even as people wait on the outside of the building for the doors to open.

Many have been the times when I have felt like taking the shoes from off my feet, knowing that the ground on which I stood was Holy Ground. Many are the times when the Power of the Holy Ghost is so present in my own body that I have to struggle to remain on my feet. Many are the times when His Very Presence healed sick bodies before my eyes; my mind is so surrendered to the Spirit, that I know the exact body being healed: the sickness, the affliction, and in some instances, the very sin in their lives. And yet I could not pretend to tell you *why* or *how!*

From the beginning, as now, I was wholly sure of two things: first, that I had nothing to do with what was happening, and second, I *knew* that it was the supernatural power of Almighty God. I have been satisfied to leave the why and the how to Him, for if I knew the answers to those two questions, then I would be God!

In the light of God's great love, tenderness and compassion, the Holy Spirit revealed to me my worthlessness and helplessness of self. His greatness was overwhelming; I was only a sinner, saved by the Grace of

God. The Power was His and the Glory, and this Glory, *His* Glory, He will not share with any human being.

If you can once grasp the concept of the Holy Trinity, many things which may once have puzzled you become clear. The Three Persons of the Trinity, God the Father, God the Son and God the Holy Ghost are a Unity. They are co-existent – infinite and eternal. All Three were equally active in the work of creation, and *are* equally active and indispensable in the work of Redemption. But although the Three work together as One, each has at the same time, His own distinctive function.

God the Father planned and purposed the creation and the redemption of man, and is in our vernacular, the Big Boss. God the Son provided and purchased at Calvary what the Father had planned in eternity. He made possible the realization of God's eternal plan. All that we receive from the Father *must* come through Jesus Christ the Son, and that is why at the heart of our faith is a Person – the very Son of the very God. When we pray, we come before the Father's Throne in Jesus' Name. We cannot obtain an audience with the Father, except as we come to Him in the Name of His Son.

But the Holy Spirit is the *power* of the Trinity. It was *His* power which raised Jesus from the dead. It is that *same* Resurrection power that flows through our physical bodies today, healing and sanctifying.

In short, when we pray in the Name of Jesus, the Father looks down through the complete perfection, the utter holiness, the absolute right-eousness of His only Begotten Son, knowing that by Him, the price was paid in full for man's redemption, and *in* Him, lies the answer to every human need.

God honours the redemptive work of His Son by giving to us through Him, the desire of our hearts. Thus, while it is the Resurrection power of the Holy Spirit which performs the actual healing of the physical body, Jesus made it perfectly clear that we are to look to Him, the Son, in faith, for He is the One who has made all these things possible.

Permission sought.

Oral Roberts, who began as a traditional healing evangelist, eventually developed a theology of healing that brought divine healing and medical healing into harmony. ORU is Oral Roberts University.

4.9 O. Roberts, *Expect a Miracle: My Life and Ministry*. *Oral Roberts, an Autobiography,* London: Nelson, 1995, pp. 254–61, abridged

A physician joins a healing evangelist

After graduating from the University of Tennessee College of Medicine and practicing general medicine in private practice, Dr. James E. Winslow was trained to be an orthopedic surgeon with the famous Campbell Clinic in Memphis, which specialized in turning out topflight surgeons in orthopedics.

Time passed until 1969, when Jim's wife was diagnosed with ovarian cancer. Although the cancer specialists did not say it with words, Jim knew from the tone of their conversations that Sue was going to die.

Sue's dad, a manufacturer in Mississippi, came to Tulsa, and he and Jim discussed what they were going to do. Between them, they had the money to get the best medical care in the world.

Jim told me later they both believed that a person has some control over her illness by the approach she takes to it. Jim's mother thought a person could either fight the disease or lie around until it killed her – one or the other.

His father-in-law's mother was once a temporary devotee of Mary Baker Eddy, and she read all of her works and believed much of them. She taught her son that a person could influence her state of health by her state of mind and beliefs.

He and his father-in-law discussed that and decided they would try to set in motion a circumstance that would cause everyone who came in contact with Sue to be positive, not negative.

Sue was a Methodist layperson. She began attending a prayer group and received the charismatic experience of speaking in tongues. She told Jim about it, who felt he needed to do a lot of reading and studying on it. He wasn't for it or against it; he was just unschooled about it.

During that time, strange things began happening. Sue did not get terribly sick with radiation therapy, and the chemotherapy did not bother her much. She did not even lose her hair. Jim accused the medical oncologist of not giving her any chemotherapy. But her doctor said that he was giving Sue about twice the usual dose.

Sue told us later that as she lay on the table taking chemotherapy she was saying, 'Lord, let Your healing power go into every cell of my body.' Soon she recovered.

Jim and Sue have been married many years, and she has not had a problem with cancer since then. This incident would play an extremely important part in what God was about to do in helping Jim understand God's call on my life to merge prayer and medicine.

One night Jim brought Sue and their three children to a basketball game at ORU. Our team had a player from Chattanooga, Tennessee, the state where Jim came from. His name was Richard Fuqua, and he was averaging thirty-six points a game. The ORU basketball team was leading the NCAA Division I in points made and in rebounds.

That night our leading rebounder, Eddie Woods, fell and hit his head on the floor and was carried off. Jim got up and went to see about Eddie. Soon Eddie recovered and went back in the game. Coach Ken Trickey asked if Jim could provide medical care for the ORU basketball team, and Jim told him he would do it.

Two years later, in 1972, I injured one of my knees playing golf, and Coach Trickey said I ought to go see Jim Winslow, an orthopedic surgeon.

After Jim examined my knee, I asked him if he ever prayed *with* any of his patients. Jim thought I said *for* the patients, so he told me that sometimes he did. I asked if he would pray for my knee.

Jim told me later that the thought went through his mind: *If I can't pray for Oral Roberts, I can't pray for anybody.* So he said, 'Yes, I guess I can pray for you.' And he did.

After he finished, we got into an argument as to how much I owed him because he said his office didn't charge ministers. Finally, I said, 'If you won't take my money, will you play golf with me at Southern Hills?' He said yes. That summer as we played several times late into the evening, important things began to happen.

I remember most that Jim and I became friends, and soon we were talking at great length about healing – what it really meant to come at healing from an alternative perspective, which was the one I believed God had given me. Jim and I stimulated each other's thinking, probing healing from what he thought of it from his background and his medical practice, and what I thought of it from my healing ministry.

I added, 'I don't know how the American Medical Association elects its leaders, but to me, the tragedy in most denominations I know is that they seek out good administrators rather than their most spiritual people and those who have the most proven results of helping people come to know and serve God and also to expect His supernatural intervention in their lives.'

Jim said, 'There is some of that in the way medicine chooses its leaders. One of the chief weaknesses is that the mind is so finely trained, there is little emphasis placed on how physicians can encourage their patients, talk with them, and cause the patients to be comfortable in their spirits in getting their medical care.'

I said, 'This is the first time I've heard you mention the spirit of a person. Doctors do believe people are more than minds and bodies, don't they? That they have souls?'

He said, 'I can't say I have thought very much about the spiritual over-tones of the way doctors help people get well. I know it is not in our train-ing in medical school or in our residencies. I suppose it depends on the individual doctor and whether or not he or she is a spiritually minded person.'

I said, 'And if he or she is not?'

He said, 'That's one I hadn't thought about, either. I can only say that when doctors don't have some belief in God, and in involving the spirit of a person with the treatment, it could leave a void.'

I explained to Jim that probably as much as or more than most people, I've had to fight for my health and continue fighting for it. It's the reason I want the best of medical care and the most anointed people of God pray-ing for me. What had been the most defeating to me is that doctors seem to see me as a physical and mental being only, and praying people see me as a spiritual being only. Yet they are both in the process of bringing healing to me. It was very frustrating, and God had been dealing with me about it. 'In fact,' I told Jim, 'He has spoken to me that He wants His healing streams of prayer and medicine merged and that His time has come for me to be a forerunner in getting it done.'

I told him how I had been near death's door with tuberculosis, and God had spoken audibly to me that He was going to heal me, that I was to take His healing power to my generation, that someday I was to build Him a university based on His authority and the Holy Spirit, and that I was also to build a medical school for the combining of medicine and prayer.

That almost stopped the golf game. Jim grew very quiet. We played several holes without any more conversation on the subject of medicine as he practiced it or prayer for the sick as I had been doing it.

Finally, Jim said, 'Now I know why we met. I know why we've been having these talks. And I think I understand that my wife's recovering from cancer, with all due respect to my medical colleagues, was also due to her faith and a divine intervention from God. I've never put all this together before. I hadn't even thought about it.

'She first received everything we could get done for her by the oncolo-gist, by radiation, chemotherapy, and so on. We left no stone unturned.

She had received what you call the charismatic experience, the baptism of the Holy Spirit with tongues, and she was receiving direct healing prayers from her prayer group. One day I woke up and saw my wife was healed. The cancer was gone. She glowed with health. As I said, she's not had a sick day since. Sue's combining medicine with prayer was better than either one of them alone.'

That was a powerful moment!

Right here is the rub, as I see it. Who do you trust as your Source? Who, indeed, is the Source of all healing?

I believe the Bible, in which God teaches He alone is the Source of our total supply: 'But my God shall supply all your need according to his riches in glory by Christ Jesus' (Phil. 4.19); and 'I am the LORD that healeth thee' (Exod. 15.26). Our total supply most certainly includes our deliverance from sickness and disease. Therefore, both healing coming through supernatural intervention, through believing the gospel and the prayer of faith, and healing coming through medicine or surgery really come through God our Source.

As far as supernatural intervention is concerned, it can come – as I know it – in two different ways. One, God acts sovereignly; that is, God is entirely on His own without anybody doing anything. This is really under God's control, and although it happens, it doesn't occur often. Two, a believer or a group of believers pray and agree in prayer for supernatural intervention to heal a sick person or destroy a disease. That is the way supernatural healing most often happens as I know it.

After 48 years of continuous healing ministry, I am familiar with both ways. But I am also familiar with receiving healing through the principle and process of medicine. When I have been under medical care by a doctor, or in a hospital as a patient, I have come with faith in God, basing my hope of a cure on God as my Source working through the physician, the nurses, the medicine, and medical equipment. Never once have I looked to any man, however skilled, or medical facility, whatever the state of the art, as the Source of my recovery or health. I have trusted God as my Source, whether in medicine or in prayer, or in both together.

John Wimber developed a somewhat holistic view of divine healing and located this healing within an evangelistic context.

4.10   J. Wimber with K. Springer, *Power Healing*,
London: Hodder & Stoughton, 1985, pp. 84–6

The New Testament also has many illustrations of the relationship between spiritual sickness and other types of problems. Mark 2.1–12 describes how Jesus healed a paralytic. The paralytic had been brought to a crowded meeting by his friends (they had to lower him through a hole in the roof). Jesus, recognizing the friends' faith, said to the paralytic, 'Son, your sins are forgiven' (v. 5).

There were teachers of the law in the room at the time who thought to themselves, 'Who can forgive sins but God alone?' (v. 7). Jesus said, *'Why* are you thinking these things? Which is easier: to say to the paralytic, 'Your sins are forgiven,' or to say, 'Get up. Take your mat and walk'?' (vv. 8–9). Then, just as he had done with the paralytic's sins, Jesus declared him healed: 'I tell you, get up, take your mat and go home' (v. 11). The fact that Jesus forgave the man's sins first indicates that Jesus understood spiritual sickness, caused by sin, was the primary issue in the paralytic's life, and that his paralytic condition was directly related to it.

John 5.1–15 describes one of Jesus' greatest miracles, the healing at the pool of Bethesda of a man who had been an invalid for thirty-eight years. He was an embittered, lonely man who seemed angry with life and people, and was without hope (v. 7). Like many who suffer from chronic illness, he was full of unbelief, fuelled by years of failed healing attempts ('he had been in this condition for a long time' (v. 6)).

Jesus asked the man if he wanted to get well, that is, if he wanted to turn away from his bitterness and anger as well as be healed of his physical problem. The invalid answered by trying to shift the blame for his unbelief: 'I have no-one to help me into the pool. While I am trying to get in, some-one else goes down ahead of me' (v. 7). That is, he thought that God could not heal him because of others' failure to help. This man illustrates our problem, that our faith and expectations are limited. Commenting on his response, John Calvin wrote, 'This sick man does what we nearly all do. He limits God's help to his own ideas, and does not dare promise himself more than he conceives in his mind.'

Christ responded to the invalid's litany of self-pity and unbelief by heal-ing him. What Jesus said when he healed him is very important. First, Jesus commanded that he 'Get up!' (v. 8). Through these strongly spoken words the invalid's thoughts were jolted away from others' failures and on to taking responsibility for his own life. Then Jesus told him to 'pick up [his] mat and walk' (v. 8). This call was to obedience and faith – obedience to Jesus' words, faith in Jesus' power. In commanding the invalid in this way, Jesus asked him to believe that God could still heal. As the invalid acted on Christ's words, he was healed.

What is often overlooked in this story is how Jesus later found the man at the temple and instructed him, 'See, you are well again. Stop sinning or something worse may happen to you' (v. 14). Apparently Jesus knew in this instance that the root of his problem was spiritual sickness brought on by sin. God's healing grace was abundantly given, but the invalid still had to believe and turn from the sin that had held him captive for thirty-eight years.

About five years ago a woman in her late forties asked me to pray for her healing. She suffered from chronic stomach disorders and arthritis. When I started to pray over her I received an insight that she was bitter. So I asked her if she was feeling hostility, anger or bitterness towards someone; and I felt led to ask specifically if she felt that way towards her sister.

She stiffened up, then said, 'No. I haven't seen my sister for sixteen years.'

I enquired further: 'Are you sure?'

Then she told me how years ago her sister had married a man she loved, then later divorced him. 'I cannot forgive my sister for that,' she admitted.

'If you don't forgive her,' I told her, 'your "bones will waste away", just as David complained his did when he kept silent about his sin of adultery with Bathsheba.'

When she heard my words she relented. 'What should I do?' she asked.

I told her to write her sister a letter, forgiving her and asking to renew their relationship. She wrote the letter immediately, but she did not post it for several weeks. During that time she became more ill, until she thought she was going to die. Then she remembered the letter. Somehow she summoned the strength to drive to the post office and post it. The very *moment* she dropped the letter into the box, she experienced relief, and she was completely healed by the time she reached home.

Used by permission of Hodder & Stoughton, 338 Euston Road, London NW1 3BH, UK.

5 Baptism in the Spirit and Charismatic Gifts

W. K. Kay, Introduction

Baptism in or with the Holy Spirit is central to the Pentecostal and charismatic movements. Reference to this baptism comes from the lips of Christ himself within the book of Acts (1.5). In Acts 1 Christ tells the apostles to wait in Jerusalem until they receive power from heaven and in Acts 2 this promise is fulfilled on the day of Pentecost. On that occasion there are the signs of wind and fire but also speaking in tongues. The term 'speaking in tongues' is taken from the Authorized Version of the Bible where the word 'languages' was then translated 'tongues'. So the phrase simply means 'speaking in languages'. On that first Pentecostal day the international crowd of pilgrims thronging the streets of Jerusalem understands the languages spoken by the disciples. The visitors were amazed because 'each one heard them speaking his own language' (Acts 2.6).

The experience of the baptism in the Holy Spirit is most fully described in the book of Acts, and Pentecostals have been assiduous in assembling the textual evidence to build up a composite picture of the baptism's nature, purpose and significance. Although there has always been theological debate over how the text of Acts might be related to the Gospels and to the Epistles, the outlines of discussion are described in the following two paragraphs.

While early holiness Christians looked for spiritual power and experiences of sanctification, they largely followed a Wesleyan framework that presumed two basic stages within the Christian life: the first stage, conversion or the new birth, and the second stage sanctification, or holiness, or perfect love. The first stage occurred when someone came to saving faith in Christ and the second took place after prolonged spiritual exertion and attempts to eliminate sinful habits and dispositions.[1] A wide variety of views were held about the nature of the post-conversion spiritual experience but the term 'baptism' was frequently used to indicate the overwhelming sense of the divine that was its essence. The Scottish cleric

---

[1] The best description of the fit between the Wesleyan and Pentecostal theological frameworks is to be found in Donald W. Dayton (1987), *Theological Roots of Pentecostalism*, Peabody, Mass.: Hendrickson.

Edward Irving, often seen as the nineteenth-century precursor of Pentecostalism, wrote with theological power and originality about the baptism with the Holy Spirit and his writings and preaching led to an outbreak of speaking with tongues in the churches for which he was pastorally responsible (5.1).

How widely known Irving's theology was within holiness and Wesleyan groups in the United States is uncertain but the term 'baptism' referring to something more than water baptism was current at the revivalist fringes of Christianity. The difficulty for these groups was to find a criterion that might identify the experience unequivocally. In one church prayer meeting someone who claimed to have received a dynamic baptism of power jumped over the wood stove heating the building. Thereafter, those who also jumped over the stove were thought to have received the same spiritual experience![2] So when, after theological reflection and dispute, a consensus grew among the emerging Pentecostal denominations that the baptism in the Holy Spirit was *marked* by speaking with other tongues, clarity was achieved.[3] Whether this clarity was achieved at too great a cost and with spurious precision is part of an ongoing debate within the Pentecostal and charismatic movements.

The connection between Spirit baptism and speaking with tongues is usually traced to the students of Charles Parham's Bible College in Topeka, Kansas, in 1901. W. J. Seymour had been a student at Parham's College and took this teaching to Los Angeles and to Azusa Street where he maintained it against those who argued either against the possibility of speaking with tongues in the modern era or against those who argued that baptism of the Holy Spirit was simply synonymous with sanctification. To understand the Pentecostal and charismatic movements, one must appreciate the basic position taken at the beginning of the twentieth century by Seymour and others in order to appreciate the variants that developed subsequently in some Pentecostal denominations and especially within the charismatic movement.

---

[2] In discussion during a paper given by Jeffrey A. Trexler at the Society for Pentecostal Studies, Dallas, 1990. See also J. A. Trexler (1990), 'From Chaos to Order: G. F. Taylor and the Evolution of Southern Pentecostalism', 20th Annual Meeting of the Society for Pentecostal Studies. The paper shows that the criterion of tongues, rather than being a cause of dispute, settled a chaotic situation at the beginning of the twentieth century by replacing subjective spiritual claims with an objective phenomenon.

[3] The Assemblies of God, for instance, accepts speaking with tongues as the 'initial evidence' of the baptism in the Holy Spirit. The Elim Pentecostal Church simply accepts 'signs following' without specifying tongues. There is a large popular and academic literature defending, attacking and modifying the various positions.

W. Durham (5.2), a powerful early Pentecostal preacher who came to believe that there was no separate and decisive crisis of sanctification after conversion, describes his own baptism in the Spirit and gives an indication of the overwhelming nature of this event. Roswell Flower, a key member of American Assemblies of God, realized early on that speaking with tongues, or the baptism in the Holy Spirit, must point beyond itself and, in his view, be related to missionary activity (5.3). Donald Gee, a key representative of British Assemblies of God, provides a standard account of the classical Pentecostal position about speaking with other tongues. This is a relatively late extract (1963) but it represents a view that he had held for at least 40 years and that was central to classical Pentecostalism all over the world (5.4). This view has been re-expressed and defended by David Petts but he also picks up some of the hermeneutical issues that have become part of contemporary debate (5.5). The issue here is whether the book of Acts, as an historical account of the early Church, is a suitable text from which to deduce to doctrine.

Dennis and Rita Bennett writing relatively early in the charismatic movement and in a popular book take up the issue of the nature of the tongues spoken by those who claim an experience of the baptism (5.6). This is a contentious issue in some circles since linguistic and psychological research has found difficulty in recording and identifying utterances in tongues that are clearly part of a language system and foreign to the speaker. The problem is complicated by the fact that there are approximately 3,000 languages in existence and when somebody speaks in a language they have not understood, detractors of speaking with tongues can argue that this is enabled by subconscious acquaintance with foreign words. Alternatively, linguists have analysed patterns of vowel and consonant sounds in tongues speech to determine whether or not they are indicative of known language groups. None of the research by William Samarin has been reported here, partly because it needs to be read at length and partly because we do not find his case convincing.[4]

J. Rodman Williams wrote a report on the baptism in the Holy Spirit for the guidance of the Presbyterian Church in the United States in 1971 (5.7). The report is interesting because it partially reinterprets classical Pentecostal theology and demonstrates how charismatic theology loosens the Pentecostal conclusions that had been keenly defended and established since the inception of Pentecostal denominations. For instance, Williams argues that, while baptism of the Holy Spirit may be indicated by certain

---

[4] e.g. W. J. Samarin, (1959), 'Glossolalia as Learned Behaviour', *Canadian Journal of Theology* 15, 60–4; (1972), *Tongues of Men and Angels*, New York: Macmillan; (1973), 'Glossolalia as Regressive Speech, *Language and Speech* 16, 77–9.

phenomena (e.g. speaking with tongues), it would be a mistake to say that it *must* be indicated in this way. Similarly he defends the practice of infant baptism on the grounds that such baptism can – and this was argued by Calvin – be indicative of grace to be appropriated more fully at a later date. In this way infant baptism has a theological meaning referring to admission to the Church without shutting off the possibility that further spiritual phenomena inherent in the original baptism might be embraced at a much later date: both the early sacrament and the later experience are equally valid and neither negates the other.

Frank Macchia writing from within the classical Pentecostal tradition provides a more recent and original consideration of speaking with other tongues (5.8). He expands the significance of the phenomenon and understands it against a background of a new kind of 'acoustic sacrament' expressive of the freedom of the Spirit that gives to Pentecostal spirituality elements of countercultural protest. The argument here is not about the meaning of particular biblical texts but rather about concepts that are building-blocks of theology.

A similarly thoughtful piece of writing from Peter Hocken, speaking within the Roman Catholic charismatic stream, indicates both the role of David du Plessis (1905–87) in popularizing the terminology of 'baptism in the Spirit' during the formative years of the charismatic movement and his focus on Jesus as the baptizer in the Holy Spirit, the administrator of the experience itself (5.9). So baptism in Holy Spirit is importantly focused on Christ who acts sovereignly to bestow the gift on the needy Church.

Speaking with tongues is connected with other gifts of the Spirit mentioned in 1 Corinthians 12 and 14. T. B. Barratt, in an early extract, deals with prophecy and differentiates between degrees of inspiration as well as the linkage between tongues and prophecy (5.10). Mike Bickle, writing on prophecy within New Churches, shows how this gift may function within the life of a thriving congregation (5.11). The problem for Pentecostals and charismatics is that prophetic utterances can be a powerful element in strengthening collective faith while, at the same time, being susceptible to exploitation and unspiritual rivalry. Utterances may cause fresh kinds of pastoral problems for church leaders but the extracts give an indication of the participative life of the Pentecostal charismatic congregation at its best. Men and women may come to the front of the church to address the whole body of believers because the conduct of the church is not simply in the hands of professional clergy. Hallowed liturgies which pre-specify what will be said and done by every person joining in an act of worship can be replaced by free-form worship styles that are altogether more adventurous.

The leader of what has been the largest church in the world for 20 years gives the final extract (5.12). Yonggi Cho in South Korea has built up a cellular megachurch and demonstrates his understanding of the operation of the Holy Spirit in creating dreams and visions by which the work of God may be led forward. He does not specifically say whether he takes these visions to be words of wisdom or knowledge consistent with the terminology of 1 Corinthians 14. Rather, he demonstrates a general sense of openness to the Holy Spirit that indicates a largely non-rational apprehension of Christian guidance. Interestingly, too, he does not deny that individual or collective unconsciousness may be at work within this process. He only pleads that the Holy Spirit should sanctify this aspect of our humanity in the same way as the rest of our lives. Nevertheless, as Cho makes clear, the spiritual mind must exercise discernment so as to avoid self-gratification and self-deception.

Eloquently and presciently, Irving begins to develop a theology of the baptism of the Holy Ghost.

5.1   Edward Irving, *The Day of Pentecost , or, The Baptism with the Holy Ghost,*
Edinburgh: John Lindsay & Co, 1830

Now, the third work, which I have named inhabitation, and which is the proper subject of this discourse being what is called the 'baptism of the Holy Ghost', 'the promise of the Father', and the gift of 'power from on high', is superinduced upon the two other, but neither stints nor supersedes them. They go on beneath: the mighty hand of the Father sustaining the nothingness of the creature's being; the mighty hand of the Son redeeming the sinfulness of it; and now the mighty hand of the Holy Ghost comes in to fill it with Divine attributes of wisdom and knowledge and power. The Father gives the materials, the Son frames them into a living temple, the Holy Ghost fills them with the glory of God. This work of the Comforter is the most wonderful of all. That what came out of and in itself is nothing should be capable of producing the various sensations, emotions, and affections of human life, is wonderful: that what is become mortal, pressed down on all sides with the law of sin and dissolution, should be recovered, against itself, to bring forth the fruits of holy living, is still more wonderful: but that it should be made capable of receiving and sustaining the life of God, of having his mind, and of working his works, is a thing which passeth understanding, being in very deed the mighty power of God. The great account which is made of the resurrection of Christ, in all the Scriptures, as 'the exceeding greatness of God's mighty working' (Eph. 1), and of the baptism of the Holy Ghost, which is the first-fruits thereof – called 'the power from on high', as if nothing else were worthy of that name – do prove how much more vast is this than every other manifestation of Godhead unto men. To make this erroneous mind of ours capable of discerning truth infallibly, to make this trembling and stammering lip capable of uttering words before which death and the grave and the devil stand discovered and dismantled, to make this fearful heart capable of confidence in the face of all ungodly confederations, and to strengthen this palsied hand with all the power of God – these are things which far surpass the speculation, and almost the belief, of man. And had we not seen it accomplished in the feebleness of Jesus Christ, who calleth himself 'a worm, and no man', we should not have believed it possible to be done in mortal man: and had we not the assurance of Him who is the Truth, that the like works, and greater were to be done in them who believe, we should have thought it a very wonderful thing, done once, upon an extraordinary occasion, for an extraordinary end, by one who was an extraordinary person, God as well as man, and never to be renewed again: but having his word and the facts of all the Apostolical history for it, we believe, as we have written, that this is the third and highest sphere of God's operation in man, carried on under the hand of the Holy Ghost, whose part it is to bring both the Father and the Son, or the Son indwelt by the Father, the life of glorified manhood, into all the members of the body, that is, into all who believe.

1. The true use to make of the life and ministry of the word and work of the Son of Man, is, therefore, this: As the model of the man baptized with the Holy Ghost, unto which all who afterwards should be in like manner baptized, are to be conformed. In all things he must have the pre-eminence; and in this also, of showing forth the holy manner and operation of fallen mortal flesh when baptized with the Holy Ghost. To him it appertained, not only to bear the burden and penalty of a transgressed law, and to over-come the curse of death, but also to receive and to occupy; with God's own husbandry to economize, and for God's own ends to dispense, the new endowment of power from on high, with which our nature was now to be gifted. He must not only see us out of the narrow straits into which we had brought ourselves but also navigate before us the open seas, through which we must win our way to our eternal safety and rest. This is what he did after his baptism: he, being man, showed forth in all human life and

action the manner of the Holy Ghost's operation, exactly as God would have it always to be shown forth; and without such a prototype, we should have been all at sea in respect to what is right and proper in persons so endowed . . . Without both the understanding and the application of Christ's ministry of the Holy Ghost as a model to all the baptized therewith, I perceive that the gifts now bestowing upon the church will not be without peril and evil, as at Corinth, and that Satan will gain an advantage over us.

2. Now, then, let us see what in Jesus the baptism with the Holy Ghost led to: how that super-human inspiration moved and actuated this man. And first, negatively: it did not move him to violate any of the ties and obligations of nature, so as that he should not be bound to honour father and mother, to keep covenant between man and man, and, in one word, to love his neighbour as himself; nor to break any ordinance of the law, of which he was ever most observant. Because creation . . . is an effect and operation of the Spirit, and so is that most holy law of God: now the Spirit will not in his highest operation make void his lower ones, but always act consistent and harmonious with himself. . . .

Used by permission of the Donald Gee Centre, Mattersey Hall, Mattersey, UK.

Durham, once intrigued by seeing renewed lives in those claiming a baptism in the Spirit with tongues in Chicago, travelled in 1906 to see for himself the baptism in the Spirit at Azusa Street. This extract conveys something of the spiritual experience he found.

5.2   William H. Durham, taken from *Pentecostal Testimony* and reprinted as a booklet

Personal Testimony of Pastor Durham

I was born and raised in the state of Kentucky, where I united with the Baptist church about the year 1891. I was sincere at the time but I was not converted. Therefore my experience was a great disappointment to me, for I know that, as a member of the church, I ought to have an experience; but I had no joy or peace, or knowledge of salvation. In the year 1898, in the

State of Minnesota, the Holy Spirit deeply convicted me of sin. This came about through reading the Word of God, and being convinced of its truth, I was made to see that I was a guilty sinner. The Spirit was so faithful in dealing with me that I could find no rest or peace, until I resolved to yield myself to God the best I knew how, and call upon Him for mercy. The moment I did so, the Holy Spirit revealed Jesus Christ to me hanging on the Cross, and said to me 'Christ died for your sins.' Faith instantly sprung up in my heart to accept Him as my full Savior, and the moment I did so, I felt the quickening power of the Spirit, was made a new creature in Christ, and unutterable joy filled my soul. The Spirit bore faithful witness to me, that I was a child of God. I knew beyond doubt, that I was washed in the Blood of Jesus, and the peace that passes all understanding filled my soul. I would have as soon met God as my dearest friend.

I had no one to tell me that the next step was to be buried with Him, in whom I had died and had been made alive. Had I been taught the truth, as the Apostles taught it, had I been baptized and had hands laid on me, I would have at once received the Holy Ghost. I should have been taught to reckon that I was 'dead indeed' and that I was to live and walk only in the Holy Spirit; but I could not walk in Him Whom I had not yet received. Like thousands of others, I drifted. After two years of investigating the theories of men and struggling in every way known to obtain the experience of sanctification and failing in all, I finally had grace given me from God to yield myself to Him, and trust the merits of the Blood alone, just as I had done three years before, when as a trembling sinner, I stood before the Cross and had a glimpse of the glorious Son of God, who died thereon, given me. To my unutterable joy, this step brought me back into the same state of entire sanctification and heavenly rest, peace and joy, which I had the first time I stood in the same place. As in the case of all who remain under the Blood, the Spirit dealt wondrously with me. The influence of His presence with me was so real and precious, that I really thought I had received the gift of the Holy Ghost. My greatest difficulty was in harmonizing my experience with that in the Acts of the Apostles. My difficulty was that I took soul rest and peace, and the sweet holy joy of salvation, and the witness, and influence of the Spirit for the gift of the Spirit. O, how many are making this sad mistake! I knew my experience did not measure up to the standard of the Acts of the Apostles, but like all holiness teachers and people, that I have met, I either kept out of the books of Acts, or confounded the wonderful outpourings of the Holy Spirit recorded there, with sanctification. What a sad mistake. What could be more ridiculous than the teaching, that it was sanctification or any other work of grace the Apostles received on the day of Pentecost?

In the spring of 1906, I heard of the mighty outpouring of the Holy Spirit in the City of Los Angeles, accompanied by the speaking in other tongues. It brought joy to my heart, and I told the people that I had no doubt that it was a mighty work of God. I believed in all the gifts of the Holy Spirit, including tongues, and had longed to see them in operation in the church. But when I heard the teaching that speaking in tongues was the evidence of the Baptism in the Holy Ghost, it stirred me to the depths. I fearlessly denounced this point of the doctrine as false; but when I saw the people who were filled with the Spirit and speaking in tongues, I knew that their experience was genuine. I simply thought they were wrong on this point. If this teaching were true, I had not the baptism. This would mean, that I would have to come down and take the place of a seeker. It is easy to see how hard it would be for me to do this, as I had preached the Gospel for about five years, and all the time professed to have the Holy Ghost, and tried to lead others into the same experience. So I said, 'No man can ever convince me that I have not received the Holy Ghost.' No man ever could have done it; but God did it.

In the fall of 1906, the Spirit began to fall on people here in Chicago. Among the first to be baptized in the Spirit and speak in tongues were a number that I had labored with for three years and had never doubted that they had the same experience I had. I saw that they were filled with a joy, power and glory, they never had before; that they had a love for God and souls they had never had before; and when I saw them stand up, with their faces shining with the light of Heaven, and heard them tell of the increased love and power, and then heard them speak and sing in tongues, it settled the question with me. I saw and heard for the first time in my life something that measured up to the teachings of the Book of Acts. I at once went down before God and became an earnest seeker; I found at once that the old 'claim' theory was exploded by this movement. I could not kneel at the altar, and claim the Holy Ghost and go away. This was a real experience. I must wait until He came. Finding it necessary to drop my pastoral duties for a time, I did so, and went to Los Angeles to tarry before God until He met me.

I shall never forget my first day in Azusa Street Mission. As soon as I entered the place, I saw that God was there. There were hundreds of people present, yet no man seemed to have anything to do with what was happening. The Holy Ghost seemed to have perfect control. My soul was melted down before the Lord. After a few hymns had been sung, a wave of power and glory seemed to sweep over the place, and a song broke forth in the Spirit, known in the movement as the Heavenly Anthem. It was the sweetest music that ever fell on my ears. It was the Spirit of God Himself, and I knew it. I could not sing in the choir, though I would have given much to do so. I had not received Him who was doing the singing. I saw clearly, for the first time, the difference between having the influence and presence of the Spirit with us, and having Him dwell within us in person.

Now began a time of waiting and real heart-searching. I became more helpless from day to day. Everything seemed to slip away from me. The works that I had formerly rejoiced in, and the experiences that I had glorified in could not help me now. I reached the place that I could truly say with David, 'My heart and flesh crieth out for the living God.' I had done everything I knew to do, and refused to struggle more. I simply waited, claiming God's promise, trusting in the merits of the Blood of Christ alone.

On the 26th day of February, 1907, I went to the afternoon service. I was at the end of everything; and the Lord knew it. There were thirty or more people present in the prayer room. Three of God's dear children came to me, and as they stood over me, one of them said, 'Just cease trying to do anything, and surrender all to God.' I did so; when O, joy, a thrill of power went through me, followed by another. Instantly it appeared as if every one of my pores were suddenly opened and a mighty current of power turned into me from every side; and so great was the infilling that it seemed as if the physical life would be crowded out of my body. I literally gasped for breath, and fell in a heap upon the floor. Strength was gone, but I was perfectly conscious of everything; so kept lifting my heart to God and earnestly entreating Him to finish the work. So intense was my longing to have the work finished, that I was reaching Heavenward with one hand all the time. God knows best how to do His work, I am glad He did not finish the work, the first time the power came upon me. My experience has been much more valuable as He gave it to me. No tongue could ever tell, what passed between God and my soul these first two hours I was under His power. It was glorious and wonderful. It was heaven. Such love, such sweetness, such a revelation of the Blood as the only remedy for sin, such a revelation of Christ as the only Savior, and many things that it is impossible for me to tell. After two hours He withdrew, leaving me the great benefit I had received from His visit, but with a consciousness that He Who had so wondrously wrought, had departed from me. I was disappointed but knew he would return and finish His work. I now understand why he paid me this wonderful visit and left me, without finishing the work. I meet many people, who have had some wonderful experience in their lives, which they called the baptism in the Holy Ghost; and this blessed experience enables me to locate them. God has visited them, and when they contend that it is the baptism, I remember how the glory filled my own soul, and how everything within me seemed to be turned into love and sweetness and how I walked more than a mile, with my very spirit within me whispering, 'Glory to Jesus,' at every step. I also remember, that He made me to know that this was simply my own spirit's being brought into a state of rapture, and that the baptism was not yet completed.

The Lord permitted me to walk in this state for two days and nights. Then as I knelt before Him, the Spirit again fell on me. . . . This continued for some time, when finally my throat began to enlarge and I felt my vocal organs being, as it were, drawn into a different shape. O, how strange and wonderful it all was to me and how blessed it was to be thus in the hands of God. Last of all I felt my tongue begin to move and my lips begin to produce strange sounds, which did not originate in my mind. In a few moments he was speaking clearly through me in other tongues, and, then I heard Brother Seymour, the Pastor, say, 'He is through now,' etc. He said that he had retired to rest early in the evening, and that the Spirit had spoken to him and said, 'Brother Durham will get the baptism tonight,' and that he had arisen and come down. Then he lifted up his hand and prophesied that where I should preach the Holy Spirit would fall on the people. The Lord then permitted me to rise to my feet, and He, for Whom my soul had longed, did not leave me this time, but remained, and for a long time I could not help speaking in tongues.

Used by permission of The Flower Pentecostal Heritage Center, Springfield, Missouri, USA.

J. Roswell Flower (1888–1970), a key figure in American Assemblies of God, linked the baptism in the Holy Spirit with mission.

5.3   J. Roswell Flower, *Pentecost,* untitled editorial, August 1908, p. 4

The Baptism of the Holy Ghost does not consist in simply speaking in tongues. No. It has much more grand and deeper meaning than that. It fills our souls with the love of God for lost humanity and makes us much more willing to leave home, friends and all to work in his vineyard, even if it be far away among the heathen . . . 'Go ye into all the world and preach the gospel to every creature.' This command of Jesus can only be properly fulfilled when we have obeyed that other command 'Tarry ye in the city of Jerusalem till ye be endued with power from on high!' When we have tarried and received that power, then and then only are we fit to carry the gospel. When the Holy Spirit comes into our hearts 'the missionary spirit' comes with it. They are unseparable as the missionary spirit is but one of the fruits of the Holy Spirit. Carrying the gospel to hungry souls in this and other lands is but a natural result of receiving the baptism of the Holy Spirit.

Used by permission of The Flower Pentecostal Heritage Center, Springfield, Missouri, USA.

Donald Gee (1891–1966), a key figure in British Assemblies of God, wrote numerous books and articles. He saw himself primarily as a teacher and, in this article, sets out his reasons for believing in association of the baptism in the Holy Spirit with speaking in tongues.

5.4   D. Gee, 'The Initial Evidence of the Baptism of the Holy Spirit', *Redemption Tidings*, 31 May 1963, pp. 10–12

The doctrine that speaking with other tongues is the initial evidence of the baptism in the Holy Spirit rests upon the accumulated evidence of the recorded cases in the book of Acts where this experience is received. Any doctrine on this point must necessarily be confined within these limits for its basis, for the New Testament contains no plain, categorical statement anywhere as to what must be regarded as THE sign.

The conclusion that the proper initial evidence of the Baptism in the Spirit is speaking with other tongues is most simply arrived at by a logical sequence of reasoning as follows:-

Scriptural foundation

1. The New Testament reveals that the baptism in the Holy Spirit is a definite personal experience, alike conscious to the recipient and manifest to any others who may be present on the occasion.

(a) Now that which makes this so definite an experience and spiritual crisis in the New Testament cannot possibly be those results which afterward appear in character and ministry as an outcome of receiving the Spirit's fullness, for these will obviously take some time to manifest themselves.

(b) Neither can it only be some inner personal consciousness of the recipient, for that would be entirely unknown and inconclusive as evidence to any others who might be present at the time.

(c) It follows then that it must plainly be some conscious and outward manifestation given at the moment of the believer's baptism in the Spirit: and this is exactly what we find did take place in the New Testament.

Outward manifestation

2. Having settled it that the Scriptural evidence of the baptism in the Holy Spirit must consist therefore of some such outward manifestation, it only remains to define what that manifestation should be.

This must be arrived at, as we have already pointed out, by carefully examining the records of the specific cases mentioned in the book of Acts, which we will now proceed to do.

(a) The Day of Pentecost (Acts 2). The outstanding supernatural manifestation of the Spirit on this occasion is, without controversy, speaking with other tongues. The fact that tongues were the Divinely chosen attestation to this initial outpouring of the Holy Spirit for the present dispensation carries great weight for all future occasions, when believers receive their personal birthright on this same line, according to the universal promise of verse 39.

Peter plainly recognizes the fact in Acts 11.15 that the Day of Pentecost had established accepted precedent. The outpouring of the Spirit then under consideration was accepted as authentic by all, when it was proved to be the same as in 'the beginning'. But the only outward link that bound together the two occasions, and stamped them as identical, was the fact that in both they spoke with tongues. This one manifestation of the Spirit, standing quite alone, was considered conclusive evidence. The argument that we equally recognize it is almost overwhelming.

(b) Samaria (Acts 8.14–18). In this instance there is no indication whatever as to the precise nature of the manifestation given. Simon's observation and amazing request (verses 18, 19) prove conclusively that it was something quite obvious and definite. In the face of a perfectly open question such as this incident affords, we are as much justified in believing it was 'tongues', as believing it was anything else; indeed, we are more justified because of the weight of the example of other definite instances. The initial evidence of speaking with other tongues would meet all the requirements of the context here.

(c) Saul of Tarsus. The actual reception of fullness of the Spirit by the apostle to the Gentiles is not separately recorded at all. It is implied as part of the necessary fulfilment of the commission given in very definite terms to Ananias (Acts 9.17). But we have Paul's personal testimony in 1 Corinthians 14.18 that he permanently enjoyed speaking with tongues to an abounding degree; and there is every reason to believe that he first received this particular manifestation of the Spirit at the same point in his spiritual experience that the other apostles first received it – when being baptized in the Ghost.

(d) The company in the house of Cornelius (Acts 10.44–7). It is stated as plainly as possible here that the evidence that satisfied the surprised and prejudiced Jewish believers that these Gentiles had indeed received the Holy Spirit was speaking with tongues. The phrase 'FOR they heard them speak with tongues' in verse 46 is so emphatic that it approaches a definite statement of the doctrine we are considering. Some unmistakable evidence to place the authenticity of the Gentile experience beyond question was palpably needed here: it was supplied by 'tongues', and this fact reveals the unique place this sign had already taken in the New Testament Church.

(e) Ephesus (Acts 19.1–6). Here again the initial evidence that this little company had received the Holy Ghost is plainly stated: – 'They spake with tongues and prophesied.' Nothing could be plainer. Several years had elapsed since the Day of Pentecost, and even since the outpouring upon the first Gentiles in Caesarea, but we find the same identical initial evidence accompanying the gift of the Holy Spirit.

What, then, is the result of our examination of evidence? That in three cases out of five it is plainly stated that the particular manifestation accompanying the baptism in the Holy Spirit was speaking with tongues; and that in the other two cases, though left an open question, there are at least preponderating reasons for believing they spoke with tongues then also.

We submit, therefore, that the evidence is entirely sufficient for the conclusion expressed in the doctrine that 'speaking with other tongues is initial evidence of the baptism in the Holy Spirit'.

Confirmation of the truth of this doctrine is certainly happily supplied by the experience of many thousands of believers in every corner of the world today.

There are three main objections to this doctrine, which it is now advisable fairly to consider: One founded on Scripture; one on experience; and one on observation.

'Do all speak with tongues?'

The doctrine is sometimes questioned on Scriptural grounds because of Paul's statement in the subjunctive mood made in 1 Corinthians 12–30 'Do all speak with tongues?'

It should be carefully noted that in any case this Scripture can never be used to question the fact of the initial evidence of the baptism in the Holy Spirit being 'tongues'; at the most it can only be used to question whether we should expect this evidence in every case.

But on examination of the context we find that Paul is dealing here exclusively with the subject of spiritual gifts as granted to the various members of the body of Christ for the edification of the whole. The question of the experience of believers when personally receiving the fullness of the Holy Spirit does not come up here at all, and any attempt to wrest this statement from its proper application must result in confusion.

For our information concerning the manifestation given to believers when baptized in the Spirit we are entirely shut up to the instances already noted in the book of Acts. On the Day of Pentecost and in the house of Cornelius the Scripture plainly uses the word 'ALL'; and in both cases the obvious meaning is that 'ALL' received the fullness of the Spirit, and 'ALL' spoke with tongues (Acts 2, 4, and 10.44–6). Yet no one would wish to infer that they 'all' then received the one particular GIFT of diversities of tongues for regular exercise as members of the body of Christ; this was only allotted to some – which is exactly what Paul says in 1 Corinthians 12.30.

To recognize a proper distinction between speaking with tongues as the initial evidence of the baptism in the Holy Ghost, and the Gift of Tongues in the Church is both justifiable and necessary to prevent confusion in doctrine and application. The book of Acts deals with the first phase of this manifestation; the epistle to the Corinthians with the second, and we note the following plain distinctions: – (a) The initial evidence is spontaneous (Acts 10.44–6), whereas the Gift is controllable (1 Cor. 14.28); (b) The initial evidence can be given to any number on one occasion, as for instance 120 on the Day of Pentecost (Acts 1.15 and 2.4), a room full of people (Acts 10.24), and at least twelve (Acts 19.7); whereas the use of the GIFT is limited on one occasion to 'two or at the most three' (1 Cor. 14.27). The above passages completely contradict each other unless we recognize a distinction between tongues as an initial evidence of the Baptism in the Spirit, and tongues as a gift in the body of Christ.

The divine pattern is the standard

An objection, not Scriptural in the least, but worthy of frank consideration, is one founded upon experience. Namely, that if this doctrine be true, why are so many spiritual believers today without this experience, especially those who claim to have received a definite baptism in the Holy Spirit?

Our answer to this is that the principle holds good here as everywhere in the spiritual realm, 'according to your faith be it unto *you*'. We have good reason for presuming that, for various reasons, these friends either do not believe they could have such an absolutely Scriptural experience today, or else they do not want it. Of one thing we are assured, that 'The Promise' (of a Pentecostal Baptism as recorded in the New Testament) is still for 'all that are afar off, even as many as the Lord our God shall call' (Acts 2.39).

But to make the experience of these friends – or even the experience of great leaders of the Church in bygone generations – a standard by which to judge a doctrine and measure the plan and willingness of God is plainly wrong, and would prove fatal to the progress of the Church as a whole.

We submit that the only standard of Christian experience permissible to the believer is the pattern which God has caused to be written for the Church of every generation upon the pages of the New Testament. To fix our eyes upon the best of men limits us to never rising beyond the experience of the one we happen to admire; but to fix our eyes upon the Scriptures leaves us free to rise into all the fullness of God's plan.

This objection should never find any place among those who claim to make the Scriptures their only rule of faith and practice.

The gift of tongues and the fruit of the Spirit

A final objection we will consider is one founded upon observation, namely, the inconsistent lives of certain who claim to have spoken with tongues as an evidence that they have been baptized in the Holy Spirit.

This objection is one we admit with deep sorrow in so far that lack of holiness in a child of God professing to be filled with His Spirit is never excusable on any ground. It must be carefully pointed out, however, that this provides no Scriptural argument whatsoever against the truth of the doctrine or experience we are considering. Inspiration does not sanctify.

We have every reason to believe that Ananias and Sapphira had shared in the full Pentecostal blessings of the Early Church. In the Corinthian Assembly which Paul commends as coming behind in no gift (1 Cor. 1.7), we find among its members quarrelling, immorality, intemperance, serious error concerning such a fundamental doctrine as the resurrection. We simply state the naked facts which every student of the New Testament will verify. There was no need for these failures, there was every provision made to prevent them, but that some did, and some still fail of the grace of God is patent beyond argument. Those who reject a Scriptural doctrine because of the lamentable failure of some of its exponents can find no possible justification before an open Bible. To maintain logically the position with consistency we must justify an unbeliever who refuses to become a Christian because he has unfortunately met professing believers who live inconsistent lives. God forbid.

The Fruit of the Spirit comes by walking in the Spirit (Gal. 5); and it is evident from 1 Corinthians 13.1–3, that it is possible for a believer to speak with tongues and exercise other gifts of the Spirit without walking in love. Their gifts then become profitless and vain, just 'sounding brass tinkling cymbal', but this does not prove that they were not genuine at the outset and when they were first filled with the Holy Spirit. Paul never suggests that they had counterfeit gifts from the evil one; they were right gifts but used without the love of God in the heart. The sad picture is of believers who once had a genuine anointing of Spirit but have backslidden. The remedy is obviously a return to the first Anointing and exercise of the gracious gifts of the Spirit in love and holiness.

While we therefore believe that this doctrine is so Scriptural that it may be put forward with all boldness and certainty, yet we also feel that it should be advanced with great modesty and love. It has sometimes suffered much (what Scriptural doctrine has not!) by being pushed egotistically and rashly. A truth and an experience which should have been welcomed as a privilege has thereby unhappily become a means of offence.

Those who have, in accordance with the Scripture, received the initial evidence of speaking tongues when they were baptized in the Spirit and the writer is happy to include himself among them, have nothing whereof they may boast in themselves. All the glory is due both now and ever to the Gracious Lord who bestowed the Gift.

Used by permission of Assemblies of God Publishing, Nottingham, UK.

David Petts (b. 1939), Principal of The Assemblies of God's Bible College UK (1977–2004), addresses questions relating to the Pentecostal tendency to derive doctrine from the book of Acts.

5.5   D. Petts, 'Baptism in the Holy Spirit: The Theological Distinctive', in K. Warrington (ed.), *Pentecostal Distinctives*, Carlisle: Paternoster Press, 1998, pp. 99–119, abridged

. . . In summary, the Pentecostal understanding of the four passages in Acts which are seen as instances of the baptism in the Spirit is that since tongues is the one repeated phenomenon in Acts 2, 10, and 19, and since it was 'almost certainly' the phenomenon that Simon saw (Acts 8.18), speaking in tongues should be viewed as the initial evidence of the baptism in the Spirit.

Challenges – and a response

The Pentecostal belief that the baptism in the Spirit is an experience which is both distinct from regeneration and accompanied by tongues has been challenged, on both counts, from a variety of perspectives. . . . Broadly speaking, challenges fall into two categories, hermeneutical and exegetical, and I shall deal with these in turn.

Hermeneutical challenge

. . . Pentecostals derive their doctrine of the baptism in the Spirit largely from the Book of Acts where a pattern is seen to emerge from a series of select passages. The underlying assumption is that contemporary experience should be identical to apostolic Christianity. The experience of the disciples in Acts 2.4 is thus the pattern for believers for the whole church age. . . .

Having, therefore, argued that Acts is suitable as a source of Christian doctrine, it is now appropriate to ask how doctrine may be derived from it. The major issue here is the use of historical precedent. To what extent is it legitimate to see in Acts a pattern for the church today? In this connection, Fee[1] offers three principles:

1. The use of historical precedent as an analogy by which to establish a norm is never valid in itself.
2. Although it may not have been the author's primary purpose, historical narratives do have illustrative, and sometimes 'pattern', value.
3. In matters of Christian experience, and even more so in Christian practice, biblical precedents may be regarded as repeatable patterns – even if they are not to be regarded as normative.

Although I am broadly in agreement with these principles, it is important that they are applied with care. It is clear, of course, that we cannot take a

---

[1] G. D. Fee, 'Hermeneutics and Historical Precedent: A Major Problem for Pentecostal Hermeneutics', in R. P. Spittler (ed.), *Perspectives on the New Pentecostalism*, Grand Rapids: Baker, 1976, pp. 128–9; see also G. D. Fee, 'Acts: The Problem of Historical Precedent', in G. D. Fee and D. Stuart, *How to Read the Bible for All It's Worth*, Grand Rapids: Baker, 1982, pp. 87–102; G.D. Fee, 'Baptism in the Holy Spirit: The Issue of Separability and Subsequence', *Pneuma*, 7.2 (1985).

single historical incident and insist that all Christian experience must conform to it in every detail. To argue that because the Christians in Acts 2 received the Spirit in Jerusalem, therefore all Christians must go to Jerusalem to receive the Spirit, would be absurd! Thus Fee is right in saying that the use of historical precedent as an analogy by which to establish a norm is never valid in itself. But that does not mean that frequently repeated historical incidents may not be understood to be normative.

. . . What I am arguing here is that, if we accept the premise that Luke's intention in Acts is theological, that he is intending to teach us something, then the understanding that Luke's narrative must be viewed in a teaching context will radically affect our exegesis of Acts.[2]

Accordingly, it seems to me, Fee's statement that biblical precedents may be regarded as repeatable but not normative is too general and consequently too weak. Indeed, if a precedent is consistently repeated in a didactic narrative, then the precedent ought to be considered normative. To illustrate, I consider the phenomenon of the sound of a violent wind at Pentecost (Acts 2.2) to be repeatable, but not normative. But that speaking in tongues should be expected as evidence of the baptism in the Spirit, I consider to be normative because of the consistency with which Luke refers to it.

In this connection, I believe that the case for the Pentecostal position is far stronger than is usually allowed. It is usually argued that the case for tongues is based on three of five incidents in the Book of Acts. But to argue this is to ignore two important facts. First, it is clear from the context in Acts 8 (where tongues is not mentioned) that the passage is not a full description of what took place. (We are told that Simon saw that the Spirit was given through the laying on of the apostles' hands, but we are not told what he saw. The passage itself makes clear that it is not a complete description of events.) The same is true of the account of Saul's conversion in Acts 9. We are told that Ananias came that Saul might be filled with the Spirit, but there is no description of Saul's reception of the Spirit. If these two passages were intended to be full descriptions (which they clearly are not) and if as full descriptions they failed to mention tongues, then the Pentecostals' case for insisting on tongues would be disproven. But the passages are not full descriptions and this fact actually strengthens Pentecostals' position. For wherever there is a fuller description of events in connection with the baptism in the Spirit, the first recorded manifestation is speaking in tongues (Acts 2.4, 10.46, 19.6). But this leads to my second point.

---

[2] See also John's helpful comments with regard to narrative theology. D. A. Johns 'New Directions in Hermeneutics', in G. B. McGee (ed.), *Initial Evidence*, Peabody: Hendrickson, 1991, pp. 153–6.

The argument that the Pentecostal position is based on three of five cases is also fallacious because it considers occasions rather than individual baptisms in the Spirit. The precise numbers are not important, but it is usually assumed (on the basis of Acts 1.15) that there were some 120 disciples present on the Day of Pentecost. If that be the case, then Acts 2.4 describes 120 baptisms in the Spirit. All 120 were filled with the Spirit and all 120 spoke in tongues. Similarly in Acts 10.44–6, the Spirit fell upon 'all who heard the message' (v. 44) and they spoke in tongues and magnified God (v. 46). In Acts 19.6–7, we are told that the number of Ephesians upon whom the Spirit came and who spoke in tongues and prophesied as a result was about twelve. This means that in the three passages in Acts where there is a fuller description of people being baptized in the Spirit, some 150 people received the Spirit, and on each occasion, the first phenomenon Luke records is speaking in tongues. In the light of these considerations, if we accept as I have already argued that Luke's intentions were didactic, we must conclude that tongues is to be viewed as the normative accompaniment to the baptism in the Spirit.

Dennis (1917–91) and Rita (b. 1934) Bennett enumerate practical purposes of speaking in tongues.

5.6   Dennis and Rita Bennett, *The Holy Spirit and You*,
Eastbourne: Kingsway Publications, 1971, pp. 85–8

The gift of tongues is not a sign to the believer since he doesn't need a sign, but it may be a sign to the unbeliever (usually unsought for), causing him to accept the Lord Jesus Christ. 'Wherefore tongues are for a sign, not to them that believe, but to them that believe not . . .' (1 Cor. 14.22 KJV).

How the gift of tongues can be a sign to the unbeliever:

a) The tongue may be a language known to the unbeliever with God speaking directly to him.

b) The tongue may not be a known language, but the powerful impact of the message in tongues, normatively accompanied by interpretation, may speak to the unbeliever, and be a sign to him.

When tongues are a message from God, coming to the unbeliever either by his knowing the language (a translation), by the inspired interpretation through a believer, or in some rare cases even without benefit of interpretation or translation, they are a sign to the unbeliever that God is real, alive, and concerned about him.

In a Full Gospel church in Oregon, there was a young man who had married a Japanese girl while stationed in Japan with the armed forces. The young couple returned to the United States, and were doing well, except that the young lady flatly resisted her husband's Christian faith and held steadfastly to her Buddhism. One night, after the evening service, the couple was at the altar, he praying to God through Jesus Christ, and she praying her Buddhist prayers. Next to them was kneeling a middle-aged woman, a housewife from the community. As this woman began to pray out loud in tongues, suddenly the Japanese bride seized her husband's arm:

'Listen!' she whispered in excitement. 'This woman speak to me in Japanese! She say to me: "You have tried Buddha, and he does you no good; why don't you try Jesus Christ?" She does not speak to me in ordinary Japanese language, she speak temple Japanese, and use my whole Japanese name which no one in this country knows!' It is not surprising that the young lady became a Christian!

We have known of many similar cases. What actually happened in this situation is that as the American housewife was yielded to God in *praying in tongues*, the Holy Ghost chose to change the language from prayer to God – to a message *from* God – through the *gift* of tongues.

Ruth Lascelle (then Specter) had been brought up in an Orthodox Jewish home. When in her early adult life, her mother accepted Jesus as her Messiah, Ruth thought her mother had lost her mind. She went to her mother's Full Gospel church to try to disprove their beliefs. At one meeting there was a message in tongues which, although uninterpreted, had such a great impact on Ruth that she knew in that moment that Jesus was real, and she too accepted Him as her Messiah.

Here is an example of the gift of tongues, although neither understood nor interpreted, yet being a sign of such strength that Ruth was converted on the spot. Ruth says: 'I asked God to give me a sign to show if the Christian faith was really true. At the time of course, I had never heard of the New Testament Scripture: "The Jews required a sign"' (1 Cor. 1.22 KJV).

Another interesting scene took place in 1964 in Northern California at a charismatic Episcopal church service. A college student had come to the meeting with her father, an important ecclesiastical official. This young lady had known Jesus in her childhood, but had gotten further and further away from Him during her college years. Her faith had been pretty much smashed and she was under psychiatric care. Near the close of the meeting the gifts of tongues and interpretation were manifested in love and with power. Tears began to pour down her face as she made her way to the altar for prayer. She told the person counselling with her:

'When I heard speaking in tongues for the first time tonight, and the message that followed, I knew once again without a doubt that God is real and He loves me!'

This last is an example of these gifts as a sign, not to an unbeliever, as previously recorded, but rather to a temporarily unbelieving believer.

The gifts of tongues and interpretation may also be a message from God to bless and exhort faithful people. Examples are numerous; we will take time to give only one. One Friday night about a year after Rita was renewed in her experience of the baptism in the Holy Spirit she was attending a prayer meeting. She prayed for a friend who was working as a missionary nurse in Africa, and was having some difficult trials. As she finished praying for Dorothy, there was a gift of tongues and interpretation, which said in effect: 'If you, yourself, are willing to go and help your friend, your prayer will be answered much more quickly.' Then the Lord asked Rita three times, just as Peter had been asked: 'Do you love Me?' She had been walking closely with Him, and had been an active witness for Him ever since her renewal; it was such a surprise to be asked if she loved Him, that she began to weep. Rita told God, then and there, that she loved Him so much that she was willing to go wherever He wanted her to go. So convincing was the message the Holy Spirit had given that at the end of the meeting her friends gathered around to bid her farewell! As it turned out, although she was willing to go to Africa, two months later the Lord sent her instead – to Texas!

Used by permission of Kingsway Publications, Lottbridge Road, Eastbourne, Sussex BN23 6NT, UK covering permission for Coverdale House, but for the USA attempts at contacting Bridge Publishing, South Plainfield, New Jersey were unsuccessful.

This report illustrates how a charismatic approach to the baptism in the Holy Spirit may be different from a Pentecostal approach. In addition to the New Testament, this report draws support for the modern doctrine and experience of the Holy Spirit from Calvin's Institutes and key documents of the Presbyterian Church. It clearly rules out, however, the proposition that the baptism in the Holy Spirit must be accompanied by speaking with tongues.

5.7 Report given in the Minutes of the 111th General Assembly of the Presbyterian Church in the United States, Massanetta Springs, Virginia, 13–18 June 1971, pp. 104–17

This is reproduced in K. McDonnell (ed.) *Presence, Power, Praise: Documents of Charismatic Renewal,* Collegeville, Minnesota: Liturgical Press, 1980, pp. 312–17 and is the concluding section of the document. The role of J. Rodman Williams in the production of the report is acknowledged in M. W. Wilson, *Spirit and Renewal: Essays in Honour of J. Rodman Williams,* Sheffield: Sheffield Academic Press, 1994, p. 17.

An evaluation of contemporary events involving a 'baptism of the Holy Spirit' must begin, as the structure of the report implies, with the guidance furnished us by the Scriptures. . . .

A. As we seek to give an expression of our faith in the Holy Spirit that will be an aid in comprehending the experiences which have prompted the present study, there are several basic principles which we must bear in mind. First, as the Scriptures repeatedly affirm, the Holy Spirit is the Spirit of the holy God, the God of the Bible. All our speech about the Holy Spirit is therefore speech about God. We shall make no attempt to define the concept of 'spirit' in general and then move to an understanding of the Holy Spirit based on our ideas about the essential properties or characteristics of 'spirit.' Rather, our task is to discern the meaning of God's action, in the person of his Spirit, in the lives of his people.

Second, as the New Testament makes clear, and as Calvin aptly reminds us (*Inst.* III, i, 4), there is no understanding of the Spirit apart from faith. This means that all our statements about the Holy Spirit are in essence affirmations of faith. They are not 'factual' statements in the sense that they purport to give objective data or information which may then be tested for accuracy by scientific means. In speaking of the Holy Spirit we speak *from* faith to faith.

Third, since the Holy Spirit is the spirit of the God whom we know only through Jesus Christ, we are compelled, in regard to the contemporary spiritual phenomena, to 'test the spirits to see whether they are of God' by the measure of their confession of Jesus Christ (1 John 4.1–3). Nothing that contradicts what we see in Christ can rightly be regarded as the activity of the Spirit; on the other hand, whatever bears witness to Christ and his work of the redemption of mankind exhibits the incontrovertible evidence of the Spirit's presence.

B. With the foregoing principles in mind, and with constant reference to the Biblical teachings, the Standards of our Church, and the contemporary situation, the Permanent Theological Committee offers the following statement for the guidance of the Assembly.

1. The greatest emphasis in the Bible, and the most prominent aspect of our Reformed tradition, is to be found in the work of the Spirit in bestowing upon man all the benefits of God which come to him in Jesus Christ. Faith in Jesus Christ is the way whereby all benefits are received, such as justification, sanctification, and eternal life (1 Cor. 6.11; John 3.16; Confession of Faith XVI, 2), and through the Holy Spirit this salvation is a reality.

2. The Holy Spirit accordingly dwells in all who thus believe. If anyone does not have the Spirit of Christ, he does not belong to him (Rom. 8.9). Thus it is impossible to speak of a transition within Christian existence from the state of Spirit's being *with* to being *in*. The Spirit indwells all Christians.

3. Baptism with water is a means of grace whereby the grace of salvation is not only offered but conferred by the Holy Spirit (Confession XXX, 6). However, according to the Confession, the significance of baptism is not tied to the moment of administration, for, though God's saving grace is conferred thereby, such grace may become efficacious at a later time, or it may have become efficacious earlier. For example, there are those who do not come to an appropriation of this grace (especially if baptized in infancy) until a later date. Calvin speaks (particularly regarding infants) of being 'baptized into future repentance and faith' (*Institutes* IV, 20), and urges that this should fire us with greater zeal for renewal in later years. From this perspective it is possible to say that baptism with water may very well be separated from salvation, or at least from full entrance upon it. Though baptism is a channel of God's grace, this grace is not automatically efficacious. Accordingly, there may be special need in the Reformed tradition to lay stress on later occasions (such as entrance into communicant membership) on which God's grace may also be appropriated. Reformed teaching about baptism must be held in creative tension with all that is also said about the importance of conversion and regeneration, and the practice of our church should be in harmony therewith.

4. 'Baptism with the Holy Spirit,' as the Book of Acts portrays it, is a phrase which refers most often to the empowering of those who believe to

share in the mission of Jesus Christ. The significance of 'baptism with the Spirit' is also represented in terms such as 'outpouring,' 'falling upon,' 'filling,' and 'receiving,' being for the most part attempts to depict that action of God whereby believers are enabled to give expression to the gospel through extraordinary praise, powerful witness, and boldness of action. Accordingly, those who speak of such a 'baptism with the Spirit,' and who give evidence of this special empowering work of the Spirit, can claim Scriptural support. Further, since 'baptism with the Spirit' may not be at the same time as baptism with water and/or conversion, we need to be open-minded toward those today who claim an intervening period of time.[1] If this experience signifies in some sense a deepening of faith and awareness of God's presence and power, we may be thankful.

5. We are called upon to recognize a work of the Spirit, which involves the application of special gifts and benefits to the members of Christ's church. The Confession of Faith suggests this in Chapter IX, 4 where, following the paragraph on the Spirit's work in redemption, the words, in part, read, 'He calls and anoints ministers for their holy office, qualifies all other officers in the church for their special work, and imparts various gifts and graces to its members.' Here is a special work of the Holy Spirit of calling and anointing that is peculiarly related to the life of the believing community. We would add that it is important for the church constantly to bear this work of the Holy Spirit in mind so that there will be a continuing readiness for, and recognition of the calling, the qualifying, and the imparting of the gifts and graces of the Holy Spirit to the community of faith. Both a fresh confrontation with the biblical record and contemporary spiritual experience, we believe, are bringing us into a fuller understanding of the work of the Holy Spirit.

6. The 'baptism of the Holy Spirit' may be signified by certain pneumatic phenomena, such as speaking in tongues and prophecy (Acts 2.4; 10.46; 19.6). In the Old Testament, as we have noted, the Spirit is understood at times as an invading power, a charismatic fury; also it is frequently associated with ecstatic prophecy. However, since the Spirit came only to certain exceptional persons, this was quite limited. With the New Testament dispensation the Spirit is now available to all who believe in Jesus Christ. Hence such signs of this invading power as ecstatic language and prophecy

---

[1] We here call attention to the 1965 General Assembly declaration on *Glossolalia* which includes this statement: 'Scripture in several cases clearly distinguishes between a baptism with water and a baptism with the Holy Spirit (Matt. 3.11; Mark 1–8; Luke 3.16; Acts 1.5). We would agree that, since Pentecost, baptism and receiving the Spirit belong together in a single experience (Acts 2.38). But both Scripture and Confession face the possibility that there may be a lapse of time between the two (Acts 8, 10, 19; Confession XXX, 5).'

could occur with anyone who has experienced this visitation. Clearly it would be a mistake to say that all upon whom the Spirit comes *must* manifest specific pneumatic phenomena. The Spirit usually manifests himself in other ways. However, that such extraordinary manifestations *may* occur – and in so doing give evidence of the Spirit's working – is quite in accord with the witness of the New Testament.

7. There may be further bestowal of the Holy Spirit. 'Baptism with the Spirit' signifies the initial outpouring of God's Spirit wherein the community and/or person is filled with the presence and power of God. But also there may be later bestowal in such fashion as to signify implementation of the original event, whether or not accompanied by pneumatic phenomena (cf. Acts 2.4 with 4.31). This renewed activity of the Spirit ought not to be designated 'baptism' (at least, the New Testament never uses this term for it), but as 'filling,' wherein the empowering Spirit moves to renew the believer and believing community.

8. The bestowal and reception of the Spirit or the gifts of the Spirit, does not signify a higher level of spirituality nor ought it to suggest that some Christians have more of the Holy Spirit than others. Such expressions as 'baptism', 'filling', and the like point rather to the Spirit's implementing activity: endowment for the witness to the gospel. The Spirit is active in all believers, and they may be 'filled' with the Spirit in various ways for the mission of the Church. It should be added that such expressions as 'having' or 'filled with' the Spirit are not to be construed as obviating the possibility and actuality of growth in grace and knowledge.

9. Both the coming of the Spirit himself and the various abilities or charismata which he may bestow upon men are, above all, to be received as the benefits of God's free grace. Neither the Spirit, then, nor his gifts may be considered 'possessions' of the believer; he does not own them, nor can he presume that they are, or will be, at all times (or at any given time) available. Each occasion on which the Spirit's presence is known or his gifts made manifest is to be an occasion for new thanksgiving and praise to God. Hence, there should be no jeopardizing of the peace, unity, and fellowship of the church because of special experiences of the Holy Spirit, but a rejoicing together in all those ways whereby God leads His people into fuller apprehension of the riches of His grace.[2]

---

[2] The UPUSA Church 1970 declaration, 'The Work of the Holy Spirit,' in the section entitled 'Guidelines,' begins thus: 'We believe the Church needs to pray for a sensitivity to see the manifestations of the Holy Spirit in our world today.... We believe that those who are newly endowed with gifts and perceptions of the Spirit have an enthusiasm and joy to give, and we also believe that those who rejoice in our traditions of having all things done "decently and in order" have a sobering depth to give. We therefore plead for a mutuality of respect and affection.'

10. An experience of the Spirit can neither be validated as such, nor evaluated with respect to its theological significance, by any scientific (i.e., psychological, sociological, etc.) means. It is to be acknowledged that such events, just as any other human events, may become the legitimate objects of scientific inquiry without prejudging the results of such inquiry. But regardless of the scientific conclusions which may be reached, the question of the theological significance of these phenomena will remain, and it may be answered only within the context of the Christian faith. The Corinthians' ability to speak in tongues, for example, may have a perfectly good psychological explanation; but whether the Spirit of Jesus Christ was active in that phenomenon is a question which neither psychology nor any other science can answer. But this conclusion leads also to the observation that the extraordinary or unusual nature of an experience (and the same would apply to gifts) is no criterion by which to judge its significance for faith. Ecstasy is not in itself an unambiguous occurrence. Not every dramatic event, experience, or ecstasy is necessarily a work of the Spirit.[3]

11. It is clear that there is Biblical and Reformed witness concerning baptism of the Holy Spirit and special endowments of the Holy Spirit in the believing community. Of course, it is impossible to make any general pronouncement concerning the validity of particular claims made, since multiple factors may be at work. But where there is divisiveness, judgment (expressed or implied) on the lives of others, an attitude of pride or boasting, etc., the Spirit of God is not at work. However, where such an experience gives evidence of an empowering and renewing work of Christ in the life of the individual and the church, it may be acknowledged with gratitude. This means above all that Christ should be glorified, his own Spirit made manifest in human lives, and the Church edified. For such evidences of the presence of the Holy Spirit the Church may rejoice.

Used by permission of The Liturgical Press, Collegeville, MN 54321, USA.

[3] Compare this statement from the 1965 General Assembly declaration on 'Glossolalia': *'The Gift of the Spirit can be counterfeited or sought for the wrong motive* (1 John 4.1). There is no reason to suppose that forms of utterance voiced at the prompting of the Spirit cannot be initiated or cultivated by men and women variously motivated. While there may be among us some who "speak in tongues" as the Spirit gives them utterance, there may also be present among us those who, succeeding in the effort to "speak in tongues," unwarrantedly assume their utterance to be an evidence of the Spirit of Christ. The gift may be sought and its counterfeit achieved from wrong motives.'

Although writing within a classical Pentecostal framework, Macchia offers fresh thinking about the value of speaking with tongues

5.8   Frank D. Macchia, 'The Question of Tongues as Initial Evidence: A Review of *Initial Evidence*, edited by Gary B. McGee'[1] first published in the *Journal of Pentecostal Theology* 2, 1993, pp. 117–27 (extract is pp. 120–3, abridged)

Sociologically, restorationism through charismatic signs, such as evidential tongues, can be viewed as a kind of countercultural movement that arises out of a basic disillusionment with the mainline churches and their formalized links with the apostolic heritage. It is, in the minds of devotees, a restoration created by God – and maintained by God alone. This is the reason that frenzied charismatic activity often accompanied fringe or persecuted groups such as the Montanists, Canisards or Pentecostals! I do not wish to limit tongues to sectarian or fringe movements, nor to limit institutional/liturgical forms to mainline religious movements. But the emphasis on charismatic signs among groups dissatisfied with the ecclesiastical mainstream helps to explain Burgess's observation . . . that a theological dualism often accompanied devotion to signs initiated by the Spirit.[2] Those devoted to sectarian or fringe groups often harbor some kind of dualistic vision of reality in order to distinguish themselves from mainline institutions and to keep themselves pure from contamination. I have been convinced for some time that the whole issue of charisma and institution will be important for the future of Pentecostal theology.

There are, of course, numerous theological dangers in dualisms, which I cannot explore here. The major theological challenge for Pentecostals is how to channel the protest element in their spirituality into a constructive form of social renewal and ecumenical dialogue, in a way that is true to the spiritual and cultural openness of Acts. As Murray Dempster has noted, tongues in Acts always accompanies the elimination of economic, racial and religious barriers. Robeck's provocative description of Seymour's stress on fruits of love and holiness as 'evidences' of the Spirit's work can help Pentecostals to integrate evidential tongues and the evidence of a liberated life. These two kinds of evidence need not be played off against

---

[1] G. B. McGee (ed.), *Initial Evidence: Historical and Biblical Perspectives on the Pentecostal Doctrine of Spirit Baptism* (Peabody, Mass.: Hendrickson, 1991).

[2] e.g. S. M. Burgess, 'Evidence of the Spirit: The Ancient and Eastern Churches', in McGee, *Initial Evidence*, pp. 9–13.

each other (as Robeck presents Seymour as having done), since they occur in two different contexts (worship and life). But their integration is necessary for a proper understanding of both. What is tongues other than a sign of a renewed and yielded language (and life!) under the liberating direction of the Spirit? What would it be without love and holiness in life to fulfill it? On the other hand, what is holiness without the renewing and liberating power of the Spirit implied in tongues worship (and in other forms of worship)? . . .

What links tongues with Spirit baptism for Pentecostals? Pentecostals support initial evidence, not through external laws or guarantees through some kind of integral connection between Spirit baptism and the experience of tongues. As W. T. Gaston stated in 1918, 'tongues seems included and inherent in the larger experience of the Spirit baptism'.[3] Whether the accent be on the overwhelming power or mystery of the Spirit, the power of language to express a person's innermost being, or the significance of a tongue yielded to God, implied is the assumption that tongues flows naturally from the kind of divine–human encounter initiated in Spirit baptism. Tongues not only 'signifies' Spirit baptism in the simplistic understanding of this term, but also participates in the experience itself, as an aspect of it. This integral connection between tongues and Spirit baptism illuminates the many statements of Pentecostals, such as Donald Gee, that connect the departure of the glory and power of our experience of the Spirit with the abandonment of evidential tongues.

What would help us to understand how Pentecostals maintain both initial evidence and the freedom of the Spirit is the realization that tongues functions for them more as a 'sacramental sign' than as rationalistic 'evidence'. Both William Samarin[4] and Walter Hollenweger[5] have referred to tongues as an 'acoustic sacrament' for Pentecostals. Paul Tillich remarked that Christianity requires a 'sacramental element', distinct from the individual sacraments of baptism or communion. For Tillich, this element is not primarily sustained by a law or command but by an integral connection between the experience of God and the physical/acoustic reality used as a visible sign of this experience. In my opinion, tongues provides Pentecostals with this kind of sacramental element. As Tillich noted, the Protestant principle, most consistently carried out in the Reformed tradition, seeks to replace the sacramental element of Christian spirituality with a radical emphasis on the freedom of the Spirit, in order to

---

[3] H. I. Lederle, 'Initial Evidence and the Charismatic Movement: An Ecumenical Appraisal', in McGee, *Initial Evidence*, pp. 128–9.

[4] W. J. Samarin, *Tongues of Men and Angels* (New York: Macmillan, 1972), p. 232.

[5] W. J. Hollenweger, *Geist und Materia* (Munich: Chr. Kaiser Verlag, 1988).

avoid a demonic objectification of the Spirit in sacramental means of grace.[6]

To my mind, Pentecostal sacramental spirituality is unique in its effort to push beyond this impasse between the Protestant principle and an elimination of the Spirit's freedom through the Spirit's 'objectification' in sacramental means of grace. Pentecostals insist on the freedom of the Spirit, since tongues itself is a sign of the Spirit of God as unrestrained and beyond human manipulation. Yet, without limiting the freedom of the Spirit, there is a genuine emphasis among Pentecostals on consistent visible signs (especially through tongues) that are integral to the experience of Spirit baptism. Tongues is a kind of primary sacrament for Pentecostals, the 'new sign of the Christian Church', according Thomas Barratt,[7] the 'root and stem' out of which all spiritual gifts grow and by which they are nourished, according to Edward Irving (who is, perhaps, the first Pentecostal!)[8] or the 'spiritual rest of the new covenant'.[9] How else can we account for the emphasis of Pentecostals on tongues as 'initial' evidence? Also, since tongues is not solely granted at the hands of an ordained minister, there is a strong tendency in the sacramental spirituality toward democratization in worship.[10]

Used by permission of the Editors of the Journal of Pentecostal Theology, *J. S. Land et al., Church of God, 900 Walker Street, N. E. Cleveland, Tennessee, USA.*

---

[6] P. Tillich, *The Protestant Era* (Chicago: University of Chicago Press, 1947), ch. 7.

[7] Quoted in G. B. McGee, 'Popular Expositions of Initial Evidence in Pentecostalism', in McGee, *Initial Evidence*, pp. 117–30.

[8] Quoted in D. W. Dorries, 'Edward Irving and the "Standing Sign" of Spirit Baptism', in McGee, *Initial Evidence*, pp. 41–56.

[9] Quoted in J. L. Hall, 'A Oneness Pentecostal Looks at *Initial Evidence*', in McGee, *Initial Evidence*, p. 181.

[10] Quoted in G. B. McGee, 'Popular Expositions of Initial Evidence in Pentecostalism', in McGee, *Initial Evidence*, p. 123.

Writing from within a Catholic charismatic context, Hocken reflects on the interaction between Pentecostal and charismatic understandings of the experience of the Holy Spirit.

5.9   Peter Hocken, *The Glory and the Shame*, Guildford, Surrey: Eagle Publishing, 1994, pp. 46–50, abridged

The first Pentecostals believed that this baptism in the Holy Spirit was the recurrence in the twentieth century of the experience of the first Christians. They were convinced that their experience of a second (or even third) blessing subsequent to regeneration–conversion reflected the pattern of Christian experience recorded in the Acts of the Apostles. While Pentecostals undoubtedly did seek to understand the objective data of the New Testament, especially Acts and 1 Corinthians, inevitably perhaps they read back into the Scriptures contemporary patterns of Evangelical and Holiness experience.

It is possible however to recognize that the Pentecostals were led by the Spirit in this identification with Pentecost and their naming of this central experience, without accepting all their exegesis. This can be done by insisting that the original Pentecostal use of the term 'baptism in the Spirit' was primarily prophetic. It is an interpretation of contemporary experience in the light of the Scriptures rather than exegesis of the Scriptures illuminated by present circumstances. The designation of this work as baptism in the Spirit was not simply the result of study of the New Testament, but was a spiritual interpretation and prophetic proclamation that 'This is That' which was spoken of by the prophet Joel and initially experienced on the day of Pentecost.

It is true that Charles Parham was largely responsible for the teaching that speaking in tongues is the biblical evidence for baptism in the Spirit. He was in a way the father of the doctrine of 'initial evidence' that has characterized the majority of Pentecostals. But it was at Azusa Street that we find the first manifestation of the full range of characteristics that have since marked the world-wide Pentecostal movement: eschatological expectation, restoration of the spiritual gifts, spiritual equipment of every believer, explosive praise, power for evangelism, revelation of the Saviour. Unlike Topeka, it was a public manifestation of the dynamic power of the Spirit reconciling people of different races and sending witnesses throughout the world, whose meaning was most deeply expressed in the prophetic declaration 'This is Pentecost'. In this light, it is significant that the prophetic statement 'This is That' was made in a corporate context, an outpouring of the Spirit on an incredibly diverse gathering of believers at Azusa Street, rather evocative of the diversity recorded in Acts 2.

That the use of the term baptism in the Spirit is primarily prophetic is saying:

- negatively, it is not in its essential reality simply an individual experience located within a series of experiences;
- positively, it refers to a sovereign intervention of God in the life of the Church, and points to a particular work of God at a specific point in Christian history;
- thus a Christian baptized in the Spirit has been plunged by the risen Lord Jesus into the unlimited torrent of the Spirit's life, and thereby participates in a sovereign grace being poured out on the Church; this is understood in faith to be a contemporary experience of the grace that characterized the foundation of the Church and which looks for its completion at the second coming.

Charismatic usage

From the beginning of the charismatic movement, participants readily used the Spirit terminology of the Pentecostals. The dominant Pentecostal doctrine concerning baptism in the Spirit was criticized from opposite angles – from the Evangelical side, by those insisting on the simultaneity of regeneration and the gift of the Spirit; from the Catholic side, by those concerned to uphold baptismal regeneration and the objective gift of the Spirit in the sacraments of initiation.

Despite the theological objections, the majority stuck, perhaps somewhat obstinately, to the terminology of baptism in the Spirit. If this prophetic interpretation is correct, such obstinacy could represent a tenacity of the Spirit in the face of powerful pressures, both doctrinal and pastoral. It no doubt represented a deep instinct that this was an appropriate term, despite the real difficulties raised by Church leaders and theologians. This sense of its appropriateness probably flowed from an awareness of the link between this contemporary grace and the event of Pentecost. The charismatic movement with eruption in almost every Christian tradition appeared an outpouring of the Spirit 'on all flesh' as prophesied by Joel and applied in Acts 2.17. Humanly speaking the extent of this usage owed much to the distinctive ministry of David du Plessis.

From 1959, du Plessis circled the world announcing this outpouring of the Spirit on Christians of every Church and every continent. Central to his message was Jesus' role as baptizer with the Spirit and the identity of this blessing with the earlier Pentecostal outpouring. What Christians in the mainline Churches are experiencing, he announced, is the baptism in the Holy Spirit, the same grace as the Lord poured out at Azusa Street. Just as the Pentecostal usage of Spirit-baptism was prophetic, so David du Plessis's distinctive ministry was prophetic. He embodied the essential link between identification of this grace as baptism in the Spirit and affirmation of its universal and unitive character. Du Plessis grasped the importance of the same term being used to describe the central grace common to all streams.

The significance of being baptized in the Holy Spirit today

If this reflection is on the right lines, the significance of the Pentecostal and charismatic movements lies above all in two related points: (a) the sovereign manner of God's action through the risen Jesus baptizing with/in the Holy Spirit and (b) the heavenly uncreated character of the life poured out. Just as the events of Pentecost and Caesarea gave the primitive Church a strong sense of the eschatological and heavenly character of the Church and of the Christian life, so this outpouring of the Holy Spirit in the twentieth century is restoring to the Church a dynamic faith in, and a direct knowledge of, the risen and glorified Lord who, bearing the wounds of Calvary, pours out from the divine throne streams of living water. . . .

The spiritual gifts which are evidently a distinguishing feature of the Pentecostal–charismatic outpouring are best seen, not as the essence of the phenomenon, but as characteristic signs of the divine sovereign intervention of baptizing with the Holy Spirit . . .

This contemporary grace of God directly addresses our present spiritual malaise. To a Church in which many people hardly believe that God acts in any identifiable way, or who think that such direct manifestations of God's love and mercy are reserved for the few or for the past, this current of divine life is a clear sign that 'Jesus Christ is the same yesterday and today for ever' (Heb. 13.8). The sense that the Church is on the defensive, constantly yielding ground to secularist trends, her influence ever more ineffective, is strikingly reversed by this sovereign manifestation of divine life and power. The increasing restriction of Christian life to a private sphere with minimal impact on the world is dramatically challenged by the public character of these outpourings and the communities and ministries to which they give rise.

Used by permission of Eagle Publishing, 6 Kestrel House, Mill Street, Trowbridge, Wiltshire BA14 8BE, UK.

From the beginning of the Pentecostal Movement teaching on NT Prophecy was needed. This extract by T. B. Barratt of Norway (1862–1940) demonstrates the thinking and teaching of a key European Pentecostal.

5.10　T. B. Barratt, *In The Days of the Latter Rain*,
London: Elim Publishing House, 1928, pp. 108–9, 112–14, abridged

Individuality not eliminated

We may plainly recognize the style used by Paul, and distinguish it from that of Peter and John. So also in the Old Testament, we notice the difference between the writings of David, Isaiah, Ezekiel and others. The words spoken, or written, are truthful and reliable, but have the unmistakable characteristics of the speaker or writer.

This then seems to prove that the Holy Spirit does not break or disregard the individuality of the prophet, but sanctifies it, and uses it as a channel for the message to be given.

But there appear to be various *degrees* in the intensity of the Spirit's operations through the prophets. We may expect that the Spirit will illuminate the mind, and fill it with the thoughts to be revealed, and give it the words whereby these thoughts are to be made known to the people, and give the power to speak the words with divine authority. Or the Holy Spirit may even use the vocal cords without any brain work on the part of the speaker. This would then be a 'Thus saith the Lord!' – Inspiration in its highest form, a case of verbal inspiration. But between this and the least inspired prophecy there may be several degrees of intensity, making it more or less a work of the Spirit through the brain or the mind, or without it. The message given need not be reckoned as a human message merely, because it passes through the mind. It bears a definite mark probably of the human instrument used, but the message is nevertheless from God; that is, if it is consistent with the general teaching of the Bible, and is therefore not to be despised (1 Thess. 5.20, 21).

. . .

To remain in the Church

There seems to be no doubt in the mind of the apostles that this gift of prophecy, as all the other gifts of the Spirit, was to remain with the Church throughout this dispensation. The same arguments may be used to prove this, as those used to prove the existence and the necessity of the *tongues* and other gifts of the Spirit throughout the 'last days'.

Prophecy at times in tongues

On the Day of Pentecost, Peter made the statement that the speaking in tongues in Jerusalem was of a prophetic nature, because, as far as we can see, there was no prophetic speaking of the kind we classify with prophetic speech, but merely tongues. Still, he says the prophecy of Joel was fulfilled, which said: 'And it shall come to pass in the last days, saith God, I will pour out of My Spirit upon all flesh: and your sons and your daughters shall prophesy' (Acts 2.17).

There must, therefore, not merely have been worship and adoration in the 'tongues' heard, but also messages to the people, similar to those mentioned in 1 Cor. 14.3. Their character of 'prophecy' arose from this fact, those present understanding what was said.

Tongues and prophecy give mutual help

Tongues and prophecy are twin brothers, and brought about by the same mighty Spirit. There was no necessity, as we have already shown, for tongues, as is generally supposed, on Pentecost, in order to reach the different nationalities assembled in Jerusalem at that time, as almost everybody knew the chief languages generally spoken, which is seen from the fact that they all understood Peter, without his making use of an interpreter. The miracle of tongues gave his message that peculiar background, that divinely supernatural stamp, without which he would have had no solicitous crowd to speak to, and certainly not the same influence over the masses that he had.

Used by permission of Elim Foursquare Gospel Alliance, PO Box 38, Cheltenham, Glos. GL50 3HN, UK.

Where the laity is empowered by the Holy Spirit, prophecies will occur during church services. Mike Bickle shows how he dealt with problems that can arise.

5.11   Mike Bickle with Michael Sullivant, *Growing in the Prophetic*, Florida: Strang Communications, 1996, pp. 178–81

Correcting unanointed prophecies

Most pastors and leaders have at one time or another experienced the fear of strange or unbiblical words being voiced in the church in the name of prophecy. But if there is an established process of correcting such fleshly words, there will be less pressure on both the leaders and the people.

There are several different types of correction that will periodically need to be employed. Although most of the prophetic words in our church come through the microphone up front, that procedure is not established as a hard and fast rule. Asking people to speak their prophetic word over the microphone serves three purposes. First, it allows the entire congregation to hear the word clearly. Secondly, it gives us the ability to tape record it. Thirdly, it gives the leaders a chance to talk with the person when necessary before the prophetic word is spoken. However, someone will occasionally give a word from the congregation that does not edify the body; there seems to be no inspiration, no life or relevance. I do not like to call this a false prophecy, for that might imply that the person is deceived by a demon. In 1 Corinthians 14.3 it says, 'He who prophesies speaks edification and exhortation and comfort.' The word may not do any of those things, but if it's not a directional prophecy, and if it doesn't represent a doctrinal error, then even though it is unanointed we treat it as a less serious problem.

We will usually let it go the first time and probably the second. However, after two so-called prophetic words that seem to contain no anointing or edification, we will go to the person and gently suggest that they submit their word to the leaders sitting at the front. If it happens a third time, we then require them to submit their prophetic words to the leadership before speaking them out in the church service. If the person does not heed this third private correction from the leadership, we will stop them on the fourth time and correct them publicly. This has only happened a few times in twelve years. On each occasion we have taken time to explain to the entire congregation the process that evolved with that person. If the whole process is not explained to the congregation, then other prophetic people may have a paralysing fear of being publicly corrected. But when the people understand the whole process, it gives them security to know that the leadership will not deal harshly with them if they make a mistake when they begin to step out. They must not be afraid that they might prophesy something wrong and be suddenly corrected for it before the whole church. The church needs to be able to trust the leadership to deal with such things in a spirit of gentleness or else the spirit of faith and liberty in the church will diminish quickly. If this happens, then the prophetic ministry will surely dry up and shut down.

Instant correction

There are two types of prophetic word that we publicly correct immediately, but as gently as possible. The first type is a prophetic utterance given as a rebuke or correction to the church without first going through our leadership team. For example, I would never go to another church and give a prophetic word that was a correction or redirection without giving it first to their leadership. If the leadership of the church agree with the word, I would ask them to present it to the church. It is usually more effective if the local leadership team speak the corrective word instead of a visitor, who is not well known by the local church. However, they might ask me to share it with the church, but I would do so only after it was made clear to everyone that I was speaking at their request. If, in our private discussion, the leaders rejected the prophetic word, yet I was convinced that I had unmistakably heard from God, I might warn them in the pastor's office, 'I think you people are in real trouble.' But I would never speak a corrective word publicly in a church outside their leadership and authority structure.

If a person stands up and gives a prophetic word that suggests a new direction, a rebuke or correction for our church without first submitting it to the leadership, I would desire to respond gently in this way: 'I appreciate the fact that you are trying to hear from God for this church and that you care about us. However, I would like you to take this word, share it with the leadership team and let us discern it together. We also invite you to be a part of this process if you wish, but for now we are not going to move in that direction. We will come back and give you a report later.' It is very important to teach people to stay within proper lines of spiritual authority when bringing a corrective or directive word to a local church.

The other type of prophetic word we would correct immediately is one that contains unorthodox doctrinal implications. Again the correction must be done with kindness and gentleness. This is not the time for the pastor to seek to look macho by showing how many bullets he has in his pastoral gun. We must always remember that we are dealing with precious human beings who are redeemed by Jesus' precious blood. If you deal harshly with the individual's error, that harshness will also destroy the liberty and openness in the church. If a person's prophecy included some kind of significant doctrinal error, then I would have to correct it on the spot. I would begin by saying, 'I'm sure he meant well, but the word spoken calls into question a doctrine that we esteem as biblical'. Then I would clearly state the accurate doctrine that was called into question.

Paul (David) Yonggi Cho (b. 1934), of South Korea, shows how Christians can enter what he calls the 'fourth dimension', a spiritual plane, and so envision the future.

5.12   Paul Yonggi Cho with R. Whitney Manzano, *The Fourth Dimension: More Secrets For a Successful Life*, vol. 2, Plainfield, NJ: Bridge Publishing, 1983, pp. 50–5

Visions and dreams: the instruments of the fourth dimension

If a man understands what he is, he will desire to know how he can grow in his fourth-dimensional capabilities. If the Holy Spirit has come to lead us and guide us into all truth, how does He operate?

The age of the Holy Spirit began on the day of Pentecost. Peter preached his first message the day that the Holy Spirit came in clear manifestation. His text was from Joel 2: 'And it shall come to pass in the last days, saith God, I will pour out of my Spirit upon all flesh; and your sons and your daughters shall prophesy, and your young men shall see visions, and your old men shall dream dreams' (Acts 2.17, KJV).

Dreams and visions are very similar in nature. Young men have a tendency to envision the future; old men naturally dream about the past. However, both dreams and visions work within the framework of the imagination.

Before we can understand how visions and dreams operate, we should understand something about the framework within which they operate: the imagination.

The imagination: the soul of the vision and dream

In 2 Corinthians 10, Paul tells us that we are to walk in the Holy Spirit and not in the flesh. The King James Version uses the word 'imagination' in the fifth verse. However, the word could be better translated 'reasonings' or 'logic'. Paul does not mean that we should not reason, but he does tell us not to rely on our natural logic that has not been sanctified by the Holy Spirit. Our problems are greater than just natural ones and the solutions must be found by using our spiritual minds. 'For the weapons of our warfare are not carnal but mighty in God for pulling down strongholds, casting down arguments and every high thing that exalts itself against the knowledge of God, bringing every thought into captivity to the obedience of Christ' (2 Cor. 10.4–5, NKJV).

Paul uses military language when referring to the realm of the imagination. The unregenerated mind uses natural reason which cannot understand spiritual things. Paul refers to these natural reasonings as strongholds or fortifications which the spiritual mind must bring down in order for the Christian to live victoriously.

When the Bible refers to the heart, it is referring to the area of our soul which comprises the imagination. Jesus said, 'Let not your heart be troubled' (John 14.1, NKJV). There are seven areas which Jesus revealed were problems in the heart:

1. The heart can be hardened to spiritual reality (Mark 6.52).
2. The heart can be blind, incapable of seeing what would be obvious to the spiritual person (John 12.40).
3. The heart is where sin begins (Matt. 15.19).
4. Words spoken are first conceived in the heart (Matt. 12.34).
5. Satan operates his tempting powers in the heart (John 13.2).
6. Doubts begin in the heart (Mark 11.23).
7. Sorrow and trouble work within the heart (John 14.1; 16.6).

Therefore, Paul's teaching the Corinthian Christians to guard their hearts was based on the clear emphasis which Christ gave to this important part of the soul.

I liken the heart of man to a painter's canvas. What a man dreams and envisions is the paint. If the Christian takes the brush of faith and begins to paint on the canvas of his heart the pictures that God has revealed to him, those revelations become reality.

The unconscious mind

What is referred to as the subconscious is really the unconscious mind. The unconscious mind is the motivational force that causes men to act or to behave without conscious perception. I have noticed a number of books on this subject in recent years.

Carl Gustav Jung, the son of a clergyman and a student of Sigmund Freud, developed the field of psychology known as analytical psychology as a reaction to Freud's psychoanalysis. In his view, man was not only motivated by conscious thought and reasoning, but also by his unconscious mind. He broke down the unconscious into two categories: 1. the personal factor or one's individual unconscious; 2. the collective factor or one's collective unconscious that is inherited from one's ancestors.

There developed a sociological belief that man's collective unconscious was inherently good. Society's rules were thought to tend to inhibit man. Anthropologists, artists and philosophers began traveling to primitive cultures searching for the goodness and simplicity in man which had not been spoiled by the prohibitions of Western culture.

The belief in man's inherent goodness is in direct contradiction to Scripture. 'The heart is deceitful above all things, and desperately wicked; Who can know it? I, the Lord, search the heart, I test the mind, even to give every man according to his ways, and according to the fruit of his doings' (Jer. 17.9–10, NKJV).

God reveals to man in Jeremiah 3 things about his heart: (1) The heart is not inherently good, but inherently evil. This is because of sin; (2) Man is not naturally capable of understanding his own heart. Only the Lord knows a man's heart and is capable of revealing it to him; (3) A man's actions will reveal his heart.

If our actions and accomplishments result from a motivating force that is beyond our conscious perception, then should not the Holy Spirit choose to work within this realm in order to sanctify it and cause it to motivate us to do God's will?

The ability to see and dream

The Holy Spirit is pictured by Peter at the day of Pentecost as a river. God had promised to pour this river into humanity irrespective of social standing, gender, or age. Joel prophesied that the moderate former rain and the stronger latter, or harvest, rain would both fall at once in 'the day of the Lord'. The torrents of God's Holy Spirit forming a spiritual river would fill every believer and bring forth spiritual fruit.

When the final day of the first fruits, (first harvest) festival arrived, the

Holy Spirit descended in a forceful manner. It must be remembered that the Pentecost feast (fifty days after the wave offering of the Passover festival) was a feast of anticipation. If there was a good grain harvest, then the fruit harvest, celebrated as the Feast of Tabernacles, would also be good.

The Church was born within the festival of anticipation. The anticipation will be culminated at the Second Coming of Jesus Christ. By that time, the Church will have accomplished her divine purpose of bringing the gospel of Jesus Christ to every creature. The success of the Church is assured because the Holy Spirit has empowered her with supernatural ability.

The Holy Spirit came on the day of Pentecost not only to cause men to be able to prophesy (speak forth the Word of God), but also to give the ability to have visions and dreams.

In the Old Testament we often see God giving visions and dreams concerning future events. In fact, Samuel was called a seer (1 Sam. 9.9). Daniel was able to see from Babylon the development of successive kingdoms and looked into the Church age and beyond. Ezekiel could see beyond his land into a foreign land.

This phenomenon was not limited to the Old Testament. In the New Testament, Ananias, Paul and even a Roman, Cornelius, had prophetic visions and dreamed dreams.

This does not necessarily mean that we should all remain in ecstatic states. However, it does mean that we are to participate in God fulfilling His will in our lives by first envisioning His purpose and then filling our imagination with it through dreaming.

Consequently, the believer should not be limited to the three-dimensional plane, but should go beyond that into the fourth-dimensional plane of reality. We should live in the Spirit. We should guard our minds from all negative and foolish thinking. This keeps the canvas clean for the artwork of the Holy Spirit to be painted on our imaginations. Creativity, perception, intelligence, and spiritual motivation will be by-products of an imagination which has been activated by the Holy Spirit.

Used by permission of Bridge Publishing, PO Box 141630, Gainesville, FL 32614, USA.

PART 3
THEOLOGY IN PRACTICE

6 Holiness in the Eyes of Pentecostals and Charismatics through the Twentieth Century

A. E. Dyer, Introduction

Origins

Before ever the Pentecostal Movement was formally recognized, before there were any tongues speakers . . . there were the Holiness groups. Some even included 'Pentecostal' in their title. During the nineteenth century many groups grew up from Methodist revivalist preachers in the USA, and in UK from the Keswick conventions. The former were following Wesley's sanctification teaching, whereby some derived crisis experiences of 'becoming perfect', sinless. Such encounters with the Holy Spirit were even termed 'Baptism in the Holy Ghost'. On the other hand the more Calvinistic Keswick teaching stressed seeking power for service, and the same phrase 'baptism in the Holy Ghost' could mean endowment with power, de-emphasizing the cleansing aspect of the experience. Holiness became a pre-requisite to power for service for some groups' teachings. As Blumhofer writes, 'Those strongly for a second blessing for sanctification warned of the danger of spiritual power being channelled through "unsanctified vessels".'[1]

The next debate: crisis or process?

In fact this led some of the Pentecostals to advocate not one crisis but two such experiences post-conversion – one for holiness and one subsequently for power, with tongues. Already by 1909 there was some teaching being published on this in *Confidence* by the German Pentecostal leader Jonathan Paul (1853–1931) (6.1).

William Durham of Chicago went to investigate Azusa Street in 1907. He received a powerful experience of the baptism in the Spirit (see 5.2) and returned to spread the Pentecostal teaching in Chicago. Later he found

---

[1] E. Blumhofer, *The Assemblies of God: A Chapter in the Story of American Pentecostalism*, vol. 1: *To 1941*, Springfield, Mo.: Gospel Publishing House, 1989, 217ff.

Azusa Street in opposition to his teaching that everything the Christian needed was accomplished at once on the cross of Christ so salvation and sanctification were 'already ours in Christ' (6.2). Some thought that Durham's teaching on the finished work of Calvary meant that it granted Christians licence to live as they pleased. 'People who have the Holy Ghost in an unsanctified vessel', warned Charles Parham, 'find that their flesh becomes the medium through which fanaticism and wild fire work!' (*Apostolic Faith*, August 1912, p. 4).[2] Parham taught that sanctification had to precede Spirit baptism and felt justified after Durham's death in recounting his prayer that whoever was wrong – either he or Durham – would die.[3]

In *Word and Witness* (December 1913) E. Bell (who later became a General Superintendent of Assemblies of God, USA) discussed this, concluding, 'The present possession (those who claimed a Second Blessing) is but the earnest [guarantee]. . . . There are rich effusions of the Spirit yet to be received . . .'. Both parties concluded that they held to the necessity of holiness, as separation from sin and separation to God, in a progressive way, not as a result of baptism in the Spirit.

Taboos and lifestyles

The next outcome was the outward expression of this holiness or separation from the world. It led to the question of a dress code – not that plain dress equals holiness! 1 Peter 3 was interpreted puritanically: a list of taboos was made of 'Thou shalt not . . .'. Taboos originated in 'economic dislocation' according to Robert Anderson.[4] The proponents of such taboos, not having material goods, defended their lowly social position, while implying an attack on those who did have more to flaunt in apparently 'unworldly manners'. Parham even threw sarcastic comments at church picnics, in *Apostolic Faith*. Wacker stresses the ridiculousness of the taboos and customs for rejecting the world (6.3). Blumhofer defends the Assemblies of God (AG), considering they had balanced views; they stressed the nurturing of a love relationship with Christ as more important than the taboos because 'Effective soul winning and spiritual power

---

[2] See Blumhofer *Assemblies of God*, p. 219.

[3] F. Bartlemann, *Azusa Street* first published Plainfield NJ: Bridge, 1925, pp. 151, 155–6; see also, E. Blumhofer, 'The Finished Work of Calvary, William H. Durham and a Doctrinal Controversy' Assemblies of God Heritage, 1983 pp. 9–10, p. 217.

[4] H. Goss, *Winds of God: The Story of the Early Pentecostal Days (1901–1914) in the life of Howard A Goss as told by Ethel E. Goss*, New York: Comet Press Books, 1958, p. 78.

mattered most.'[5] Nevertheless holiness proponents thought AG soft on holiness for not adopting their dress code and, in reply, AG continued to assert that they *were* 'believers in holiness'.

On reflection it is not surprising that these people, born as they were in the Victorian era, found it hard to adjust their moral and ethical stance to the rapid social changes that arrived with the twentieth century. The ideal of 'separation from the world' was not simply an ideal or an attitude but a reality to be expressed by clothing, eating styles and innocent recreational activities. To holiness believers the issues were clear-cut. Yet, clear-cut issues became all too likely to merge into the safest and most conservative of social norms. Even the mixing of blacks and whites that had characterized the early revival at Azusa Street was soon lost in Durham's church. This may be because black Pentecostals took Parham's 'holiness first' position rather than Durham's power and holiness together, not for any colour bar reason. It still took years before different races were welcome in each other's pulpits.

Definitions

Out of these debates came several denominational strands, especially in the USA.[6] One of these, the International Pentecostal Holiness Church (IPCH) has a statement of belief that shows how they have balanced the 'sinless perfection' impossibility with the possibility of living without sinning (6.4). They still maintain that, 'Pentecostal baptism of the Holy Ghost and fire is obtainable by a definite act of appropriating faith on the part of the fully cleansed believer' (Article 11). This implies three stages: conversion, sanctification and baptism of the Holy Ghost with tongues as the initial evidence.

The fledgling Assemblies of God USA made a statement in 1916 and revised it in 1961, dropping the word 'entire', simply stating that, 'Sanctification is an act of separation from that which is evil and dedication unto God. . . .' The Assemblies of God in the USA thus stressed the continuing work of the Holy Spirit as the result of Spirit baptism. According to M. Pearlman,[7] who quotes R. M. Riggs (also Assemblies of God General Superintendent), 'To be filled with the Holy Spirit means to allow the Holy Spirit to search out and condemn and destroy the impurities of the nature and spirit.'

---

[5] Blumhofer, *Assemblies of God*, p. 155.

[6] See V. Synan, *The Century of the Holy Spirit*, Nashville: Thomas Nelson, 2001, for the history of these groups.

[7] M. Pearlman, in *Paraclete* 7.4, p. 22.

E. S. Williams, also at one point an Assemblies of God General Superintendent, tried to define holiness as 'A habitual condition' to be 'full of the Holy Ghost'. . . in the daily life of a spiritual person by which character reveals the fruit of the Spirit (cf. Eph. 5.18).[8] The British AG leader, Donald Gee, emphasized the power aspects of the believer's relationship to the Holy Spirit. He still insisted, however, on a daily experiential relationship between the believer and the Spirit. 'The fruit of the Spirit will thus be seen as the manifestation and outcome of the divine life put within the believer at regeneration.'[9]

Charismatic appraisals

These positive views of holiness seem to swing with the pendulum to the negative outworking of lifestyle holiness. If it was not presented as a list of taboos, it appears that a holy and righteous lifestyle had to be taught to new converts – even as to how they ran their bank accounts, apparently. This may have started as logical, practical teaching but became an enforced lifestyle by 'heavy shepherding' during the latter part of the 1970s and early 1980s in charismatic circles (see 8.4; 8.5; 8.6).

Other neo-Pentecostal or charismatic groups appear to try to balance out these views, if John White is representative of the 1990s. He brings the corrective to a hope for quickly endowed holiness. Rather it is an altogether longer-lasting and more deeply embedded aspect of growing to maturity in the life of the Holy Spirit in the believer. He sees the Church is far from holy so the purpose of holiness is his concern for the world to see God's glory. Jesus' bride is to be 'a radiant church without stain or wrinkle or any other blemish but holy and blameless (Eph. 5.27)'.[10] He goes on to develop the theme through repentance, worship and the way the Holy Spirit works. The excerpt given (6.5) illustrates the need he sees for constant filling(s) with the Holy Spirit in the process of sanctification.

Colin Urquhart, an ex-Anglican founder of Kingdom Faith Revival Ministries, wrote *Holy Fire* in 1984. Here he emphasizes holiness as a part of revival lifestyle (6.6). However, this does not share the same taboos as were found at the start of the twentieth century. In other streams of charismatic renewal at the turn of the millennium, concepts of holiness have not

---

[8] E. S. Williams, *Systematic Theology*, Springfield, Mo.: Gospel Publishing House, 1953, vol. 3, p. 57.

[9] Cf. D. Gee, *Concerning Spiritual Gifts*, Springfield, Mo.: Gospel Publishing House, 1972, p. 65; *Fruitful or Barren?* Springfield, Mo.: Gospel Publishing House, 1961, pp. 65, 89.

[10] J. White, *Holiness*, p. 21.

been expressed by observation of outward regulations for holiness. In fact there may have been a deliberate reaction against the 'Thou shalt not' mode of teaching. Drinking alcohol, even visiting clubs is all justified on the grounds that it enables Christians to meet those who need to hear the Gospel. Again the pendulum swings!

Each time an emphasis on holiness appears in the Christian press there seems to be a realization of the world's polluting effect on the Church and of a need for repentance, of a world crisis pending with eschatological overtones (pre-1914; during the 1960s freestyle living and Cold War eras; again in the 1990s post-Gulf War?). A 'revival' of sorts occurs (Pentecostals in 1906/7; charismatic renewal movements within the denominations in the 1960s; Toronto, Pensacola in the 1990s) and then men work out the 'practicalities' of lifestyle and discipleship until that fades and another cycle starts.

In an account of the Whitsuntide convention meetings there is a summary of Pastor Paul of Germany's teaching.

6.1   Pastor Jonathan Paul, 'The Work of the Cross', *Confidence*, June 1909, p. 135

This was the underlying thought in all of Pastor Paul's addresses – victorious life in Christ the Risen Lord, through his victorious death. 'It is finished' – complete redemption. Romans 6.6 and 11 were the basis of the talk on Tuesday night. The Holy Spirit drove irresistibly home the blessed truth of our identification with the death and burial and our union with the risen Lord. This is what Pentecost means – victorious life. Simple and homely illustrations, so child-like as to be startling, made the profound truths of the Cross live and throb in the message.

The practical side was always sounded: the Holy Ghost-life must be *lived* not shouted. Paul had been caught up in the third heaven, but he didn't speak of it until 14 years after, and he didn't go off into trances when he could be of any service to the churches (2 Cor. 5.13) . . .

Sanctification means separation and holiness. The Holy Ghost could only fall upon that which was pure and purified through the Blood; then Divine Life and Healing could be claimed, and *must* follow.

A beautiful distinction was made between the old creation and the new.

God foresaw the fall. (The devil didn't know the secrets of the Lord Hallelujah!) Accordingly the first Adam was created – made out of dust; but the second Adam was begotten not made. He was pure in substance; 'that Holy Thing' (Luke 1.35). The death and grave of Jesus has separated us from sin. In His risen life we may claim complete victory over sin and the effects of sin – disease and death. If we live only to that which is 'begotten of God' then the devil has no power over us, 1 John 5.18, and the redemption of the body will become an accomplished fact.

Used by permission of the Donald Gee Centre, Mattersey Hall, Mattersey, UK.

Durham argues that there is no 'second work' of sanctification following conversion. Thus there are two stages, conversion and baptism in the Holy Spirit, and no intermediate stage of crisis sanctification or holiness, making three in all.

6.2   William H. Durham, *Pentecostal Testimony* (1907)

I believe that the time has come that God wants His people to understand His Word, and to accept it in preference to any theory. From the day the Holy Spirit fell on me and filled me I could never preach the second work theory again. I must say that in theory I still held to it, but was restrained in the Spirit from preaching it any more. From the first, the Spirit dealt with me and revealed clearly in my heart the plain Bible truth of the finished work of the Cross of Calvary; but it took months for me to get it clear enough in my mind to be willing to entirely discard the old theory, and take my stand on the simple living truth of God. I moved with great care out of respect for many recognized great men, including Wesley, who had taught sanctification as a second work of grace. I waited until I was sure that there was no possibility of my being mistaken on the subject from a Scriptural standpoint. Then, in the fear of the Lord, I preached the finished work of Calvary – one work of grace. From the first, God wonderfully honored it and the Spirit fell in power wherever it was preached.

I have preached on this subject to thousands of people since then. I honestly believe that ninety-nine out of every hundred of them accepted it. Not one has ever come and told me that what I preached was not the Bible. Some who did not see it at first have said, 'Yes, what you preach is the

Scripture, but I am going to search the Scriptures to see if I cannot find another work taught somewhere.' I say humbly, not one has ever come to point out the other work to me in the Bible.

Death, burial and resurrection

The plain teaching of the Word of God is identification with Jesus Christ. The thought of God concerning our salvation is expressed in a death, burial, and a resurrection. Our faith in God's plan is clearly expressed in the ordinance of baptism. We believe that we are dead with Christ, therefore we are buried with Him; and if we have been planted together in the likeness of His death, we believe that we shalt be also in the likeness of His resurrection. Romans 6.6 says that our 'old man' was crucified with Christ, that the body of sin might be done away. The seventh verse says, 'For – he that hath died is justified from sin.' Col. 2.11–13 says, 'In whom ye were also circumcised with a circumcision not made with hands, in the putting off of the body of the flesh in the circumcision of Christ; having been buried with Him in baptism, wherein ye were also raised with Him through faith in the working of God, who raised Him from the dead. And you being dead through your trespasses and the uncircumcision of your flesh, you did He make alive together with Him, having forgiven us all our trespasses.' Please notice that the body of the flesh is put off in the circumcision of Christ. Please notice in the twelfth verse, that we were buried with Him in baptism and raised with Him through faith in the working of God. Please also notice in the thirteenth verse, that we are made alive together with Christ. The first verse of the Third Chapter of Colossians tells us 'we are risen with Christ.' The third verse says, 'For ye died, and your life is hid with Christ in God.'

Old man crucified

Now all the teaching of the second work people has to do with the destruction or removal of the 'old man'. They teach that a saved person has a dual nature. That while we are made a new creature, yet the 'old man' is in us, and that the Adamic nature is removed in the second work of grace.

Now as soon as it is established that the 'old man' is crucified and slain in conversion, the whole foundation from under their theory is entirely removed, and their structure tumbles to the ground; yet the plain teaching in all the Scripture is to the effect, that the 'old man' was crucified with Christ, and that we are justified on the ground that Jesus Christ took our place and died in our stead. Now, why was it necessary for Jesus Christ to die for us? Because the sentence of death pronounced upon Adam the first, the 'old man' was handed down to us and must be executed before we could be justified. So when Jesus Christ went to the Cross He not only took our sins upon Him, but He, in the fullest sense, became our Substitute and took our place, and the sentence of death which hung over us was executed in Him; or, in other words, our 'old man,' the Adamic nature, was crucified with Christ that it might be destroyed or done away.

Used by permission of The Flower Pentecostal Heritage Center, Springfield, Missouri, USA.

In hindsight these 'taboos' to establish holy living seem somewhat ridiculous but they should be understood in the context of the times.

6.3   G. Wacker, *Heaven Below: Early Pentecostals and American Culture*, Cambridge, Massachusetts: Harvard University Press, 2001, pp. 122–6

Mouth taboos began with forbidden foods and drinks. They included meat in general and shellfish and hog products in particular, soft drinks in general and Coca Cola in particular. Mouth taboos also included coffee, tea, ice cream, chewing gum and, of course, medicinal drugs. Both the definition and the enforcement of these proscriptions varied from time to time and from group to group. At the Assemblies of God's 1914 organizing meeting, for example, elders decided that eating meat was so controversial that they would leave it to individuals to decide for themselves.[1] Though no Holy Ghost sect ever endorsed the use of tobacco, Church of God elders wrangled for years about the scope of the evil. Was it moral to grow tobacco if that was the only way to earn a living? Was it permissible to work in a store that sold cigarettes?[2] Whatever the variations, the main point is that Pentecostal leaders sought to outlaw many consumables other Christians quietly tolerated or simply took for granted.[3]

Some went a good deal further. In the early days many stalwarts fasted

---

[1] Minutes of the General Council of the Assemblies of God, 1914, p. 6.

[2] Mickey Crews, *The Church of God: A Social History* (Knoxville: University of Tennessee Press, 1990), pp. 52–5.

[3] See for example Coffee: Milton Grotz, *Eat and Drink to the Glory of God*, Christian Workers Union, Words of Life Tract, 1914, p. 9.

regularly.[4] The students at Charles Parham's Bible School in Topeka reportedly had gone without food for six days before Agnes Ozman (and then others) spoke in tongues on January 1, 1901.[5] The black saints who received Holy Spirit baptism at the Bonnie Brae house on April 9, 1906, just before the Azusa Mission outpouring, had been fasting for ten days before 'Pentecost fell'.[6] The diary of Henry L. Fisher, the founding patriarch of the United Holy Church in North Carolina, revealed that he often fasted on Friday, apparently in preparation for the evening service.[7] In 1910 three zealots in the western part of the United States reputedly starved themselves to death by trying to go without food for the biblically sanctioned forty days.[8] Such deprivation represented many things, some of them prudential. But the most obvious included a primitivist yearning for direct contact with God, regardless of social conventions. 'Fast days carried people out of ordinary time – or out of time's decay – back to that moment when all things were new' is how David D. Hall describes the practice's aims in colonial New England. He might well have said the same about early Pentecostal culture.[9]

Mouth taboos extended to what came out of the mouth as well. Again, the appropriateness of lying, swearing, and telling racy stories never arose. Pentecostals treated such behaviors as they treated cannibalism: too obviously evil to require explicit condemnation. But they did worry about the frivolous use of the tongue. The latter included idle talk, foolish talk, jesting with friends, and telling tall tales. Aimee McPherson – never at a loss for words herself – scorned the practice of reciting limericks at a grade school play. A child of God, she insisted, should not utter 'one idle word (let alone foolish words).'[10] Faith home director Martha Wing Robinson chastised herself for indulging in 'general conversation' when she could

---

[4] See for example L. P. Adams, in *Present Truth*, December 1909, p. 6; Albert Norton, in *Triumphs of Faith*, September 1909, pp. 195–200.

[5] C. W. Shumway, A Study of 'the Gift of Tongues', AB Thesis, University of South California, 1914, p. 166. Presumably fasting for extended periods meant living on soup or gruel, not complete absence of food.

[6] Ibid., p. 175.

[7] See for example Henry L. Fisher, 'Diary,' March 3 and May 19, 1922, Professor William C. Turner's private collection.

[8] *Confidence*, December 1910, p. 278. *Confidence* noted this event in order to condemn it.

[9] David D. Hall, *Worlds of Wonder, Days of Judgement* (New York: Alfred A. Knopf, 1989), p. 171.

[10] Aimee Semple McPherson, *This is That: Personal Experiences, Sermons and Writings* (New York: Garland, 1985, original 1919), p. 41.

have been better occupied in prayer.[11] The same proscriptions applied at the grass roots. One sister's congregation in Alamo, Texas, rebuked this otherwise faceless soul for using tobacco and 'carrying on foolish & gesting.'[12] A Chicago correspondent allowed that a Christian should be 'cheerful, light-hearted, free and sunny, but not over talkative.' Too much prattling, she explained, 'interrupts the spirit of devotion.'[13] The ban on inappropriate speech extended even to euphemisms, what one earnest partisan called 'Sugar-Coated Swearing.' Offending terms included 'My goodness, good gracious, Sakes alive, Gee-whiz.'[14] A Lytham, England, newspaper reported in 1913 that a local missioner placed 'foolish talking and jesting' on the same plane with fornication and idolatry.[15] In this context we can appreciate A. J. Tomlinson's otherwise inexplicably dour insistence that much of the friction within the church 'germinate[d] in lightness and frivolous conversation around the fireside.'[16]

The misuse of the eyes and ears seemed just as bad. At one time or another partisans censured the reading of novels, newspapers, and comic books.[17] They attacked 'worldly music' with vehemence. The latter included ragtime, tunes played on the fiddle, and classical violin.[18] The British firebrand Stephen Jeffreys dismissed Tony Music in church as 'nothing but rubbish.'[19] Admittedly, if the number of inquiries directed to editors of the various publications can be taken as a reliable index of the way many among the faithful felt, the laity seemed reluctant to give up music with a snappy rhythm. But leaders insisted. So it was that one questioner, who asked if it was all right to play waltzes on the piano at home, learned that it was better to play 'sacred music' at all times.[20] Another leader allowed that temperance and patriotic songs might be acceptable

---

[11] Martha Wing Robinson, 'Diary', typed June 8, 1907, p. 21, AG.

[12] Minutes of the Church of God, Alamo, Texas, April 24, 1932, COG.

[13] Elizabeth Timmermann, in the *Pentecostal Herald*, March 1917, p. 3.

[14] C. M. Padgett, in the Church of God *Evangel*, October 13, 1917, p. 2.

[15] *Lytham Times*, April 18, 1913, page not available, AGUK.

[16] [Church of God] General Assembly Minutes 1906–1914 (Cleveland, Tenn.: White Wing Publishing House, 1992), 1913, pp. 212–13.

[17] See for example *Confidence*, April 1908, p. 13; *Word and Witness*, May 1915, p. 2; Church of God *Evangel*, March 1917, p. 1.

[18] See for example McPherson, *This is That*, p. 38; Zelma Argue, *Contending for the Faith*, 2nd rev. edn (Winnipeg: Messenger of God Publishing House, 1928, original 1923), pp. 8–11; *Apostolic Faith* [Calif.], January 1908, p. 3; classical violin: Gordon P. Gardiner, *Radiant Glory: The Life of Martha Wing Robinson*, 2nd edn (New York: Bread of Life, 1970, original 1962) p. 92

[19] Reported by A. A. Boddy in *Confidence*, April–June 1920, p. 26.

[20] E. S. Williams in *Pentecostal Evangel*, July 20, 1929, p. 9.

under certain circumstances, but in general one should stick with Christian tunes.[21]

The way that a true child of God clothed and adorned the body also fell under the wary eye of Pentecostal watchdogs. This issue was more complicated than one might suspect. Several sources suggest that the earliest partisans actually displayed a measure of openness to secular clothing styles. According to Howard Goss, a founder of the Apostolic Faith movement in the Southwest, 'lady workers' in particular adopted the styles of the day. Bedecked with silks, satins, and jewels, they were, he remembered, 'very smartly turned out'.[22] But things soon changed. By 1910 or 1915 at the latest, Pentecostals had largely adopted the 'POOR-DRESS-GOSPEL,' as one writer put it.[23] Elders particularly worried about superfluous items of adornment, including watches, rings, hatpins, neckties, and brass buttons. At the Azusa mission, one writer declared, God's Spirit literally grabbed the hands of converts and compelled them to pull the rings from their fingers and hatpins from their hair.[24]

Alluring clothing warranted repeated condemnation – which suggests, of course, that the problem would not go away. Neckties and abbreviated sports attire for men earned occasional rebuke,[25] but, predictably, writers found women's attire more worrisome. The main problem was the plain fact that women's clothing – or the lack of it – attracted men's attention. An unnamed writer for the Kansas *Apostolic Faith* assailed 'scant attire, peekaboo waists, hobble skirts and flimsy silken stockings.' Brushing aside any possibility that men might be responsible for the rise in sexual misdeeds, the author placed the blame squarely on the heads of 'mothers and daughters themselves.'[26] Females shared males' concerns. 'Women who want to please Jesus,' asserted one Church of God matriarch, 'will never make their clothes so attractive as to draw the attention of men.'[27]

---

[21] A. W. Orwig, in *Bridegroom's Messenger*, November–December 1919, p. 4.

[22] Howard A. Goss, *The Winds of God: The Story of the Early Pentecostal Days (1911–1914) in the life of Howard A. Goss as told by Ethel E. Goss* (New York: Comet Press Books, 1958), p. 38.

[23] *Word and Witness*, June 20, 1913, p.2.

[24] *Apostolic Faith* [Calif.], September 1907, p. 2.

[25] Neckties: Harold Dean Trulear, 'The Mother as Symbolic Presence: Ida B. Robinson and the Mt Sinai Holy Church,' in *Portraits of a Generation: Early Pentecostal Leaders*, ed. James R. Goff, Jr, and Grant Wacker (2002); sports attire: *Apostolic Faith* [Kans.] January 1913, p. 5.

[26] *Apostolic Faith* [Kans.], May 1913, p. 15, quoting remarks of Lutheran Pastor J. H. Keller.

[27] Mattie Lemons, in *Evangel*, August 9, 1914, p. 5, quoted in Crews, *Church of God*, p. 56.

Pentecostal Bible schools went out of their way to regulate female students' dress. The Peniel Bible Institute in Dayton, Ohio, for example, required female students not to cut or curl their hair, to forgo cosmetics, and to wear uniforms.[28] Items of adornment could be almost as dangerous as beguiling clothing. For the Quaker Pentecostal Levi Lupton, no Holy Spirit-filled woman would degrade herself with any form of adornment, however innocuous by worldly standards. 'What does that gaudy ribbon ... on your dress say? ... TAKE CARE [Y]ou might just as well write on your clothes: 'No truth in religion.'[29]

Pentecostals' determination to articulate and enforce behavioral codes based on biblical or direct Holy Spirit prescriptions rather than convenience or convention emerged with particular force in the realm of sexual behavior. In order to understand this process of self-definition, we first need to ask how the contrary image arose in the popular imagination.

The stereotype of Pentecostals as libertines ... is almost as old as the revival itself. Saints themselves bore much of the blame, for they used charges of immoral sexual activities as a club for thumping each other in intramural power struggles. Charles Parham, for example, claimed that lewd behavior had disgraced Holy Ghost missions in the Midwest and southern California. 'The wild, weird prayer services in many of these fanatical meetings, where the contact of bodies in motion is as certain and damning as in the dance hall, leads to free-love, affinity-foolism and soul-mating.'[30] Parham asserted – without a trace of evidence, one might add – that some leading Chicago workers had found themselves in a 'delicate condition' because unorthodox views of sanctification had eroded their moral standards. *Word and Witness* repudiated Parham himself for unspecified 'sins.'[31] Still more damaging was the charge or implication by some factions that others espoused free love teachings and practices. This indictment cropped up in the early issues of the Azusa *Apostolic Faith*, reappeared in periodicals throughout the United States and in Britain, and troubled black as well as white fellowships.[32]

---

[28] *Peniel Advocate*, August 1929, p. 3.

[29] Levi Upton, in *New Acts*, October 5, 1905, p. 7. The quotation purportedly came from Charles G. Finney.

[30] Charles Parham, in *Apostolic Faith* [Kans.], December 1912, p. 4–5.

[31] Probably the editor E. N. Bell in *Word and Witness,*October 20, 1912, p. 3.

[32] *Apostolic Faith* [Calif.], September 1907, p. 2.

This is taken as a key characteristic for the 'holiness churches'.

6.4   International Pentecostal Church of Holiness, statement on Sanctification, 13 March, 2003
http://www.iphc.org/docs/theology/exeg3.html

Article Ten

We believe in sanctification. While sanctification is initiated in regeneration and consummated in glorification, we believe that it includes a definite, instantaneous work of grace achieved by faith subsequent to regeneration (Acts 26.18; 1 John 1.9). Sanctification delivers from the power and dominion of sin. It is followed by life-long growth in grace and knowledge of our Lord and Savior Jesus Christ (2 Corinthians 4.16; 2 Peter 3.18).

Article Eleven

We believe that the Pentecostal baptism of the Holy Ghost and fire is obtainable by a definite act of appropriating faith on the part of the fully cleansed believer, and the initial evidence of the reception of this experience is speaking with other tongues as the Spirit gives utterance (Luke 11.13; Acts 1.5; 2.14, 8–17; 10.44–46; 19.6).

Sanctification

The derivation of this word, from root to stem in both Hebrew and Greek languages (the original languages in which the Word of God was first written) may help to some extent in the definition of its meaning, but is not sufficient to set forth the vast scope of truth embraced by the word as used in both Old and New Testaments. The historico-ethical revelation of the word as connected with the manifestation of Jehovah to the patriarchs, to Israel, the elect nation, and to and through Jesus Christ in fullness, is the only way by which the full knowledge of the word as to its meaning can be obtained. . . .

Kadesh is the Hebrew word for sanctification and its equivalents. Its verbal stem is derived from the root *dash*, which primarily signifies to 'break forth shiningly' (Cremer's Lexicon). . . .

This manifestation was clearer and more abundant in Christ Jesus who was the effulgence of his Father's glory (Hebrews 1.3). It also characterizes the fullness of the work of the Holy Ghost. From the root and stem significance of the Hebrew word *kadesh* and its equivalent in Greek, we learn by its historic development that holiness ('that which breaks forth shiningly') is the fundamental essence and perfection of God's being in infinite fullness. He embodies all holiness absolutely. There is none outside and independent of Him. Everything is holy as related to Him. On the basis of, and to the extent of this constituted relationship, we are holy.

We now come to consider holiness in the sphere of relationship. The Hebrew and Greek terms, as defined above in relation to God, take on other shades of meaning in the sphere of divine relationships. As applied to persons and things, it signifies to be solely and completely devoted to a divine service. 'Every devoted thing in Israel shall be holy' (see Leviticus 27.28). This devotion is necessarily preceded by a separation from everything in the previous life. This separation covers all sins and sinning, and all inherited sin – the old man – since sin in all forms is of no service to God. The former separation is done in repentance and the latter in crucifixion. This crucifixion is wrought in the heart of the one who is alive to God; that is, the regenerated. Separation from all the former life, inward and outward, places us in the position to be forever devoted to God.

The original word signifies divine appropriation as a result of the act of devotion. This appropriation makes us holy. Then begins the 'breaking forth shiningly' of the sanctification of the divine Being wrought within us. We become luminaries in the world. The holiness of God shines in us to the degree of our relationship to Him.

Used by permission of The International Pentecostal Church of Holiness, Statement of Belief IPCH Articles 10 and 11.
http://www.iphc.org/docs/theology/amp3.html, IPCH, research@iphc.org

White brings balance with an understanding of the purpose of holiness.

6.5   J. White, *Holiness: A Guide for Sinners*,
Guildford, Surrey: Eagle Publishing, 1996, pp. 91–100, abridged

As you receive both imparted righteousness and holiness, they become all of a piece once again. You are equally grateful for both, just as for all God's kindness. Gratitude and worship flow almost uninterrupted from your heart.

. . . To follow the path of progressive holiness is not a matter of passing examinations by dint of great effort but of discovering the kindness of a God who wishes to share his holy nature freely with us. He wants us to be like Himself, so that he can have pleasure with us. He says, 'You are to be holy to me because I the lord am holy, and I have set you apart from the nations to be my own' (Lev. 20.26).

Mysterious wind

There are two broad ways in which the Spirit works. God awakens, converts, saves and sanctifies; that is one operation. He empowers; that is a different operation. This book is about the sanctifying process. But because some people, particularly those in the holiness tradition, believe that baptisms or anointings of the Spirit are the highway to sanctification I want to present an alternative point of view. Because the two operations of the Spirit are different, and because the Spirit's power is more necessary today than it has ever been, I devote this chapter to the differences and similarities between the two. . . .

. . . In the traditional holiness view, holiness ('entire sanctification') arose from a second work of grace. You had an instantaneous experience by which the Holy Spirit conveyed holiness. Proponents of this view claimed validating from John Wesley's teaching in his little book *A Plain Account of Christian Perfection*. The doctrine had its true beginning however with George Fox (1624–1661) who founded the extreme left wing of the Puritan movement in the mid-seventeenth century. It was called the Society of Friends and has become known as 'the Quakers'. From the fact that when the Holy Spirit fell on people they would shake. . . .

There seem to be sanctifying spin-offs from the Spirit's empowering work, and power 'spin-offs' from his sanctifying work. We cannot have any experience of the Holy Spirit's power without something of God's character imparting itself to us. In the wake of renewal you feel more like praying, reading the scripture more, sharing your testimony with others and you do all this more and more. Unhappily the feelings do not endure. . . .

Empowering and sanctification

Some Christians have no use for instantaneous visitations of the Holy Spirit, even suggesting that they are from the pit. This is very sad. Some of the sanctifying effects of a 'close encounter' with the Holy Spirit may not last; but we still need power. And we cannot expect much power without the Holy Spirit's repeated 'falling' on us.

Used by permission of Eagle Publishing, 6 Kestrel House, Mill Street, Trowbridge, Wiltshire BA14 8BA, UK.

God's standards are to be taken at heart level; this brings real revival in Urquhart's estimation.

6.6   Colin Urquhart, *Holy Fire*, London: Hodder & Stoughton, 1984, pp. 12–13

Fire purges, consumes and tests. Becoming a Christian is not the completion of God's purpose for the believer. He wants him to build and be fruitful so that his work survives the testing.

Jesus Himself will be 'revealed from heaven in blazing fire with his powerful angels' (2 Thess. 1.7). Those who love the Lord will not need to fear His coming for they know they shall be taken to rejoice with Him in His glory. However, 'if we deliberately keep on sinning after we have received the knowledge of the truth, no sacrifice for sins is left, but only a fearful expectation of judgment and of raging fire that will consume the enemies of God' (Heb. 10.26–7).

The Christian does not need to live in fear of judgment, only in awe of God, his holy and almighty Father who has shown such love, mercy and grace to him. 'Therefore, since we are receiving a kingdom that cannot be shaken, let us be thankful, and so worship God acceptably with reverence and awe, for our God is a consuming fire' (Heb. 12.28–9).

The believer will not resent the refining; he is only too conscious of the need for it. It may come through various difficulties or trials. These God allows, 'So that your faith – of greater worth than gold, which perishes even though refined by fire – may be proved genuine and may result in praise, glory and honour when Jesus Christ is revealed' (1 Pet. 1.7).

Peter advises: 'You ought to live holy and godly lives as you look forward to the day of God and speed its coming. That day will bring about the destruction of the heavens by fire, and the elements will melt in the heat. But in keeping with his promise we are looking forward to a new heaven and a new earth, the home of righteousness' (2 Pet. 3.11–13). We cannot imagine the immense power of this fire that will destroy the elements. No wonder Jude urges his readers: 'Snatch others from the fire and save them'' (v. 23).

In the Book of Revelation, the Lord is described as having eyes like blazing fire (1.14, 2.18). The Spirit counsels the church in Laodicea to 'buy from me gold refined in the fire, so you can become rich' (3.18). Better that refining than the lake of fire which is the second death (20.14). 'If anyone's name was not found written in the book of life, he was thrown into the lake of fire' (20.15).

Jesus came to give men that life and to save them from the eternal judgment they deserved because of their sin. How could the holy, righteous, just, perfect God be made one with sinners? How could they be saved from the lake of fire and be made like the Lord instead? How can the holy fire of God's love purge and cleanse their lives making them fit for heaven? It is obvious that we have the option of inviting the refining fire of God's love in our lives now, or of experiencing the fire of His judgment later. Better the refining!

Although this is a process needed in our lives, we do not necessarily welcome it. In the following pages we will be concentrating on the refining that God desires to bring into our lives through the holy fire of His Spirit. Do not resist what He wants to do in you; He has your welfare, as well as His glory, at heart.

I counsel you to buy from me gold refined in the fire so you can become rich.

Used by permission of Colin Urquhart, Kingdom Faith Ministries, Old Crawley Road, Horsham, West Sussex R12 4RY, UK.

7 Worship

A. E. Dyer, Introduction

Worship has always held a central place in Pentecostal and charismatic circles. While freedom of expression and extempore prayer have been preferred, there is often an underlying oral liturgy in Pentecostal services. Musically, the early tone was set by a medley of old time Methodist and Sankey hymns from the nineteenth-century Evangelical/Holiness traditions and these might be supplemented by songs or hymns written by Pentecostals themselves (e.g. Harold Horton or Alex Tee). By the middle of the century, or at least from the start of the charismatic movement in the 1960s, there was a burst of new song-writing. The songs were popularized in phases and reflected various musical styles. As the charismatic movement spread across the world, these songs might emanate from Australia and New Zealand as easily as from England or California. The simple *Scripture in Song* worship choruses (often accompanied by guitar rather than piano or organ) gave way to more complex rousing songs reflecting a triumphalist theology within the New Churches or independent Pentecostal churches and, later, to songs that were written to accompany Marches for Jesus or other forms of outreach. At about the same time, in the 1980s, Vineyard songs became popular and these followed the rhythms of Country and Western music and the intimacy of worship rather than the stridency of evangelism. Into this experientially rich environment, Pentecostals and charismatics could weave manifestations of gifts of the Spirit, especially around the Celebration of the Lord's Supper, or Holy Communion.

The first excerpt shows how the Anglican Alexander Boddy ensured that Sunderland Conventions (1908–14) managed to combine Pentecostal exuberance and liberty with decorum and order. Boddy provided rules for the worship, and everyone who attended had to agree to accept them (7.1). Donald Gee and John Carter later commended the style of worship found at the Conventions because Boddy's rules had no quenching effect on the gifts of the Spirit; rather they encouraged 'organized spontaneity'.[1]

---

[1] See D. N. Hudson, 'Worship: Singing a New Song in a Strange Land', in *Pentecostal Perspectives*, ed. K. Warrington, Paternoster Press, 1998, pp. 177–87.

Donald Gee describes his 1935 world tour in *Upon All Flesh*. The tour began in London and started with a typical meeting held at Sion College. The excerpt gives an insight into the style of British Pentecostalism at that time (7.2).

In the USA, especially in the early 1900s, musical worship might have included spontaneous dance as advocated by Maria Woodward Etter, the American evangelist around the turn of the twentieth century (7.3). However, as Pentecostal churches became larger and more established, choirs were formed and worship took on a liturgical or even 'performance' aspect. Some of these choirs were used evangelistically to accompany radio broadcasts, but they could hardly function without sophisticated instrumental backing and this prepared the way for the use of bands of musicians of 'rock' or orchestral nature.[2] There is often a fine line between devotional expression and entertainment value. Thomsen's abridged article 'A Broken Spirit: The Key to Acceptable Worship' is indicative of the concern even in 1934 that the early sincerity and simplicity of Pentecostal worship was in danger of being lost (7.4).

Before the advent of the overhead projector, Pentecostal worship made use of hymnbooks. Each religious movement has its own theological emphases and, though Pentecostals shared much with Methodist revivalism and Baptist evangelistic doctrine, they made new collections of hymns that picked up Pentecostal themes, even if these had originally been composed in Methodist or Baptist contexts. The preface to the joint British Assemblies of God and Elim publication of *Redemption Hymnal* (1952) sums up the intentions of their committee (7.5 and 7.6).

Black Pentecostalism has developed a variation in its worship music style that has been labelled Black Gospel. An excerpt from Joel Edwards' book *Let's Praise Him Again* illustrates their style. Their distinctives lie in the feel of Negro Spirituals but also have affinities with Jazz and Blues. Choirs are lively and skilled in harmonies and often used evangelistically. Experience, often experience of freedom from slavery, rather than reformed or Wesleyan theology, has always been at the root of their singing and this gives it a characteristic sound and appeal (7.7).

The charismatic movement stimulated experiments with musical and worship styles. By the 1980s it was common to find music groups with a recognized person to lead worship, and this was a role quite distinct from that of the church's minister. Chris Bowater developed a model for this at the Lincoln New Life Church (UK). His comments in his 1986 book were replete with warnings about the dangers of charismatic worship in

---

[2] 'Revival Time' choirs were formed for radio broadcasts in the UK and similarly in the USA.

practical and spiritual terms. His emphasis also lies in 'prophetic worship'. By this he means that while in God's presence there can be a freshness of communication from God, that worship deepens relationship (7.8).[3]

Worship, as Matt Redman has written, 'is all about You Jesus'[4] and for this reason charismatics who have composed and led great celebrations of worship advocate a *lifestyle of worship*. They are keen to stress that worship is not just a matter of singing the right songs. Neither is the purpose for introverted 'bless me' times. Graham Kendrick of Ichthus, London, introduced a wider concept into worship. Kendrick's style makes worship a public witness as a declaration of praise of Jesus, his love, his power. The excerpt (7.9) shows that Kendrick advocated a lifestyle of worship that affected all life's activities. This was demonstrated in his Marches for Jesus organized locally and finally globally from 1987 to 2000. Creative ways of expression were encouraged from Pentecostal clapping to charismatic dancing with flags and ribbons. From 1985 to 2000 Kendrick stimulated public worship and intercession through songs like *Shine Jesus Shine,* starting locally and reaching globally; hundreds and thousands of Christians declared God's goodness while marching through their city streets. Even Christians in nations like Malaysia, where public Christian witness is forbidden, managed to stage a declaration in a park area. From this declaration of the Church's existence by way of declaring the goodness of God in public many Christians have been renewed and many others brought into the kingdom of God!

Charismatic worship accepts that enjoyment is part and parcel of the whole community experience. Jack Hayford defends a mode of charismatic worship that might appear to be too anthropocentric, too concerned with the needs of worshippers (7.10). He denies this and asserts that knowledge of God comes this way, because worship is 'for' people. Yet it is also for evangelism since, where there is genuine worship, 'Kingdom power' is evident.

An interesting aspect of the development of global Pentecostal/charismatic styles of worship is that, although there is some cultural variety, there is an amazing uniformity in the American style of 'how to do church' from Singapore to Korea and probably to Africa's more westernized areas; it had great effect on lifestyles. Africa still incorporates much more dance and repetitive song than elsewhere. Latin America has its own version of celebratory worship, again using its own version of guitar music.

---

[3] This is further emphasized by Terry Laws in an influential book, *The Power of Praise and Worship,* Tulsa, OK: Victory House, 1985, both for personal and corporate benefit in the Church, and over its enemies.

[4] Matt Redman, 'When the Music Fades' 1997, Kingsway's Thankyou Music.

Globalization has helped Wimber's Vineyard's quieter adorational personal songs (7.11) and Australia's Hillsongs (7.12) big choir/band to flourish; they have set another trend for churches worldwide to adopt. Thousands of songs were composed in the 1980s–1990s; churches catch on to the latest ones and drop the rest as if they belonged to yesterday's secular pop-charts. It is difficult to detect an underlying trend here. Perhaps the most that can be said is that ripples of change that flow through Pentecostal and charismatic worship have been driven by a fresh appreciation of the Holy Spirit's work in the Church and the world.

In the early times of Pentecostal fervour, Alexander Boddy of Sunderland, England, an Anglican vicar, felt he had to maintain order and only invited those who could agree to his instructions as given in his magazine Confidence.

7.1   A. A. Boddy, 'Rules for Whitsuntide Conventions',
Confidence, April 1908, p. 2, abridged

As these meetings are for Conference and not for controversy, we admit by ticket, which will be freely given to those who can whole-heartedly sign the following (which is printed on the Admission Card):-

DECLARATION.
I declare that I am in full sympathy with those who are seeking 'Pentecost' with the Sign of the Tongues. I also undertake to accept the ruling of the Chairman.

Prayer and Praise should occupy at least one-third of even our meetings for Conference. It is suggested that everyone should make a point of being very punctual, and, if possible, to have a quiet time of prayer before the meeting and that there be as little talking as possible in the room before the meetings, but silent prayer only while waiting.

As to choruses, etc., it is suggested that, as far as possible, they should be left to the Leader to commence or control, and friends are asked so to pray (silently) that he may be led aright. Confusion is not always edifying, though sometimes the Holy Spirit works so mightily that there is a divine flood, which rises above barriers.

The Chairman's ruling should be promptly and willingly obeyed in cases of difficulty. There should at those moments, if they occur, be much earnest prayer (in silence) that God may guide aright and get glory through all.

Earnest and victorious prayer is asked for, that all may be done in accord with the will and purpose of God, and to His glory only.

Used by permission of the Donald Gee Centre, Mattersey Hall, Mattersey, UK.

Gee described the worship he saw as he set out around the world in the 1930s.

7.2   D. Gee, *Upon All Flesh: A Pentecostal World Tour*,
Springfield, Missouri: Gospel Publishing House, 1935, p.10

One distinctive feature of British Pentecostal meetings will be the singing of many, many choruses, most of them bright and catchy expressing the joy of salvation, but others very sweet and beautiful full of worship and all about the Lord Jesus. They love the old Methodist hymns also and the congregational singing of the British assemblies is always thrilling to a visitor.

Before very long there will probably be an utterance in 'tongues' that will be duly interpreted usually by the leader of the meeting; for the two gifts of the Holy Spirit, tongues and interpretation, are exercised very generally in the British Assemblies of God. Quite often you will hear the gift of prophecy also.

Exuberant joy can result in expressions of praise beyond words; Maria Woodward Etter defends dancing in praise.

7.3   Mrs M. B. Woodward Etter, 'Sermon on Dancing', 4 December 1915

Where dancing in the Bible is mentioned, it always signifies victory for the Lord's Hosts. It was always done to glorify God. The Lord placed the spirit of power and love of the dance in the Church, and wherever the Scripture speaks of dancing it implies that they danced by inspiration, and were moved by the Spirit, and the Lord was always pleased, and smiled His approval: but the devil stole it away and made capital of it. In these last days, when God is pouring out His Spirit in great cloud bursts and tidal waves from the floodgates of heaven, and the great river of life is flooding our spirit and body, and baptizing us with fire and resurrection life, and divine energy, the Lord is doing His acts, His strange acts, and dancing in the Spirit and speaking in other tongues, and many other operations and gifts. The Holy Ghost is confirming the last message of the coming King, with great signs, and wonders, and miracles. . . .

Moses also led the hosts in the same way, with music and dancing, and a new song given for the occasion by the Spirit. So the Holy Ghost is falling on the saints of God today, and they are used the same way. Those who never danced one step are experts in the holy dance, and those who do not know one note from another, are expert musicians in playing many different instruments of music, and often the sounds of the invisible instruments are heard from the platform, the sounds can be plainly heard all over the house. And I say in the fear and presence of God, the singing and demonstration puts the fear of God on the people, and causes a holy hush to come over the people. The strange acts are coming more and more, showing they are something new, and that Jesus is coming soon, and the Lord is getting His bride ready to be translated, and dance and play at the great marriage of the Lamb, which will soon take place, for the bride is making herself ready.

Luke 15.25; his elder son was in the field. When he came near the house he heard music and dancing; he asked what does all this mean? They said, 'Thy brother has come home, and thy Father has killed the fatted calf, because he has received him safe and sound', and he was angry and would not go in, but the feast and rejoicing went on just the same. The Father said, 'It is meet that we should be merry and rejoice, for thy brother who was dead and who was lost, we have received him safe and sound.' All will agree with me this was an old fashioned Holy Ghost revival. The lost son is a sinner whom the Spirit brought out of darkness to light; the saints are filled with the Spirit.

I was very slow to accept the dancing in the Spirit, for fear it was in the flesh, but I soon saw it was the 'cloud of Glory' over the people that brought forth the dancing, and playing invisible instruments. The sounds of sweet, heavenly, music could often be heard. Several times I asked that those of the congregation, who heard this music from the platform (where they knew there were no instruments to be seen), be honest and raise their hands. Many hands went up from saints and sinners. The stillness of death went over the people when they heard the sounds of music, accompanied with the heavenly choir. Often a message in tongues was given in one or more languages, and the interpretation. As I saw the effect on the people by the Holy Ghost, in convincing them that they were in the presence of God, I concluded that this is surely the Lord's strange work, and his strange acts. I saw as many as nine of the most noted ministers dancing at one time on the platform; they danced single, with their eyes closed; often some fell, slain by the mighty power of God. These things convinced me. I also saw men and women who have been crippled join in the dance, with wonderful grace. One lady, who was on crutches five years who got healed in her seat, afterwards danced over the platform, singing heavenly music. The virgins, the young men, and the old men, all joined in the dance together. Praise the Lord. 'Let us be glad and rejoice,' for the marriage of the Lamb is come, and His wife hath made herself ready (Rev. 19.7). The Lord is quickening our mortal bodies for the translation.

Used by permission of The Flower Pentecostal Heritage Center, Springfield, Missouri, USA.

Meditative worship balances and leads to exuberant praise once hearts are right before God.

7.4   Niels P. Thomsen, 'A Broken Spirit: The Key to Acceptable Worship', *The Latter Rain Evangel*, January 1934, abridged

I wish to direct your thoughts to Psalm 51.16 and 17: 'For Thou desirest not sacrifice; else would I give it: thou delightest not in burnt offering. The sacrifices of God are a broken spirit; a broken and a contrite heart, O God, thou wilt not despise.'

In this material day and age, when materialism is gripping the hearts not only of the people of the world but frequently gripping the hearts of those in the church of Christ, in days when we seem to be seeing everything from the material point of view, it is good to be reminded of what God really desires of us. . . .

. . . Sin could be cleansed only when God could see a broken spirit behind it all. Our prayers, our praises, our preaching or whatever we attempt for the Lord will never please Him unless he sees a broken spirit accompanying it. . . .

. . . God is looking for contrite hearts. What constitutes a contrite heart? One that has all resistance taken out and is absolutely yielded. If you are presenting that kind of a heart with your worship today, then your offering is acceptable to Him and His heart is pleased. Let us never forget that nothing else will please Him. We may give glorious testimonies, we may even be winning souls and working along many lines of Christian service and still not be satisfying the heart of God, for He is pleased only with the offering given by a broken spirit and a contrite heart. And when He sees that, then little becomes much; then our worship is acceptable to Him. And I rather think that when the heart is right, even though the person be ignorant of correct forms of worship, the Lord will overlook the ignorance. He is pleased because He sees a heart that is yielded to Him. That is the worship He seeks.

Used by permission of The Flower Pentecostal Heritage Center, Springfield, Missouri, USA.

In post-war Britain, Pentecostals felt the need for devising their own hymnbook, to include some of their own distinctives in worship.

7.5   *Redemption Hymnal*, London: Elim Publishing House, 1951, reprinted 1952, 1954, 1960, 1964

Preface (*abridged from the Music Edition*)

This collection of hymns has been compiled to meet the need of companies of believers all over the British Isles who are rejoicing in a scriptural experience of the grace and power of the Holy Spirit similar, they humbly affirm, to that received by the early Christians on the Day of Pentecost, and enjoyed throughout the primitive churches. The inconvenience of not possessing an adequate compilation of hymns in one book suited to their distinct testimony eventually led to a decision to prepare and publish such a collection. The widely representative Committee that was appointed now present the result of their labours of several years.

These hymns emphasize the Deity of the Lord Jesus Christ, and glory of His cross as central in the redemption, by His blood, of sinful men. They provide for the worship of the Father in Spirit and in truth, and express the aspirations of those who long to be holy as He is holy. Their basis of doctrine is belief that the Bible is the Word of God that liveth and abideth forever, by which they are born again and through which they grow in grace and in the knowledge of our Lord and Saviour. All these truths have new and deeper power and beauty through the baptism in the Holy Spirit received as a definite experience with scriptural evidence. Because existing hymn books contain an inadequate selection of hymns that embody this vital testimony, one special aim in compiling this collection has been to supply that which is lacking.

A hymnal is now proffered that combines rich devotional hymns in abundance with stirring revival hymns that present the Gospel in all its depth, winsomeness and simplicity. It is equally suitable for the regular life and work of the local churches, for great conventions and for evangelistic campaigns.

The hymns of the Methodist Revival, many of the best of which will be found in this collection, served to impress its great doctrinal and experimental truths upon the multitudes who sang them. In publishing this grand collection in the middle of the Twentieth Century the Committee believe that these hymns also will indelibly impress the burning truths of the Pentecostal Revival upon the many thousands who will sing them with the spirit and with the understanding also.

Examples of hymns used mid-twentieth century.

7.6   *Redemption Hymnal*, London: Assemblies of God Publishing House, 1951

243

1. In Thy name, O blessed Saviour,
   Gathered in this sacred place;
   Here we seek a Father's blessing,
   Plead and pray for needed grace;
   From the ocean of Thy fulness,
   Boundless, fathomless and free;
   Let a tidal wave come sweeping.
   Setting hearts at liberty.

   Lift the floodgates, lift the floodgates,
   Let the tide come sweeping in
   Blessed tide of full salvation,
   Washing, cleansing, from all sin.

2. Lift the floodgates, let salvation
   In tremendous currents flow,
   To the uttermost fulfilling
   Thy blest mission here below;

   Until myriads of sinners,
   Borne on love's resistless tide,
   Shall be swept into the kingdom
   And believers sanctified.

3. It is coming, we believe it,
   Thou dost hear and answer prayer;
   It is coming, we shall see it,
   Thine almighty arm made bare;
   Tides of power, tides of glory,
   Holy tides of perfect love,
   Satisfying, overflowing.
   Coming on us from above.

   Mrs C. H. Morris

249 (verse 1 of 4)

They were gathered in an upper
   chamber
As commanded by the risen Lord,
And the promise of the Father
There they sought with one accord
When the Holy Ghost from heav'n
   descended
Like a rushing wind and tongues
   of fire
So, dear Lord, we seek Your blessing
Come with glory now our hearts
   inspire.

Let the fire fall, Let the fire fall
Let the fire from heaven fall;
We are waiting and expecting
Now in faith dear Lord we call:
Let the fire fall, Let the fire fall
On Thy promise we depend;
From the glory of Thy presence
Let the Pentecostal fire descend.

H. Tee

Variations in worship style around the world are most evident in the 'black' churches and Edwards as a member of such describes these. He was General Secretary of the African and Caribbean Evangelical Alliance from 1988 until he became the General Director of the British Evangelical Alliance in 1997.

7.7   Joel Edwards, *Let's Praise Him Again*,
Eastbourne: Kingsway Publications, 1992, pp. 70–4

Music and worship

As in most worship settings, music plays a central role. In many black churches it dominates worship, creating the sense of movement and spontaneity. Songs punctuate the various segments of worship and creatively camouflage any restless moments in the order of events.

In the traditional black church, hymns still underpin biblical teaching and make doctrine accessible to the worshipper. Preachers quote songs or choruses as readily as Bible texts. Songs set the scene for the sermon and act as a concluding feature of the preacher's address. In some cases, a relevant hymn or chorus enhances a focal point during a sermon. This was powerfully illustrated by the preacher, Lennox Powell, when during a sermon on the Crucifixion he spontaneously led the congregation in a well-known song based on Isaiah's prophetic statement:

> *He was wounded for our transgression*
> *He was bruised for our iniquity*
> *Surely, he hath borne our sorrow*
> *And by his stripes we are healed.*

In the black church the song is the worship property of all members, who may use it to express their deepest joys or sorrows. Those least comfortable with words will often 'borrow the words of the song' to express their experience. Indeed, Iain MacRobert contends that in the black church the song is one of the most unifying and peculiar features of the church's life. This he regards as one of the distinguishing marks of black worship, one which has survived its cross-Atlantic passage from Africa via America and the Caribbean. This dependence on song is one of the unique characteristics of black Christianity, and gives it a universal coherence. (MacRobert is comfortable about using the term 'Black Church' as this, he feels, properly identifies the churches that share this common liturgical feature.) The significance of Negro spirituals and songs in the black American experience has also been usefully documented by many writers including James Cone in his *God of the Oppressed* and *Spirituals and the Blues*.

Even the more articulate rely on songs as an acceptable mode of communicating their true feelings. The song provides a legitimate alternative for the spoken testimony. As a result, it is not unusual to hear someone say, 'For my testimony, I would like to sing . . .' This is not an abdication of personal testimony or necessarily an unwillingness to speak. It is simply a recognition that the song has already fully represented one's own thoughts in an art form conducive to worship. It is both real and biblical.

In recent years much has been written about the slavery heritage and the use of song. Undoubtedly, black Pentecostalism has inherited much of the culture conveyed through the Negro spirituals. This influence has certainly stamped a quality of 'other-worldliness' on the liturgy of the black church. 'Separatedness' is also deeply imbedded in the songs, influenced by a curious combination of the revivalism of the Southern States Holiness movement of the nineteenth century and the survivalism of the American Negro in slavery. It is important to recognize that this emphasis is not wholly negative. The longing for a better world that still pours from popular songs was the source of a valuable hymnology of anticipation. The slaves' hope was as real as their suffering, and in a sense the song became a means of salvation.

The message of hope has been aided by the repetitive style of the music, which lends itself to a powerful form of oral indoctrination. Historically black churches have been associated with the poor. Consequently, it has been a main education centre for thousands of black people, their education coming from the Bible and the spoken word. Because repetition is both biblical and practical, it reinforces truth and seals abstract concepts in the mind. Black Pentecostal worship has drawn deeply from this historic well to water the tired spirits of its adherents, whose natural method of learning was the spoken, repetitive word.

Currently a powerful transition is taking place in Pentecostal worship. This change is coming about largely through the music of the younger Christians. The traditional hymns of Sankey and Moody and the *Redemption Hymnal* are quietly giving way to the American choir sound. Even the more recent Country Western style of the Chuck Wagon Gang and popular denominational hymnals loved by many senior adults is gently being set aside for the more contemporary sounds of black American songs or the worship chorus culture of British Christian songwriters like Graham Kendrick.

The wealth of creative talent which has learned and faithfully reproduced black American gospel music is having the greatest single impact on the worship of black churches today. Relatively few churches are without a gospel or youth choir; a Sunday morning comparison between the youth choir and the senior adult choir tells its own story. Moreover, there are very few churches in which young adults are being fed from the youth choir into the senior adult choir. The average age of a senior choir is likely to be over forty-five, with little hope of survival beyond the next ten years. This means that black Pentecostalism in Britain will lose a part of its identity that was very prominent in the 1960s and 1970s. The quartet and hymnal culture is seriously under threat of extinction in some sectors of the church.

Evidently, some adults would argue that this older style is the authentic 'sound of Zion' and therefore the true representation of black Pentecostal worship. However, as mentioned earlier, many of these hymns were borrowed from a combination of old negro spirituals, Southern States writers of early Pentecostalism, and from the strong influences of mainstream churches. In each case these selections were further transformed by the oral traditions and culture of Caribbean Christians, which gave them a rhythm and movement never intended by the original songwriters! The biblical truths of these great hymns were owned but their mood was subject to cultural surgery when the songs reached the Caribbean.

The truly authentic Caribbean song is to be found much more in the numerous choruses known throughout the black church that have no identifiable author. They convey a distinct cultural and worship environment, which is unmistakably Caribbean – they are even sometimes exclusive to particular pockets of the Caribbean:

> *Better get right with God, Come and do it now,*
> *Under the Cross of Jesus – Lay your burdens down.*
> *Better get right with God. Come and do it now.*
> *Get right, get right – Better get right with God.*

Such a song incorporates a bold simplicity and urgency conveyed by the repetitive and uncompromising directness; it is the confrontation of the Cross. The song lives because it harmonises simple words with a compulsive melody. Only a spiritually indifferent person hears this chorus, understands it, and still rejects the Cross.

Used by permission of Kingsway Publications, 33 Lottbridge Road, Sussex BN23 6NT, UK.

Chris Bowater has taught many how to worship 'in the Spirit' all around the world; here he introduces the subject with some warnings.

7.8   Chris Bowater, *Creative Worship: A Guide to Spirit-Filled Worship*, Basingstoke: Marshall Morgan & Scott, 1986, pp. ix–xi , 18–23, abridged

Introduction

'Not by might, nor by power but by my Spirit, says the Lord Almighty' (Zech. 4.6).

Methodology scares me sick. As soon as labels are put on people and activities we suddenly become experts at knowing the right names: words like 'restoration', 'apostle', 'body ministry' readily spring to mind. They flow off the tongue so effortlessly. The problem with labels is that they don't always represent the truth.

God is not so concerned with methods of worship. He is looking for worshippers. God is looking for people who have hearts that reach out to Him, lives that are open to His leading, ears that are sensitive to His voice. He is looking for children who will take time to develop a relationship with their father.

God is looking for 'doers' not 'knowers'. It's as if in John 14.15 Jesus was saying, 'If you love me, then do what I say.' An outworking of love is more important than an understanding of it.

Prejudiced opinion will always destroy. It will destroy relationships and will act like a tourniquet on the life-flow of the Spirit of God. God is bigger than our puny imagination. He is not restricted by our way of doing things.

I offer this book as an encouragement. It is not a textbook, but hopefully a stimulus to worshipping creatively the God of all creation. It is written on the basis of two major observations: the dangers in charismatic worship and the essentials for 'flowing' in worship.

Four dangers in charismatic worship

1. Worship that is merely response to an atmosphere: 'Worship that depends on the externals for existence is not real worship at all; true worship is what you have left when the externals are taken away' (Graham Kendrick, *Worship*).
2. 'Play church' mentality: an attitude of programme filling, where there is plenty of 'form' but little 'power'.
3. Worshipping worship: into the latest songs but not taken up with God.

4. Unreality: a failure to take off the masks and be real. Worship involves the burning up of pretence.

Three essentials for 'flowing together' in worship

1. The body: Church is about people, people who are 'dwelling together in unity' (Ps. 133), who are prepared to move with God-given visions. God cannot work through rebellious unco-operative people.
2. The eyes: leadership with vision, a sense of direction, tuned in to the heart and plan of God.
3. The legs: those who help carry the vision, priests who carry the Ark, musicians and singers with a clear calling after God in their lives and hearts.

Spirit and truth

Because God is, there is worship. God is Spirit and desires spiritual worship from a spiritual people. In a sense, Jesus removed much of the need for discussion and debate about worship when He declared in John 4.24 that, 'they that worship the Father must worship Him in spirit and in truth'. The options are removed. Sure, you can choose what you worship: money, ambition, power and position or whatever, but when Father God is the object of devotion, adoration and reverence, we no longer choose how we worship Him. We must worship Him in the way He desires. Furthermore, He is looking for those who will do just that (John 4.23).

What, then, is it to worship in Spirit and in truth?

It appears that it is not related to a place or a tradition. The woman of Samaria, on recognising Jesus as out of the ordinary, 'a prophet' (John 4.19), albeit that hers was a partial revelation, immediately began to enter a Samaritan versus Jewish debate on worship: 'Our fathers . . . this mountain . . . you say . . . Jerusalem' (John 4.20).

Have you noticed how people become defensive of their traditional positions when the person of Christ is under discussion? In reply to 'What do you think of Jesus?', along with hurried barrier constructions comes, 'Well, of course, we've always been Baptists . . .' or, 'You know, we like the way the Church of England do it.' Spirit and truth worship has nothing to do with the building, liturgy or lack of it. How often, though, do we become astonishingly building-orientated. I've even heard someone say at a housegroup fellowship, 'It's not like being at church!' We are the Church – and God is building it. It's not made up of pews and chairs, pianos and organs, stained glass windows and pulpits, even hymn books and overhead projectors, beautiful or necessary though these can be. You and I are joined together, not merely in fellowship, but in a miraculous 'limb-ship', into the body of Christ, of which He is the head. God is seeking a flow of worship that comes from His body, each member in glorious, loving harmony with each other.

One hears these days, and maybe it has ever been so, certain people lamenting, 'It's not like it used to be.' What isn't? God? Has He changed? Maybe they have! Perhaps they are not so diligent, so fervent, so determined to worship the Lord as they once were. Perhaps their relationship with God is not what it used to be!

'They that worship the Father . . .' (John 4.23). You see, the true worshippers are those who are living in the reality of their relationship with God. It is a now relationship. I am secure in His Fatherhood but I must never become complacent in it.

> Abba Father, Abba Father, my soul delights in You,
> Abba Father, Abba Father, my soul delights in You,
> Hallelujah my heart has cause to sing,
> I'm a spirit-born, blood-bought, child of The King,
> Abba Father, Abba Father, my soul delights in You.

Worship must emanate from a current, ongoing, intimate relationship with God. When was the last time your spirit shone as you whispered, 'Father I love You, I worship and adore You'?

. . . True worship is a throne ministry. Songs like 'Majesty', 'Jesus, we enthrone You', 'He is the King of Kings' freely pour from our lips but our minds are on so much more than the One who is enthroned in the midst of the praises of His people. We get taken up with all that is peripheral. Even the songs themselves, intended to be vehicles for our own worship, become intrusions. There is a very real danger of worshipping worship – the new songs, the atmosphere. We must see the Lord, upon the throne, and concentrate on Him alone.

Used by permission of the author, C. Bowater, dB Studios Ltd., The Old Brickyard, Brant Road, Lincoln LN5 9AD, UK. Reprinted as Believers Guide to Worship, *available in French, Korean, Polish, Portuguese, Romanian.*

Kendrick teaches that worship is not just for services on Sundays.

7.9   G. Kendrick, *Worship*, Eastbourne: Kingsway Publications, 1984, pp. 31–9, abridged

Dethroning the gods

Worship is not just a matter of what happens between set hours on a Sunday. If we fail to realize this, we are fooling ourselves. It is not even a question of whether it is ancient, modern, staid or enthusiastic, creative or boring. What we so often fail to recognize is that worship is at the heart of a radically different way of living. To adopt new freedoms of expression – new music, dance, drama and so on in our worship – is by no means to guarantee the reality of it or its acceptability to God, and in many places we are in serious danger of mistaking these outward developments for true worship in the sight of God. To worship implies far more than participation in a series of devotional acts at regular intervals.

Even when we talk comfortably in terms of presenting our very selves as living sacrifices, feeling that we have understood this as being true worship, I wonder whether even then we have seen its full implications. This is because of a popular tendency to 'spiritualise' our faith at the cost 'earthing it', of abstracting it rather than seeing it right through to its practical application. Of course the worship that the Father desires is worship 'in spirit', but we must mind ourselves that the Bible sees us as whole people, and consequently a 'spiritual' act can never be separated from simultaneous actions in the body. Thus 'spiritual' activities that bear no relationship to the way in which we live our everyday lives are shown to be at best little more than sentiment, and at worst, blatant hypocrisy. . . .

Spiritual self-gratification

It is also far too easy, within the current upsurge of creative input in the realm of worship, to find ourselves chasing spiritual or aesthetic experiences, as if the highest achievement of our whole pilgrimage on earth was to enter some kind of praise-induced ecstasy! I am in fact all in favour of spiritual experiences when they are genuine, and welcome ecstasies that are gifts of God and not artificially induced, but if such things become the aim of our gatherings for worship, then we have turned the gospel upside down. The gospel is for the salvation of the world, and we are sometimes in danger of locking ourselves inside the rescue-shop and plundering the stock of blessings for the sole purpose of spiritual self-gratification, while millions stream empty-handed past the closed doors into eternal darkness, hearing the joyful sounds and seeing the advertisements, but never being given a chance to test the goods.

Worshipping in a fallen world

There is a desperate need to place renewed forms of worship in the wider context of what worship is and to work through the social, economic and political implications that worshipping God inevitably creates. Worship, or rather misdirected worship, is in fact the issue at the very heart of the world's problems. It should be obvious that worship is not the exclusive property of the Christian, or of the adherents to other religious faiths. The practice of worship is an inescapable part of being human; even an atheist is a worshipper of something, because there is built into all of us the vacuum left by our loss of communion with God that took place at the Fall. We were created to worship, and having rejected the rightful worthy object of worship, mankind has continued through his sad history substituting every variety of false god, and serving successions of them in fear and misery. . . .

Worship is a political act

How often do we blandly sing, 'Jesus is Lord!' in apparent blindness to the implications of that enormous statement? To genuinely worship Jesus as Lord of all is immediately to challenge all false gods, and to pose a threat to their dark and dingy domains. Bearing in mind that the gods of this world are intricately bound into the godless political and social systems that surround us, it is absolutely true to say that worship is a political act. If Jesus is Lord, then every other 'lord' is excluded from that title and subservient to him.

For many of the early Christians, to voice the glorious affirmation 'Jesus is Lord' was to pronounce their own sentence of death. Such a statement, linked to a life that practised Christ's lordship, was seen as an act of political treason and punished as such!

We have similar situations today under strict atheistic regimes where a denial of the 'lordship' of the State is treated as a treasonable offence because it undermines the very ideological foundations upon which the security of such states are built. It is true that, in Western 'free' society, the cry – 'Jesus is Lord!' is all too often ignored by the authorities. But that should not in any way be taken as a sign that democratic states acknowledge or tolerate his lordship. Closer to the truth would be the explanation that our presence in society reflects so little of the radical challenge of the statement that we are tolerated as a peculiar but fairly harmless sect. . . .

A vision of Christ. . .

From all our activities, battles and campaigns, we need constantly to return to worship the greatest champion of the poor and oppressed, of truth and justice, Christ Himself. In Him we discover the true motive for changing society, which is not our own idealism, despair, frustration or self-image as would-be 'liberators', but the God who says, 'Be holy because I the Lord your God am holy' (Lev. 19.2). It is in worship that we concentrate upon the One who laid down his life for the world, and trusted neither in the power of political activism nor in mystical escapism under the title 'spirituality'.

We Christians are in the business of building the kingdom of God on earth, in expectation of its culmination in an eternal kingdom; but if this kingdom does not have its roots in heaven right now, it will turn out to be little different from the world's kingdom which will not survive the 'shaking of all things'. Only that which cannot be shaken will remain, and surely anything that does not have its roots in heaven, and in the worship of heaven, will not continue into eternity.

Because we love the King

Many of us are worshipping the King in apparent ignorance or disregard of the justice and righteousness of his kingdom, while others are trying to build the kingdom while neglecting to worship the King. The King and his kingdom are inseparable, the kingdom being no less than a practical extension of his character, and we must not forget that it is built for his glory anyway! We should build the kingdom because we love and worship the King, or we may discover too late that we have been building not his kingdom, but ours.

The implications of worshipping God in a world of false gods are numerous and costly. Worship is a new way of living, and we inevitably feel the violence of its pull as we turn against the tide. Yet in the very act of worship – from the setting of the will to obey in a small matter of truth or honesty, to the exercise of the spirit and voice in corporate praise – there are tremendous resources of strength, healing and inspiration to be found.

It is 'Christ in us' who is the 'hope of glory', our hope and the world's hope, and it is in lifting him up that those without hope are drawn to him. There is no doubt that our forms of worship can be used to misdirect us into a false spirituality that cuts us off from the outside world, and many may have become disillusioned or critical of it for that very reason.

Worship, however – that is, an encounter with the living, caring, suffering Christ – will always send us out into the world to be more like him. Our motive for changing the world must be Jesus himself; his example, his teaching, his sacrificial giving of himself, and his presence inside us by the Holy Spirit. It is only his love in us that can possibly bear the crushing load of problems and pain that face us as we try to reach out. It is our love affair with him that gives us inspiration to love others, and his lordship in our lives that is the only power that has ever overcome the world and its gods.

Used by permission of Kingsway Publications, Lottbridge Road, Eastbourne, Sussex BN23 6NT, UK.

Usually worship is toward God but Hayford argues for the benefit it gives to people.

7.10   Jack W. Hayford, *Worship His Majesty*,
Ventura, CA: Word Publishing, 1987, pp. 57–8

Sequence is the issue. God's gift is first.

1. God has given worship to everyone as a privileged resource, not as a private regimen to be performed for His scrutiny.
2. The gathering of people in His Name is still intended to be an occasion when hungry and searching souls find an atmosphere of warmth and acceptance.

I've decided to risk the protest of the spiritual purist: 'Humanistic! Idolatrous! Anthropocentric! Vanity of vanities!' However, before flashing red lights explode in the halls of ecclesiastical orthodoxy, let no one mistake me.

In saying that worship is *for* man, I haven't said worship is *to* him; and, in saying worship is a gift to man, I didn't say it is not to be expressed unto God.

He – the Transcendent and Eternal One – is still the Person in our worship. But in approaching the task of leading worship as I have declared it here, each time I step before my flock, I sense God's pleasure. I am leading them to Him, but I am doing it by means of a gift He has given for their blessing. Worship is for them, and I learned that they experience growth in every way as they receive this gift of worship as something that is theirs.

I think you'll find the same, for thousands who joined with me in this discovery have come to attest to the vitality of these facts:

1. God has provided worship as a means of entry to our rejoicing in the presence of the Ultimate Reality.

2. Worship introduces dimensions of possibility in every life that transcend our sin and our self-imposed limitations as we welcome the Transcendent One.

3. Worshiping God brings the highest sense of dignity humanity can know, for the regal nature of His Majesty begins to flow downward and inward.

The greatest issue we face is not so much that we immediately perceive the depth of our sin and weakness or even the greatness of God's grace and power. The primary issue is whether we will come – will we be led before His Throne and seek Him. Because if we do, heaven will break loose *on earth.*

In our church, the passage of nearly two decades has seen tremendous growth in people, an increase in attendance to nearly 10,000 each week, a garnering of nearly 30,000 for Christ during that time span – all flowing from this mindset concerning worship's priority and its purpose.

And during those years, time and again in my study of the Scriptures, the Holy Spirit has unveiled notable personalities of the Bible as case studies in the power and purpose of worship.

The song for which Jack Hayford is most well known is the following:

> Majesty, Worship His majesty
> Unto Jesus be glory honour and praise
> Majesty, Kingdom authority
> Flow from His throne unto His own
> His anthem raise
> So exalt, lift up on high the Name of Jesus
> Magnify come glorify Christ Jesus the King
> Majesty, Worship His majesty,
> Jesus who died, now glorified, King of all Kings.

Used by permission of Gospel Light/Regal Books, Ventura, CA, USA.

Apart from forming a church network across the world, Wimber continued using his own musical skills to provide worship songs that bear their own devotional distinctives.

7.11   John Wimber, *Vineyard Songs*, Mercy Publishing/ Maranatha Music (USA); Word Music (UK), 1979

O let the Son of God enfold you with his Spirit and his love
Let Him fill your heart and satisfy your soul
O let Him have the things that hold you
And His Spirit like a dove will descend upon your life and make you
    whole.

Jesus, Oh Jesus, come and fill your lambs. (repeated)

O come and sing this song with gladness
As your hearts are filled with joy
Lift your hands in sweet surrender to His name.
O give Him all your tears and sadness,
Give Him all your years of pain,
And you'll enter into life in Jesus' name.

Used by permission, 'Spirit Song' by John Wimber, © 1979 Mercy Vineyard Publishing, Administered by CopyCare, PO Box 77, Hailsham, East Sussex BN27 3EF, UK.

Hillsong worship from Brian Houston's Church, Sydney, Australia, also had a global influence on Christian worship.

7.12   Darlene Zschech, Hillsong, Australia, 1993

My Jesus My Saviour
Lord there is none like You
All of my days I want to praise the wonders of Your mighty love
My comfort my shelter
Tower of refuge and strength
Let every breath all that I am
Never cease to worship You.

Shout to the Lord all the earth let us sing;
Power and majesty
Praise to the King
Mountains bow down and the seas will roar at the sound of Your Name
I sing for joy at the work of Your hands
Forever I'll love You forever I'll stand
Nothing compares to the promise I have in You.

Used by permission of Kingsway Music, Lottbridge Rd, Eastbourne, Sussex BN23 6NT, UK.

8 Dynamics of Church Life

W. K. Kay, Introduction

This section is concerned with the inner inter-personal life of Pentecostal and charismatic churches. It gives an insight into how leaders and congregational members might relate to each other and it gives examples of the way ecclesiastical hierarchy can be redefined.

These excerpts fall into two groups. The first area covered is Church Leadership and the role of apostolic, prophetic and other ministries. The first excerpt shows how the Apostolic Church combined teaching on modern apostles with a strong written constitution (8.1). The idea of restoring the 'five-fold ministry gifts of Christ' (apostles, prophets, evangelists, pastors and teachers) (Eph. 4.11) was part of the 'latter rain' eschatological understanding of the Pentecostal 'outpouring' in the early 1900s. Nevertheless most Pentecostal groups did not officially recognize apostles or prophets within their ecclesiastical polity: they usually only spoke of pastors and evangelists. Yet the idea of five-fold ministry persisted through the Latter Rain movement in the 1940s and again in the Restoration Movement under men like Bryn Jones in Britain; it gained more credibility in a wider sphere in the 1990s. The issue is live and current within the Pentecostal and charismatic movements, particularly because the emergence of apostles and prophets would be able to challenge ecclesiastical hierarchies based upon established structures. Yet there are also issues within those networks that accept the contemporary apostles, prophets, evangelists and teachers, namely that succession of leadership is much more difficult to predict. The second excerpt, by Arthur Wallis, leaves the matter in abeyance and is content simply to argue for the continuing need for the existence for these ministries (8.2). This raises issues such as: What happens when a particular apostle becomes elderly and unable to carry out his (and usually it is a man) duties? How is the new apostle recognized?

Larry Christenson deals with the beneficial influence of the charismatic movement upon the Lutheran Church. Christenson shows how Church life within an Episcopal congregation assumes an altogether more relational and friendly face as a result of acceptance of the charismatic movement (8.3). The church moves from, at its worst, being authoritarian and rigid to being concerned that each member contributes in ways most suited to his or her gifting. By this conception, leadership becomes a particular calling, and the church becomes a family where each member has appropriate tasks.

The second group is concerned with the New Churches, churches that were set up after the 1970s from scratch. The excerpt by Derek Prince speaks to the New Churches and, perhaps, to Pentecostal churches (8.4). Here the biblical text is expounded to indicate the original Greek meanings of New Testament words to allow the dynamics and interrelations between members and leaders to be recreated. Effectively the office of bishop that, by definition, is central to Episcopal forms of government is shown to be relevant only to local congregations. Elders, overseers, bishops or pastors are shown to be almost completely synonymous, with a result that local church autonomy becomes normative. A further result of this with independent churches was a 'covenant' relationship idea that networked leaders as described by David Tomlinson of the UK Restoration Movement in a way more typical of the kind of practical teaching preferred by the New Churches (8.5).

Both Prince and Tomlinson in their own ways raise crucial issues about the nature of the Church. Although they do not criticize ecclesiastical bureaucracy or institutional machinery, they indicate what New Testament norms were and they presume that Christians should return to the simplicity of early Church government.

To end the topic of Church dynamics, two excerpts are included; the first by Mike Bickle of Kansas City shows how Ministry giftings – pastoral and prophetic – can clash and be resolved (8.6).

In the last, Larry Christenson shows how the very concept of 'Church' is changed in a Charismatic atmosphere when members are servants of one another and the world, and as they understand the role of being the suffering servant (8.7).

ळ)༙

8.1 *The Constitution of the Apostolic Church UK,*
3rd edn revised, originally published in 1937, abridged

THE TENETS OF THE CHURCH
I. STATEMENT

The following are [some of] the fundamental Tenets of The Apostolic Church, based on the Holy Scriptures and stated in summarised form.

Such Tenets, accepted and confessed, shall be an essential basis of the fellowship and union of the members thereof.

. . .

5. The Baptism of the Holy Ghost for believers, with signs following.

6. The Nine Gifts of the Holy Ghost for the edification, exhortation and comfort of the Church, which is the Body of Christ.

7. The Sacraments of Baptism by immersion, and of the Lord's Supper.

8. The Divine Inspiration and Authority of the Holy Scriptures.

9. Church Government by Apostles, Prophets, Evangelists, Pastors, Teachers, Elders and Deacons.

II. NO ALTERATIONS

The Tenets as set out herein shall for ever be the doctrinal standard of The Apostolic Church, and shall not be subject to any change in any way whatsoever.

DEFINITION OF TERMS

. . .

APOSTLE means one of the Gifts of Christ in the Ascension Ministries and is the first Office in Church government.

APOSTLESHIP means the whole Council of Apostles in whom there are vested: –

a) The responsibility for the clarification of doctrinal matters.

b) The sole power to call, ordain and locate ministers.

c) The authority to control administrative affairs at General Council (including the affairs of non-autonomous countries whose business is under the control of the Overseas Department in the United Kingdom), Regional, Area, District and Local levels.

d) The right to apply discipline as detailed in the relevant sections of this Constitution.

e) The right to attend and chair any business meeting or church service within the sphere of their jurisdiction.

The term Apostleship also means an Apostle or a number of Apostles serving in a Region, Area or District.

AREA means a number of Districts, grouped together in one part of the country. Government will be by Ascension Ministers.

AREA ADMINISTRATION means a group of Ascension Ministers appointed to govern a particular Area as defined in Chapter 6 of this Constitution.

ASCENSION MINISTERS means the gifts of men to the Church by

the ascended Lord viz. Apostles, Prophets, Evangelists, Pastors and Teachers.

EVANGELIST means one of the Gifts of Christ in the Ascension Ministries.

. . .

. . .

GENERAL EXECUTIVE means a representative group of Apostles appointed by the General Council, and whose duties and powers are defined in this Constitution.

. . .

LEADING ELDER means an Elder appointed by an Area Administration to give leadership to the other Elders in a local church. This appointment to be reviewed annually.

LITERATURE AND PUBLISHING DEPARTMENT means the department responsible for all Church magazines and literature.

LOCAL CHURCH means a number of the members of The Apostolic Church gathered together for Public Worship. A church will consist of a minimum of ten members inclusive of two Elders.

LOCAL PRESBYTERY means the Pastor together with a group of Elders who have been appointed for the administering of the affairs of a local church.

MINISTERS OF THE CHURCH means those who have been duly ordained to the salaried and non-salaried ministry of the Church.

. . .

PASTOR means one of the Gifts of Christ in the Ascension Ministries.

. . .

PROPHET means one of the Gifts of Christ in the Ascension Ministries and is linked with the ministry of Apostles in the government of the Church.

. . .

SUPERINTENDENT APOSTLE means an Apostle who is appointed by the Apostles of an Area as the Chairman of that Area Administration. Such an Apostle has the right to chair the meetings of any Committee that is functioning under the control of an Area Administration or any other business meeting or church service that might be held in that particular Area.

TEACHER means one of the Gifts of Christ in the Ascension Ministries.

. . .

Wallis came from an independent evangelical background where leadership was non-hierarchical; here he advocates restoration of Apostleship to the Church.

8.2   Arthur Wallis, 'Apostles Today? Why Not?'
Restoration, November–December,1981, pp. 2–5, abridged

Ever since the pentecostal movement broke in upon the church more than 75 years ago, other branches of the professing church have been at pains to explain why they do not themselves have spiritual gifts, such as tongues, interpretation, prophecy, healing etc. 'It is very evident', they tell us, 'that God never intended such things to be permanent. They were only necessary for the church in its primitive state'.

. . . Similarly, when asked for an explanation as to why there are no apostles or prophets today, the same somewhat tattered argument is produced. Apostles and prophets gave us our New Testament, and now that we have a complete Bible these men are no longer needed. . . . Doesn't Paul tell us that they are part of the foundation (Eph. 2.20)? And where in the New Testament is it implied that apostles were any less needed in God's own plan for the church than, say, evangelists, shepherds and teachers?

The onus clearly rests on those who assert that apostles were only intended to be a temporary institution, to prove it from the Scripture.

Apostles, prophets and Scripture

Behind so much wrong thinking in relation to apostles and prophets is a totally inadequate concept of apostolic and prophetic ministry. They are viewed as having a glorious role in the past in being the human channels through whom God gave us the inspired New Testament, but little else. Hence the argument that with the completed Scriptures in our hands they are superfluous.

Though the giving of the Scriptures was a task of the greatest importance, it cannot be identified exclusively with the ministry of New Testament apostles or prophets. It is far from certain that all the inspired writers belonged to either of these two categories. In addition, there were several apostles named in the NT, and a great host of NT prophets, who never gave us a single line of Scripture. What then did they do for a living?

. . . We need to see these men as primarily those who brought the word of revelation and direction into the living situations where God was building his church. It was by comparison a very small though eminent band among them, plus inspired historians like Mark and Luke, who were chosen to give us the sacred writings. Unless we understand this we shall miss completely the significance of such men today and the indispensable role they still have in the building of the church.

The view that apostles and prophets have passed away, and that spiritual gifts have ceased, both rest on the faulty premise that the completion of Scripture rendered them obsolete. Though we have inspired writings we still need inspired utterances, and having the Word of revelation we still need the men of revelation.

. . .

Three classes of apostle

To understand what God is now saying about apostleship we must distinguish in the New Testament three classes of apostle. In the first there stands, solitary and unique, *our Lord himself,* who is described as 'the apostle and high priest of our confession' (Heb. 3.1). There is a sense in which all the ministries of Ephesians 4 find their perfect expression in Christ.

The Greek word for apostle has its root in the verb 'to send', so that an apostle basically means 'a sent one'. In John's gospel we read that Jesus was constantly telling men that he was 'sent' by the Father. He continually lived and moved and ministered in the consciousness of his commission from heaven. That is the heart of apostleship. . .

In the *second* group we have 'The Twelve'. Judas Iscariot's place was taken by Matthias. Some would have us believe that Paul was to be the replacement for Judas, and that Peter acted prematurely in raising the issue when he did, and then casting lots with the result that Matthias was appointed. We never again hear of Matthias, they tell us, but the great apostle God raised up was Paul. But then, how many of 'The Twelve' do we ever hear of again individually after Pentecost? And as for Paul, he was ineligible for the choice, according to the conditions laid down in Acts 1.21–22. He was not even converted till some time after Pentecost. 'The twelve apostles of the Lamb' were destined to be the foundation stones of the new society (Rev. 21.14). How could Paul have been a foundation stone in the historical sense that 'The Twelve' were, since he was not around when the foundations were laid at Pentecost? Quite apart from this, the Holy Spirit clearly endorses Peter's appointment of Matthias as the twelfth apostle in Acts 2.14 and 6.2, and later Paul is careful to distinguish himself from 'The Twelve' in 1 Corinthians 15.5, 8. In considering the question, 'Apostles today?' it is crucial to see that Paul belonged to a third distinct class of apostle.

Apostles of the Ephesians 4 order

This third category of apostles referred to in Ephesians 4.11, are, according to Paul, the *gifts of the ascended Christ* (Eph. 4.7–11). They are thus to be distinguished from 'The Twelve' who were appointed and commissioned by Christ in the days of his flesh. In a word, the appointment of 'The Twelve' was *pre*-Pentecost; that of the Ephesians 4 apostles was *post*-Pentecost.

Paul was, of course, the outstanding apostle of the Ephesians 4 order, and he loved to recount his personal meeting and commissioning by the ascended Christ. But we have several other apostles who were not among 'The Twelve'. There was James, the brother of our Lord (Gal. 1.19). He, and our Lord's other human brothers, appear to have been unbelievers during our Lord's earthly ministry. But after Christ appeared to James in resurrection (1 Cor. 15.7) he was numbered amongst the apostles, and became, it would seem, the leading apostle in Jerusalem, taking precedence even over Peter (Acts 15.13; Gal. 2.9).

Jude, who wrote the epistle by Jude, was the brother of James and of our Lord, and was most likely an apostle, though he is not actually named as such. Others specifically mentioned are Barnabas (Acts 14.4, 14), Silvanus (Silas?) and Timothy (1 Thess 1.1; 2.6), and the unknown Andronicus and Junias (Rom. 16.7). In addition, Paul referred to the members of his team as 'apostles' (1 Cor. 4.9).

More than fifty years after Pentecost, the Patmos vision that we call the book of Revelation was given to John. In chapter two we have the message of Christ to Ephesus: 'I know . . . that you have tested those who claim to be apostles but are not and have found them false.' If the only authentic apostles in NT times were The Twelve and Paul, why ever was it necessary, more than 50 years after Pentecost, for the Ephesian church to be testing apostles to discover whether or not they were genuine? The implication is that the head of the church was still giving this gift to men.

Until we all attain

The strongest argument for a continuing apostleship is in our understanding of *the purpose* for which this gift was given. In contrast with the absence of any clear indication that apostles were to cease, we have strong biblical evidence that in fact they were to continue till the purpose for which they were given was fulfilled. Apostles, as well as the other gifts of Ephesians 4, were 'to prepare God's people for works of service, so that the body of Christ may be built up, until we all reach unity in the faith and in the knowledge of the Son of God and become mature, attaining to the whole measure of the fullness of Christ' (Eph. 4.12–13).

The key word is 'until'. This grand objective has not yet been realised. The body of Christ has not yet reached 'the unity of the faith'. It has not yet come to the place of corporate maturity. The full-grown corporate man has yet to emerge in the earth. It didn't happen even in NT times. We have still a long way to go, and apostles, together with the other ministries, are given until that glorious goal is reached. It is illogical to argue that we still need shepherds and teachers but not apostles and prophets. . . .

End-time shaking

For many, 'Apostles today?' is nothing more than a hypothetical question. If, as we believe, the end-time shaking is upon us, then the ministry of the apostles will become increasingly crucial. Jesus spoke of the house built on the rock and the house built on the sand. What a house is built on may seem of insignificant importance until the storm breaks, then it becomes a life-or-death matter. It is surely in preparation for the coming storm that God is highlighting this theme at this time. We shall not need the experts to tell us in that day, which are the churches which have been built on the foundation of the apostles and prophets. The day will declare it.

Used by permission of Covenant Ministries International, Nettle Hill, Brinklow Road, Ansty, Coventry CV7 9JL, UK.

A Lutheran minister, Christenson sets out how the charismatic movement has changed attitudes in church life.

8.3   Larry Christenson, 'The Church: An Ordered Body', in *Welcome, Holy Spirit*, Minneapolis: Augsburg, 1987, pp. 309–12, abridged

Order in congregational life

A charismatic Lutheran pastor who has the support of the lay leadership can exercise considerable freedom in bringing changes to a local congregation. This is the level at which the charismatic renewal has had its greatest impact in the Lutheran church, especially in the United States. At regional and national levels the overall influence of the renewal has had some effect on the church as a whole, but, generally speaking, regional and national church leadership has not included charismatics.

Concern for congregational order in the charismatic renewal has been an extension of its emphasis on the lordship of Christ. If Christ is truly Lord of the church, then its structure and operation cannot be a matter of indifference or mere preference, but should be reflective of his will in the matter.

Scripture, the point of departure

. . .

On the one hand, as we have noted earlier, it seems clear that the New Testament does not present a single, universally normative structure for a Christian congregation. On the other hand, Scripture is certainly not silent in regard to questions of order, structure, and authority in the church. What the Holy Spirit led the church to do in its formative years in regard to order ought not be turned over to antiquarians with never a sideward glance. It is part of the apostolic witness, part of canonical Scripture. We cannot assume *a priori* that the Spirit will not apply the same or similar wisdom to our situations.

It is true that 'situations change,' but parroting that slogan should not be our point of departure in establishing the order of a congregation. For it is also true that the Spirit is able to apply the same basic truth in a great variety of situations. The Spirit may indeed set aside some patterns from the past and utilize present-day practices in ordering the life of a congregation, but he is not bound to do so, nor are we free to do so if he wills something else. We must at the very least take into account the possibility that the Spirit may find some of his own precedents in the church more to his liking than the latest fad from the political or management marketplace.

Alternative concepts for ordering congregational life

If one were to look for a touchstone of the charismatic movement's teaching on congregational order it would probably be focused in words like elder or church council. This stems first of all from the study of Scripture. The role of elders figures prominently in governing structures in both the Old and New Testaments. The other side of this is the fact that charismatics have recognized some of the weaknesses inherent in a congregation that structures itself after the model of a democratic assembly. . . .

A change in concept is sometimes described as a transition from democracy to kingdom. . . .

A related concept for understanding congregational order has been that of family. The model of family tends to produce in a congregation an ordered set of relationships rather than simply a procedure for handling issues. The church council answers to the role of parents; the congregation, to the role of children. At first glance this seems to lead to a more central-ized, authoritarian structure, but the opposite is more usually the case. Loving and sensitive parents probably listen more sympathetically to their children than an elected official does to his or her constituency. They listen because they love and seek the best for their children, not because the children have the leverage of a vote in the next election. A typical church constitution might permit a church council to do certain things with a majority or two-thirds approval of the congregation. Charismatic congre-gations that have developed the family concept, on the other hand, might well decide to wait if as few as 10% of the members feel uneasy about a par-ticular action; in a family, maintaining unity is normally more important than pushing through a particular decision.

A charismatic Lutheran congregation that had experimented with a family model of church government for about 10 years included the following statement in its annual report:

. . .

1. *Leadership is a particular calling.*

. . .

What we have come to see is that leadership is a particular gift and calling in the Body of Christ. While there will inevitably be some real development in any person who serves on the council, the council is essentially a ministry for those who have already demonstrated the gift and calling for leadership. Our concern in nominating people for the council is . . . to discern the ones whom the Lord has given the calling of leadership in the congregation.

We must set aside the worldly notion that leadership is a place of higher status, while those not in leadership occupy a lower status. . . . The calling of each and every one is to serve. Leadership is simply a necessary function in the Body of Christ to which some members are called, because God has gifted and equipped them for serving in this particular way.

. . .

We do not see the evolving of a small cadre of leaders in our congre-gation as a sign that we are in a rut, or having the same old people run everything. Rather, we believe this is the result of a definite leading of the Spirit. It has resulted from his work among us, to strengthen and build up the Body of Christ.

2. . . .

A political system is a poor model for church order. Far better is the model of a family, 'the household of God' (1 Tim. 3.15). The nature of a Christian congregation is much more akin to a family than to a democratic government. According to the family model, the leaders of the congregation fulfil the role of parents. They are responsible for the leadership and direction of the family.

Prince, a Classics scholar, sets this argument for a strong church leadership; it led to a style that became known by its opponents as 'heavy shepherding', whereby ministers apparently dictated the lifestyle of their congregations.

8.4   Derek Prince, *Discipleship, Shepherding, Commitment*, Fort Lauderdale: Derek Prince, 1976, pp. 11–15

CHURCH LEADERSHIP

1. In New Testament congregations, all Christians (i.e. disciples) were expected to be under the rule of duly appointed leaders. The leaders of each local church were always referred to collectively, in the plural. They had three distinct, but related, titles: elders; overseers (or bishops); shepherds (or pastors). In the King James Version, 'overseer' and 'bishop' are two different ways of translating the same Greek word *episkopos*, 'shepherd' and 'pastor' are two different ways of translating the same Greek word *poimen*.

2. Three Greek verbs for 'ruling' are used:

(1) *hegeomai* to 'lead,' as a shepherd leads his sheep or a general leads his army. In KJV, as a noun, this word is translated 'governor' in Matt. 2.6; Acts 7.10.

(2) *poimaino* = to 'shepherd' (from the noun *poimen* = 'a shepherd'). In KJV this word is translated to 'rule' in Matt. 2.6; Rev. 2.27; 12.5; 19.15; and to 'feed' in John 21.16; Acts 20.28; 1 Cor. 9.7; 1 Pet. 5.2; Rev. 7.17. In other words, the concept of 'shepherding' includes both 'ruling' and 'feeding.' In

Rev. 2.27; 12.5; 19.15 the phrase 'to rule with a rod of iron' carries over the metaphor of the shepherd's 'rod,' but the fact that the 'rod' here is one of iron (not wood) denotes wrath and judgment, in place of grace and mercy.

(3) *proistemi* = to 'be set over' or 'at the head of' (see Rom. 12.8; 1 Thess. 5.12; 1 Tim. 3.4, 5, 12; 5.17). In 1 Tim. 3.4–5 there is a direct parallel between a man ruling his family and a man ruling the church, for Paul says that a bishop (overseer) must be 'one that ruleth well his own house, having his children in subjection with all gravity. (For if a man know not how to rule his own house, how shall he take care of the church of God?)' Thus, the authority of a father in his family is a pattern for the authority of a leader in the church.

3. The following are some further scriptures indicating that in the New Testament Christians were expected to be ruled by leaders: '. . . know them which labour among you, and are over you in the Lord, and admonish you . . .' (1 Thess. 5.12). 'Let the elders that rule well be counted worthy of double honour . . . ' (1 Tim. 5.17). 'Remember them which have the rule over you . . . Obey them that have the rule over you, and submit yourselves . . . Salute all them that have the rule over you . . . (Heb. 13.7, 17, 24).

4. All the scriptures quoted above indicate plurality of leadership. Here are some other scriptures that indicate the same: 'the elders' (Acts 11.30); 'they had ordained them elders in every church' (Acts 14.23) 'the apostles and elders' (Acts 15.2, 4, 6, 22, 23) 'the elders of the church' (Acts 20.17); 'the Holy Ghost hath made you overseers' (Acts 20.28); 'all the elders were present' (Acts 21.18); 'the bishops (overseers) and deacons' (Phil. 1.1); 'ordain elders in every city' (Titus 1.5); 'let him call for the elders of the church' (James 5.14).

5. To understand the relationship between elders, overseers (bishops) and shepherds (pastors), we may set the following scriptures side by side: Acts 20.17, 28; Titus 1.5, 7; 1 Pet. 5.1–2.

(1) In Acts 20.17 Paul 'called the elders of the church' (at Ephesus); in Acts 20.28 he said to these same elders, 'Take heed therefore unto your selves, and to all the flock, over which the Holy Ghost hath made you overseers, to feed (shepherd) the church of God . . .' Thus these elders were also overseers, whose responsibility was to shepherd the flock (the church).

(2) In Titus 1.5 Paul instructs Titus to 'ordain elders in every city . . .' In Titus 1.7, describing the kind of man qualified to become an elder, Paul says, 'For a bishop must be blameless . . .' Thus Paul uses the two titles 'elder' and 'bishop (overseer)' interchangeably to refer to one and the same person.

(3) In 1 Pet. 5.1–2 Peter writes, 'the elders which are among you I exhort, who am also an elder [literally who am a co-elder] . . . Feed [shepherd] the flock of God. . . taking the oversight thereof . . .' Peter's usage agrees with that of Paul. Writing to elders, he tells them that their responsibility is to shepherd the flock and to take the oversight of it – i.e. to be its overseers.

The above scriptures show that elders were also overseers (bishops), responsible to shepherd the flock (i.e. the congregation).

6. In the light of the scriptures quoted above, any Christian who accepts the pattern of the New Testament church as still applicable today, would do well to ask himself the following questions: Who are the leaders who rule over me in the church? Do I know them? Do they know me? Is there a right relationship between them and me?

7. In Rom. 12.6–8 Paul lists various special 'gifts' (*charismata*), among which he includes 'ruling.' 'He that ruleth let him do it with diligence . . .' Once the basic plurality of leadership in the church has been established, the Holy Spirit will normally impart to one of the leaders this *charisma* for 'ruling' – a special gift for administration and direction within the collective leadership. It will not necessarily be permanent. There may be a time when the Holy Spirit will transfer this charisma from one leader to another, but this will not affect the overall functioning of the group. It is the responsibility of all the leaders to recognize this *charisma* and to submit to it, irrespective of the person upon whom it rests.

8. So long as a man functions with this *charisma*, he is the mouthpiece and the representative of the whole group of leaders. However, the final responsibility for all major decisions still rests with the collective leadership. In the conference described in Acts 15.1–29, it appears that the *charisma* of leadership rested upon James – who was an apostle (see 1 Cor. 9.5). However, the final decision was expressed in the words, 'It seemed good to the Holy Ghost, and to us . . .' In other words, it was a unanimous decision of the whole group, expressing the mind of Christ imparted by the Holy Spirit to His Body, the Church, as it functioned in divine order (see 1 Cor. 2.16). Experience has shown that leadership functioning according to this pattern can achieve similar unanimity today.

Used by permission of Derek Prince Ministries International, PO Box 19501, Charlotte, North Carolina 28219–9501, USA.

Here Tomlinson, in the 'Restoration Movement' (UK) discusses the need for a network for leaders of relationships under the term 'covenant'. Some independent new churches began to relate across geographic norms to leaders across the world.

8.5   David Tomlinson, 'Loyalty: Covenant Relationship', *Restoration*, March–April 1978, p. 27, original emphasis retained

Covenant relationship – what is it?

Talking about loyalty leads us inevitably into the subject of commitment and covenant relationship. 'Is there a valid place for David and Jonathan type covenants today?' I am often asked. 'Don't they lead to cliquish, exclusive relationships?'

Personally I prefer the term 'commitment' to 'covenant' because I find it less misleading. The New Testament is absolutely clear: *there is only one covenant* – the new covenant in the blood of our Lord Jesus. No other context exists for any commitment amongst believers. Jesus made His covenant with all His followers and therefore the only valid boundary for exclusiveness is *all of God's people*! 'Right then,' you say, 'how can you possibly justify a form of commitment less than you've outlined?' Simple, really. Let's bear in mind that the new covenant is not merely of general application but also of specific application. If I could operate a committed relationship with all of my brothers and sisters in Christ that would be great, but I can't. In practical terms, I must know those with whom I am working out the intimacy of the covenant.

Beware. Unhealthy relationships develop out of exclusiveness and superiority. Recognize and seek a working relationship with other works you see God doing in your locality, even though their emphasis or expression may be somewhat different from your own. The separation which should exist, and no doubt will increase as time goes on, is not between one 'brand' and another but between life and death.

Having offered the cautions, now let me be perfectly clear, not only is specific commitment scripturally permissible, it is absolutely essential if real building is to proceed. I am currently a member of a local body of Christians in which every individual has personally expressed his commitment both to God and to one another. Let me share with you just two of the points we defined as important for working out a committed relationship. Number one was the point I mentioned earlier: 'Vision of a church which is a healthy, caring, Spirit-gifted community, free from fears and insecurity, showing the government of God among us and to the area around us, bringing others to Christ and building them into the body, co-operating with other Christians in the area to express the unity of the church.' Point number two is surely the very essence of commitment: '*Loyalty*'. Always looking for the best in one another, not passing on criticism but lovingly confronting where necessary; praying for and encouraging one another and seeking the blessing and progress of others.

Used by permission of Covenant Ministries International, Nettle Hill, Brinklow Road, Ansty, Coventry CV7 9JL, UK.

The difficulty of charismatic giftings clashing in team church leadership is illustrated by this abridged account of Duelling Prophets.

8.6　Mike Bickle with Michael Sullivant, *Growing in the Prophetic*, Florida: Charisma House, 1996/Eastbourne: Kingsway Publications, 1995, pp. 160–7, abridged

Duelling Prophets Sunday

During the second year of pastoring our new church plant in Kansas City, I had sat and watched five or six prophetic people regularly compete for the microphone during the Sunday morning services. I was starting to get exasperated because it was becoming clear to me that there was a lot of hype in what had been going on for the last few months. Some of the people were growing tired of feeling manipulated by these prophetic people and were starting to voice their feelings. On one Sunday morning in December 1984, two of the main prophetic people got into a 'prophetic duel' right in front of the church. One stood up and proclaimed something to this effect: 'Thus saith the Lord, "A great thing is going to happen."' Then the second man stood up and said, 'Thus saith the Lord, "Better things are going to happen."' Then the first prophetic guy topped him. Not to be out-prophesied, the second man answered back by giving something even better. They went about three rounds each.

　. . .

Another leader and I got both of these prophetic men together and had what turned out to be a very strong and direct confrontation. Both of them were defensive, and threatened that if I didn't accept their ministry style and what they had to say, the Holy Spirit's blessing would leave our church. . . .

Normally I would have been intimidated by people who had previously prophesied with such dramatic accuracy. But I was provoked and offended, so I rose up and told them both to leave. . . . That was such a disillusioning time for me that I was tempted to do away with all of the prophetic ministry, the miracles, the supernatural confirmations – everything, and we would no longer have prophetic ministry in our church.

. . .

But God doesn't abandon you because a prophetic minister feels offended. He can be used mightily and effectively by the Holy Spirit, but he is not the mediator between us and God. Only Jesus is.

These two men went out from our meeting to complain against me to some of the key people in the church. But these people called me and congratulated me, saying, 'Thank you, thank you, thank you!' That's when it dawned on me that it was not the prophets who had the gifting and call-ing of governmental leadership in our church. I also realised that if leaders don't stand up and speak the pastoral wisdom God has given them, prophetic people would not only destroy the church, they would destroy their own ministries as well. Much of what happened on 'Duelling Prophets Sunday' was my fault, because I had not exercised my leadership gift and responsibility. . . . I realised that the team of governmentally gifted people in our church had a lot more pastoral wisdom than the prophetic men did about church life and how people respond to the word of God. In one short week, the way I viewed my own ministry and that of our pastoral leadership team totally changed.

Within two weeks both of those prophetic men had come back and repented to me of their ambition and carnal motivations. This put a new confidence in me that some of those deep uneasy feelings I had had about their ministry style were really wisdom and discernment. I determined that I was no longer going to dismiss or quench those feelings. Since that encounter, I have decided that whenever I have a nervous feeling about what the prophetic people are doing, I am not going to ignore it. To neglect the responsibility to lead the prophetically gifted people will usually result in harm to the church and to the prophetic ministers.

The motivation of rejected prophets

Most prophetic people are in touch with their giftings long before they cultivate the corresponding wisdom, humility and character that are necessary to succeed in prophetic ministry. . . . The average person who has been in the prophetic ministry for ten years is pretty beaten up and bruised. This is especially true if the prophetic gift was active in their early years. By the time they are forty or fifty they are often very guarded and suspicious of authority figures. Those coming into prophetic ministry later in life may also have problems with rejection. These past histories of dysfunctional relationships with leaders in the church cause prophetically gifted people to put a lot of extra pressure into gaining honour and acceptance. Several problems can develop if they give in to those temptations.

. . .

Insecure pastors and leaders

Knowing where and how to draw the line with prophetic ministry minimizes the insecurity and fear that a pastor normally experiences when first encountering such people. If a pastor understands how to deal with these people, he is less afraid of them. Most pastors don't mind if things are a little messy if it is going to be profitable at the end of the day. . . . For the most part, pastors don't want to be embarrassed, and they don't want their people becoming hurt and confused. They are trying to protect their people and keep peace in the church.

Prophetic people often have a very keen sense of being answerable to God. Pastors have that sense too, but they are also very aware of being answerable to people. A pastor probably feels both concerns differently from the prophetic minister. The pastor realises he is answerable to God, but knows that, if there is a problem, on Monday morning he's going to hear it from the elders and from half of the congregation. The pastor also has the conflicts and practical pressures of meeting the budget. And when people get upset, they often leave and disrupt the economics of the church. What that means to the pastor is that he might have to fund part of the ministry staff. The prophets don't usually live in that arena or with those pressures.

Many pastors yield to insecurity and the fear of man. They have seen too many churches fail and so many people hurt by it. They sometimes take their eyes off God and yield to fear when things go beyond the comfort zone. They must learn to lead without fear and yet keep balanced in the area of risk-taking without sacrificing pastoral wisdom.

. . .

The prophet's biggest fear is that he might not get everything unloaded that God wants unloaded. The pastor's biggest fear is that he doesn't want to get the church into hype because he has to maintain a long-term relationship with them. Prophets and pastors have the same motivation, being afraid of missing God, but from different points of view.

One of the greatest benefits of having prophetic ministry in the church is that we need the input from proven, gifted people who carry the prophetic burden of God's heart without the same fears and anxieties that often accompany the pastoral leadership team. Many times those fears and anxieties serve as blinders to the pastor. It may be harder for a pastoral leader to recognize a flaw in the church if it has been there a long time. This flaw seems so obvious to the prophetic people. Perhaps the pastor is more acutely aware of all the problems that will arise from trying to fix the problem. On the other hand, a general understanding of pastoral and administrative problems associated with leading the church should enable prophetic people to understand the pastor's dilemma more clearly.

The church's greatest effectiveness is realised when the diverse gifts and personalities work together as one team ministry. But it takes a lot of patience and honouring of one another to deal with the pressures that come with nurturing and leading a church with a variety of giftings. Unless we learn to show honour to each other and the unique work that the Holy Spirit is doing in each person's life, we may end up in a holy war, especially if the gifts and personalities are strong. Without team ministry, none of these gifts would be able to prosper. I believe this is especially true for the prophetic ministry.

Used by permission of Strang Communications for Charisma House, Creation House, 600 Rhinehart Road, Lake Mary, Fl, USA.

A different approach to understanding church life biblically and in a charismatic scene is given by Christenson; the suffering servant has a lot to teach us.

8.7　Larry Christenson, 'The Church: A Servant', in *Welcome, Holy Spirit*, Minneapolis: Augsburg, 1987, pp. 334–9, abridged

The church: a servant

Jesus came into the world to serve (Mark 10.45). Every believer is called to serve. Christians serve each other; they also serve those who are not yet believers.

Serving underlies all Christian life and activity. This is a profound truth, but one easily corrupted by legalistic posturing. A recital of human needs, calculated to induce a guilt reaction, does not produce a servant church. Serving is a gift of the Holy Spirit. Jesus' serving is incarnated in those who live near him in his church, responsive to his lordship, built up by his forgiveness, by his Word, and by his body and blood. Serving comes by the working of the Spirit, not humanistic imperatives.

Serving is a gift as truly as are the signs of prophecy, tongues, healings, visions, and revelation. The more spectacular gifts are not higher or more valuable than the humbler gifts of helping and serving. Both are *gifts* which means that they are not produced by human talent or in response to legalistic demands, but are the result of the Holy Spirit's gracious visitation and empowering.

A charismatic Lutheran pastor in Scandinavia reported:

We have seen more or less dead Christians and congregations come alive in serving as an answer to their prayers for the Holy Spirit.

Rich people say: 'My money isn't mine. It is God's. I am only a steward.' They are happy to give to the poor people, to evangelistic and missionary work. They not only share their money, but their homes and tables too.

But not only rich Christians share – also people in ordinary circumstances. The Holy Spirit lays other people's needs on their hearts. They help each other in a practical way, take care of each other when anyone is sick. They look after each other's children and dogs. They comfort each other when they feel sorrow, and so on.

When their pastor or fellow Christian is persecuted, they gather in prayer and let the one who is under attack by mass media or the children of this world know that he or she has their and God's love.

We have seen Christians who have served an unfortunate neighbour, hit by mental disease, by taking them 50 or more miles to visit their home church when there was an intercession service. Others have given their time to known and unknown prisoners, alcoholics, and drug addicts.

Eyes have been opened to see others. Feet have become willing to go to others. Hands have been lifted to serve others.

Why do people do this? Why do they bother about each other in this unselfish way? The answer is: the Holy Spirit has worked it in them. He has given them new hearts. He has given them the gift of serving – not as something they must do to qualify as 'good Christians,' but as the living presence and power of Christ in the heart.

The servant church

The church early recognized that service lies at the heart of the Christian life and mission. This came to practical expression in the wide-ranging use of the word deacon (one who serves) as a designation for every form of ministry, from apostle to those who wait on tables (see Acts 6.1–4). Paul understood and taught that spiritual gifts, which are given to every believer (1 Cor. 12.7), are instruments of service. It is a theological insight of far-reaching significance. It describes the basic attitude that motivates the use of spiritual gifts.

The servant mentality runs contrary to human nature. When the flesh reasserts control, the desire to dominate others crops up in every area of the church's life – in relationships between individual believers, in groups of Christians, within the local church, and beyond. Pastors try to lord it over their congregations, congregations over their pastors, men over women, women over men. Sometimes spiritual gifts are misused as instruments of domination. Missionary work can be twisted into a means of manipulating people. Especially dangerous have been attempts by the church to exercise power in the world and over society, instead of simply serving.

. . .

How can the church determine its servant role? It cannot serve everyone everywhere; it must be selective. The Spirit-led church looks to the Holy Spirit for guidance. The question then is this: Where does the Holy Spirit want us to serve? Through revelation and confirmation by the Spirit the church must be guided into those places where he calls it to serve.

The gifts of the Spirit are valuable spiritual tools both in discerning the Lord's will for the servant church and in carrying it out. Spirit-led service is not simply a human or humanitarian ministry. It is a divine work, accomplished through human instruments in spiritual power.

Suffering

A servant church will inevitably be a suffering church; the two cannot be separated.

Suffering has not been a prominent theme in the charismatic renewal. Serious critics from within the movement cite this as one of the renewal's major weaknesses. Teaching on spiritual power and faith has not been balanced with a biblical perspective on suffering. This is ironic, inasmuch as some of the greatest suffering of Christians in our day has been among those who share a charismatic spirituality and perspective – in China and some Third World countries. Their experience, however, did not begin to receive major attention in the charismatic renewal until the late 1970s. In the beginning, the formative influences of the movement came more from the United States and Western Europe.

Suffering is not something alien to the life of Christians. God chooses it for us. It is one of the ways that we share the life of Christ. It is not a call to heroism but to humble dependence on the Spirit, who enables us to walk in the suffering that belongs to our calling.

. . .

Paradoxically, suffering is twin to hope. The believer's hope emerges in the midst of suffering – hope not only for the age to come, but also for this life. Suffering helps prepare us to share in the reign of Christ (Rom. 5.2–5.17).

. . .

The more Christians are filled with the Holy Spirit, the more powerfully they bear witness, the more heartily they live the Christian life, the more consistently they follow Jesus, the more suffering will come their way. A movement that urges people to be filled with the Spirit cannot avoid the consequences: it must help prepare them for suffering.

This does not mean training people in survival techniques. It means extending the central theme of the charismatic renewal into this area of life also: we enter times of suffering, like everything else in the Christian life, totally dependent on the Holy Spirit. We do not shrink from suffering. We recognize it as an integral aspect of Christian experience. In the power of the Spirit we resist the temptation to avoid or ease the suffering by accommodating ourselves to the world. We trust the Spirit to maintain our fellowship with the serving, suffering Christ.

Used by permission of Larry Christenson, editor, Lutheran Renewal Center, 2701 Rice Street, St Paul, MN 55113–2200, USA.

9 Evangelism

A. E. Dyer, Introduction

The Evangelists

The distinctive Pentecostal contribution to reaching those not yet believing in Christ as Lord and Saviour, and what distinguished them from Baptist or Methodist evangelists of the eighteenth or nineteenth centuries, was to be found in their expectation that miraculous signs, usually healing, would accompany the preaching of the Gospel. The pattern was taken from the end of Mark's Gospel 'The disciples went out, and preached everywhere, and the Lord worked with them, and confirmed his word by the signs that accompanied it' (Mark 16.20, NIV).

Donald Gee wrote *The Ministry Gifts of Christ*, providing a theology of ministry for the five-fold giftings (Eph. 4.11); an excerpt explains 'an evangelist' (9.1). An account of the activities of the brothers Stephen and George Jeffreys – arguably Britain's two greatest Pentecostal evangelists of the twentieth century – is provided (9.2). Meetings were held in hired halls or tents, advertised by posters or newspaper advertisements. After the conventional gospel preaching an 'appeal' was given for conversion healing and people responded. Crowds heard and came; a revival atmosphere grew. Many of the Elim and Assemblies of God (AG) churches of the UK were initially established in this way.[1]

By the middle of the twentieth century many North Americans like T. L. Osborn (4.7), W. Branham and Oral Roberts (4.9), had taken their tents and loudspeakers all over the world.[2] Radio evangelism and teaching continued alongside ministries that filmed their campaigns for television. Reinhard Bonnke campaigns were only different from others in their sheer scale. Thousands of people have claimed healing, and there have been reports of people being raised from the dead. In the excerpt from

---

[1] Cf. Willie Hacking's account, in *Joy Magazine*, August 2001, pp. 34–5; and W. Hacking, *Faith's Venture*, self-published 1988, pp. 20–2.

[2] As recorded in *Voice of Healing* magazine published by Gordon Lindsay of Christ for all Nations, Texas, 1947–64.

Evangelism by Fire Bonnke explains 'How to plunder hell and populate heaven' (9.3).

Local church

Alongside the more obviously Pentecostal forms of evangelism that stressed healing, evangelism at local church level was more prosaic. In the UK Willie Richards, the pastor who founded Slough AG, wrote two books, one a narrative and theory of evangelism (*Pentecost is Dynamite* – 9.4) and another that was a practical manual (*Doorbell Evangelism*). A wider context was developed at the World Pentecostal Conference in 1955 when Leonard Steiner of Switzerland made the Pentecostal theology of Spirit-baptism central to evangelism (9.5). Over against the concerns for tongues, interpretation, prophecy and the other charismata of 1 Corinthians 14 to be manifested in local congregations, he emphasized the Spirit's role in evangelism. Anglican David Watson, a representative of the 1960s UK charismatic movement, wrote *I Believe in Evangelism* where he developed this 'larger' theology (9.6).

Personal work

John Wimber found that spiritual gifts could operate anywhere with evangelistic effect and taught it at Fuller Seminary with a more comprehensive theological rationale than had been taught in previous decades. His books *Power Evangelism* and *Power Healing* brought signs and wonders to the forefront of evangelical attention once again for bringing the power of God home to non-Christians (9.7).

Meanwhile other para-church movements encouraged personal Pentecostal evangelism as with the Full Gospel Businessmen's and Women's Aglow meal evangelism. Members would invite friends to a meal where a person would tell of their personal encounter with Jesus Christ. Prayer for those responding for conversion or healing or other needs would be made at the end of a talk.

Church growth

Yonggi Cho of South Korea triggered the use of 'cells' for evangelistic church growth (9.8) but Ralph Neighbour (*Where Do We Go from Here? A Guide for Cell Group Churches*) and Lawrence Singlehurst of Youth With A Mission (YWAM) took the model further. Many charismatic churches have adapted this across the world; cells – as in biology – are meant to multiply themselves and therefore grow into congregations. Since then

César Castellanos in Colombia has developed a variation of this in his 'G12' pattern (cf. 21.1). Cells are home groups that function like mini-churches although these form congregational groups for collective worship, usually on Sundays.

Pentecostal or charismatic people expect signs and wonders to accompany their witness on three levels, mass, local and personal. Each Christian is encouraged to seek God's Holy Spirit power for witness according to Acts 1.8. On this basis Pentecostal and charismatic individuals and teams have spread the Good News of Jesus Christ from their homes across the world.

Ministry gifts were described at length by D. Gee (British AG leader) but 'Evangelist' was the most obvious one of the early decades in Pentecostal circles.

9.1 Donald Gee, *The Ministry Gifts of Christ*,
Stockport: Assemblies of God, 1930, pp. 30–3

The Evangelist

The word 'Evangelist' only occurs three times in the New Testament: 'Philip the Evangelist' (Acts 21.8); 'He gave . . . some evangelists' (Eph. 4.2); 'Do the work of an evangelist' (2 Tim. 4.5). Its meaning, of course, is one who brings the Evangel; a Preacher of the Gospel; literally – 'a messenger of good tidings.' In spite of these somewhat scanty references, Ephesians 4.11 makes it plain that 'Evangelists' constituted in the Early Church a distinct and well-recognized order of ministry, separate from either Apostles, Prophets, Pastors or Teachers.

The Gift of the Evangelist

Fortunately for us, the ministry of an Evangelist needs no laboured definition. The popular conception of the office has kept very close to the truth. We all know, and love, men who seem to have the Good Tidings of God's redeeming grace burning in their souls. Whenever they preach, their favourite theme is Salvation in its simplest sense. At times they may choose other subjects, but it is very obvious that here they are most at home.

The whole Bible to men with this Divine Gift seems to contain nothing but the one Message; they find it in type in all the stories of the Old Testament, it sings to them out of the Psalms, and inspires them from the Prophets. They revel in the New Testament, for here they are most of all at home. Sometimes they amaze us, however, by the way they find Gospel truth in parts of the Bible where we have seen nothing but pure history, or prediction, or doctrine applicable to believers only. Like Philip, their classic example, they are ready to commence at almost any portion of the Bible you please, and preach – JESUS! (Acts 8.32–5). It is a glorious Gift.

Their Gift is plainly a direct endowment from the Lord. Philip had been chosen by the Church, and ordained by the apostles, as a 'deacon' (Acts 6): he had been given no commission to evangelise; yet immediately he found himself in Samaria the heavenly gift urged him to a preaching of the Gospel, with glorious results. The same occurred at Azotus, and right through to Caesarea. We are sometimes asked to plead with young men to become evangelists. If the divine gift and calling is within them they will need no such plea: they will preach the Gospel of necessity and spontaneously; and it is just such Evangelism we need (1 Cor. 9.16). Sometimes, perhaps, we may be rightly concerned as to whether a divine gift is being quenched, but the impulse to all genuine ministry must be Divine. It can be ours to make an opening, but even when the Church fails here (as perhaps it did with Philip in Jerusalem), we are persuaded that a real gift from Christ will always somehow find or make its own opportunity.

Marks of true Evangelism

Philip stands before us in the inspired Word as our model Evangelist, and it is fortunate that in Acts 8 we really have a wealth of material.

(a) Supernatural advertising

Miracles of healing were a prominent part of his ministry. In view of this fact we are more than surprised at those who boast of such loyalty to the Scriptures, and yet violently oppose and condemn Evangelists who pray with the sick to-day. Surely in doing this they have the highest of precedents. Our Lord Himself adopted the same methods, and personally sent the seventy out with explicit instructions to do this very thing (Luke 10.9). It is plainly stated that this was the main reason why the people gave heed to what Philip said (Acts 8.6). God had evidently equipped him with those particular Spiritual Gifts needed for his ministry.

The principle also stands strikingly revealed that a display of Divine Power and Blessing upon any ministry is the very finest form of advertising. No fleshly, worldly flourishing of trumpets can ever take its place if we want Revival in the Power of the Holy Spirit. There is a place for legitimate publicity, but we have seen advertising 'stunts' in evangelistic work which are nauseating, and can only result in completely grieving the Spirit away. Divine Power soon draws crowds.

(b) The 'Word' essential

The signs and wonders caused them to 'take heed' (verse 6), but it is significant that soon after, and before they were baptised as professed believers, it says they 'believed' Philip's preaching (verse 12). Miracles arrest and compel attention, but it is the preaching of the word that converts and saves. Philip was no mere sensationalist, just satisfied with drawing the crowds. He preached solid Gospel truth to them, and it was in believing this that they were really saved. That the work of grace in their hearts was real in the sight of God is proved by his immediate gift of the Holy Spirit as soon as Peter and John prayed for them (verse 17).

True evangelism must 'preach the word' as its central and essential factor, whatever place may be given to personal testimony, healing, or other legitimate features. The authoritative and loving call to repentance and faith must aim at moving the will of the sinner; not merely stirring the emotion, or tickling the intellect. It is the glorious secret of the message of the cross that it does move the will, and in this is contained the ministry of the highest 'Word of Wisdom' which Paul exercised with such effect when he evangelised Corinth (1 Cor. 2).

(c) The individual decision

Conversion is an individual matter. Every New Birth is something personal between a human soul and God. Perhaps this is partly the reason why, after the story of the mass conversions at Samaria, real though they were, the chapter finishes with the exquisite story of the Evangelist and the Ethiopian – just one soul.

Herein undoubtedly lies the supreme gift of a real Evangelist; the power to bring individual souls whether in a crowd or not, to a personal determination. Someone has defined it as 'The power to precipitate decision.' A prophet may move the hearts of a whole company, a teacher may instruct them; but it is particularly the part of the Evangelist to compel by Divine Grace to an immediate surrender of the individual will to Christ. Who would not covet such a gift? Who has not felt deeply stirred whenever they have seen it in exercise?

Used by permission of Assemblies of God Publishing, Nottingham, UK.

Edward Jeffreys wrote the story of his father and uncle who founded the Elim Pentecostal movement in Britain in 1915. They were amazing evangelists with healing gifts demonstrated in their campaigns.

9.2   E. Jeffreys, *Stephen Jeffreys: The Beloved Evangelist*, Luton: Elim Movement Ablaze, Redemption Tidings Bookroom, 1945, pp. 59–61

What wonderful things would take place to-day if we did really take God at His word and act upon it! This my father did, and his remarkable faith in God brought innumerable blessings to burdened souls and diseased bodies wherever he went.

Many outstanding cases of healing took place at Hendon, one of them being the remarkable healing of a man who had been deaf and dumb for forty years. The following report appeared in the *Hendon and Golders Green Gazette:*

FAITH HEALING WONDERFUL SCENES AT WEST HENDON

The Revival Mission undertaken, by Pastor Stephen Jeffreys at the Alexandra Hall, Brent View Road, West Hendon, has met with enthusiastic reception. The opening meeting last Sunday evening was well attended, and many who went to scoff departed convinced. Meetings have been held throughout the week, and have been attended by an atmosphere of devotion rather than ridicule. The blind, the lame, the deaf, the dumb, and the diseased have all been represented at the Pastor's meetings, while people have arrived from places as far distant as Barking so that their children might come into touch with that Divine Power which it would seem, is associated with the work of the Mission.

At the meetings Pastor Jeffreys makes a great point of impressing upon his hearers the fact that they must not look to him, personally, for aid. He was unable to do anything, but he believed Jesus could. If the hearers believed in Him, the Pastor expressed his willingness to pray for them. The body was, he said, the Temple of God, and God did not want defiled or deformed temples. Disease was the product of sin, but if the afflicted believed, then, and then only, could they hope for deliverance. The object of the mission was not to heal bodies, but to save souls.

A representative of the Gazette attended the Pastor's meeting on Tuesday afternoon, and witnessed many remarkable scenes.

This earnest little minister was undoubtedly the instrument of some Higher Power. While the congregation sang, he prayed for the deliverance of many souls. A woman who had suffered from paralysis threw away her sticks; another, who had been crippled through a diseased bone resulting from an accident in Hendon, walked around the hall. A woman who had suffered for five years with a withered arm held it up and used it in visible sight of the congregation. Sufferers from tuberculosis and cancer declared to those present that the pain had left them, and still the people sang and an atmosphere almost unreal in its intensity, prevailed throughout the hall.

[Headlines included] THE DUMB SPEAK, HENDON MAN'S CURE AFTER FORTY YEARS OF SILENCE, A REVIVAL WAVE
Amazing scenes have been witnessed this week in West Hendon where faith healing meetings have been held by Pastor Stephen Jeffreys in connection with a great revival campaign. Pastor Jeffreys, the well-known Elim Revivalist, has occupied the Alexandra Hall, Brent View Road, since Sunday, and has held services each evening and on several afternoons, in the course of which the truth of his claims for faith have been fully brought home to the crowds who have visited the building.

One of the most remarkable cases of cure was that of Mr. W. J. Palmer, of 22, Herbert Road, West Hendon, who has been deaf and dumb for over forty years. Mr. Palmer attended a meeting on Monday evening and submitted himself among many patients for healing. In a few moments he was seen to be talking with the pastor, and such was the amazement among those who knew of his misfortune in the past that quite a number of people followed him home in the hope of hearing him speak.

Calling on Mrs. Palmer, a representative of the *Hendon and Finchley Times* was told that her husband was able to talk to her for the first time for forty-two years. One can imagine the joy which the fact has brought into the little household! Mr. Palmer speaks rather softly, and with a little hesitation after so long a silence, but his voice, Mrs. Palmer told us, appears to be improving rapidly.

In the same evening the cures effected included those of a cross-eyed boy and a little dumb girl. This child, who is staying with friends in Wilberforce Road, West Hendon, had been dumb for a very considerable time, and her recovery was a matter for great rejoicing.

On Tuesday, Wednesday, and Thursday afternoons special Divine healing services were held, and our representative was a witness of some remarkable changes. One young woman whose case is well-known in West Hendon, came to the meeting – her second visit – with the assistance of a stick, and leaning on her brother's arm. She had been a cripple for many months. After the laying-on of hands she was able to abandon her stick and walk round the hall without assistance. She was later seen walking home. Her brother subsequently showed us the surgical bandages which she had been able to discard. Another crippled woman threw her stick aside before she tried to walk, so great was her faith that she had been healed. She descended from the platform unaided and walked away. There were many similar cases, including one of a girl who had been practically paralysed for five years.

Another person testified to a cure of rheumatoid arthritis after many years, while a person who had been under an operation for cancer, without success, told the meeting she had been able to do all her housework since first visiting Pastor Jeffreys, whereas she was previously incapacitated.

The campaign had been attended by marked enthusiasm, and we understand that a very large number of people have been converted. Pastor Jeffreys impresses upon all that he is not the healer. 'My business is to put you right with God,' he says. (*Hendon and Finchley Times*).

Used by permission of Assemblies of God Publishing, Nottingham, UK.

Bonnke, a German Healing Evangelist, has been holding campaigns ever since the 1970s, particularly in Africa. Here he links faith with evangelism.

9.3   Reinhard Bonnke, *Evangelism by Fire*,
Eastbourne: Kingsway Publications, 1989, pp. 88–9, 116, abridged

How to plunder hell and populate heaven

For over six years I ran a Bible correspondence school. That was in Lesotho, Africa, from 1968 to 1974. The purpose was, of course, to reach the lost people of the country for Christ. The enrolment grew to approximately 50,000 students.

To keep this project going put great demands on my faith. I was only a missionary. I needed an office, and the monthly rent was only $30. But one day I couldn't pay, and I prayed and groaned all day, 'Dear Lord, let me have $30 to pay the rent.' The hours passed, evening came, but I still had no money. Slowly, I walked down the road to the house where we stayed as a family.

Suddenly, in the middle of that road, the power of the Lord came upon me. I heard His voice clearly inside my heart, 'Do you want Me to give you one million dollars?' One million dollars! My heart raced the Formula One circuit. What I could do with that amount of money! Why, with one million I could bombard the whole world with the gospel, I thought.

But then, a different thought struck me. I am not at all a weepy person, but tears began running from my eyes, and I cried, 'No, Lord, don't give me one million dollars. I want more than that. Give me one million souls. One million souls less in hell and one million more in heaven – that shall be the purpose of my life.'

Then the Holy Spirit quietly whispered into my very spirit words I had never heard before -'You will plunder hell and populate heaven for Calvary's sake.' That day, a determination gripped me. I knew God had greater plans for my life, and I set out to fulfil them in progressive stages. God has granted me ever-increasing blessing and grace.

How often since then have I seen the devastating power of the gospel crash against the gates of hell, storming the dark domains of Satan. I often saw, within one week, 300,000 precious people respond to the call of salvation in our gospel crusades. I joked with my co-workers: 'If Jesus keeps on saving souls at this rate, one day the Devil is going to sit alone in hell.' I'm glad to make Satan sorry.

Knowing the power of the gospel, we don't need to be frantic. Jesus is equal to the need. The world is sick, and Jesus has the only remedy – the gospel. Our part is simply that we must carry this medicine to the patients. Jesus commanded it – 'Go ye!' That is not a suggestion or a recommendation, but an order. We had better obey, or else miss the greatest joy known to man.

How to have an effective gospel

The message is Jesus. What He does shows who He is. The former is all-important. Jesus saves from sin. We are not moralising. We are not giving descriptions of sin. An American President went to church one day, and later his wife asked him what the preacher's sermon was about. 'It was about sin,' he replied. 'And what did he say about sin?' his wife enquired. 'Oh, he was against it,' the President told her.

People expect that. The question is: What can be done about it? People need victory over sin in their personal lives. They need to feel clean, forgiven. They need to feel less disgusted with themselves. Many a man will tell you he knows he's not going to heaven, but he has no idea what to do.

We must major on how to get people out of the mire, how to get them cleansed by the precious blood of Jesus, how to receive assurance and the witness of the Holy Spirit. These are mighty themes.

I constantly stand before vast crowds. To say anything less than the gospel would be wicked. Thank God I have a gospel, a positive message of power and hope. Then I find the fountain of the love of God springing up. Healing waters flow in all directions. That love touches human hearts. Men and women open up to God. They often have little of this world's goods, but it matters less when they possess the riches of God; assurance, peace and joy which no factory makes, no shop sells, no affluence provides.

. . .

You cannot expect to live a successful Christian life if you are not in the Spirit for that is how God arranged for you to live. Wherever we are we can be in the Spirit and that is the important fact . . . In our element of the Spirit we are unconquerable, invulnerable going from victory to victory, our life hid with Christ in God. The man moving in the Spirit; the church moving in the Spirit; workers, evangelists, pastors and teachers moving in the Spirit – that is the only formula I know for success. In the Spirit of God we can win the world for Jesus.

Used by permission of Kingsway Publications, Lottbridge Road, Eastbourne, Sussex BN23 6NT, UK.

An example of a Welsh Pentecostal Evangelist as an equipper of churches is W. H. T. Richards. A church planter before the term was invented, he tells his story. Healing played a vital part in this ministry, but he also equipped others for the task too throughout the AG denomination in the UK during the 1960s.

9.4 W. H. T. Richards, *Pentecost is Dynamite*, London: Lakeland, 1972, pp. 35ff.

Right from the beginning I felt the urge to go and found churches but how was I to start? It's one thing to have vision and zeal but to achieve anything worthwhile we need definite guidelines. Now I may have been naïve but for me there was no other way – I decided to take my directions from the New Testament. I saw that the disciples went forth with neither purse nor scrip. That encouraged me, for in my case I had no option but to go forth with neither purse nor scrip. My parents were out of work and there was no support from any organization. I read of the exploits in the Acts of the Apostles and how the early Church went about the task of winning people to Christ. I could see no reason then, when I started my ministry, nor can I see any now, why the church should not follow the same general pattern as the early Church in spreading the message of the gospel.

God's guidance

So I went forth, without any money, not knowing where I was to lodge and with no committee behind me (looking back now, I think that was in the providence of God). I am not suggesting that it is wrong for young men to enter the ministry backed by their friends and supported by organization, but what I am saying, is that when these are not available it will not hinder those who have received God's call.

I shall not set down in these pages very much about the battles, setbacks and triumphs, but I would like to mention an incident which led to the commencement of the church where I now serve as minister. Twenty-eight years ago, during the Second World War, I was pastor of a church in the suburbs of London. I have vivid recollections of those terrifying days when the capital was subject to nightly bombing raids for three months. I lived through the blitz and saw suffering and death in its stark reality almost every day. It was during this period, whilst I was in prayer, that the Holy Spirit impressed a word upon my soul. It was the name of a town that I had never visited and knew nothing about. It was a unique experience for me. I have known nothing like it, before or since. The incident recurred several times during the following days. I felt that God was telling to me to go to this particular town to establish church. The name of the town was Slough, in Buckinghamshire.

So with only twelve pounds in my pocket, I set out to visit the district and this I did several times. I was a little disheartened, for all the public halls had been commandeered by the government. Then I found an old dilapidated Scout hut that nobody seemed to want. There were only about twenty chairs; the windows were boarded up; mice were running around on the rafters; the wooden sections had no lining on them. It was a very cold place indeed. The place that I decided to use as my 'vestry' was filthy with old socks and other junk! But I was grateful for this haven where I could receive my potential converts. I spent the twelve pounds on a month's rent, two thousand handbills and fixing a notice board to announce the services.

I found four or five Christians who were interested in my plans and I contrived to follow the principles laid down in the Acts of the Apostles regarding the founding and building up of a local church. The same thing happened as in the other churches I had known – in a few months we began to grow. We increased to twenty, then fifty, then one hundred, until today we have over five hundred members with eight hundred children and teenagers in our twenty-five branches of Sunday Schools and youth activity. We have, of course, had our casualties and dropouts, and many have moved elsewhere. Today about twenty members are engaged in full-time or part-time Christian work. We built a church which has had to be extended four times and we have started other churches. We have an outreach ministry based upon the teaching of the Acts, in conjunction with which we run an International School of Evangelism correspondence course to train folk in evangelism. There are over eight thousand students enrolled, covering about twenty denominations, including hundreds of ministers. We have centres on the continent and throughout the world. These students have themselves won thousands to the Christian faith. We publish a national magazine called *Dedication*, which is sent to thousands of ministers. The whole of this ministry is offered freely to the Church of Christ, costing thousands of pounds each year. In addition, we have seen a repetition of what occurred in the early Church – conversions, healings, demonic power dealt with, and the Holy Spirit coming upon the believers in the same way as related in the Acts of the Apostles. For twenty-eight years we have witnessed constant growth each year as a result of following the pattern of the early Church. We should expect a ministry of the miraculous.

Simple faith in the words of Christ has worked miracles in many lives. I am thinking of one man who had hernia trouble for fifty years. After prayer the large lump completely disappeared. Then there was a man who had been bedridden for years and who was almost bent double for eighteen months, unable to straighten himself. Two members called at his home, offered to pray for him and urged him to yield his life to Christ. The man willingly did so. They prayed for him and immediately he straightened up, got out of bed and was wonderfully healed. He jumped up and down, shouting in his excitement, 'I am healed. I am healed!' This man became a sound convert to the Christian faith, and so did his wife and her two friends, who are still with us today.

Not long ago a lady was pushed into our church in a Bath chair. She had been like this for years and was gradually getting worse. I prayed for her many times, and nothing happened, but she said to me, 'It's all right, Pastor, I know God is going to heal me!' although she was getting worse all the time. Then she was taken to a little Mission Hall in the country one Sunday afternoon and during the service she suddenly felt the presence of God come upon her. She got out of her Bath chair and was completely healed in a moment of time. It was the faith of this simple soul that brought the miracle into her life. These are just a few instances of the many miracles that have taken place.

I take no credit whatsoever for this, . . .

I am firmly convinced that the great need of the twentieth-century Church is to adopt the first-century methods of evangelism. . . .

Used by permission of A. W. Richards, Kings Church Windsor, Central Administration, 631/4 Ajax Avenue, Slough, Berks. SL1 4AF, UK.

Leonard Steiner of Switzerland preached at the World Pentecost Conference in 1955 and encouraged evangelism as the Pentecostal contribution worldwide.

9.5 L. Steiner, 'The Pentecostal Movement and World Evangelism', *Pentecost*, 20 June 1955

Evangelism is the one great task given to the Church in this world, the chief reason why we as Christians are still on earth. Its foundation is the Great Commission of our Lord: 'Go ye into all the world and preach the Gospel to every creature.' 'To every creature!' This means, to every creature with a human soul, or, to every individual human being. You will agree with me that today, over nineteen hundred years since the Commission was given and, as we believe, at the close of this dispensation of grace, it is far from having been accomplished. . .

In a world where there is a rising tide of nationalism, scientific scepticism and Communism he [Professor Lamott] sees the hope of a religion that creates the greatest passion in the individual and keeps him most closely in touch with the actualities of modern life. Christianity is the religion that can meet the challenge of revival of a revolutionary nature.

Do we know where that is? Praise God it has come in this blessed worldwide Pentecostal Revival! You all may have read that lovely and timely article by Rev. A. G. Osterberg of California on the beginning of this revival at Azusa Street reminding us who are of the younger generation that Pentecost at its beginning was a 'Revival with tears'. And I like those closing sentences in his article, which run like this:

A heaven-born Revival given by the Holy Spirit which at the same time was a revolution did its God-pleasing work in the hearts . . . The high and the low, the rich and the poor, clergymen and laymen, surgeons, professors, carpenters and masons all were lying humbled upon their face before God . . . As a result they were melted together as one family over which the banner of Christ and of Pentecost was waving without a shadow or a spot so pure and so healthy in their relations as fresh snow, a unity in life purpose and testimony to spread the wonderful message unto the ends of the earth.

The Pentecostal Movement and World Evangelism! I am humbly but firmly convinced that the truth embodied in our movement supplies the answer to the problem of World Evangelism. It is the baptism in the Holy Ghost in its Scriptural fullness and purpose that enables the Church as well as the individual Christian to meet the challenge of a world still filled with heathen darkness. Without boasting we can be proud of the fact that our Movement from its beginning has been a Missionary Movement. And we do well to remind all our assemblies and followers that all other aspects of the spiritual life and growth – as e.g., sanctification, edification, Christian perfection, and even our preparation for the Coming of our Lord, are never an end in themselves. They are just means to make us more fit for the great task. I think we do well to remember with gratefulness to God the noble contribution to World Evangelism in the past fifty years by our over 2,000 missionaries in all parts of the world. We ought not less to praise God for the tireless efforts of the fine company of Evangelists and faithful Pastors to seek and win the lost for Christ. Ought we not also as a Conference to thank God for what has been accomplished in these past years through the ministry of our brethren in the so-called healing movement? I think we ought to assure them of our united prayers.

There is another reason to praise God. In spite of all criticism, our Movement is now getting growing recognition from other Churches. I do not believe that this is something to make us conceited. Prof. Blanke of Zurich University (an authority among all Churches) speaks in one of his recent publications of the Pentecostals as the 'brave and successful spearheads of Protestantism in South Italy and South America.' Even a notable Catholic author in France [Ch. Chery] cannot hide his admiration of the dynamic strength of the Pentecostal Movement in his country.

Used by permission of the Donald Gee Centre, Mattersey Hall, Mattersey, UK.

David Watson, an Anglican minister who saw an empty church in York grow tremendously in the 1970s enlarges on evangelism theologically.

9.6   D. Watson, *I Believe in Evangelism*,
London: Hodder & Stoughton, 1984, ch. 10, pp. 168ff., abridged

The Spirit in Evangelism

The Acts of the Apostles records an astonishing growth-rate of the first-century Christian Church. . . . What were the reasons for this extraordinary evangelism explosion? . . .

In the first generation of the Church we must not forget the uniqueness of the apostolic witness and the clearly exceptional effusion of God's grace for the period when the foundation of the entire Christian Church was being laid. Paul wrote that the household of God was 'built upon the foundation of the apostles and prophets, Christ Jesus himself being the chief cornerstone', therefore, when 'many wonders and signs were done among the people by the hands of the apostles', so that the sick were brought out into the street in the hope that at least Peter's shadow might fall on some of them, and when 'God did extraordinary miracles (even Luke recognized that these were not "ordinary" miracles!) by the hands of Paul, so that handkerchiefs or aprons were carried away from his body to the sick, and diseases left them and the evil spirits came out of them', it is not to be assumed that the same astonishing power is available to all Christians in every generation. Of course God in his sovereignty may give quite remarkable signs and wonders at any time, and the history of the Christian Church up to the present day contains numerous evidences (persuasive to all but the determinedly sceptical) that healings and miracles and other less common gifts of the Holy Spirit did not die out with the apostles. However, there was no doubt a special and unusual cluster of miracles surrounding the apostolic testimony to the resurrection of the Lord Jesus.

Having said all that, the manifest power of God that was demonstrated so fruitfully in the New Testament Church was, of course, the power of the Holy Spirit. There are no less than forty specific references to the Spirit in the first thirteen chapters of Acts. If Luke's second volume bears the right title, as it is largely an account of the various activities of the apostles, a fuller and more accurate title would be 'The Acts of the Apostles through the power of the Holy Spirit'. . . .

1. The Holy Spirit and the Great Commission

The Spirit of God is essentially a witnessing Spirit. 'He will bear witness to me, and you also are witnesses,' said Jesus. 'I will send him to you. And when he comes [to you], he will convince the world of sin and of right-eousness and of judgment.' This is the great purpose of God's gift of his Spirit to us: to make us more effective in our witness and evangelism. 'You shall receive power when the Holy Spirit has come upon you; and you shall be my witnesses.' Indeed, whenever and wherever the Spirit is present in power, the evangelistic work of the Church will flow naturally and spontaneously.

The urge to witness is inborn in the Church, it is given with her nature, with her very being. She cannot not witness. She has this being because of the Spirit who indwells her. Pentecost made the Church a witnessing Church because at Pentecost the witnessing Spirit identified himself with the Church and made the Great Commission the law of her life . . . From this it could be said that having to stress the Great Commission, and having to urge people to witness, is not a sign of spiritual life, but a sign of spiritual decadence.

Certainly from Pentecost onwards, evangelism inevitably happened. It was not long before the accusation came to the Church leaders from the high priest: 'You have filled Jerusalem with your teaching.' And yet we find no reference at all in the early Church to that Great Commission. Nowhere does Luke suggest that they reminded one another or exhorted one another to 'go and preach the gospel'. . . . The encouragements to evangelise were unnecessary when the witnessing Spirit was so powerfully working amongst them. The irresistible missionary expansion of the Church was inevitable from the precise moment that the Spirit descended upon those disciples in that upper room. In the various calls to mission from Church leaders today, the seeming ineffectiveness of much of the subsequent evangelism may well be due to a failure to appropriate the power of the Spirit. Only the Holy Spirit can bestow spiritual life, and if there is no life there will be no powerful preaching of the gospel, and where there is no powerful preaching of the gospel there will be no trans-mission of life to others. . . .

2. The Holy Spirit and power

Shortly before his ascension, Jesus said to his disciples:

> Thus it is written, that the Christ should suffer and on the third day rise from the dead, and that repentance and forgiveness of sins should be preached in his name to all nations, beginning from Jerusalem. You are

witnesses of these things. And behold, I send the promise of my Father upon you; but stay in the city, until you are clothed with power from on high.

It is useless to attempt to witness to Christ, in obedience to his command, without the power of his Spirit. It is out of the abundance of the heart that the mouth will speak. For example, if you are carrying a glass full of some liquid and if I bump into you, what will spill out? Naturally, whatever is in that glass. In the same way, when people 'bump into' us each day in the street, shop, office, lecture room or hospital, what will spill out of our hearts? Obviously whatever is in them. That is why the disciples were told to wait until their hearts were filled with the Spirit; without this they would have been empty and powerless to communicate Christ. Nor was the coming of the Spirit at Pentecost sufficient for them on all subsequent occasions. Shortly afterwards, feeling their weakness under the threat of persecution, they prayed to God for boldness, 'and they were all filled with the Holy Spirit and spoke the word of God with boldness . . . And with great power the apostles gave their testimony to the resurrection of the Lord Jesus.' Indeed the power of the Spirit is indispensable to the proclamation of the gospel. Anyone can preach words; some can preach convincing and persuasive words; but only God can change lives . . .

In all these instances the power of the Spirit was manifestly present because these men were totally committed to Christ and also to one another, regardless of the personal consequences. This, by and large, is what is lacking in the Church today, and consequently there is so little power, or even motivation, when it comes to evangelism. Taking the Church as a whole, we are not single-minded when it comes to our commitment to Christ or to the Body of Christ. Either we have many interests and ambitions, the Kingdom of God being only one of them, in which case the Church becomes simply one of many clubs to which we belong, and our involvement is determined by our inclination at that time; or we are committed to Christ in a personal and private fashion, but not to the Body of Christ. We remain individualists, and avoid one of the immediate implications of being filled with the Spirit, namely 'submitting to one another out of reverence for Christ'. However, God's power is for God's people. It was when the disciples 'lifted their voices together to God' and were 'of one heart and soul', and 'had everything in common' that 'great grace was upon them all'.

3. The Holy Spirit and communication

The Spirit is concerned not primarily with religious experiences, but with the truth of the gospel of Christ and with the truth of God's word. Jesus called him the Spirit of truth who would guide the disciples into all the truth. Now the truth without the Spirit can be depressing and damaging in its deadness; but the Spirit – or rather spiritual experiences – without the truth can quickly slide into all kinds of excesses, abuses and counterfeits. The Spirit is bound to the word . . . A Church which abandons the link with the word and tries to rely only on the Spirit falls a prey to all the evils of spiritualistic enthusiasm. Conversely, a Church which tries to rely only on the word and tries to reduce the Spirit to the word, falls a prey to all the evils of a verbalistic enthusiasm. Donald Gee says the same thing more simply and arrestingly: 'All Word and no Spirit – we dry up; all Spirit and no Word we blow up; Word and Spirit – we grow up.' Church history has repeatedly shown that, where there has been both a powerful and a continuous renewal of the Spirit, spilling over into effective evangelism, there has also been a firm stress on the truth of God's word, particularly in the preaching and teaching ministry, and in the growth of small house-groups. 'Virtually every major movement of spiritual renewal in the Christian Church has been accompanied by a return to the small group and the proliferation of such groups in private homes for Bible study, prayer, and the discussion of the faith.' Conversely a tragic number of genuine movements of the Spirit have suddenly disappeared, or gone sour, or become heretical, owing to a neglect of the truth of God's word. The Paraclete passages in John, Chapters 14–16, make it clear that the Spirit who was coming to be with the disciples, to bear witness to Christ and to convict the world of sin, would do so by being the Spirit of truth. It is impossible to separate the teaching and witnessing aspects of the Spirit's work . . . .

Used by permission of Hodder & Stoughton, 338 Euston Road, London NW1 3BH, UK.

Signs and wonders followed Wimber's ministry, not just in church. This he defines as 'Power Evangelism'.

9.7   John Wimber with Kevin Springer, *Power Evangelism*, London: Hodder & Stoughton, 1985, pp. 44–7

Power evangelism

Shortly after take-off, I pushed back the reclining seat, and readjusted the seat belt, preparing to relax. My eyes wandered around the cabin, not looking at anything in particular. Seated across the aisle from me was a middle-aged man: a businessman to judge from his appearance, nothing unusual or not about him. But in the split-second that my eyes happened to be cast in his direction, I saw something that startled me.

Written across his face, in very clear and distinct letters, I thought I saw the word 'adultery'. I blinked, rubbed and looked again. It was still there. 'Adultery'. It was not with my natural eyes, but in my mind's eye. No one on the plane, I am sure, saw it. It was the Spirit of God communicating to me. The fact that it was a spiritual reality made it real.

By now the man had become aware that I was looking ('gaping at him' might be a more accurate description).

'What do you want?' he snapped.

As he spoke, a woman's name came clearly to mind, more familiar to me; I had become accustomed to the Spirit bringing things to my awareness through these kinds of things.

Somewhat nervously, I leaned across the aisle.

'Does the name Jane [not her real name] mean anything to you?'

His face turned ashen. 'We've got to talk,' he stammered. The plane we were on was a jumbo jet, the kind with a small upstairs cocktail lounge.

As I followed him up the stairs to the lounge I sensed the Spirit speaking to me yet again. 'Tell him if he doesn't turn from his adultery, I'm going to take him.'

Terrific. All I had wanted was a nice, peaceful plane ride to New York. Now here I was, sitting in an aeroplane cocktail lounge with a man I had never seen before, whose name I didn't know, about to tell him God was going to take his life if he didn't stop his affair with some woman.

We sat down in strained silence. He looked at me suspiciously for a moment, then asked, 'Who told you that name?'

'God told me,' I blurted out. I was too rattled to think of a way to ease into the topic more gracefully. 'Who told you?' He almost shouted the question, he was so shocked by what I had said.

'Yes,' I answered, taking a deep breath. 'He also told me to tell you . . . that unless you turn from this adulterous relationship he is going to take your life.'

I braced myself for what I was sure would be an angry, defensive reaction. But to my relief, the instant I spoke to him defensiveness crumbled and his heart melted. In a choked, desperate voice he asked me, 'What should I do?'

At last I was back on familiar ground. I explained to him what it meant to repent and trust Christ, and invited him to pray with hands folded and head bowed, I began to lead him in a prayer: 'O God', was as far as I got. The conviction of sin that had built up in him seemed virtually to explode. Bursting into tears, he cried out 'O God, I'm so *sorry. . .*' and launched into the most heart rending repentance I had ever heard.

It was impossible, in such cramped quarters, to keep hidden what was happening. Before long everyone in the cocktail lounge was intimately acquainted with this man's past sinfulness and contrition. Even the stewardesses were weeping with him!

When he finished praying and regained his composure, we talked for a while about what had happened to him.

'The reason I was so upset when you first mentioned that name to me', he explained, 'was that my wife was sitting in the seat right next to me. I didn't want her to hear.'

I knew he wasn't going to like what I said to him next.

'You're going to have to tell her.'

'I am?' he responded weakly. 'When?'

'Better do it right now', I said gently.

The prospect of confessing to his wife was, understandably, somewhat intimidating, but he could see there was no other way. So again I followed him, down the stairs and back to our seats.

I couldn't hear the conversation over the noise of the plane but I could see his wife's stunned reaction, not only to the confession of infidelity, but also to his account of the stranger sitting across the aisle who had been sent by God to warn of the consequences of his sin. Eyes wide with amazement (and probably terror) she stared first at her husband, then at me, then back at her husband, then back at me, as the amazing story unfolded. In the end the man led his wife to accept Christ there on the aeroplane.

There was little time to talk when we got off the aeroplane in New York. They didn't own a Bible, so I gave them mine and we went our separate ways.

This might seem like an unusual – if not bizarre – event, yet I could write hundreds of other accounts like it – both from my own experience and from that of others whom I know. I call this type of encounter 'power evangelism'; it has been seen in periods of great missionary expansion and renewal throughout history.

By power evangelism I mean a presentation of the gospel that is rational but also transcends the rational. The explanation of the gospel comes with a demonstration of God's power through signs and wonders. Power evangelism is a spontaneous, Spirit-inspired, empowered presentation of the gospel. Power evangelism is that evangelism which is preceded and undergirded by supernatural demonstrations of God's presence.

Through these supernatural encounters people expect the presence and power of God. Usually this occurs in (such as the man on the aeroplane experienced) healing, prophecy, and deliverance from evil spirits. In power evangelism, resistance to the gospel is supernaturally overcome, and receptivity to Christ's claims is usually very high.

Used by permission of Hodder & Stoughton, 338 Euston Road, London NW1 3BH, UK.

These two excerpts provide an insight into the formation and growth of what became the largest Pentecostal church in the world. The first is taken from the church's own website and the second is from an article by Vinson Synan in the IPCH's cyberjournal.

9.8   Yoido Full Gospel Church
http://davidcho.com/NewEng/bd-1.asp

Yoido Full Gospel Church (YFGC) started in the form of a home worship service in the living room of Pastor Ja-Sil Choi in Daejo-dong on May 18, 1958. There were five participants: Dr. Cho, Pastor Choi and her three children. One day in late June, a month after the foundation of the church, a woman suffering for seven years from a stroke was healed. Because of this healing, the church grew rapidly. Even shamans, fortunetellers, and street hooligans came to the tent church to seek a new life. When the membership of the church reached 800, God allowed the completion of Full Gospel Revival Center at Seodaemun in November 1961. Dr. Cho, having received pastoral ordination, changed the name of the church to Full Gospel Central Church in 1962.

As the membership kept growing and reached 3,000 by 1964, four services were held on Sundays. With the membership reaching 8,000 in 1968, the church decided to build a new church. On August 19, 1973, Yoido Church was completed and the first worship service was held. The membership, which had increased to 100,000 by October 1979 doubling in two years, grew to become the largest church in the world. World-known press including *The New York Times* began to notice the growth of YFGC. The membership increased to 400,000 by 1984. By then the church was renamed Yoido Full Gospel Church and the membership rose to 700,000 by 1992, about the time when Dr. Cho was elected chairman of the executive committee of the World Assemblies of God Fellowship.

Vinson Synan: http://members.cox.net/pctiicyberj/synan.html

In October of 1994 Dr. Cho hosted the 'largest prayer meeting in history' when the International Assemblies of God convened in the Yoido church for a world evangelization program of prayer and planning to win the world for Christ. At the climax of the rally, over 1,000,000 persons massed in Yoido Plaza for the climactic prayer session. In a move that recognized the importance of the Korean church in the world pentecostal and charismatic movements, Dr. Cho was named Chairman of the International Assemblies of God.

Many researchers have studied the phenomenal growth of the Korean pentecostal churches and especially that of Cho's Yoido congregation. The best answers have been offered by Young Hoon Lee, one of Cho's associate pastors. Lee singles out the following five causes of the 'wonderful growth' of the church:

1. a strong positive message
2. a powerful healing ministry
3. the Prayer Mountain movement
4. the baptism in the Holy Spirit and speaking in tongues
5. home cell group meetings
6. the use of mass media

By the 1980s the charismatic movement had begun to permeate the traditional Protestant and Catholic churches of Korea, bringing pentecostalism into the mainstream of the churches. Church growth specialists noted the incredible growth of all the Korean churches and the central role of the Holy Spirit renewal in their growth. By 1990 such researchers as David Vaughan were listing the largest churches in the world, five of which were in Seoul and all of which were classified as 'charismatic' to some degree.

They included the following:

Yoido Full Gospel Church 200,000 in Sunday worship services
Kum Ran Methodist Church 50,000 in Sunday worship services
Nambu Full Gospel Church 47,000 in Sunday worship services
Soong Eui Methodist Church 40,000 in Sunday worship services.

In addition to these 'superchurches' thousands of congregations exploded throughout Korea in one of the most remarkable revivals in the history of the Church. Among these were the Korean Catholics who also experienced a powerful charismatic renewal during the last two decades of the century. By 1990 it was estimated that over 350,000 Korean Roman Catholics had been baptized in the Holy Spirit and were active in the Charismatic Renewal.

By the end of the century, it was clear that South Korea was well on its way towards becoming a Christian nation. By 1992 the percentage of Christians in the population of the nation stood at 40.7. From small beginnings in the early years of the century, the Korean pentecostals added their spiritual fervor and organizational skills to the massive growth of the church in the nation. By 1995, the pentecostals had grown to be the third largest church in South Korea with almost 2,000,000 members. The record of Korean church growth was unparalleled in any other part of the globe. The growth from a tiny persecuted minority to an almost certain majority of the population is a quantum leap that can only be explained in spiritual and supernatural terms. The pentecostals and charismatics, with their gifts and zeal, have led the way in Korea as they have in many other parts of the world.

Used by permission of Dr H. Hunter (ed.), Cyber Journal for Pentecostal-Charismatic Research No. 2 (July 1997) at *www.pctii.org/cyberj/index.html*

10 Missions

A. E. Dyer, Introduction

Mission to the 'uttermost parts of the Earth' was fundamental to Pentecostal thinking. Pentecostals simply had to share their good news. Based on verses like Acts 1.8 they coupled this commission from Jesus with 'the Father's promise' of power, by which God would enable them to witness to all parts of the world. Early in British Pentecostal circles – which were still led by the Anglicans A. A. Boddy and Cecil Polhill – the purpose of this experience and the new phenomena of the Holy Spirit was seen to be for missions. Since Polhill had been one of the Cambridge Seven who set out for China with the China Inland Mission (1887) as a missionary to Yunnan (south-west China), he assumed the position of organizer of a new mission – the Pentecostal Missionary Union (PMU). The inauguration of this mission is described in the January 1909 first copy of *Confidence*, a magazine edited by Boddy (10.1)

As missionaries already abroad received this Pentecostal experience they joined this mission if other 'Boards' did not accept them any longer. The first British Pentecostal missionaries set out in 1909 for India and China.[1] Others left America, often via Azusa Street, Los Angeles. One of the intriguing ideas of the new missionaries was that their new spiritual gift of speaking in other unlearned languages (*glossolalia*) was for the purpose of calling them to a specific people or at least for spreading the gospel (*xenolalia*). Revd and Mrs A. G. Garr left Kentucky's Asbury College to pastor a Burning Bush Mission in Los Angeles. There, after visiting Azusa Street, he received the baptism in the Spirit and felt called to India; they tried various places in India and on to China, unsuccessful in finding the language of their tongues speech.[2] Polhill refutes the idea of evangelistic *xenolalia* in an article in *Confidence* (1911) (10.2). The vocation to be a missionary was more than the ability to speak in tongues.

Other young men, W. F. P. (Willie) Burton and James Salter, with 'Daddy' Armstrong set off apart from the PMU to Africa where by 1915 they

---

[1] In early 1909 Miss Kathleen Miller and Miss Lucy James left Britain for India.

[2] See the *Dictionary of Pentecostal and Charismatic Movements*, Zondervan, 1988, p. 329

established the Congo Evangelistic Mission. Over forty years later W. F. P. Burton was still in Africa, as was his colleague Teddy Hodgson, who was to be martyred at the hands of Congolese rebels in 1960.[3] Included in the excerpts then is a letter from Burton in 1919/20 telling of the results of their work in Lubaland (today's central Congo) (10.3). Another excerpt gives an account of Burton himself by a later colleague, Harold Womersley (10.4).

Many missionaries left Western shores (UK, USA, Scandinavia, etc.) for long and short terms, many venturing in faith with little support, and few hit headlines at home. However, those who did hit headlines for reaching many nations were the international healing evangelists including George Jeffreys (UK/Europe), Smith Wigglesworth (from the UK), T. L. Osborn (USA), W. Branham (USA), A. C. Valdez, R. Cerullo and later M. Cerullo, and many others, from the 1930s and especially the 1950s.[4] Others like Benny Hinn, or Marilyn Hickey, have continued this into the twenty-first century, filming it for tele-evangelism, whereby they appeal for finance for humanitarian programmes.

With regard to long-term mission in 1931, the British Home Reference Missions Council (HRMC) decided to adopt an 'indigenous church' policy. This had the aim of enabling indigenous church members to take on leadership, financial and propagating responsibilities for churches which missionaries had planted. This ideally allowed missionaries to move on to fresh fields. Roland Allen, an Anglican Missionary to China and later Africa, was very influential in promoting this policy from the early 1900s and included in it an emphasis on dependence on the Holy Spirit. Burton was much impressed by his writings and adapted them from the original Chinese application to his Congo situation. Melvin Hodges (AG America) repopularized this policy afresh in 1953 (10.5).

By the 1950s a new generation of Pentecostals were beginning to lead their churches, taking over from the pioneers. During the 1950s eschatological warnings appeared in the Christian press and echoed the concern for nuclear proliferation. There was a strange tension between these underlying anxieties and the unequalled prosperity that began to diffuse through Europe and North America. There was a new attitude in the world concerning material benefits. This meant that raising financial support for mission needed highlighting again, especially as many new as well as experienced missionaries were sent out immediately after the war.

---

[3] See *Redemption Tidings*, 23 December 1960, for a report of the martyrdom in the Congo on 23 November 1960.

[4] See *Voice of Healing*, published by G. Lindsay of Christ for All Nations, Texas, in the 1950s, for accounts of these healing evangelists. See Healing and Evangelism sections.

As a result of the missionary movement there were small but growing Pentecostal churches all over the world. Numbers of missionaries increased during the 1950s and onwards. The American AG alone sent out 1,464 Pentecostal missionaries in 1987 alone.

Other Americans, like Donald McGavran, C. Peter Wagner and Charles Kraft from Fuller Seminary, have had much worldwide influence too, especially since the 1970s in areas to do with church growth. This has led the latter to emphasize signs and wonders and spiritual warfare. They also promoted prayer for missions in the '10/40 Window'. This referred to the geographical area covered roughly by the latitudes 10° to 40° north where there were the least christianized areas in the world. Later the emphasis changed to the 40/70 window, as Europe and Russia were perceived as post-church. Wagner, Kraft and others like them have come to represent 'The Third Wave'; they have had influence over a much broader spectrum of denominations compared to the first two waves of Pentecostals and independent charismatics or neo-Pentecostals.

David Barrett has drawn up statistics that illustrate the incredible growth seen among Pentecostals like no other denomination.[5] C. P. Wagner gives a summary of Pentecostal growth, stressing the factors he sees in good growth as belonging 90 per cent to Pentecostal churches/ missions, more than any other group. In 1991 he gave the following figures:

Worldwide

1945	16 million classical Pentecostals
1965	50 million including charismatics
1975	96 million all
1985	247 million all
2000	562 million[6]

By 1987 autonomous national Assemblies of God had become the largest or second largest Protestant denomination in no fewer than 30 nations of the world. Wagner thinks this is a result of wise application of indigenous missionary strategy producing over 90,000 national ministers in local

---

[5] C. P. Wagner considers that 90 per cent of churches where he notes church growth factors are Pentecostally inclined. Cf. C. P. Wagner, in *Called and Empowered: Global Mission in Pentecostal Perspective*, ed. M. A. Dempster, B. D. Klaus and D. Petersen, Peabody, Mass.: Hendrickson, 1991.

[6] Estimated by D. Barrett, (1982), *World Christian Encyclopedia: A Comparative Study of Churches and Religions in the Modern World* AD1900–2000, Oxford: Oxford University Press.

congregations worldwide. The growth of Pentecostal churches worldwide from the 1950s onward is exemplified by Yonggi Cho's church in Korea (600,000 by the 1990s). Now many nations like Korea and Singapore are surpassing western nations in sending more missionaries per capita of church membership.

Pentecostal theology is seen most clearly in pulpits and on street corners. In summary the following characteristics can be seen in Pentecostal missions: Bible-based evangelism; faith in prayer for provision and guidance; a supernatural worldview that can relate to non-western societies; compassion with supernatural means of meeting needs as well as social concern; church-based outreach; and strong leadership enabling congregational participation, with good training schemes.

Along with far better training in understanding cross-cultural communication, better communication lines of technological import, and the fact that mission is increasingly 'everywhere to everywhere', not just 'the west' to elsewhere, 'Spirit-filled' Christians have many advantages. They have a 'theology on the move' as L. Grant McClung, Jr, has said. They encourage an experiential theology of God. Now that even the western nations are more open to 'spiritual phenomena' than the Enlightenment Age of Reason and Modernity had given space for, there is room for displaying God's power, providing experiential spiritual encounters. This is the reason for C. Kraft's analysis of 'Power Encounter' (10.6), a term originally used by Alan Tippett when studying supernatural phenomena in conversion processes in Polynesia.

While normal in Pentecostal circles in terms of healings and prophetic revelations or visions for guidance this has become more widespread in charismatic or third-wave circles, thus globalizing it further. The 'normal' Christian, filled with the Spirit, cannot not be involved in declaring and demonstrating God's power in missions from their doorstep to the other side of the world.

Confidence *magazine was used to promote mission by Pentecostal missionaries; here is the announcement of the inauguration of the Pentecostal Missionary Union.*

10.1   Cecil Polhill, 'The Pentecostal Missionary Union',
Confidence, January 1909, pp. 13–15

The Pentecostal Missionary Union
(For Great Britain and Ireland).

EXECUTIVE COUNCIL:
Mr. Cecil Polhill, Howbury Hall, Bedford, Secretary for England, and
  Treasurer.
Rev. Alex. A. Boddy, All Saints' Vicarage, Sunderland, Editorial Secretary.
Mr. T. H. Mundell, 'Everstone' 25, Avondale Road, South Croydon.
Mr. Victor Wilson, 11, Merry St., Motherwell., N.B., Secretary for Scotland.
Mr. Andrew W. Bell, 11, Abbey Place, Dunfermline.
Mr. Andrew Murdoch, Edengrove, Kilsyth.
Mr. H. Small, East Wemyss, N.B.

At a preliminary Council Meeting held in All Saints' Vicarage, Sunderland, on Saturday morning, January 9th, 1909, there were present Mr. Cecil Polhill, Mr. Andrew W. Bell, Mr. Harry Small, and the Rev. Alex. A. Boddy. After a season of earnest prayer for guidance a long sitting followed, and it was felt that the Holy Spirit indeed helped at every point, so that there was perfect unity.

The following were the Resolutions adopted by the Council:

1. The name of this Society shall be 'The Pentecostal Missionary Union for Great Britain and Ireland.'
2. The above shall form the Executive Council, with power to add to their number.
3. A larger General Council shall also at once be formed, and shall meet (if not sooner) at the Whitsuntide Conference at Sunderland. The members of this Council shall consist of Representatives, one from each Pentecostal Centre in Great Britain.
The Centres are asked to appoint these at once, and furnish the names and addresses to the English or Scottish Secretaries. It is suggested that such Representative should become the local Missionary Secretary and Treasurer.

4. Pentecostal Centres are invited to send in at once, through their own Representatives, the names of suitable volunteers for Foreign Service. Printed questions will then be sent to two friends (whose names should be given at the same time as the names of the candidates).

5. Pentecostal Centres are invited to have regular times for offerings for the support of the Missionaries. Missionary Boxes will be supplied on application to the English or Scottish Secretaries through the Representative. The funds will be acknowledged once a quarter in *Confidence*.

6. Bible Schools with a course of some months' study will be arranged for in Scotland and London as soon as possible. The
candidates or their Centres are asked to help towards expenses. The Society's funds will also be partly devoted to this.

7. All our Missionaries on going into the Foreign Field will receive the following Certificate, renewable from time to time (or revocable by the decision of the Council in extreme cases):

PENTECOSTAL MISSIONARY UNION (FOR GREAT BRITAIN AND IRELAND). MISSIONARY'S CERTIFICATE. This is to certify that

....

....

of ....

having been accepted as a (Probationer or) Missionary of this Union by the Members of the Executive Council is hereby authorized to act as its Representative.
    Signed

      ....

      ....

      ....

Members of the Executive Council.

N. B. – This Certificate is for ..... years or less period if the Council see fit.

---

8. Salary. No salaries guaranteed. The Home Centres will do their best to support the Missionary work by alms and prayer, and at least to supply necessaries.

9. Religious Tests. Candidates must be from those who have received the Baptism of the Holy Ghost themselves. They must be sincere believers in the Atonement through the Blood, with both pardon and full deliverance, and succeeded by the anointing of the Holy Spirit with the Signs and Gifts. They must be believers in the infallibility of the Holy Scriptures.

10. Educational Standards. They must have a fair knowledge of every Book in the Bible, and an accurate knowledge of the Doctrines of Salvation and Sanctification.

It was mentioned that Mr. Cecil Polhill was arranging for a house in London, where soon they would receive English Candidates accepted by the Council. Mr. H. Small, of East Wemyss (Fife, N.B.), hopes to receive accepted Scottish Candidates when arrangements are perfected.

11. Cecil Polhill hopes to lead out to Western China and Tibet the first contingent of Pentecostal Missionaries in September next and settle them with a leader, to return to England after a while. The Council thought it might be well for the forces at first to be united and working in the same district, within reach of one another.

The question of Centres supporting Special Missionaries was thought of, and it was felt that while funds might be so given, they should pass through the channel of the Union. They could be specially devoted, according to the request of the donors. Those who go abroad in connection with other societies or independently could not be Missionaries of our Union, though they would be followed by our earnest prayers and sympathy.

The first meeting of the General Council (p. 15 *Confidence*, JAN., 1909.) will be (D. V.) at 2 p.m. on Wednesday, June 2nd, in All Saints' Parish Hall, Sunderland.

For all information apply to Mr. Cecil Polhill, Howbury Hall, Bedford, Secretary for England; Mr. Victor Silvosos, Motherwell, Secretary for Scotland.

O Lord, give us a heart of love for the Heathen in Asia, Africa, America, and the Islands of the Sea. Bless our Missionary Union. Show us, each one, what we may do, and give us grace to do it as unto Thee. Choose Thine own Messengers, and may none of us refuse to hear a call. Guide the Council and those who shall train and teach the Missionaries. May the World in some way be blessed through our Pentecostal Blessing and Thou shalt have all the glory, for Thou wast slain, and Thou alone art worthy, O Master, to receive all we have, for all blessing comes from Thee, and only of Thine own do give unto Thee. Amen.

Used by permission of the Donald Gee Centre, Mattersey Hall, Mattersey, UK.

Pioneer movements have teething problems – as in the use of tongues and mission!

10.2   Cecil Polhill, 'Calls to Foreign Service', *Confidence*, January 1911, p. 8

Calls to Foreign Service

There are members of Pentecostal Gatherings and others who feel that they base a call to the Foreign Mission Field because they believe that they speak in Chinese, Indian, or African languages etc. They should, however, be very careful not to go before God. Before leaving home they should take steps to verify the fact that they really have a complete language in which at all times they can preach the Gospel.

I feel it only right to say that from among the very many who have gone abroad after the Pentecostal blessing we have not yet received one letter stating that they have this miraculous gift in any useful fullness.

This is a strong call to prayer and trust for this gift of language. But to many who possibly have a spirit of unrest I would quote the apostle's words (1 Cor. vii. 24) 'Let every man wherein he is called, therein abide in God.' The speaking of words in Chinese or other languages may be the Lord's sign that such an one is to be an intercessor for that particular field: a home missionary. The call may come one day in a much clearer way to go to the foreign field. But wait for it.

Used by permission of the Donald Gee Centre, Mattersey Hall, Mattersey, UK.

This quotes a letter from W. F. P. Burton, pioneer of the Congo Evangelistic Mission, when based in Mwanza, Belgian Congo, on 20 January 1920. At last God had answered prayer.

10.3   W. F. P. Burton, 'A Luban Pentecost', from *Missionary Pioneering in Congo Forests*, compiled by Max W. Moorhead, 1922, Ch. 11, pp. 198–207, abridged

My heart is so full of praise to God that I scarcely know where to commence in telling you of the great blessings of the last fortnight. I have repeatedly asked your prayers that God's Holy Spirit might be poured out upon Lubaland. Let me tell you how wonderfully, our Father has answered.

. . . for a number of little lads would gather at Sister Toerien's house to pray for the baptism of the Spirit; or, having been filled with the Spirit themselves, to pray others into blessing. This would proceed until nearly midnight, but so eager were some youngsters that, though they had to start work at 6.30 a.m. we could hear voices of earnest prayer coming from one hut long after midnight.

So with earnest crying to God, and with hearts brimful of love for all parties, we raised a definite note from the commencement of convention, upon the supreme necessity of God's children being endued with power from on high. Moreover, we determined to cast the matter on the Lord, that we would willingly work with one native entirely surrendered to God, and filled with the Holy Spirit, rather than with a thousand who powerlessly blindly follow the Scriptureless traditions of men, and ignore the simple instructions of the Word of God. Thus, then, for the first four days of the Conference, we ceaselessly hammered upon the one dominant note of submission to God's Word.

On the fourth day of the Convention, Thursday, in our morning meeting there were about 160 present, to whom we spoke on Mark 16.15–18: 'These signs shall follow them that believe.' There was a solemn, heart-searching time, and God's power was wonderfully felt as those present frankly acknowledged that they did not bear the hallmark of Scripture, in that these signs did not accompany their ministry. Then at the Invitation to come forward to pray for, and to receive the Holy Spirit, almost the whole of the congregation came forward. Even the most stubborn opposers were ashamed to hold back. At once the whole of the front of the chapel was a tightly wedged mass of earnest natives with their woolly heads down and their shiny black backs heaving with the emotion of prayer.

. . . it was not many minutes after we started praying that the first few were filled with the Spirit. And then they helped us by laying hands upon, and praying with others. It was only those on the outskirts of the crowd that were within reach. The whole of those in the centre of the crush were out of our reach, but not out of God's. Oh, how they cried, and groaned, and grovelled in the dust, as they wrestled their way to victory. The noise of this great visitation was heard in a village one and a half miles away. Truly the mountains of pride and self-esteem were broken down, and the valleys of fear and mistrust were filled up, the crooked places of schisms, quarrels, suspicions, and party spirit were made straight, and the result is the same as in John the Baptist's time, that all flesh is seeing God's salvation (Luke 3.5–6). There sat one middle-aged woman apart on her little stool (in all our assemblies the women and men prefer to sit apart), and as she nursed her baby, the look of her face was one of pharisaic disdain, as much as to say, 'Fancy, disturbing yourselves like that! I'm sure I'm far too dignified for anything so grotesque.' But as the power of God came down, and dozens of little lads were crying and beating their breasts, or rolling their perspiring little faces in the dust in the agony of their appeal, or magnifying Jesus in Luban, or in the new and heavenly language of the Spirit, there were very few in the room who were untouched, and it was utterly impossible to tell how many received the Holy Spirit. Presently the portly woman, mentioned above, began to feel the movings of the Spirit, and stool and baby went anywhere, as she abandoned herself to God. This was not the only baby that Sister Toerien rescued during the service. Oh, what a different woman was this once haughty negress next day, when she received the Holy Spirit, and walked up and down with hands uplifted, praising God in new tongues.

We have grieved much over the haughtiness of one or two older Christians, but what a change the Spirit has wrought. One old man always took a front seat and lost no opportunity for impressing upon everyone in truly native fashion, the greatness of his own importance and piety, but from the time that the Spirit fell upon him, he has taken his place at the very back of our chapel, to keep the door and to keep the noisy children quiet, while when later in the services, I asked for some volunteers among the youngsters, to clear the pool which we used for baptism, from mud and slime which had silted into it, he was the first to offer for this undignified and dirty job.

That first wonderful meeting lasted from 10 a.m. to 3 p.m. For three hours the whole place was swayed by God's Spirit. Many fell as though dead and those who had no room to fall on the floor fell on each other.

At least two cases occurred of those who praised God in beautiful English, and I also heard snatches of French, and Dutch or German. And almost all who spoke in tongues had languages with beautiful clear R sounds, – which is significant, since in the natural a Luban cannot properly pronounce this sound. Then when all was quiet, of course I had to explain it all from Acts 2, that 'this is that,' and that Christ Jesus 'being by the right hand of God exalted . . . hath shed forth this which ye now see and hear.' Since then it is hard to say which has been the most wonderful meeting. Natives have been coming and going all the time, so that one cannot give an accurate number of our visitors, for some would stay for two or three days and go away, others would go and come back again. But it was manifestly unwise to let all the believers go back home after a week's meetings as originally intended, since some remained cold, hungry, and unblessed, while others in the full flood tide of a new found power and blessing, were in danger of being carried into excitement and folly, unless taught from Scripture more of God's purpose and desire in pouring out His Spirit. But an average of considerably over 100 visitors must have been here for the fortnight's meetings. Moreover, since this is the busiest part of the gardening season, when every day's labour will give big returns at the end of the rainy season, almost half of the believers were unable to attend, and those who did come only did so at a big personal sacrifice which, however, God wonderfully rewarded.

. . . The hours between the meetings were fully occupied in answering questions, giving advice and encouragement, and in listening to confessions of sin. This last is all the more wonderful since hitherto horses could not drag confessions from a Luban. All their lives long they have lived in such deception and hypocrisy, that to confess a sin, when they had not been caught red-handed, would appear to them the height of absurdity. But 'when He (the Spirit of Truth) is come, He shall convince the world of sin' John. 16.8), and during this convention the burdened ones have forced themselves upon me whether I would or no. And, oh, what fearful pages of crime were unfolded. But against the hideous background of disgrace and shame, the Cross of the Lord Jesus is all the more resplendent. How precious it was to kneel with these stricken, guilty lads, pour out our heart's burden to God, and see them go away humbly, gratefully rejoicing, yet still amazed at the stupendous fact that 'The blood of Jesus Christ, God's Son, cleanseth us from all sin.'

Used by permission of Central Africa Missions, 355 Blackpool Road, Preston, Lancashire PR2 3AB, UK.

Harold Womersley worked alongside Burton in the Belgian Congo and gives an insight into the qualities of the superior pioneer Pentecostal missionary that Burton epitomized.

10.4   H. Womersely, *Wm F. P. Burton: Congo Pioneer*,
Eastbourne: Victory Press, 1973, ch. 8, pp. 71–7, abridged

A vision with a task

Samuel Chadwick's definition of a missionary has always intrigued me: 'A vision without a task makes a visionary. A task without a vision makes

for drudgery. A *vision with a task* makes a missionary.' If this is true, then
W. Burton was an ideal missionary: no hazy visionary . . .

. . . William Burton certainly had a vision, and the vision revealed the
task. And he went at it with all the strength, intelligence, dedication, spiritual perception and power that God supplied constantly, according to his
need. He was to a great degree inspired by the example of Hudson Taylor
and the scriptural pattern of the China Inland Mission, though he did not
rigidly copy others, realising that every country, every people and every
age would require modification of methods in preparing a people and
building a church that would please the Lord.

He bought a copy of Roland Allen's *Missionary Methods St. Paul's or
Ours?*, and read it with fascination and approval. It seemed so similar to
his own ideas, yet he saw clearly that many things which applied to China
and its peoples did not necessarily apply to Central Africa and the Bantu,
particularly in Christian Education as no one in Mwanza knew anything of
books, or even of writing and reading. . . .

. . . First, William Burton's vision was of an *indigenous Church*. This was
a revolutionary idea in those days. Missionaries to primitive peoples
whom the tentacles of European civilisation were scarcely yet reaching
considered that a strong, if benevolent, parental control was essential and
usually imposed a copy of their own particular denomination in doctrine,
worship and organisation upon their converts. William Burton and James
Salter endeavoured from the start to form a church that was reliant on God
and that looked to Him and His Word rather than to the rigid rules of man,
and one that would begin to share the burden of responsibility right from
the start. Even before they could even read or write, the converts were
encouraged to witness. . . .

It was a long and uphill task, but well worth the struggle, and whatever
success our missionaries have had through the years in developing indigenous principles, it is almost entirely due to the insistence and encouragement of Willie Burton. At first, the aim was not to establish Mission
Stations, but to camp in a village and preach till a nucleus of believers
could be formed into an assembly, then pass on to another and so on until
we had covered the Field.

However, we soon found that we should never get round the thousands
of villages, often miles apart, in this way. We had to establish a base from
which to work and from which to replenish our stocks. We were obliged to
have a centre where we could systematically teach believers to read, write
and do simple arithmetic so that they could read the Word of God, enter up
their records and reckon up church offerings. We needed a place where we
could train national workers, by whom our labours could be multiplied
indefinitely, and the country covered with the Gospel as quickly as pos-

sible. The key to the indigenous church was the indigenous worker, and such had to be trained. There were also complications of mail and delivery of goods that would greatly hamper a totally itinerant preacher in a land of long distances, remote forests, no motor roads (at that time) and few means of communications.

Secondly his vision was of a simple *Church.* Many societies had complained that their older stations had developed into small 'towns' and that many of their missionaries were so involved in the central organisation that they knew little of the way of life in the bush areas, and less of the mental processes of the Congolese. From the start, William Burton determined to have small de-centralised stations.

Not only simplicity of organisation but simplicity in worship was his aim. The Breaking of Bread, as he conducted it, lacked any suggestion of ritual: he encouraged the people in their assemblies to use a lump of their stiff manioc mush or pudding for the bread. It was just as much their daily bread as a wheaten loaf to the European, or the unleavened cake of the Jews. He also found that the sticky red pods or buds of the 'mwilembwe' plant, a variety of 'rosella', mixed with water, was a practical and easily obtained substitute for wine. The plant was grown behind most of the people's huts for the sake of the edible leaves. Better still he gave them slips of hedge-mulberry; [which] . . . made a still more acceptable wine. . . . He felt that the memorial remembrance of Christ's body and blood was more important than the material emblems, . . .

All the meetings Burton held were simplicity itself; no frills, no formulae, no special uniform, no titles other than, 'elder' or 'deacon'. Even funerals, dedication of believers' children, water baptisms and weddings were completely informal. . . . But although he reduced formalities to the absolute minimum, it had to be the Scriptural minimum, and nothing less than the Word declared or the apostles taught. . . .

Thirdly his vision was of an *instructed staff.* New workers were invariably allotted to older ones, he and Mrs. Burton taking a good share. When younger missionaries from other stations visited Mwanza, he missed no opportunity of instructing them by all sorts of interesting means in missionary life, the country, the people and their customs, the language, what to do and what not to do in dealing with the Congolese themselves, with white traders and with Government officials. Not to mention fascinating items of information about birds, beasts and butterflies. . . He loved to teach and had such a charming manner that we all, young and old, never tired of his tales, his folk-lore, his fables and his proverbs. He certainly helped us to understand the people of the country, their fascinating language and background. He saved us from many pitfalls and rid us of wrong ideas about the land in which we had come to work.

He was particularly helpful in regard to the language. By *1923* he had prepared very detailed notes in duplicated form of its structure and vocabulary, and by *1928* a rule was applied in the Mission, which continued until the big evacuation during the war of independence in *1960–61*. This rule said:

1. That no new worker shall use English in any contact with the Congolese or preach through an interpreter after the first welcome meeting, where such was held. (There was no such fuss made at Mwanza itself!)

2. That every new missionary must study the language and pass successfully two written examinations, one after six months and the other after twelve months.

3. That every missionary must make an attempt to preach in public in the local language no later than six months after arriving on the Field. Failing this he or she would be sent home.

All this put people on their mettle; they realised the necessity of speaking the language of the country and the seriousness of their calling. 'No man worth his salt will waste God's money by fooling around,' Willie Burton would say, 'and remember that the saints of God have sacrificed to send you out. Be your best for Jesus!' Down went noses to the grindstone! Out came paper and pencils to jot down every new word and phrase! Every opportunity was seized to try to talk with the Bantu and understand them. Some managed to splutter out a testimony or a sermonette in three months, others just scraped in with something more polished within the six months, but not one missionary failed the stiff examination, though it may have been pretty close!

. . . Burton told us of the surprising richness of the language. In 1915 he had collected 1,500 words, which had been increased to 15,000 by 1920, all of which were in regular use. This latter figure, he said, was double the usual vocabulary of many Bantu tribes and compares more than favourably with the average Englishman's vocabulary. His collections of fables and of 1,800 proverbs are unrivalled and were published by the judicial revue of Katanga (*La révue juridique du Katanga*) as was his 'L'âme Luba' (*The Luban Mind*), a treatise used today as a text book in universities.

Used by permission of Central Africa Missions, 355 Blackpool Road, Preston, Lancashire PR2 3AB, UK.

✺

With mission as a fundamental to Pentecostals, Hodges worked out a theology of Pentecostal mission.

10.5 Melvin L. Hodges, *A Theology of the Church and Its Mission: A Pentecostal Perspective,* Springfield, Missouri: Gospel Publishing House, 1977, pp. 32–6, abridged

Pentecost vital to the Church and its mission

The coming of the Holy Spirit, which was experienced in its fullness on the Day of Pentecost, was anticipated for two reasons. First, it was seen as the fulfilment of long expectations throughout the Old Testament that God would indwell His people (Ezekiel 37.27; cf. 1 Corinthians 6.19; 2 Corinthians 6.16). Second, it was seen as the means through which the knowledge of God would come to the world (Joel 2.28, 29; Acts 2.1–4, 16–18).

J. Herbert Kane observes:

> . . . To the early church, the Holy Spirit was not simply a power to be employed, but a person to be loved, trusted, consulted, and obeyed.[1]

The Feast of Pentecost symbolized the descent of the Spirit

. . . the Feast of Pentecost was not an isolated event but followed in sequence the previously mentioned feasts. In fulfilment, Pentecost is not an isolated experience but depends on the sacrifice of the Son of God at Calvary and His subsequent resurrection.

Without the offering of the Son of God as God's sacrifice for sinful man, there could be no descent of the Holy Spirit. Therefore, the coming of the Spirit on the Day of Pentecost is seen as the fulfilling of God's purpose in Calvary. Calvary is significant because the price for man's redemption was paid. The Resurrection Day was of immense significance because Christ, having risen from the dead, became the Head of the new creation. It was on that day that He inbreathed His resurrection life into the awestruck disciples and said: 'Receive ye the Holy Ghost' (John 20.21). Peter refers back to that day as marking the time of his rebirth unto a lively hope by the resurrection of Jesus from the dead (1 Peter 1.3, 4). Though having been made new men by the resurrection of Jesus from the dead, the disciples

---

[1] Herbert Kane, *Understanding Christian Missions*, Grand Rapids: Baker Book House, 1974, p. 44.

were still commanded to wait for the enduement of the Holy Spirit (Acts 1.4, 5). On the Day of Pentecost He came in power both to fulfil God's purpose in taking full possession of the waiting disciples and also to make them instruments of blessing to the world (1.8). . . .

The presence of God had come closer, dwelling no more in a tabernacle made with hands, but in the human body of His incarnate Son.

God had come closer to man than ever before, but still His full purpose was not yet attained. For this reason, Jesus told the disciples it was better (expedient) for them that He go away, because if He did not go away the Comforter could not come (John 16.7), but if He went away He would pray the Father and He would send them another Comforter that would abide with them forever. At that time He said that He dwelt with them, but He would be in them (John 14.16, 17). So on the Day of Pentecost the great purpose of God dwelling in His people was realized for the first time when the believers 'were all filled with the Holy Ghost' (Acts 2.4). Paul referred to this when he stated that Christians grow up to be part of a holy temple for the habitation of God through the Spirit (Ephesians 2.19–22).

It is one of the tragedies today that many Christians stop with Calvary and rejoice in sins forgiven; others see the victory of a new life, as they partake of Christ's resurrection. God's purpose, however, is that the road that begins at Calvary be followed through the resurrection and on to Pentecost, so that the believer's body becomes a temple of the Holy Ghost, filled with and baptized in the Holy Spirit. John the Baptist in giving testimony concerning Christ emphasized these two points: He was the Lamb of God that would take away the sins of the world (John 1.29), and He was the baptizer in the Holy Spirit (John 1.33). Jesus was insistent that the disciples wait until the Day of Pentecost before they begin their ministry to the world (Luke 24.46–49; Acts 1.4, 5, 8).

Pentecost – essential to missionary outreach

Christ had given the disciples the Great Commission. He had explained that they were to preach the gospel to all the nations and the power of the Holy Spirit would come upon them for this purpose. The missionary endeavour of preaching the gospel to the whole world could not be carried out simply as loyal obedience to the commands of Jesus. The apostles and early Christians needed an inward impulse – they must become co-labourers with God and find an inward compulsion for the fulfilling of this command. This dynamic for world evangelism came on the Day of Pentecost. Roland Allen said:

Acts does not begin with 'the Lord Jesus said go'; but with 'ye shall receive power and ye shall be witnesses.' St Luke fixes our attention *not on an external voice but upon an internal Spirit* [italics ours].

The Spirit given to the apostles is thus seen to have created in them an internal necessity to preach the gospel.

Harry R. Boer states:

The idea of Pentecostal endowment of the Church with power for her missionary labours makes Pentecost contemporaneous, as it were, with all the ages of the Church's history. The Spirit is the continuing dynamic in the life of the witnessing church and of her witnessing servants.

He points out that even Peter would not have gone to the Gentiles simply on the basis of the Great Commission, but required a special revelation and direction of the Holy Spirit to accomplish God's purpose toward the Gentiles.

The contemporary Pentecostal movement and missions

Perhaps at this point it would not be amiss to answer an oft-repeated question as to why the Pentecostal movement is so successful in its missionary labours while other sincere missionary efforts have not always enjoyed the same success. It can be pointed out that according to the Church Growth Study Team, which gave their report in the volume entitled *Latin American Church Growth*, 63 per cent of all Protestants in Latin America are Pentecostals. Many have inquired as to the reasons for this. No doubt the fact that most Pentecostal missionary efforts are among the poor has something to do with it. God may use sociological and economic factors to prepare a land for greater receptivity to the gospel. Nevertheless, Pentecostals would affirm without hesitation that the reason for progress in missions is that the Pentecostal people endeavour both in preaching and experience to give the place to the Holy Spirit which the New Testament indicates should be given.

The Pentecostal missionary movement is prospering for the very reason that it is Pentecostal. Some recent writers have attempted to show that the results Pentecostal churches experienced on the foreign field could be achieved by simply adopting some of the practices which are more appealing to the masses without necessarily becoming 'Pentecostal' in experience. It is questionable that one could find a Pentecostal who would agree with this premise.

The Day of Pentecost

The Day of Pentecost is seen by all Christians as of special significance for the Church. First, because it might be considered the Church's official birthday, for from this time on there was no need to wait for anything further in the plan of God to be accomplished before the Church could launch out on its mission. Second, it was on this day that the Holy Spirit was poured out in His fullness, and thus fulfilled the promises given by the prophets, John the Baptist, and Jesus himself.

Used by permission of Mrs Lois Hodges.

Having seen apparent failure in his mission career in Nigeria, Kraft made a paradigm shift in his missiology once he encountered the power of the Holy Spirit. However, he affirms commitment and truth encounters have to be essential for true conversions. He is Professor of Anthropology and Intercultural Communication at Fuller Theological Seminary.

10.6   C. H. Kraft, 'What kind of Encounters do we Need in our Christian Witness?' in R. D. Winters and S. C. Hawthorne (eds), *Perspectives on the World Christian Movement*, Carlisle: Paternoster Press, pp. C71–8, abridged

What kind of encounters do we need in our Christian witness?

. . . My task in this article is to offer an approach to power encounter that is biblically balanced with two other encounters that evangelicals have always emphasized.

The basic concept

The term 'power encounter' comes from missionary anthropologist Alan Tippett. In his 1971 book, *People Movements in Southern Polynesia*, Tippett observed that in the south Pacific the early acceptance of the gospel usually occurred when there was an 'encounter' demonstrating that the power of God is greater that that of the local pagan deity. This was usually accompanied by a desecration of the symbol(s) of the traditional deity by its priest or priestess, who then declared that he or she rejected the deity's power, pledged allegiance to the true God, and vowed to depend on God alone for protection and spiritual power.

. . . More recently the term has been used more broadly to include healings, deliverances or any other 'visible, practical demonstration that Jesus Christ is more powerful than the spirits powers or false gods worshipped or feared by the members of a given people group'.[1] The concept of 'taking territory' from the enemy for God's kingdom is seen as basic to such encounters.

According to this view, Jesus' entire ministry was a massive power confrontation between God and the enemy. The ministry of the apostles and the church of succeeding generations is seen as the continuing exercise of the 'authority and power over all demons and all diseases' given by Jesus to his followers (Luke). Contemporary stories about such encounters come from China, Argentina, Europe, the Muslim world, and nearly everywhere else where the church is growing rapidly.

Tippett[2] observed that most of the world's people are power-oriented and respond to Christ most readily through power demonstrations. Gospels about faith, love, forgiveness, and the other facts of Christianity are not likely have nearly the impact on such people as the demonstrations of spiritual power. My own experience confirms Tippett's thesis. Therefore, cross-cultural workers ought to learn as much as possible about the place of power encounter in Jesus' ministry and ours.

Additional encounters

. . . We need to focus on the close relationship in the New Testament between these three encounters. Here's an outline that will help:

JESUS CHRIST CONFRONTS SATAN

1. *Concerning power.* This results in power encounters to release people from satanic captivity and bring them into freedom in Jesus Christ.

2. *Concerning commitment.* This results in commitment encounters to rescue people from wrong commitments and bring them into relationship to Jesus Christ.

3. *Concerning truth.* This results in truth encounters to counter error and to bring people to correct understandings about Jesus Christ.

---

[1] C. Peter Wagner, *How to Have a Healing Ministry* (Ventura, Calif.: Regal Books, 1988, p. 150. See also John Wimber, *Power Evangelism* (New York: Harper-Row, 1985), pp. 29–32; and Charles Kraft, *Christianity With Power* (Ann Arbor: Servant, 1989).

[2] A. Tippett, *People Movements in Southern Polynesia* (Chicago, Ill.: Moody Press, 1971), p. 81.

Throughout the world many Christians who have committed themselves to Jesus Christ, and who have embraced much Christian truth, have not given up their pre-Christian commitment to and practice of what we call spiritual power. The powers of darkness which they formerly followed have not been confronted and defeated by the power of Jesus. So they live with a 'dual allegiance' and a syncretistic understanding of truth. Therefore, some mistakenly assume that if they confront people with healing and deliverance campaigns to show them Christ's power, they will turn to him in droves. They assume that those who experience God's healing power will automatically commit themselves to the source of that power.

However, I know of several such campaigns that have produced few, if any, lasting conversions. Why not? Because little attention was paid to leading the people from an experience of Jesus' power to a commitment to him. These people are accustomed to accepting power from any source. Therefore, they see no greater compulsion to commit themselves to Jesus than to any of the other sources of power they regularly consult.

I believe Jesus expects power demonstrations to be as crucial to our ministries as they were to his (Luke 9.1, 2). However, any approach that advocates power encounter without giving adequate attention to the other two encounters – commitment and truth – is not biblically balanced. That many people who saw or experienced power events during Jesus' ministry did not turn to him in faith should alert us to the inadequacy of power demonstrations alone as a total evangelistic strategy.

. . . The nature and aims of the encounters

The three encounters – power, commitment, and truth – are not the same; they are each intended to initiate a process crucial to the Christian experience aimed at a specific goal.

1. The concern of the truth encounter is understanding. The vehicle of that encounter is teaching.

2. The concern of the commitment encounter is relationship. The vehicle of that encounter is witness.

3. The concern of the power encounter is freedom. Its vehicle is spiritual warfare.

Truth and understanding have a lot to do with the mind; commitment and relationship rest primarily in the will; and freedom is largely experienced emotionally.

. . . A diagram of what I have been saying about the nature and aim of truth encounters looks like this:

START		PROCESS		AIM
Awareness	→	Leading to knowledge	→	Understanding of truth

The initial commitment encounter leads a person into a relationship with God. Through successive encounters between our will and God's, we grow in intimacy with and likeness to him, as we submit to his will and practice intimate association with him. Initial commitment and the relationship that proceeds from it are tightly linked to truth, both because they are developed within truth encounter and because a relationship with God is the true reason for human existence.

Implied in the commitment encounter is the cultivation of the fruits of the Holy Spirit, especially love toward God and man. We are to turn from love of (or commitment to) the world that is under the control of the evil one (1 John 5.19) to God who loved the world and gave himself for it. As we grow in our relationship with him, we become more like him, conforming to the image of Christ (Rom. 8.29).

The commitment encounter looks like this:

START		PROCESS		AIM
Commitment to Jesus	→	Growth in relationship	→	Character of Jesus Christ

Power encounters contribute a different dimension to Christian experience. They focus on freedom from the enemy's captivity. Satan is the blinder (2 Cor. 4.4), restricter, hinderer, crippler – the enemy who attempts to keep people from commitment to God and truth. Though he works on all human faculties, the enemy seems particularly interested in crippling people emotionally. If people are to move into commitment to Christ they need emotional freedom.

The power encounter process may be diagrammed as follows:

START		PROCESS		AIM
Healing, deliverance, etc.	→	Increasing freedom	→	Victory over Satan

For the one who is healed, delivered, blessed, or otherwise freed from the enemy's grip, the major payoff is freedom. However, for an observer, the impact is likely to be quite different. If properly interpreted, the encounter communicates basic truths about God's power and love. The observer sees that God is worthy of his trust because he is willing and able to free people from Satan's destructive hold, as we see in this diagram:

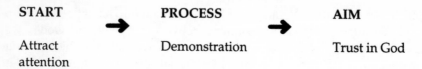

START	→	**PROCESS**	→	**AIM**
Attract attention		Demonstration		Trust in God

Although we do not call them power encounters, our demonstrations of acceptance, forgiveness, and peace in troubled times – plus a number of other Christian virtues – play the same role of attracting attention and leading people to trust God. These all witness to the presence of a loving God willing to give abundant life and bring release from the enemy.

The encounters work together

Our missionary witness needs to use all three encounters together, not separately, as we can see in this three-part circle: . . .

. . . The diagram below shows the interworkings of these three aspects of Christian life and witness in more detail.

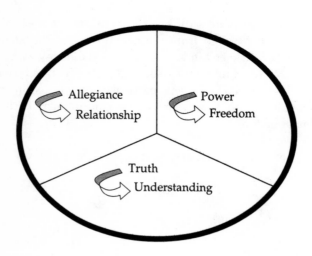

Truth Understanding

There are three stages in the process, . . .

	START	NEED	PROCESS	RESULT
STAGE I	Satanic captivity	Freedom to understand	Power encounter	Commitment to Jesus Christ
	Ignorance/ Error	Enough commitment to understanding	Truth encounter	
	Non-Christian commitment	Challenge to commit to Christ	Commitment encounter	
STAGE II	Commitment to Jesus Christ	Spiritual warfare to provide protection, healing, blessing, deliverance	Power encounter	Growing relationship to God and his people
		Teaching	Truth encounter	
		Challenges to commitment	Commitment encounter	
STAGE III	Growing relationship to God and his people	Authoritative Prayer	Power encounter	Witness to those at the beginning of Stage I
		Teaching	Truth encounter	
		Challenges to commitment	Commitment encounter	

. . . Beyond our own Christian growth lies our witness. At the end of his ministry, Jesus taught much about his relationship to his followers and theirs to each other (e.g. John 14–16) as well as about the authority and power he would give them (Acts 1.8). He carefully related power and authority to witness (e.g. Matt. 28.19, 20; Mark 16.15–18; Acts 1.8).

He told the disciples to wait for spiritual power before they embarked on witness (Luke 24.49; Acts 1.4) just as Jesus Himself had waited to be empowered at his own baptism (Luke 3.21, 22). We are not fully equipped to witness without the freedom-bringing, truth-revealing power of the Holy Spirit (Acts 1.8).

. . . As we survey the world's mission fields, we find many places where Christians still have dual allegiances. Many believers, including pastors, still go to Shamans, priests, and other spirit mediums. At the same time, charismatic and Pentecostal churches specializing in power encounter evangelism are growing rapidly in most parts of the world.

. . . We encounter commitment to other gods and spirits with the challenge to commitment to Jesus Christ. But when the people need healing, or seek fertility or when there isn't enough rain, or there are floods, too often our answer is the hospital, the school, and modern agriculture. We provide secular answers to what to them (and the Bible) are basically spiritual issues.

We have encountered Satan's counterfeit 'truths' with the exciting truths of Christianity, but often in such an abstract way that our hearers have seen little verification of that truth in our lives. In most cases, both missionaries and the local Christians are more impressed with scientific than with biblical truth.

The missing element for them and for us is the 'third arrow,' genuine New Testament power, the continual experience of the presence of God, who every day does things the world calls miracles. We must encounter Satan's counterfeit power with God's effective power. Truth and commitment alone won't do. We need all three kinds of biblical encounters, if we are to succeed in our world missionary communication.

Used by permission of the author, Dr C. Kraft, Fuller Theological Seminary, School of World Missions, 135 N. Oakland Ave., Pasadena, CA 91182, USA.

PART 4
ISSUES

W. K. Kay, Introduction

Excerpts within this section have been chosen to illustrate a range of issues facing the Pentecostal and charismatic movements. The first two concern pacifism, which was part and parcel of Pentecostalism from the very beginning (11.1; 11.2). This was not simply a reaction to the 1914–18 war although, after the war had taken place, the revulsion against killing within the trenches made it easier to restate the position. Since the 1920s and the drafting of the American Assemblies of God's minute indicating pacifism, there has been a gradual adjustment so that Pentecostal chaplains are found within the armed forces in the United States and there is far less emphasis upon opposition to war.[1] The issue is whether, in the current climate of terrorism and counter-terrorist measures, pacifism is a historical curiosity or whether it should be revived.

The second issue, represented by the 1927 article written by Roswell Flower, is one that relates to the self-knowledge of the Pentecostal movement and, by implication, of the charismatic movement (12.1). This 1927 assessment argued that it was imperative for Pentecostalism not to forget the cross of Christ, the discomfort, sacrifice and willingness to accept slander and marginalization that were the hidden strengths of early Pentecostals. How should Pentecostals and charismatics see themselves in the twenty-first century? How should they understand their history and identity?

In the middle of the twentieth century, David du Plessis (1905–87) linked ecumenism with the Pentecostal charismatic movement (13.1). His perspective was a unique one and, towards the end of his life, he worked hard to establish unity among different strands and streams of Christianity. He did not see the Pentecostal and charismatic movements in opposition to the ecumenical movement but rather as motivated and actuated by the same Spirit. This is a view that would be contentious in some Pentecostal and charismatic circles. The issue is still to be resolved.

In 13.2 Michael Harper surveys the Pentecostal and charismatic scenes and assesses their strengths and weaknesses and likely futures. He despairs of the mainline denominations, 'the enemy is at the gate if not already within the camp'. While commending the orthodoxy of the Roman Catholic and the vitality of the independent or new churches, his hopes for the western churches rest in epochal changes like those that followed the fall of the Roman empire or the Reformation.

[1] Edith Blumhofer (1985), *Assemblies of God: A Popular History*, Springfield, Mo.: Radiant Books, p. 92.

In contrast to Harper's unsentimental judgement on the Church are the hopes of the 'faith movement'. The so-called 'prosperity gospel' was associated with the healing evangelists in the post-1945 era. Kenneth Copeland (14.1) writes about the financial pressures of his TV ministry and the benefits of prayerful monetary giving as a way of confronting 'the spirit of lack'. Copeland, writing from a northern American context, presumes that the main difficulties facing his partners are from the pressures of modern life; Harper presumes that the whole of the western Church is in dire straits and only to be rescued by divine action.

Although there have been criticisms of prosperity teaching, the issue is not as clear-cut as might seem to be the case.[2] On one hand, the first-century Church was poor and Christianity does not immediately, by a series of acts of faith, lead poverty-stricken individuals or countries into a rich land of milk and honey. On the other hand, the diligence and self-discipline provided by Christian conversion does tend to provide, in the long-term, economic benefits – a discovery, named 'redemption lift', made by Wesley as a result of the Methodist revival. So to what extent, if at all, is it right to associate Christianity with material gain? And how can one separate New Testament promises of material provision (Matt. 6.30–33) from Old Testament blessings of material riches (Deut. 28.12; Ps. 112.3)?

Two excerpts provide accounts of the role of women (15.1; 15.2). There are still the divergences of opinion between authoritative and patriarchal groups within the Pentecostal and charismatic movements and those who see Scripture as encouraging openness to the ministry of women. The issue has the potential to raise substantial disputes. It is certainly notable that in the early days of the Pentecostal movement women evangelists (e.g. M. W. Etter, Aimee McPherson) were much more prominent than they are today. In theory the theology of the Pentecostal and charismatic movements, except in some limited groups and networks, does not restrict women in ministry but, in practice, women rarely have nationally prominent roles. The question is whether the issue has reached a pragmatic equilibrium or whether there are new developments to come.

An excerpt from *The Cross and the Switchblade* illustrates a Pentecostal way of dealing with social concern (16.1). David Wilkerson's extraordinary ministry came to prominence in the 1960s. It was of international importance and his book sold millions of copies. It brought the theology of the baptism in the Holy Spirit to wide notice. The excerpt here shows how Wilkerson believed the Holy Spirit could play a direct and active role in

---

[2] A. Brandon, (1987), *Health and Wealth*, Eastbourne: Kingsway; D. R. McConnell, (1988), *A Different Gospel: A Historical and Biblical Analysis of the Modern Faith Movement*, Peabody, Mass.: Hendrickson.

helping young people free themselves from the power of drugs. His success raises the issue of the relationship between the gospel-preaching Pentecostal and charismatic movement and the social work that is more commonly associated with liberal Christianity.

Television evangelism, particularly in the United States, assumed an enormously high profile in the 1980s. Christian television stations made superstars of evangelists and appeared to establish them with national status so that their pronouncements became politically important, as in the case of Pat Robertson, who became credible enough to seek Republican nomination for the US presidency. The fall of Jim and Tammy Bakker, and subsequently of Jimmy Swaggart, were memorable events, both because of the public perception that evangelists were immoral and because the cause of Christian broadcasting was set back many years. The Executive Presbytery of the American Assemblies of God dealt with the matter with dignity and sincerity and the excerpt illustrates the difficulty that Christian groups have maintaining pastoral care of ministers who outgrow their denominational beginnings (17.1).

Baptism in the Spirit has an unexpected consequence. It makes people aware of spiritual evil, and the excerpts in Chapter 18 demonstrate unresolved issues within the Pentecostal and charismatic movements. On the one side, du Plessis argues against exorcism since the cross of Christ is a victory over all evil (18.1). On the other, Don Basham provides an example of exorcism and the successful cure of someone who did not respond to conventional treatment (18.2). Terry Law (b. 1943) advocates defeating such spirits with an attitude and verbal expression of praise to God that brings faith and perception of God's wisdom (18.3).

These issues of exorcism are linked with spiritual warfare. An excerpt from G. Otis, Jnr, illustrates the notion of territorial spirits against which spiritual warfare must be waged (18.4). Those who argue for this practice point to the success of their methods over large unevangelized areas or cities.[3] Thus some Pentecostals and charismatics believe that spiritual warfare is a crucial reality; others, like Andrew Walker, believe that it is, at best, a distraction and, at worst, a deception (18.5).[4]

A dramatic outbreak of charismatic phenomena occurred within the

---

[3] C. P. Wagner, 'What Are Their Names?' pp. 48–9, and J. Dawson, 'Seventh Time Around', pp. 136ff., both from C. P. Wagner (ed.), *Territorial Spirits*, Chichester: Sovereign World, 1991.

[4] See also T. Smail, A. Walker and N. Wright, '"Revelation Knowledge" and Knowledge of Revelation: The Faith Movement and the Question of Heresy', *Journal of Pentecostal Theology* 5 (1994), pp. 57–77; T. Smail, A. Walker, and N. Wright (1995), *Charismatic Renewal*, London: SPCK.

Toronto Airport Christian Fellowship in the early 1990s. Two positive excerpts deal with the phenomena suggesting that, at heart, it was a revelation of God's love and that the physical manifestations – falling over, lying on the carpet, laughing – were peripheral to the main experience (19.1; 19.2).

Two excerpts deal with Pentecostal communities. There is a case for arguing that the early Church in the book of Acts that is used as a model for Pentecostal doctrine could also offer an example of community living. It is therefore not surprising to find charismatic groups that are also happy to pool their resources, break down individualism, equalize incomes and operate on a community basis. In 20.1 Noel Stanton gives an account of Europe's oldest existing charismatic community with which the Jesus Army church network is associated.[5] In 20.2 a brief piece outlines the basis of the Mother of God community in Gaithersburg. Cardinal Suenens provides an overview of the charismatic movement from his perspective in 1978 and finds community living and ecumenicism worthy of comment, though he is also clear in rejecting classical Pentecostal interpretations of baptism in the Holy Spirit, 'there is of course no question of a super-baptism . . .' (20.3).

The last excerpts offer insight into the megachurches that are still growing phenomenally; cell church principles in Korea are now being adapted into the Latin American G12 pattern, where every leader evangelizes and trains up to twelve people and then these new people themselves become leaders of new groups, and so on. In London Colin Dye has been taking his numerous satellite churches of the London City Church into a G12 format (21.1).

All the issues selected here could be seen as growing points for the Pentecostal and charismatic movement in the future. Some may well be resolved and the variety of positions may become acceptable without difficulty or rancour. Other issues may simply fade away even though they represent matters which, at the moment, raise questions without obvious answers.

---

[5] K. Newell, (1997), 'Charismatic Communitarianism and the Jesus Fellowship', in S. Hunt, M. Hamilton and T. Walter (eds), *Charismatic Christianity: Sociological Perspectives*, Basingstoke: Macmillan.

11   Pacifism

❧❧❧

Many of the early Pentecostals were pacifists in 1914–18. Pentecostal
denominations emerged around this time partly because pacifists did
not wish to be led by those who had supported war.

11.1   Arthur Sydney Booth-Clibborn, *Blood Against*
Blood, New York: Charles Cook, 1907

In war all things are inverted. Many a vice becomes a virtue. Lying and
spying is part of the patriotic work for which Christian governments
secretly pay great sums of money to individuals of other nations, while
ready to shoot individuals of their own nationality for similar services
rendered to the 'enemy.'

The stabbing and shooting which is wrong to the individual in private
life, becomes right in international quarrels. Reason must submit to a
thousand wrenches, and accept a whole education in false philosophy and
specious sophistry before it can accommodate itself to war, its principles,
its scenes and associations.

Here, nearly all the laws of social life are suspended, the ties of home
violated, the very idea of humanity being one great family is denied, in the
obligation laid upon husbands and fathers to slay other husbands and
fathers, and thus destroy humanity in its very centre – the home.

The very order of age and youth are inverted: as Herodotus said and
John Bright repeated with so much force, 'In peace the sons bury their
fathers, in war the fathers bury their sons.'

War is therefore a mass of hideous contradictions, and an outrage upon
reason and common sense.

There are no contradictions in true Christianity. War is therefore
anti-Christian in all its forms. The testimony of the fathers of the Church
was unanimous in this respect, and in Reformation days, Erasmus boldly
repeated that testimony, saying, 'Christ in disarming Peter, disarmed
every soldier.' 'The weapons of our warfare are not carnal, but spiritual,'
said Paul, in describing the central principle of the overcoming of evil
in the world. The words of Christ 'Love your enemies' are absolute. They
embody his description of the spirit animating the children of God on

earth, as opposed to that controlling the children of the world. And why? 'That ye may be the children of your Father who is in heaven, who maketh his sun to shine upon the evil and on the good, and sendeth rain on the just and on the unjust.' And in describing the heathen – the unregenerate – he said: 'If ye love them who love you, what reward have ye? Do not even the heathen love the same?' The difference then between the heathen and the Christian is an essential difference in spirit and disposition and in the means employed to remedy the evils in the world: to the heathen it is carnal power and worldly war, expressed in hatred and ending in death; to the Christian it is spiritual power and gospel war, expressed in love and ending in life.

In the one, man sacrifices his neighbour and sheds blood; in the other, man sacrifices himself and lets his own blood be shed. In the one it is Cain; in the other it is Abel.

In the one it is apostolic warfare; in the other it is the warfare of apostates.

War is too positive, too definite a thing to admit of any half ways or half measures. It is either from above or from below. If it is from heaven it must be absolutely heavenly, and nothing hellish in it. If it is from hell, it cannot be regarded as a heavenly obligation upon Christians, upon whom all true obligations are either of heavenly origin or of no authority whatever.

War cannot be successfully performed without deception and lying in a hundred forms. Protestant nations admit this in the politico-military domain as a necessity, while refusing to admit it in other spheres. They recognize spying and falsehood to be necessary adjuncts of war. They therefore adopt in this respect the principle of the Jesuit that the end justifies the means. This alone classifies war immediately. It forces it back within the pale of the apostate spurious form of Christianity represented in one of its culminating forms by the Church of Rome, whose Pope had, till recently, soldiers and a warship.

One of the signs of the apostasy in the book of Revelation was that the wicked woman arrayed in scarlet – the false bride of Christ – was seated upon the beast – the beast of carnal force, and national power. The power of the gospel message to the world and its authority upon mankind must have therefore been seriously reduced wherever Christian Churches or Associations have sanctioned war. If we were to inquire to what degree this injury has been caused to the gospel by its own advocates, an answer seems to be forthcoming in the case of the first evangelist, Saint Peter, previous to his receiving the baptism of the Holy Ghost.

He cut off the ear of the enemy. We may therefore conclude that sword bearing Christianity has only a one-eared audience, and that the power of the gospel is reduced by its advocates by at least *one half!*

Here American Assemblies of God demonstrate the dilemma for pacifist Christians. They want to show that pacifism can coexist with patriotism.

11.2 Minutes of the General Council of the Assemblies of God, held 21–27 September 1920 in Springfield, Missouri

RESOLUTION CONCERNING THE ATTITUDE OF THE GENERAL COUNCIL of the Assemblies of God toward any Military Service which Involves the Actual Participation in the Destruction of Human Life.

While recognizing Human Government as of Divine ordination and affirming our unswerving loyalty to the Government of the United States, nevertheless we are constrained to define our position with reference to the taking of human life.

Whereas, in the Constitutional Resolution adopted at the Hot Springs General Council, April 1–10, 1914, we plainly declare the Holy Scriptures to be the all-sufficient rule of faith and practice, and whereas, the Scriptures deal plainly with the obligations and relations of humanity, setting forth the principles of 'Peace on earth, good will toward men' (Luke 2.14): and

Whereas, we, as followers of the Lord Jesus Christ, the Prince of Peace, believe in implicit obedience to the Divine commands and precepts which instruct us to 'Follow peace with all men' (Heb. 12.14); 'Thou shalt not kill' (Exod. 20.13); 'Resist not evil' (Matt. 5.39); 'Love your enemies' (Matt. 5.44); etc., and

Whereas, these and other Scriptures have always been accepted and interpreted by our churches as prohibiting Christians from shedding blood or taking human life;

Therefore, we, as a body of Christians, while purposing to fulfil all the obligations of loyal citizenship, are nevertheless constrained to declare we cannot conscientiously participate in war and armed resistance which involves the actual destruction of human life, since this is contrary to our view of the clear teachings of the inspired Word of God, which is the sole basis of our faith.

EXPRESSION OF LOYALTY TO THE GOVERNMENT

Resolved, That the General Council hereby declares its unswerving loyalty to our Government and to its Chief Executive, President Wilson, and that we hereby restate our fixed purpose to assist in every way morally possible consistent with our faith, in bringing the present 'World War' to a successful conclusion.

Bylaws, XX. MILITARY SERVICE

As a Movement we affirm our loyalty to the government of the United States in war or peace.

We shall continue to insist, as we have historically, on the right of each member to choose for himself whether to declare his position as a combatant, a noncombatant, or a conscientious objector.

Used by permission of The Flower Pentecostal Heritage Center, Springfield, Missouri, USA.

12 Generations

Roswell Flower, an honoured and long-serving member of American Assemblies of God, looks back at the early beginnings of Pentecostalism and detects a sea change in the mid-1920s. The early radicalism was in danger of being lost. His main call, however, is to the cross and to a willingness to maintain Pentecostal distinctiveness.

12.1　J. Roswell Flower, 'The Present Position of Pentecost', *Redemption Tidings* 3.10, 1927, pp. 4–6

It has been a real burden on my heart that we might get a glimpse of the present situation in Pentecost, that we might know just where we stand. I believe that Pentecost is facing a real crisis at the present time. A crisis is not new in the history of the church. There have been crises before – lots of them; but we have a particular advantage in that we can look back over the world's history and see those high points which stand out like a beacon on a mountain. We can be so guided and helped by those things that we can avoid the pitfalls that others have fallen into.

The crisis

What about Pentecost? It is facing a tremendous crisis. We need to wake up and know just where we are. There have been three great periods in the Pentecostal movement. Pentecost was in existence in 1900, but it did not receive its impetus until 1906 when the outpouring came down there in Azusa Street in Los Angeles. From there it spread all over the world. Before that, there was a strong movement in Oklahoma, Kansas, and Texas. We find results of that strong movement still in existence. There are a number still with us who received the Baptism in the Spirit with speaking in tongues away back in 1901. Finally the Holy Spirit was outpoured down there in Azusa Street. It was more than a doctrine. If it had been merely a new doctrine, a new interpretation of the Scriptures, Pentecost would have been confined to that quarter and never would have gotten out of it. We need to know the Scriptures, but it takes more than that. There is something else besides the teaching. In this case the teaching brought action, it

brought people down on their knees before God, and there was a phenomenon produced. People received the Baptism in the Holy Spirit and fire,
with Pentecostal manifestations, and there was no question about it. It was
unusual, striking, different; and people flocked together that they might
see, and hear, and experience for themselves.

I never will forget how the first man came from Azusa Street in the
spring of 1907, walked into a Christian and Missionary Alliance Assembly
in Indianapolis, and told the assembly there that Pentecost had come, and
that he had received it, and he spoke a few words in tongues. It was just
like throwing a bombshell in there. That was just what all those hungry
people were wanting. They wanted more than teaching; they wanted
Pentecost. And it was not long until the Day of Pentecost had fully come to
Indianapolis and hundreds of people received the Baptism.

The movement was characterized by certain things. People were not
afraid to pray, and they were not afraid to fast. I myself went through three
days and nights of prayer in the church without going home or going out
for food. If such a thing should happen now we would think it most
strange. Sleep meant nothing to us. Many a night I have gone home at two,
three, or four in the morning. We did not know what God was going to do.
He did something different almost every day. We had great expectation;
we were ready for anything that happened, and it usually happened. If
you expect God to do things, He is going to do them. If you don't expect
Him to work, He probably won't. There was no formalism in those days.
We did not know very much about the workings of the Spirit, but our
hearts were open for what God might do. And that condition continued for
practically seven years.

At the end of the seven years there came a change in Pentecost and the
second phase of the work was entered into; and that phase was a sifting of
doctrine that came in 1914. Seven years of plenty, then seven years of
trouble. In 1914 papers began to appear telling of an issue which involved
fundamental doctrines of the church; it was a serious thing, and the sifting
was on; and for a time the whole of Pentecost was unsettled, everything
was shaking. We did not know where we were or what we believed, and
there was strife and division and difference [over the nature of the Trinity
– eds]. Families were divided and assembles split up; all kinds of things
happened. We could not help it; we were in it. Thank God that that day is
just about past, and those honest men who had gone off into those things
are coming out of them.

Avoiding reproach

Now we are in a new stage, and in this new stage we have a new condition. They believe fundamentally as we do. They believe in the Baptism of the Spirit with speaking in tongues. But somehow or other there is a feeling we are too radical, that we have raised up barriers which are hindering us in the development of the work, that the claims of Pentecost are too great. There is really a spirit present to avoid the cross. Let me mention what the cross means. Paul said he gloried in the reproach of the cross. The reason the cross was a reproach in those days was because that when a man was nailed to a cross he was a malefactor in the eyes of the world. And the very idea of taking a man who had been crucified, had been slain as a criminal, and holding him up as the Saviour of the world, was a most inconsistent thing from the standpoint of reason. So when the disciples preached the doctrine of the cross, it was foolishness, it was a stumbling-block. In a large measure the world now recognizes the doctrine of the cross, and the cross itself is no longer an offence. . . .

At the present time we have Modernism on the one hand and Fundamentalism on the other. Between the two there are those who take middle ground and deplore the battle going on between the two extreme factions. Modernism does away with the supernatural; Fundamentalism believes in the supernatural, provided it is in the past, but it does not believe in it in the present. We have a parallel between these movements in the Sadducees and Pharisees of Christ's day. The Pharisees believed in the supernatural, but it was in the past. The Sadducees did not believe in anything supernatural. Now then, Pentecost has come to the kingdom for such a time as this. Just as Mordecai told Queen Esther she had come to the kingdom for just such a time; so we have come to the kingdom for such a time as this. Pentecost is in a peculiar place. We can say like Paul, 'I am a Fundamentalist of the Fundamentalists, of the strictest sect of the Fundamentalists am I one.' But that is not enough. Paul was more than a Pharisee. The Pharisees believed in the resurrection, they believed in the supernatural, but it was in the past. Paul believed in it in the past and in the present too. We are Fundamentalists, but we are more than that. We believe in the supernatural right now. We believe that what God did, He can do again; and what he can do again He is doing; praise His name! So, like Esther, we are in a peculiar place.

Now then, are we going to do as all others have done? Are we going to seek to avoid the cross, taking the position that if we are to get the dear church people in we must be careful how we proclaim our message, we must be careful lest someone say 'Hallelujah!' in our meetings? And if someone falls under the power of the Spirit at our altar, cover them up quickly or else pick them up and carry them out to a back room lest the church people stumble over them and not understand? When God was doing mighty things in the earth those sort of things were happening; devils were cast out, the sick were healed, people were receiving the Baptism of the Holy Ghost and were prostrated under the power of God for days at a time, and there were visions and thunderings and lightnings and earthquakes, buildings were filled with the glory of God, till you would go around on tiptoe lest you might make a noise, because of God's presence there.

Avoiding the cross is our temptation today. Many a mighty man of God has fallen into the snare. They are afraid of reproach, of what the people might say; afraid to have something different and distinct, which will create division. They feel there is too much cross in Pentecost.

Pentecost is dispensational. We cannot understand it unless we look at it from a dispensational standpoint. This is the time of the Latter Rain. God has raised us up for such a time as this. May God help us yield to the Spirit, to get the vision. And when we see this modern trend of modification, of letting down, of putting the cross away, let us put our foot down on it and lend our influence towards the hot, spiritual movings of God on His people. We do not have to be a bigot to be true to this testimony. Some people think they cannot be true to their testimony unless their hand is against everybody. We don't have to do that. The Spirit of Christ is big and generous and kind and free. We can meet people on their own ground without compromising. We can lend them a helping hand and give them a cheery word without compromising our position. I have a letter from a Methodist missionary in which he refers to a Pentecostal missionary and says, 'He is perfectly sincere and honest, but I don't see eye to eye with him and I can't get near him. He goes his own way and won't have anything to do with us; he ignores us. If he acts free with us he feels he will be compromising his position. Why can't he be man enough to meet us half way on things that would be a mutual benefit to both of us?' That man is hindering his ministry. If he showed a freer spirit he might win the other for God and Pentecost. We can be uncompromising in our attitude toward the Scriptures and Pentecost, and yet at the same time be generous and kind. The Lord help us.

Used by permission of Assemblies of God Publishing, Nottingham, UK.

13 Ecumenism

❧ ❧

Mr Pentecost, as du Plessis was known worldwide, broke natural, denominational bounds to meet and encourage those 'spirit-filled' believers across denominations; this 'Pentecostal experience' was the answer to schisms.

13.1 David J. du Plessis, *The Renewal of Christianity Must Be both Charismatic and Ecumenical*, Oakland, California, *c.* 1975

An Ecumenical Ministry

According to Acts 2.17–18, Peter declared, 'And it shall come to pass in the last days, saith God, I will pour out of My Spirit (charismatic), upon all flesh (ecumenical) and your sons and daughters (male and female, youth), shall prophesy . . . And on My servants and on My handmaidens (male and female, labour) I will pour out in those days of My Spirit: and they shall prophesy.' In Joel's days such things had never happened nor would such things even be permitted.

The Levitical tribe was the ministering tribe and even a Levite had to be 30 years old before he could minister. The women had no say at all. Slaves did not have a say in matters of worship. Only in a culture where youth and labour played a prominent part could it be proper for them to be recognized in prophecy. Furthermore it would have to be a culture where male and female enjoy equal rights.

Joel did not say 'Last days' but used the word 'afterward'. It seems clear that it means 'after Israel had become a free nation again.' This came to pass in 1948 after World War II, when nations and cultures had changed in many respects. This also happened almost universally because national barriers tumbled and national customs changed. Another great event in 1948 was the founding of the World Council of Churches in Amsterdam, in an attempt by Protestantism to become more ecumenical.

In the church of the first century, it was the Holy Spirit that had compelled the church to become ecumenical when Peter was persuaded to go to the house of Cornelius, the Roman officer, a Gentile. To the Church in Jerusalem, Peter declared, 'The Spirit bade me go' (Acts 11.12).

So after ten years, it was the Holy Spirit that broke the racial barriers by sending Peter to Cornelius. Then some disciples began to minister to the Grecians in Antioch where the disciples were first called Christians. This caused just as many problems in the church of those days as the ecumenical charismatic movement is causing in modern day Christianity. But they only had national and cultural problems to contend with. In our day we have both national and cultural as well as denominational and traditional problems to contend with. Only the Holy Spirit can overcome these problems.

Charismatic unity

The birth of the church was by 'receiving' the Spirit (Acts 2.38); the extension of the church is by 'receiving' the Spirit (Acts 10.47); the unity of the church is created by and depends on the Holy Spirit (Eph. 4.3, 13).

Early in this century, the Holy Spirit began to 'reprove' Christianity for being so divided. The consequence was the desire to seek unity. The historic Protestant bodies responded by forming the World Council of Churches. The schismatic bodies in Protestantism responded by forming the World Evangelical Fellowship. The Pentecostals responded by calling a Pentecostal World Conference. The Lord saw and He heard the prayer for unity. Suddenly there appeared manifestations of the Spirit in prayer meetings all over the world. This has come to be known as the charismatic movement.

Permission sought.

An Anglican minister, a prominent leader of the early charismatic movement in England since Fountain Trust days, gives his comments on the whole charismatic scene. Harper subsequently joined the Orthodox Church.

13.2   Michael Harper, 'Beauty or Ashes?'
The Ashe Lecture, 1979

Is there a cure?

There are some who would regard this disease as terminal. In other words, there is no hope. The trends within the Church are irreversible. The destination of the Church in the West is the grave-yard. Others point hopefully to the past, when similar conditions pertained, and an Oxford don called John Wesley saved the day. But there is one factor which makes our present situation altogether different from the past. The Church today in the West exists in an increasingly hostile environment; some call it the post-Christian era. In the past the Church could indulge itself in the luxury of unitarianism, sexual permissiveness, lax spirituality and political activism. It was protected by the State and by public opinion. It was to a large extent in the driving-seat. But those days are nearly over. The storm clouds are gathering. The enemy is at the gate if not already within the camp. Most of what goes for Western Christianity is like a beast fattened for the slaughter but seemingly unaware of the fate which is about to overtake it. What then can be done in the present situation? There seem to me to be three possibilities:

1. The Roman Catholic Church

For some non-Catholics the Roman Catholic Church is becoming an increasingly attractive proposition. Almost alone amongst Churches, it stands firmly for the fundamentals of the faith. It still holds strongly to belief in the Virgin Birth, the Trinity and the Resurrection. As a Church it has stood strongly on moral issues, such as divorce, abortion and pre-marital sex. It too has a balanced view of the relationship between the Church and socio-political issues. Vatican II committed the Church to social action, but Pope John Paul II made the Church's view clear at the Mexican Conference he attended in February 1979. 'Atheistic humanism,' he said, 'holds out to mankind only a half liberation because it ignores spiritual dynamics.' He refused to see Jesus Christ as a political Messiah. 'The Gospel and the Church,' he said, 'must transcend all political ideologies.' The Pope saw 'the better future – not through violence, the interplay of power and political systems, but through the truth concerning man.' The Roman Catholic Church continues to place a high premium on its spirituality. It encourages and believes in prayer; it emphasizes community life and vocations to it; and of all churches it has been the most welcoming and encouraging to the Charismatic Movement. It has stuck tenaciously to its own particularity whilst being more open to ecumenism than ever before, and some of its leaders when they speak, have the kind of captive audience that the true prophet attracts. In Pope John Paul II, Cardinal Suenens and Cardinal Hume, they have prophetic leaders whom many listen to.

Most of us would still have question marks about certain Roman Catholic doctrines, particularly the Pope's infallibility, Marian dogmas, etc., but if the present trends within the Roman Catholic Church towards reformation and renewal continue as they have since Vatican II, then I would predict that a growing number of Protestants will join their ranks.

2. The independent Churches

Others are turning in another direction – the formation of independent Churches, free from the shackles of tradition and institutionalism. This is very common in the Third World. The trend there began in this century. The failure of many of the Mission Churches truly to reflect the culture of the people, and the inhibiting of national initiative through the bondage of colonialism, led to the splitting off of churches of which the Pentecostal type is by far the largest. Today, they are the fastest growing churches in the world and it is impossible to understand Christianity in the Third World without understanding Pentecostalism.

But the same New World phenomenon is now present in the Old World. In Britain, the newest development along these lines is seen in what has become known as the House Church Movement. It reflects the same kind of attitudes as the Anabaptists and Quakers of the seventeenth century, the Moravians and the Methodists of the eighteenth century, the Plymouth Brethren and Catholic Apostolics of the nineteenth century and the Pentecostals of the twentieth century. These movements had a vision of God and the Church which they could not identify in the Established Church of their day. They felt compelled by their consciences to seek for an expression of it outside the historic Churches.

Christians in Britain and elsewhere are now turning for leadership and inspiration to the House Churches. Their members are growing. For some this is the only spiritually viable alternative to the historic Churches, which are increasingly guilty of apostasy and appear to have compromised the Catholic faith. Some of the finest examples of New Testament Christianity are to be found in these churches. The sad story of the ultimate defection of so many of their predecessors from the norms of orthodoxy should not deter us from seeing all that is good and noble in the House Church Movement. In the coming years more and more people, particularly young people, will be turning in this direction.

Of course, there are other and more numerous forms of independency in addition to the House Churches. There are the Pentecostal Churches, which are almost the only Churches in Britain which are growing, and the independent evangelical churches, such as the FIEC (Federation of Independent Evangelical Churches).

3. The renewal of the historic Churches

We need to respect those who, in their despair and disillusionment with the historic Churches, have opted for either the Roman Catholic Church or the independent Churches. But for some of us these are not alternatives we would easily choose. Is there another alternative?

There was a time when I believed that the Holy Spirit was going to renew the historic Churches. I cannot in honesty say that I believe this is going to happen, at least for a very long time. In that sense the disease has a terminal look about it. Only the most radical surgery would succeed, and the Western Churches have neither the will nor the capacity of bringing this about or of surviving the operation. It may be that persecution following the collapse of our society might purify the Church and rid it of the cancers which are destroying its life. But at the present time I see no hope of any substantial change in the condition of the historic Churches, corrupted as they are by their compromises and defeated by their doubts. But all is not lost. There is a faithful remnant. There are those, as in the Church in Philadelphia, who, in the words of Christ, 'have kept my word and have not denied my name.' There is Anglo-Catholic renewal taking place in the Church of England. There are the Evangelicals in all the Churches. There is the Charismatic Movement, which also is to be found in all the historic Churches, as well as the Roman Catholic Church. There are others who would not accept any of these labels. They too are faithful believers – disturbed and discouraged by what they see happening in the Churches. Wondering whether a new day will ever dawn when the Church becomes strong in the Spirit and faithful again to its high calling.

The faithful remnant needs to draw together. How that can take place remains to be seen. The weaknesses I have drawn attention to in the historic Churches are self-indulgences one can afford in a period of stability, but not in an age of revolution. Something of sterner stuff is required. The task that faces us is daunting. But it is no greater than that which faced the Church at Pentecost, or the Church after the fall of Rome when Christendom was submerged in a sea of paganism, or the Church at the Reformation corrupted by wealth, power and superstition; or the Church in Wesley's day, lazy, self-indulgent and apparently hopelessly compromised, or the Church in Poland in 1939 on the eve of its baptism of fire, or the pre-revolution Church in Russia in 1917 or in China in 1946. The choice before us is of a Church armed with spiritual power, convinced of the faith, trusting in Jesus Christ and filled with the Holy Spirit, praying, fasting, forgiving, loving, dying; or of a Church which compromises with the world, denies the faith, accepts the standards of the world, and worships at the shrine of the false god of humanism. Increasingly, there will be a division between the two. For the Truth's sake, the issues need to be seen and faced.

But the brighter future will not come by human power or organization. To look to man and his vain methods is futile. We have seen what man has done in his quest to achieve the Utopia of Communism or Socialism. Alexander Solzhenitsyn has said, 'I myself, see Christianity today as the only living spiritual force capable of undertaking the spiritual healing of Russia.' A remark which Malcolm Muggeridge has called 'a miracle, and one of the greatest.' But our form of Christianity needs to be stripped of those humanistic accretions which have diluted its message and paralysed its mission. Then Christianity will do for us what it will surely one day do for Russia – heal our land.

Now to our God, 'Who is able to do immeasurably more than all we ask or imagine, according to his power that is at work within us, to Him be glory in the Church and in Christ Jesus throughout all generations, for ever and ever, Amen' (Eph. 3.20–21, NJV).

Used by permission of the author, Michael Harper.

14 Prosperity

೧ನ

Kenneth Copeland, televangelist, Word-of-Faith leader, both shows how independent Pentecostal ministries can work (by calling on their prayer partners) and, in his discussion of finance, suggests paradoxically that the poverty (or lack) may be removed by generosity.

14.1   Kenneth Copeland, *Dear Partner,*
Fort Worth, Texas, Kenneth Copeland, 1997, pp. 115–20

December 1989

Dear Partner,

What a time we live in! Destruction and despair on one hand and revival and miracles on the other. Great pressure is being applied to the minds of men – pressure that is heavier and more oppressive than anyone alive on the Earth has ever seen before. It's driving people to do things they never dreamed they would ever do.

No one would ever drive their car over a cliff, passing sign after sign that said, 'Danger. Road Out. Stop!' unless they were not seeing the signs or were reading them wrong. That's what's happening today. People are not thinking straight. They're being blinded by depressed, fear-filled, pressure-affected minds.

But, praise God, born-again, Spirit-filled Christian people do not have to succumb to that darkness. We have the Word of faith!

Isaiah 54.15–17 says fear and oppression and terror will come, but not from the Redeemer. Fear and oppression have caused the destruction and the pressure we've been seeing around us. But, according to the Word, they're weapons against the redeemed that cannot prosper.

During times like these, it is ever so important for us to spend time in prayer and in the Word so we can be led by the Master, Jesus, instead of being pushed around by the pressures of life. For instance, the great pressure of finances is on everyone everywhere in some form or another.

Financial pressure has gotten so great everywhere that governments don't know what to do. Businesses don't know what to do. Families don't know. Churches don't know. But Jesus does! Don't try to do anything without hearing from Him.

God has commissioned Jesus and anointed Him Lord over the time and the finances of the Body of Christ. However, instead of listening to Him, too many of God's people are being influenced by outside pressures – pressures that are stronger today than ever before.

Pressure from traditions. . . . that causes us to just do what we've always done instead of following the leadership of the Holy Spirit. Traditions have made many believers content to just hand out a few tokens here and there that do little to nothing where the work of God and real needs are concerned.

Pressure from the media . . . that makes the lifestyle of giving look absurd – especially when that giving is to the Church or to the mission field or to ministries of any kind.

Pressure from ministries . . . that has misguided as much or maybe even more of God's goods than any of the other pressures. I know that this has harmed our work over the years more than any other one thing.

For example, as you know, our going on daily television greatly increased our operating budget. Now, we didn't go on more television to increase our assets or our income. We didn't do it to raise money. We went on TV to take God's Word to His people.

We stayed before God for several years until we were absolutely sure it was God's will to start the daily broadcast. Then as we stepped out and began to expand, of course, our expenses began to increase. However, so did our income. Then after a few months, our income leveled off – but the expenses kept rising.

We began to fall behind until we had to stop expanding, long before we finished what Jesus, Head of the Church, wanted us to do at that point!

Traditionally, this would have been the time to go into appeals on television and letters and really put the pressure on people, but we are not allowed to do that. Nowhere in the Word of God does it tell any ministry of any kind to put pressure on people.

We went before the Master and stayed there until we found out where we had missed His directions, and then we changed some things. We had some changing to do in our own house as a ministry and in our own lives personally. After doing all that, we were still $3 million short.

So we stayed before the Lord until we found out why.

Mostly it was because so many people are not worshiping God and not taking time to listen to Jesus' directions in their giving and receiving.

Since Gloria and I didn't get on television and talk about our needs all the time, then when God sent His angels and His Spirit to speak to those people about what to do, they reasoned away the prompting of the Spirit by saying, 'Kenneth doesn't need this. He never talks about money, so he must have all he can use. I've heard they give away millions of dollars, so they must have plenty. I'll give this over here or over there because they need it so badly.'

Now please don't misunderstand me. I'm not saying this to criticize or to take away from other ministries. God forbid! I'm simply saying that too many people have not been doing what it takes to find out from the Master what He wants done. That's a large part of the reason ministries are behind so much of the time.

If everyone would listen to Jesus and do what He says, then all of us would have more than enough to do whatever He says to do. Our giving would be blessed instead of cursed. The works of God would go forth and the power of darkness would be broken not only over the Body of Christ, but also over the world as the Word goes forth in power.

God's Word is the most important thing in this earth. It is the answer to all the darkness, all the pressure, all the drugs and all the heartache we see around us. Jesus – the Word – cannot fail to overcome all the death and destruction that's going forth in this earth at Satan's hands. Why?

Get this now. Jesus is God's most perfect and precious seed.

Think about the importance of seeds for a minute. In Mark 4.30–2, when Jesus wanted to compare the kingdom of God to something, He compared it to a seed. Since every thing comes from the kingdom of God, there is nothing that exists that didn't come from a seed. You were born from a seed. Then you were born again from the seed of God's Word. Your food and everything else comes from a seed.

Jesus Himself was 'The Seed' planted by God. God sowed Him in sacrifice. He came forth and is still growing up into many brethren. The kingdom – or seed – cannot be stopped. It will grow up and become greater.

That's the reason Satan and the forces of darkness want to drain you until you can't plant your seed in His Name.

I understand the dollar-by-dollar draining and heaviness of the flesh and mind that you, and most everyone else, are going through. Payments for this, payments for that try to drain the very life and faith out of your heart. We've been there!

What's the answer to a situation like that? Plant more seed! And as you do it, worship and praise God with all your heart. (See Philippians 4.16–19.)

Your money – or goods – is the husk of the seed. Your words of faith, worship and love are the life in the seed. Regardless of what happens to the husk – or money – the life of the seed is spiritual and it is forever. It will grow until it breaks the powers of darkness and lack.

There *is* pressure and darkness all around us these days. And we've all allowed it to affect us to some degree. But we have taken steps of faith and power and we will overcome the effects of it in this ministry – and, praise God, you can do the same thing in your own life!

In Jesus' Name, I take authority over any darkness that has attacked you and your household in any way. I stand in faith with you believing that no weapon formed against you will prosper.

Please join Gloria and me and all of us at KCM in standing against the spirit of lack. Pray with us! Stand with us. Jesus can't fail, so we won't fail. We're staying close to Him. As you stand with us, we're standing with you.

Together – you, us and Jesus. What a team!

We love you and pray for you every day. Victory is ours.

Ken

15 Women

This early and pragmatic article accepts the role of women in some ministries and debars them from others.

15.1 E. N. Bell, 'Women Elders', *The Christian Evangel*, 15 August 1914, p. 2, abridged

The New Testament, as well as the Old, gives also some examples of prophetesses. For instance, it is prophesied in Joel as quoted in Peter, in Acts 2.17, that God would pour out his Spirit on 'daughters and they shall prophesy'.

So one of the direct results of the out-pouring of the Spirit in these last days is that women shall, under the power of the Spirit, prophesy. Now, the word prophesy indicates more than mere speaking our own thoughts, or the giving of other products of our minds in preaching and teaching. In its highest sense it means that the person is wholly the mouthpiece of God, and the thoughts and utterances are both from the Lord. But as to the substance of such teaching in prophecy the Word tells us that such speak 'unto edification and exhortation and comfort' (1 Cor. 14.3). On this line the daughters of Philip 'prophesied' (Acts 21.9). Of course, Agabus mentioned in verse 10 was also a prophet. We see here a very high order of ministry opened up for any sister on whom God pours forth the mighty power of his Spirit and who he chooses to use in such a way. No one should think for one moment of forbidding such sisters from declaring and giving witness of God and to his glory whom God has unmistakeably called thereto. Of course each case must stand on its own merits as to whether God has called or not.

There were certain women also who were 'labourers in the Gospel' with Paul. But when we have admitted these things willingly and freely given them full liberty that the Word of God has given to them, we have said all on that side which the Word allows. There is no instance of any woman being put in a place of authority to rule, govern or teach in the authoritative sense, that is, by the authority of their office, anywhere in the New Testament.

. . .

But this should not drive us to a fanatical extreme as to women preaching. Occasionally God may deem it expedient to lay his hand on some good sister who is experienced in the Word of God not only to proclaim his word to a congregation of believers, but also to take temporary oversight of them till more permanent arrangements can be made. Of course, we all admit that they have the privilege to proclaim Jesus to the unsaved at all times. Sometimes we strike a sister with more talent for keeping things straight in an assembly than many of the brethren have. Certainly we should recognize such God-given gifts and allow them to be exercised to the blessing of the saints and the glory of God.

Used by permission of The Flower Pentecostal Heritage Center, Springfield, Missouri, USA.

Wallis was an early leader in the Charismatic movement, who had a church background with male-oriented ministry. Unlike his previous associates there, Wallis defended women's right to minister.

15.2   Arthur Wallis, 'Women in the Church',
Restoration, September–October 1979, pp. 28, 29, emphasis as in the original article

Sentenced to Silence?

A small but influential section of the church laid a ban of silence on their women on the ground that this is what the NT clearly teaches. One could only reach such conclusions by failing to take an unprejudiced look at all the Bible has to say. This should include the OT because God's role for men and women was determined in principle at the creation. Also, in one of the proof texts quoted by those who take this extreme view, 'Let the women keep silence. . . .' Paul adds, *'as also saith the law'* (1 Cor. 14.34, AV), and there is nothing in the law to support their interpretation. It would have meant that every prophetess was functioning contrary to the law, and that Hannnah's inspired prayer in the sanctuary courts was wholly out of order.

Turning to the NT, to collate all that it teaches on this subject is to make an interesting discovery. It is all the earlier scriptures that suggest that women may take audible part in the congregation (Acts 1.14; 2.1, 4, 17, 18; 21.9; 1 Cor. 11.5) and only the last two that might suggest otherwise (1 Cor.

14.34–6; 1 Tim. 2.11–12). It is generally agreed that there is a divine order and a progressive unfolding of doctrine in the NT, so that it is the earlier passages that lay the foundation of a doctrine, and the later that may amplify or modify, but never contradict. In other words we must construe the later passages in the light of the earlier, not vice versa.

Sharing in Pentecost

In circles where the baptism in the Spirit is openly taught and experienced the advocates for silence have never found any acceptance. When we see all around us God doing something that conflicts with our interpretation of certain scriptures, we do well to take a second look at our interpretation. It is just conceivable we could have got it wrong. Wherever the Spirit of God is moving today God's *sons and daughters* are sharing equally in the blessing of Pentecost, just as they did at the beginning. Wherever they come into that blessing, both are giving audible expression by praising God in other tongues, just as they did at the beginning. If God wanted his daughters to be silent in church is it not strange that the Holy Spirit inspired them to be so noisy at the inaugural meeting?

It should not need to be said that the prayers and praises of women in the church of God are as acceptable and precious to God as those of men. The local church is a family. It would be unnatural for a human father, when his family were gathered around him, to take delight in hearing his sons expressing appreciation or making known their request to him, but to insist that his daughters remained silent, and only came to him individually and privately. The offering up of spiritual sacrifices in the congregation is priestly ministry. We believe that the NT teaches the priesthood of all believers, not just the males.

Sharing in the gifts

Pentecost was a tremendous break-through. What God had formerly reserved for the favoured few, the men and women on whom he sovereignly put his Spirit for their special task, was now the covenant blessing of all. Sons and daughters without distinction now received the 'promise of the Father' and prophesied, just as Joel had predicted centuries before. This was the first instalment of spiritual gifts that were to play such a vital role in the subsequent edification and extension of the church, and the women shared in these along with the men. Later, when Paul listed the inspirational gifts in his letter to the Corinthians and devoted considerable space to regulating their function, he implied that they were open to all. 'It is the same God who inspires them all in *every one*. *To each* is given the manifestation of the Spirit for the common good . . . All these are inspired by one and the same Spirit, who apportions to *each one* individually as he wills' (1 Cor. 12.6, 7, 11, RSV). Again, 'You can *all* prophesy. . . . so that *all* may learn' (14.31, RSV).

In churches where spiritual gifts operate it is not uncommon for women to be used in manifestations of tongues, interpretation and prophecy. But what of the others? There is no restriction here as far as the NT is concerned, the restriction is only in our attitudes. The exhortation to 'eagerly desire the greater gifts' (1 Cor. 12.31) is to the whole church. But it is not enough for sisters to heed and respond; leaders must provide the security for these greater gifts to emerge by giving their approval and encouragement. There are women of faith who could be used, alongside men, in ministering to those, especially their own sex, seeking the baptism in the Spirit, healing, or release.

Used by permission of Covenant Ministries International, Nettle Hill, Brinklow Road, Ansty, Coventry CV7 9JL, UK.

16 Social Concern

❧ ❧

This dramatic story of how Teen Challenge found that the Holy Spirit could help break addictions became a bestseller doing much to further 'the cause' of Pentecostals internationally.

16.1   David Wilkerson, *The Cross and the Switchblade*,
New York: Pyramid Books, 1964, pp. 153–7

The tremendous hold that drugs have on the human body cannot be explained in physical terms alone. My grandfather would say that the devil had these boys in his grip, and I think my grandfather is right. The boys themselves say this, but in a different way:

'Davie,' I was told over and again, 'there are two habits you've got to kick if you're hooked. The body habit, and the mind habit. The body habit's not too much of a problem: you just stay in sheer hell for three days, put up with a little less torture for another month, and you're free.

'But that mind habit, Davie. . . that's something terrible!

There's a thing inside you that *makes* you come back. Something spooky, whispering to you. We got names for this guy: either he's a monkey on our back, or a vulture on our veins.

'We can't get rid of him, Davie. But you're a preacher. Maybe this Holy Spirit you talk about, maybe He can help.'

I don't know why it took so long for me to realize that this was, indeed, the direction we should take. The realization came about as an evolution, starting with a failure and ending with a magnificent discovery.

The failure was a boy named Joe. I'll never forget the four traumatic days I spent with him, trying to bring him through the pain of withdrawing from an addiction to heroin.

Joe was such a nice guy. Tall, blond, at one time a good athlete in high school, he had not come into his addiction by the usual route.

'I suppose those pain-killers were necessary,' Joe told me in my office at the Center. 'I know that when I needed them I was glad for the relief they brought. But look what happened to me afterwards. I never broke away.'

He told me the story. He had been working for a coal company. One day he slipped and fell down a chute. The accident put him in the hospital for several months, and for most of that time Joe was in severe pain. To help relieve his agony, the doctor prescribed a narcotic. By the time Joe was released from the hospital he was addicted.

'I couldn't get any more of the drug,' he told me. 'But I discovered that there was a kind of cough syrup that had a narcotics in it and I started walking all over the city buying it. I'd have to go to a different drugstore each time and use a fake name, but I didn't have any trouble getting all I wanted. I used to step into the nearest bathroom and down a whole eight-ounce bottle at once.'

After a while even this didn't satisfy Joe's growing need of drugs. He knew that some of his old high school buddies were using heroin, and he got in touch with them. From then on the pattern was typical. First sniffing, then skin popping, then mainline injections. When Joe came to us, he had been on heroin for more than eight months. He was deeply addicted.

'Can you stay here at the Center for three or four days?' I asked.

'No one else wants me.'

'You can live upstairs with the workers.'

Joe shrugged.

'It won't be easy, you know. You'll be going off cold turkey.'

Joe shrugged again.

Cold turkey – instantaneous withdrawal – is the method usually used in jails to take a boy off narcotics. We used it partly because we had no choice: we could not administrate the withdrawal drugs they use in hospitals. But we prefer cold turkey on its own merits, too. The withdrawal is considerably faster: three days as against three weeks. The pain is more intense, but it is over sooner.

So we brought Joe to the Center and gave him a room upstairs with the men workers. How glad I was that we had a registered nurse living at the home. Barbara Culver's room was just under Joe's. She'd keep an eye on him all the time he was with us. We also put a doctor on the alert in case we should need him.

'Joe,' I said, as soon as we had him settled in, 'as of this moment the withdrawal has started. I can promise you that you won't be alone for one second. When we aren't with you in person, we will be with you in prayer.'

We weren't just going to take the boy off drugs and let him alone to suffer. The entire four days would be coupled with an intensive, supportive prayer campaign. Prayer would be said for him around the clock. Day and night boys and girls would be in the chapel interceding for him. Others would be with him in person upstairs reading Scripture to him.

One of the first things we had to do with Joe was break the expectation of pain. Instantaneous withdrawal is bad enough by itself, without the added handicap of expecting it to be hell. I asked Joe where he got the idea the withdrawal was going to be so rough.

'Well . . . gee. . . everyone says . . . '

'That's just it. Everyone says it's rough, so you're sitting here sweating just at the thought of what's ahead. As a matter of fact, that need not be the case at all.' And I told Joe about a boy I knew who had been on marijuana and on heroin and who had been released instantaneously, without any of the withdrawal symptoms. That was rare, I admitted, and Joe had to be prepared for a rough time. But why make it any worse than it had to be? We worked hard to help Joe separate the real symptoms from the psychological symptoms that came from apprehension.

Then we had Joe learn the thirty-first Psalm.

This is a wonderful Psalm. We call it the Song of the Drug Addict. There are certain verses in particular that are just made for their condition:

Pull me out of the net that they have laid privily for me: for Thou art my strength.
Have mercy upon me, O Lord, for I am in trouble; mine eye is consumed with grief, yea, my soul and my belly.
For my life is spent with grief, and my years with sighing; my strength faileth because of mine iniquity, and my bones are consumed.
I was a reproach among all mine enemies, but especially among my neighbours, and a fear to mine acquaintance; they that did see me without fled from me.
I am forgotten as a dead man out of mind: I am like a broken vessel.

Once the real withdrawal pains began, Joe stayed up there in his room while he sweated through the symptoms. Barbara checked his condition regularly. I hated to go into that room. Joe lay on the bed gripping his stomach as the cramps hit him again and again. His body was a high flushed pink. Sweat poured off him in little rivers that left the bed soaked through to the mattress. He cried out in his pain and pounded his head with his hands. He wanted water, then threw it up. He pleaded with me to help him, and all I could do was hold his hand and promise him that we cared.

At night we set up a tape recorder by Joe's bed and played Scripture readings to him. I stayed at the Center during the trial. Often during the dead of night I would slip into the chapel to be sure someone was always there, then up the stairs to see how Joe was doing. The recorder was softly repeating portions of the Bible to the boy as he tossed in fitful sleep. Never once during those three days and nights did the torment let up. It was a terror to watch.

Then, on the fourth day, Joe seemed much better.

He walked around the Center smiling wanly and saying that he thought maybe the worst was over. All of us were happy with him. When Joe said he wanted to go home to see his parents, I was a little dubious, but there was nothing we could do to detain the boy if he wanted to leave.

And so, smiling and thankful, Joe walked out the front of the Center and turned down Clinton Avenue.

It came time for him to return. No Joe.

The next morning we learned that our Joe had been arrested for robbery and for possession of narcotics.

That was our failure. 'What went wrong?' I asked at staff meeting. 'The boy went through the rough part. He got the way through the worst three days he would ever have to spend. He had a tremendous investment to protect. And he threw it all over.'

'Why don't you talk to the boys who have come off successfully?' said Howard Culver. 'Maybe you'll find the key'.

There were several such boys I wanted to talk to. One by one I called them in and listened to their stories of deliverance. And they all spoke of a common experience.

I spoke to Nicky, who had been taking goof balls and smoking marijuana. I asked him when it was that he felt he had victory over his old way of life. Something tremendous had happened to him, he said, at the time of his conversion on a street corner. He had been introduced at that time to the love of God. But it wasn't until later that he knew he had complete victory.

'And when was that, Nicky?'

'At the time of my baptism in the Holy Spirit.'

I called in David and asked him the same thing. When did he feel that he had power over himself? 'Oh, I can answer that,' said David. 'When I was baptized in the Holy Spirit.'

Again and again I got the same report. I cannot describe how excited I was. A pattern seemed to be emerging. I felt that I was on the verge of something tremendous.

Permission sought.

17 Morality

The Executive Council of American Assemblies of God dealt with the fall-out from the disgrace of the televangelist Jim Bakker.

17.1 'Statement of the Executive Presbytery of the General Council of the Assemblies of God',
Pentecostal Evangel 3 May 1987, p. 15

First we want the public to know that we, as church leaders, are deeply saddened, ashamed, and repentant before God for the problems that have developed in our own church family, as well as in the evangelical church world. We are calling a day of fasting and prayer in our Assemblies of God churches.

We did not precipitate the developments of the past week. We have not tried either to expose anyone or to cover up any story. We have been responding, and are today responding as executives of the General Council of the Assemblies of God according to the Word of God and according to the policy which governs our church body.

Our love and compassion for Jim and Tammy Bakker remain strong. More than anything else, we want to be redemptive in our actions. It must also be understood that when ministers hold credentials with the Assemblies of God there are high standards by which those ministers must conduct their lives and their ministries. When these standards are violated, there must be an accounting. That is where we are today. Although letters of resignation have been received by the North Carolina District and this national office, the complete procedure must and will be followed to determine whether resignation or dismissal is in order.

. . . the information we have received indicates to us the high probability that there was not an effort by any person or organization to take over PTL.[1] We do not believe there is any evidence of blackmail. To the contrary, the evidence seems to indicate that effort and money have been expended to cover moral failure. We are deeply sorry to have to say this. We grieve for the impact all of this has had upon the entire Christian community.

---

[1] PTL, originally 'Praise the Lord and the People that Love', was the name of the television network inaugurated by Bakker [eds].

The Executive Presbytery also deeply regrets that national TV personalities have spoken out publicly and so boldly on matters about which they had very little information.

In conclusion, all of the information we have received has been turned over to the North Carolina District through the hands of Superintendent Charles Cookman. It will be the responsibility of the North Carolina District Presbytery to take appropriate action and pass that action on to this body. We will then act upon their recommendations.

Finally, we wish to express our thanks and appreciation to you, members of the media, for your patience with us and for the honest and straightforward manner in which stories of the past week have been handled by you.

March 26, 1987

18 Exorcism and Spriritual Warfare

☙ ❧

Against teaching that Christians can need exorcism, du Plessis argues that faith in Christ removes demons.

18.1 David du Plessis, *Simple and Profound*, Orleans: Paraclete Press, 1986, pp. 61–3

Can a Christian have a demon?

I also object to people blaming the devil for everything. Sometimes I will say to them: 'You think you're full of devils, but you're just full of yourself that's all.' When that question was put to a friend of mine, Judson Cornwall, he said: 'Christians can have anything they want.'

Now, here we have this great move today of exorcism.

How did the exorcism ministry get started?

The tradition of exorcism is built on one Scripture only – one that has a false punctuation in it. Mark 16.17 reads: 'These signs shall follow them that believe. In my name they shall cast out demons.'

'These signs will follow them that believe' – believe what? When you take out the punctuation (which is not in the original Greek and has been arbitrarily inserted by subsequent translators), it reads: 'These signs follow them that believe *in my name*, then they expel – not cast out – other people's demons.' I shall expel the demons, because the Lord says that a stronger man (Jesus) comes in and casts out the other (Luke 11.20–6, 1 Corinthians 1.25–9, also 1 John 4.4 and Hebrews 2.14–18).

And so began the tragedy that results in brethren exorcizing people, making them think that they have been helped. But I have had to deal with too many who later came back and said: 'I was helped for a few days, and then it got ten times worse than it was before.'

I said, 'It's because they did not first get you to believe in Jesus as Saviour and make your commitment to Him, faith in His name. Had you done so, you would have found that there was no devil within; you would have expelled him. You would have, in effect, become your own exorcist.'

One time, I was sitting in a meeting that Dennis Bennett arranged. An evangelist had been telling them all incidents where Jesus cast out devils. I sat and listened to him, and when he stopped, I added a few more instances to his list. Surprised, he asked: 'So you do believe that Jesus cast out devils?'

'Yes,' I smiled, and then looked at him and said, 'have you never heard that Jesus died?'

'Of course!'

'Well, after His resurrection, there was no more exorcism.'

'Ah,' he said, 'but what about His saying "in My name you shall cast out devils"?'

I said, 'Brother, I'm surprised at you! You, a Bible scholar, ought to know that there's no punctuation in the original. The punctuation put there later is wickedly crooked and wrong, and has built a tradition in Christianity. In some of the infant sprinkling churches, they even exorcise that poor little child, as if there were a devil already there.'

And now mothers are being accused – I have heard them preach and say: 'If a mother has a temper when her children are being naughty, she has a demon in her.' She's demonised! And what about the naughty child? Oh, he's demonised too! So the mothers begin casting out devils, instead of teaching their children to love Jesus. It is a shocking thing that has happened with this 'deliverance ministry.'

I turned to the speaker and said: 'On Calvary, Jesus destroyed him that had the power of death, that is, the devil. In the second chapter of Hebrews, verse 17, it says the devil. He destroyed him! And delivered those that were in fear of death all their life. Bound by fear of death. Now *there* is deliverance. The deliverance is at the cross of Calvary – there, where Jesus destroyed the devil, and destroyed him so perfectly that he could not hold Him in death. In Resurrection, He ruined the devil's power over death, and brought life.'

I turned to them. 'We say we've got that life. Then how come we still harbour devils, and we still fear death? The only people that I have exorcised are people that are demented. They are absolutely hopeless – you can't even get them to say the Lord's Prayer. In such cases, I'll take authority over the devil, because that person hasn't got even a mind to surrender to Christ. Backslidden Christians, I bring back to Calvary.'

I went back to my chair, saying, 'There is all my teaching on, not exorcism, but expulsion – expelling the devil.'

Permission sought.

Don Basham explains how he came to cast demons out of troubled Christians.

18.2   Don Basham, *Deliver Us from Evil*,
London: Hodder & Stoughton, 1979, pp. 61–4

Dawson stepped aside and once again all eyes turned to me. Still fighting panic, I asked aloud for Jesus to protect us in all that we were about to do. Then I remembered something. Before dealing with the lunatic man in Gadara, Jesus had commanded the spirit troubling him to give its name.

'According to the Bible,' I said, 'evil spirits have names – Deaf spirit, Dumb spirit, Legion . . . – names like that.' I also recalled the sentence, 'With authority he commands the unclean spirits . . . ,' so I determined to sound authoritative. I should have warned Sam first, but feeling both foolish and desperate I leaned over him and in a loud voice cried out:

'By the authority of Jesus Christ, I command you to give your name!'

Sam's reaction was immediate. He jumped high in his chair and let out a shriek.

'Sam Jenkins!' he shouted. 'That's my name, Sam Jenkins!'

Brother Dawson's gentle eyes twinkled. 'Well, he remembered his name anyhow.'

Hoping I didn't look as idiotic as I felt, I apologized. 'No Sam, you don't understand. I wasn't speaking to you, I was speaking to those . . . to that . . . ' I couldn't bring myself to say it. 'I was speaking to that thing torment-ing you. Don't you see?'

'You mean the demon?'

'Yes, Sam. I mean the . . . er . . . demon. We want to find out what it is. Now let's try again, okay? You spirit tormenting Sam,' I said in a softer voice, 'by the authority of Jesus Christ, I command you to tell me who you are!'

Sam screwed up his face. 'Forgetfulness.' I looked at the pastor. 'Forgetfulness?' I echoed.

The pastor nodded encouragingly.

I took another deep breath, then plunged ahead. 'All you spirits of for-getfulness, I command you in the name of Jesus Christ to come out of Sam!'

Sam shuddered slightly and sighed.

I watched him carefully for a moment, but nothing else happened.

'Think it came out, Sam?' Brother Dawson asked.

Sam opened his eyes. He seemed a little calmer. 'I don't know. Maybe.'

'Let's try again,' I said. I repeated the command. Once again Sam seemed to give an involuntary, mild shudder. Was anything really happening? One more time I ordered the spirits of forgetfulness to leave.

Sam trembled again, more violently this time. For several seconds it seemed as if he were having some kind of seizure. Just as I began to be frightened, the shaking stopped.

And then I saw something which amazed me, and which completely changed the mood of the scene there in that echoing basement prayer room. For an invisible mask seemed to slip from Sam's face and some lurking – did I dare say 'presence' – behind his eyes seemed to melt away. It's hard to put into words exactly how Sam changed. It was as if he had been wearing spectacles which distorted the way he really looked. Those spectacles were now removed. Sam *looked* different. With a shy smile he glanced up at the Dawsons. For the very first time I began to wonder if this were more than a meaningless performance. I had been acting in imitation of certain biblical events, but deep within me where my most honest self lives, I'd been doubtful and afraid that I was trespassing on a province that had best be left to the mystics and the powerful.

And then the thing happened which undid me altogether. For Sam began to speak.

'Bless the Lord, O my soul, and all that is within me bless His Holy name. Bless the Lord, O my soul and forget not all His benefits, Who forgiveth all thy sins and healeth all thy diseases...'

On and on in a quiet voice, Sam continued to quote Scripture.

'Those are the Bible verses we've been teaching him!' Stella said. 'He's never been able to repeat a one.'

For the next several minutes we listened in wonder as Sam recited passage after passage. Tears were flowing down his cheeks. There were some on mine too.

'Thank God,' Dawson said very softly. 'Oh, thank God.'

I was amazed. It was awesome. I felt ten feet tall.

As we made our way out of the church Sam edged over to me and gripped my hand. He looked younger.

'Thank you, Brother Basham,' he said, 'You must have great faith to be able to do that.'

'No, Sam,' I replied, 'if you want to know the truth I was just as frightened as you were. But we can thank God for what He has done for you tonight.'

'Yes,' Sam nodded. Then, almost parenthetically, he added, 'You know, for years I've been hearing a strange voice. In fact, it kept yammering at me all the way here tonight. "You go to that meeting and you'll die!" it said. Over and over it kept saying that. That's why I was so scared!'

Then he smiled. 'But the devil always was a liar, wasn't he?'

Used by permission of Chosen Books LLC, Chappaqua, NY 10514, USA.

Law taught a fuller doctrine of the effect of praise, including it as a weapon in spiritual warfare.

18.3   Terry Law, 'The Power of Praise and Worship',
in *Principles of Praise*, Tulsa: Victory House, 1985, pp. 145–56, abridged

. . . All spiritual weapons are launched through the mouth.

There is a very important lesson here. Our mouths must be watched over because no matter what we say with our mouths, we are launching weapons of one sort or another. Those weapons must be God's weapons and not the Devil's. If we don't use our mouths correctly, we simply make it impossible for us to win the battle.

What comes out of our mouth ultimately settles the conflict with the Evil One, and that is why the challenge of praise is so important for the believer. God has ordained that the believer exercises this kind of strength and it has one primary effect: It makes the Devil shut up. Our mind cannot be invaded with his thoughts. Our mouths cannot be polluted with his words.

It is important in a situation where deliverance is to be ministered to people that an atmosphere of praise be created. I have been in services when we moved into an atmosphere of high praise where the evil spirits that were oppressing people in the room began to cry out. Praise so upset them, that it demanded a response on their part. This simply revealed who they were and who they were holding authority over and a word of deliverance set the people free.

It is so important that we watch what comes out of our mouths. Our mouths are the way we cast our vote. When we praise the Lord, we are casting our vote for God and against the Devil. This moves us into a tremendous place of spiritual victory.

. . .

There are many people in contemporary society wrestling against the spirit of heaviness. This spirit is more than just heaviness. In contemporary language we would call it a spirit of depression. It is more than just an influence. It is an actual principality, a stronghold of the Devil. It is an evil personality, a spirit that grips the hearts and minds of people as they look at the negative side of life. It is a spirit that binds, that discourages, that frustrates. It is not merely an attitude, but an actual evil spirit.

How do we get free of this spiritual bondage? In my travels I have noticed this is one of the most common spirits that binds people. Praise is a spiritual garment and every believer must wear this garment at all times. But it is something we must put on. We literally have to clothe ourselves with this garment. This again refers directly to the act of the will in praising God.

. . .

Praise leads the believer into the triumph of Christ

Psalm 106.47 states, 'Save us, O Lord our God, and gather us from among the heathen, to give thanks unto thy holy name, and to triumph in thy praise.' This verse applies not only to Israel as a nation, but also to the Church itself. We are to triumph in the praise of God.

There is a great difference between victory and triumph. Victory is the accomplishment of the defeat of the enemy. It is the winning of the battle, the silencing of the Devil. Triumph involves much more than victory. Victory makes a triumph possible, but a triumph is a celebration of the victory already won.

When we come into Christ we are brought into His triumph (Col. 2.15). Notice the adverbial phrases of the verse. There is no time and no place when God does not cause us to triumph. God always causes us to triumph in Christ. A modern translation has it this way, 'it makes us a continuing pageant of triumph in Christ.'

. . .

. . . Paul uses the triumph analogy to make vivid our victory. What he says in Colossians 2.15 is that Satan and all his forces, principalities, powers, the rulers of the darkness of this world, spiritual wickedness in the heavenlies; all those forces are being led behind the chariot of Jesus as evidence of their defeat. They have been stripped of their armor. They have been spoiled. Now Paul in 2 Corinthians 2.14 says God always causes us to triumph in Christ. God causes us to join the pageant of triumph with Christ. In order to do this, we must accept a certain mindset. We do not pray to God to give us the victory. Our praise makes us a part of the victory celebration. We triumph in our praise. The battle already is won, past tense. Our praise ties us into a celebration of the victory that has been won.

. . .

The triumph directly relates to our praise. Our praise moves us into a position of triumph. We're not fighting the battle when we praise, we're praising God that the battle already has been won. This is a key.

Permission sought.

Otis explored spiritual events across the world since, to those advocating 'Strategic Spiritual Warfare', research was the first step. Here he tries to provide a theological basis for the kind of prayer he advocates.

18.4 G. Otis, Jr, *The Twilight Labyrinth*, Grand Rapids, MI: Chosen Books, 1998, pp. 281–3, abridged

The Apostle Paul makes it clear that our spiritual weapons 'have divine power to demolish (or pull down) strongholds' (2 Corinthians 10.4). It is obvious from the context of this passage that these strongholds are not demons or geographical locations, but psychic habitats. It is from these platforms or 'head-nests' that Satan and his cohorts endeavor to manipulate our inner world.

In response to such deceptive efforts we are called to 'demolish (or cast down) arguments' (v. 5). The word arguments often translated *imaginations* is an interesting one. Taken from the Greek word *logismos*, it is defined more precisely as 'calculative reasonings' over time (as opposed to random occasional thoughts). This definition, according to Colorado pastor Dutch Sheets, makes these arguments or imaginations look more like what they certainly are – religious or philosophical systems.

While I have no quibble with those who contend that mental strongholds are best attacked by truth, our challenge is to gain access to the minds of enchanted people. As Paul reminds us, the Gospel is veiled to those whose minds have been blinded by the god of this age (see 2 Corinthians 4.3–4). How then do we 'open their eyes and turn them from darkness to light, and from the power of Satan to God' (Acts 26.18)?

A potential solution to this challenge is found in another of Paul's epistles. After admonishing the church at Colosse to devote themselves to prayer, the apostle goes on to add a personal request; 'Pray for us too,' he pleads, 'that God may *open a door for our message*, so that we may proclaim the mystery of Christ' (Colossians 4.3; emphasis added by G. Otis).

In asking intercessors to petition God for an open door Paul is acknowledging three important truths:

1. Unsaved people are bound in a prison of deception.
2. God must breach this stronghold if the Gospel is to enter.
3. Prayer is an important means of persuading God to do this.

If we want to practice . . . liberating enchanted minds so they can understand and respond to the Gospel – we must first neutralize the blinding influence of demonic strongmen . . . (Mark 3.27)

We are not asking God to 'make' people Christians or to expel demonic powers that have become objects of worship. Such requests violate human free will and God will not honour them. What we are appealing for is a level playing field, a temporary lifting of the spiritual blindness that prevents men and women from processing truth (the Gospel) at heart level.[1]

Since our own strength is insufficient to bind higher-dimensional beings we must rely on the resources of the Holy Spirit. While it is true that we have been given power and authority in Christ (see Luke 10.19), this authority is not for us to use at our own initiative or discretion. It is ambassadorial authority, which means it is to be exercised only at the bidding of the Sovereign (see 2 Corinthians 5.20).[2] As servants we must allow submission to reign over presumption.

. . .

Strategic-level spiritual warfare, as with all prevailing or breakthrough prayer, can demand prodigious amounts of time and energy. We are asking God after all to temporarily suspend the logical consequences (Spiritual enchantment) of people's misplaced choices – an action that requires that He interpose Himself between deceived individuals and their spiritual masters.

Used by permission of Chosen Books, Baker Book House, Grand Rapids, Michigan, USA.

---

[1] Matthew 18.19 is often cited as evidence of unqualified authority to bind and 'loose', but this passage has nothing to do with spiritual warfare. And those scriptures that apparently do talk about binding evil spirits (see Matthew 12.29, 16.19; Mark 3.27) offer no promise that this action will result in permanent liberation. To achieve long-term relief from demonic enchantment, individuals and communities must repent of their sins – an action made easier by the temporary lifting of demonic deception.

[2] To be led by the Spirit involves more than acknowledging the general scope of God's will. It is also recognizing that He is Lord of the details, that only he can reveal the how and when of our particular mission.

Andrew Walker argues against the kind of spiritual warfare popularized by preachers like Wagner and Kraft.

18.5   Andrew Walker, 'The Devil you Think you Know',
in Tom Smail, Andrew Walker and Nigel Wright (eds),
Charismatic Renewal, London: SPCK, 1995, pp. 86–105,
abridged

It strikes me that a presupposition which underlies much charismatic understanding of the demonic is that the devil is a person, with a fiendish personality and a brilliant, albeit twisted, rationality. From this it tends to follow that the hosts of hell are *a fortiori* also personal. They are the counterfeits of heaven – fallen angels, like the unfallen ones except that they are committed to evil. Thus spiritual warfare can be seen in terms of battling against a well-organized and trained army with great powers of detection and destruction.

Such a view facilitates the sort of biblical exposition that we have briefly examined. It fuels the conspiratorial view of the devil that is so essential for the successful maintenance of a paranoid universe: for demons are more fearsome if one knows that they are everywhere, plotting to get us. It also helps facilitate novels such as Frank Peretti's *This Present Darkness*, which, while being a work of fiction, has the unfortunate consequence of being taken only too literally.

But evil, I suggest, has no real being of its own, certainly no personal ontology, for God created only that which was good. Lucifer, the morning star of God's creation, was not content to be a creature, but wished to be the creator. This desire inverted the power of love that sustained him, and the love of power was born. Here Milton is powerfully convincing in his poetic insight that Lucifer wished to reign not to serve, to be a god not a creature. This craving for ultimate power, C. S. Lewis tells us, was the sin that the devil taught the human race.

So rebellion was born out of a good creature's free choice that turned on its creator, disfiguring him and finally engorging him. Demonized by his own desire, the former angel of light is extinguished by his own darkness and the evil that emerges has no intrinsic life of its own, for it is parasitic on the forces and energies of God's good creation. Therefore the power of evil ultimately derives from the good power of God, but it is now corrupted power that has fallen away from his sustaining love. Having cast himself off from this love, that angelic being we call the devil not only loses his relationship with God, but is also out of sorts with himself – his own good nature. He drifts inexorably towards non-personhood, whose only end is nothingness – that existence of non-being which is outside the personal life of God.

As the devil has undergone his depersonalized metamorphosis – the carapace of evil hardening and usurping his good nature – he has become not more rational but irrational, not so much cunning as confused. He is diabolical but disordered, ferocious but fey, fearful but fickle, warlike but whimsical. In short, he has become all that God is not, and its instinct – for think more in terms of a mad beast than a personal agent – is to take as many of us with it as it can.

C. S. Lewis captures something of the eternal life of those who have fallen away from God in his book *The Great Divorce*, where we find that out-side the solidity and bright weight of heaven there is the Grey City where there is no substance or depth, only wraiths who cling to their illusions.

Can I furnish biblical verses to substantiate this exposition? I am sorry, but I cannot, for I hope it is obvious that I am just flying a kite: I am specu-lating on what the Bible chooses not to tell us. However, this is not an arbitrary exercise. I am trying to work through logically certain ideas based on an understanding of God's personal revelation both in Jesus of Nazareth and as the triune God. His self-revelation as perfect love and personal communion also suggests its negations – being (or, more accurately, appearance of being) without communion, hate, and non-personhood. In other words, I am trying to do some serious theology, but only in the realm of legitimate guesswork.

Nevertheless, I am persuaded that the essence of spiritual warfare is not taking on demonic forces by binding strong men, destroying amulets and charms and banning Halloween. Indeed, the passion with which some charismatics oppose All-Hallows Eve is matched only by their indifference to the celebration which follows it on All Saints' Day!

Perhaps it is only paranoia, but in my weaker moments I have a suspicion that the master Trickster has diverted us away from the bat-tlefield to the games-room, where we indulge ourselves in spiritual fan-tasies and trivial pursuits while the real evil loosed on the world devours all that is good and decent with the heartlessness and cruelty of the Canaanite god Moloch.

We may realize that we can fall prey to our own fantasies, and choose instead to step out from the closed world of our parishes and take to the streets and march for Jesus. Such a move could be a step in the right direc-tion, for 'coming out' is a way of 'coming clean' with the public about charismatic intentions. But if we do decide to leave our sanctuaries and swarm on to the streets, we must strive to leave the paranoid universe behind, for otherwise we may imagine that by the very act of marching we are 'shifting the demonic atmosphere' and 'binding the strong men' of the

City of London or the Mammon of materialistic Britain. And if we believe this, we may also come to believe that we can 'bind' – and hence solve – unemployment, racism, or environmental decay by a stamp of our feet, a clenched fist in the air, or a shout to the skies.

We need to learn that there is more to exorcizing the darkness than exercising our lungs. There is more to spiritual warfare than standing toe to toe with the devil and slugging it out. To meet like with like, or as Jesus puts it, evil with evil – or, if you prefer, power with more of the same – is to show that we have not really escaped the labyrinth of Dungeons and Dragons, He Man, and the masters of the paranoid universe. If this were to be our approach to evil in the world, then it would be better if we stayed at home.

If my speculative theology of the parasitic nature of evil is correct, then perhaps attacking demons amounts to a welcoming party for them. Even some of our charismatic services can no longer begin until the demons are first 'bound' in prayer. As an American charismatic recently put it: the devils take this as worship, and flock to hear themselves addressed. To put it bluntly, belligerence against them is not merely a welcoming, but a feast. (We can almost hear Screwtape telling Wormwood how he can wax fat on human aggression.) At the very least, to behave in this way is to descend to a sub-Christian barbarism. To exercise authority (*exousia* in the New Testament sense) over dark forces is one thing, but this is not the same as striving for greater fire-power to atomize the opposition (*dunamis,* a word rarely used in accounts of Christ's encounters with evil spirits, is over-played in charismatic vocabulary).

The violent comic-strip 'blow the enemy away' youth culture of Judge Dread Law Enforcer seems to have found a responsive echo in the triumphalist charismatic camp. At the Christian Resources Exhibition at Esher in 1992, for example, there was a hot trade in the tee shirt bearing the legend, 'Jesus Christ Demon Crusher'. I believe that genuine spiritual warfare means quite simply refusing to play the war game: we can only overcome evil with good, for if we appropriate the enemy's weapons we are lost. As Metropolitan Anthony puts it, 'The devil does not care who you hate, even if it's himself.' Power-seeking is dangerous, and the love of power is nothing less than devilish, for it corrupts Christian virtue.

Used by permission of SPCK, Holy Trinity Church, Marylebone Road, London NW1 4DU, UK.

19 Toronto Blessing

❧❧

John Arnott, senior pastor of Toronto Airport Christian Fellowship, recounts one person among thousands who experienced 'the Father's love' in one of the many meetings that still continued past the millennium.

19.1 John Arnott, *The Father's Blessing*,
Orlando, Florida: Creation House, 1995, pp. 23–5, 88–91

The greatest revelation I hear night after night is that God has come to people by the power of the Holy Spirit and revealed His love to them personally, often through visions and dreams and prophecy. They say, 'I know now that my heavenly Father really loves me.' Joel 2.28 is being fulfilled before our eyes.

Virginia Smith, a pastor's wife from The City Church in Bellevue, Washington, became newly acquainted with the love the Father had for her on the day of her birthday at our church. One of our staff pastors, Ian Ross, asked Virginia to put her hands over her heart. Then he prayed for healing of her broken heart – a heart broken by the father-images in her life. Ian told Virginia that God would never reject her, that she was accepted by Him. He said that God loved her perfectly, and nothing she could do would make Him love her more. Virginia later wrote to us and said:

> These were not new thoughts to me; I had taught these same truths to women for years. What made this encounter with God so life-changing was the transfer of knowledge from my mind to my spirit. All of a sudden I felt God's love and total acceptance – so much so, I found myself bent forward at the waist, weeping deeply from my innermost being. The tears were not tears of repentance or feelings of self-pity, but cries of joy and gratitude that God could love me so completely.

As Virginia wept, two members of the worship team came and sang over her while a violinist accompanied them. She found herself 'paralyzed' by God's anointing in the midst of this circle of worship and love.

I have never experienced such power and healing. I finally had to ask God to stop because my physical body could no longer tolerate such overwhelming love. I was immediately conscious of my frailty before the Lord and just how little of the Holy Spirit I could contain. Totally exhausted, I dropped to my knees and fell on my face. I felt a great desire to humble myself and rest in His presence. I walked in hungry to know Jesus more intimately and walked out full and overflowing with the goodness and love of God.

Do you know what that experience is worth? It changes everything. We will gladly surrender control to a Father who loves us so profoundly. That revelation breaks the strategy the enemy has so painstakingly built into our lives – the idea that not even God could love us or that God the Father is not really loving. The lie is exposed and instantly evaporates. Only the Holy Spirit can do that. It is a revelation of the heart.

The Holy Spirit will call you and endeavour to win your heart. He is usually not going to force you; it is an invitation. He knocks on your heart and says, 'How would you like to take part in the best thing that has ever been offered to the human race? It is a kingdom of love, a place where everybody loves everybody from the King on down.'

But to many people, love is just another four-letter word they don't relate to. I have asked hundreds of people if they ever heard their fathers or mothers say the words 'I love you, son' or 'I love you, daughter.' So many say no.

You might answer, 'I know my father never said it. He could not articulate those kind of things, but I know he loved me because we ate every day and we had a home to live in.' He worked to support you, but you needed more than that. You may be able to rationalize it intellectually, but in your emotional understanding, no loving, caring, providing, nurturing, affirming father was there for you. This left a deep vacuum. If parents would only emotionally touch and hold and affirm their children, they would grow up much better prepared to respond to the love of God.

Our hearts need to know how wonderful God is and how much He really cares for us. This revelation needs to reach deep into our inner beings.

....

Carol and I went to Rodney Howard-Browne's meeting in Fort Worth when we were visiting our daughters in June 1993. He called for all of the pastors to come forward. Carol was with me, and I was right at the end of the line. A couple hundred of us were all around the front of the church, and Rodney went along praying, 'Fill, fill, fill.'

While I was standing there I chose not to watch. I was just in God's presence. Rodney came along to me and said, 'Oh Lord, fill this man, come to this man.' He did not push me. I felt he honestly tried to impart the Holy Spirit to me, but I felt nothing. And he went on.

When I opened my eyes, I saw that one other man and I were still standing. That's when a person might think, 'Well, I am just not given to this sort of thing.'

Receive by faith

All of this caused me to relearn an old lesson: We receive everything from God by faith.

When we pray to receive the Spirit, He will often be very gentle, almost so that one may wonder, 'Am I imagining this, or is this really You, Lord?' That is when the step of faith is required. At this point people can resist or submit. This is the time to get out of the boat and walk on the water in childlike trust.

I had to start receiving that way – by faith instead of by feelings. That's how I should have received all along. So after I started exercising my faith, I got to the point where experiencing the manifestations and feelings was not important to me, which is a good place to be. Everybody could fall except me, and I really did not mind. I was receiving the things of God, whether I felt I was or not.

If you are one of those who are frustrated because you don't seem to be feeling much of anything, you must accept this fact: When you ask, you receive the Spirit of God whether you feel anything or not because the things of God are received by faith. The feelings are great, and I love them as much as anybody, but everyone receives by faith. The righteous will live by faith (Gal. 3.11).

I love to tell the story about Jim Robb, a Vineyard pastor from Washington, DC. He came to our meeting in April 1994 because he wanted to receive the power of the Spirit in a refreshing new way.

Jim stayed three or four days and nothing much happened. He phoned home to say he was staying longer. Twenty-three days later he went home discouraged because his perception was that he did not receive an anointing or refreshing from God. He had felt or manifested nothing.

Sunday came and Jim said to himself, 'I will pray for the people anyway, as I always used to do.' But when he went into ministry time at church, the Holy Spirit hit like a tidal wave. It was incredible. People were strewn all over the floor – some laughing, some crying. It was so wonderful and totally unexpected by him.

Pastor Robb was now excited. He did not phone or fax me, but got back on an airplane and flew to Toronto to tell me face-to-face that he really had received after all. Because he had persisted in prayer for twenty-one days, God had filled his life. It became obvious when he ministered in his church. To fall, shake a bit or to laugh was not the issue. He had really received by faith.

Empirical evidence on the benefits of the 'Toronto blessing' comes from this unique study.

19.2   Margaret Poloma, 'A Reconfiguration of Pentecostalism', in David Hilborn (ed.), *'Toronto' in Perspective*, Carlisle: Acute, 2001, pp. 101–4

Gamaliel's Test I: Social Psychological Data

TAV is Toronto Airport Vineyard, TTB is The Toronto Blessing, P/C the Pentecostal/Charismatic, TACF is Toronto Airport Christian Fellowship (the new name of TAV). Gamaliel is the rabbi who was Paul's teacher and who is referred to in Acts 5.34–9. He advised a policy of 'wait and see' to discover whether the new Christian movement was a divine initiative.

When I first visited TAV in November 1994, I felt in some ways as if I had just entered a Methodist camp meeting of the nineteenth century, or had chanced upon a meeting of William Seymour on Azusa Street in the early twentieth century. Although I had been involved in the Catholic charismatic movement during the late 1970s, and had studied classic Pentecostalism in the 1980s, I had never witnessed anything like the strange manifestations I saw all around me. My earlier cynical evaluation of TTB as simply another hyped attempt to rekindle the fire from the cooling embers of an earlier wave of the charismatic movement, was immediately challenged. TTB was a happening of greater intensity and duration than anything I had yet experienced during years of studying the P/C movement, and I wanted to research it for posterity. When I approached Toronto's pastor, John, with a plan to conduct a survey on pilgrims to the site, Arnott's immediate response was, 'What can I do to help you?' He is as eager as I was to secure some hard data with which to address the 'Gamaliel' issue.

In 1995 we conducted a non-random survey distributed through the August issue of TAV's *Spread the Fire* magazine, through the church's October 'Catch the Fire Again' programme and through its November 'Healing School Programme'. Questionnaires were returned to the author at The University Akron, Ohio, with a place for the respondent to indicate whether he or she would be willing to participate in a possible follow-up study. A total of 918 usable responses were received from 20 countries, with the largest proportions coming from the USA and Canada (26%), and England (11%). Seventy-five per cent provided a usable address for the follow-up survey, which was conducted in May 1997 and which yielded data on 364 of the original respondents.

While such non-random procedures do not permit generalizations to the hundreds of thousands of persons who visited Toronto during the on-going renewal meetings, they do permit us to describe some of the possible effects TTB has had on the respondents – conclusions that could, with caution, be extended to thousands of others who did not fill out the surveys. Responses to sets of questions will be presented in this article: those concerning increases in personal empowerment, and those addressing increases in service and outreach.

Personal empowerment

Although the doctrine and experience of glossolalia has been the focal point for many in the classic Pentecostal movement, Third Wave (out of which TTB developed) has placed less emphasis on speaking in tongues and more on empowerment by the Holy Spirit. The preliminary and exploratory questions asked in the 1995 survey indicated that the vast majority of the respondents (92%) had experienced the power of God, and that it lasted even after leaving TACF. Presumably it was this fresh touch of the power that that led 90 per cent of them to invite others to come to TACF to report that evangelism was more important to them than it had ever been before. The follow-up survey secured additional information on experiences of empowerment.

More than half of the 1997 respondents indicated an increase in receiving prophetic words (62%) while almost half reported an increase in receiving words of knowledge (47%), prophetic intercession (48%) and prophetic dreams (41%). Similar figures were reported for an increase in empowerment in praying for the physical and emotional healing of others since visiting the renewal in Toronto: 49 per cent replied that there was an increase in emotional healing and 34 per cent saw an increase in their efficacy in praying for physical healing.

In sum, it would appear that many pilgrims to Toronto did experience a fresh release of charismatic gifts, particularly in the realms of the prophetic and of healing, both of which are subjects of regular conferences conducted at TACF. On the basis of this survey, it would be safe to say that many individuals who have visited TACF believed they were moving in a much greater power of the Spirit in 1997 than they were in pre-renewal days.

Increase in service and outreach

Another area of questioning in the 1997 survey that is relevant to the Gamaliel Test is whether renewal participants were moved to action as a result of the Blessing. We have already seen that many purported to be more effective in charismatic ministry, especially in the areas of prophecy and healing. Other questions tapped an increase in service and outreach to the larger community.

Nine questions were asked to determine whether participants became more involved in outreach as a result of the renewal, with a mean or average of 3.6 and a median of 4. This statistic suggests that the model respondent increased his or her service for approximately four of the listed items. Those experiencing the Blessing reported themselves to be more likely to offer assistance to friends (64%) or acquaintances (57%) as a result of their Toronto experience. They were also more likely to increase their service to the church (55%), to give financially to missions (44%) and the poor (35%), to visit the sick (34%), to lead others to Christ (25%), to reach out to the poor and homeless (24%), and to be involved in other works of mercy (20%).

There appears to be a relatively strong relationship between experiencing an increase in empowerment and reporting increase in outreach to others. Those who have been more effective in prayers of prophecy and healing are more likely to report an increase in works of service. While these are personal data self-reports, they do suggest that there are countless individual whose ministries have been enhanced as a result of their experience of TTB.

An appropriate sociological question to explore is how personal experiences and individual outreach have generated institutions that in turn provide resources for the revitalization and the spread of the P/C movement. Assuming that institutions are the result of collective social behaviour, it is theoretically sound to expect that the recent experience of charismata through TTB would have been responsible for at least some reshaping transforming of the P/C movement.

Used by permission of Paternoster/Acute, PO Box 300, Carlisle, Cumbria CA3 0QS, UK.

20 Community

Here Stanton explains how Europe's oldest charismatic community based at Bugbrooke, UK, came about and why.

20.1 Noel Stanton, 'Christian Community',
http://www.jesus.org.uk/nccc/articles_index2.shtml (2003)

CHRISTIAN COMMUNITY

A radical, shared lifestyle is scriptural, makes economic sense, shows true justice and encourages real relationships and discipleship, . . .

There's no better way than 'big house' community. The New Creation Christian Community is the heart of Jesus Fellowship UK.

NCCC was birthed some 28 years ago when the Holy Spirit spoke to those of us who had been baptised in the Spirit, were moving in new spiritual discoveries, and began to understand the nature of a truly New Testament church. We were enthused by the Spirit to follow the teachings of Jesus without attempting to dilute them in any way. We saw the need to face up to such issues as who are our true brothers, sisters, mothers, fathers, children – as we belong together in the family of God. We read the warnings of Jesus concerning the danger of riches and the need to beware of the false security of worldly wealth and possessions. We noted how Jesus taught that we should be content with food, clothing and shelter, which God would provide as we seek first His Kingdom. We saw how Jesus emphasised the need, for the sake of our souls, to share wealth with the poor and so to produce justice, equality and kingdom brotherhood. We noted how Jesus called people to be fully committed disciples, to renounce all other things and to expect conflict with the natural family. And so we realised that we must be a 'church which Jesus builds' – and become an 'alternative society', a community (as with the first Christians following Pentecost) where we could work out the practice of God's new society in covenant brotherhood, with supernatural signs and wonders, with oneness in perfect love and with people regularly being saved. We noted how these were the things which proved that Jesus had ascended to the right hand of God as Lord and King and had sent the Holy Spirit to empower, build and spread His church.

And we saw that such apostolic communities were the proper environment for receiving disciples of Jesus Christ, drawing them into strong unity in His cause, and equipping them with spiritual gifts and character strengths to build and serve His church.

It has not been an easy path. Disciplines and standards have to be accepted by everyone and upheld by leaders. And there is the inevitable pain of building trusting relationships with a variety of people, many of whom have suffered hurts and rejections. Forgiveness, patience, and enduring love are vital qualities for successful community living.

Used by permission of John Campbell, Director of Communications, Jesus Fellowship/New Creation Christian Community, Nether Heyford, Northampton, UK.

A Roman Catholic charismatic community in the United States of America sets out its aims.

20.2   Mother of God Community, Gaithersburg
http://www.motherofgod.org/ (2003)

The mission of Mother of God Community is to be used by God to lead people into a close personal relationship with Jesus Christ through Christian formation, baptism in the Holy Spirit and follow-up teachings in a community environment, so that they may have Life and have it in abundance, now and for all eternity.

Mother of God Community is a Catholic and ecumenical charismatic community standing in a long tradition of spiritual renewal movements within the Catholic Church. Our calling is to live out the gospel and to grow in the knowledge of God through prayer, fellowship, evangelization and service. Members include Christians from all walks of life – families, couples, priests, and single people. We represent a wide variety of professions and backgrounds, yet are all united by a common desire to live out God's call in fellowship and community. With the guidance of the Spirit, the Community aspires to be a people:

- whose deepest desire is that God be reverenced, loved and honored;
- who witness to the primacy of Christ, the firstborn of all creation;
- who seek to deepen the Christian life in close fellowship under the lordship of Jesus;

- who are empowered by the Spirit to proclaim the Gospel by word and deed in anticipation of Christ's return;
- who witness to the call to Christian unity in the one Body of Christ.

The community is recognized within the Archdiocese of Washington as a Private Association of the Faithful. This is a canonical designation which indicates that a religious organization is officially approved for voluntary participation by Catholics. The process of obtaining this recognition included the writing of statutes governing the life of the community and the holding of elections for the community leadership.

Used by permission of the Mother of God Community, 20501 Goshen Road, Gaithersburg, MD 20879, USA.

Terminology like 'Pentecostal' or 'Charismatic', 'Baptised in the Holy Spirit' or 'renewed' . . . depended on one's roots ecclesiologically. However, here Cardinal Suenens acknowledges that this is a worldwide phenomenon and covers a number of issues so far examined in this chapter.

20.3   Cardinal Suenens, 'An Evaluation of the Charismatic Movement', *Renewal* 76, 1978, pp. 24, 25

Nowadays the renewal is no longer only an American phenomenon. It is worldwide. It is well worth looking at the richness which spiritual renewal can bring on the personal level as well as on the community and ecumenical levels. Here are a few reflections on each of these aspects.

Personal aspect

Without mutual contact all types of people from every corner of the world and from all walks of life witness to the fact that in letting themselves be invaded by the Holy Spirit they have had a spiritual experience which has touched them profoundly. This experience, which is at the basis and touchstone of renewal, is called currently 'baptism in the Spirit'. This comes from John's words in St Matthew's gospel where he says Jesus will baptise the disciples with the Holy Spirit and with fire (Matt. 3.11). Many theologians are at the moment reflecting on and analysing this experience, and are publishing new studies on the subject and on what should be understood by the term 'baptism in the Spirit'. For the Catholic theologian there is of course no question of a super-baptism, the Holy Spirit being given to us by the sacraments of baptism and confirmation. It is rather an experience which makes the believer pass from mere theory to reality, and which springs up from within him, releasing and freeing latent inner energies and showing itself in the depth of his life with the Lord.

One hears testimonies such as: 'I have discovered Jesus Christ in a more intimate and personal way; I have experienced a new taste for scripture as the word of life; I see the sacramental and institutional church with new eyes.'

I have before me a booklet from the Society of Jesus in which some forty Jesuits, of varied and extensive experience, testify to this new hold of the Holy Spirit on their lives, on their ministries and even on their Ignatian vocation according to the charism of the founder.

If I emphasise the central, experiential aspect of renewal, it is because it must be thought of from that angle. The criteria for the authenticity of renewal are to be found at one and the same time in the fruit of the Spirit, in the love which St Paul proclaims as the heart (or greatest) of all the gifts, and in apostolic boldness. For the Spirit is given to reveal and to bring Jesus Christ to the world; the Spirit is always at the heart of the apostolate, the inspirer of missionary zeal.

Prayer groups are too often judged by the degree of their free expression and spontaneity in prayer or praying in tongues. These things throw light on the interior when one has understood where the vital centre of renewal is truly found. It does not come from groups turned in on themselves, but from those open to the world; prayer cells whose members go out to make known the message and the living person of the risen Jesus Christ.

Community aspect

The renewal is brought alive in prayer groups, but it is also realised through the creation of communities where some Christians truly share their lives according to precise commitments, the 'covenant'; often with the sharing of goods in whole or in part. Steve Clark, one of the leaders of the Word of God community in Ann Arbor, rightly wrote: 'What the church needs today, more than new institutions or new programmes, are vital Christian communities.'

Ecumenical aspect

The groups I have just mentioned are generally ecumenical. This poses problems for it is necessary to live in mutual openness and also to respect each one's identity. It would be a negation of authentic ecumenism if Christians only met on the basis of the lowest common denominator. This would only lead to a churchless Christianity or to a super-church, without any foundation. There is a place for research into ways of entering into the visible unity which renewal opens up, responding to all the hopes of reconciliation, without doctrinal confusion and untruthfulness.

Conclusion

The Spirit blows where he wills. He is not limited by any human barrier. There have, however, been times in the history of the Church when he has worked with a particular power. St Francis, St Ignatius, St Theresa are examples of moments of this sort, which have affected the Church of their time and of the generations to come.

The charismatic renewal, which by no means claims a monopoly of the Spirit, is a grace which respects our freedom. A movement, or better a motion, of the Spirit, but experienced by men, the charismatic renewal is exposed to pitfalls like every movement which is also human. 'We carry our treasures in fragile vessels', St Paul says. In an emergency the treasure is of quality and it is that which matters.

I recall the words of Paul Verney: 'What interests me is not the foam of the waves, but the sea'. The sea has its reefs and its sandbanks, but it also has the power to carry fleets of ships and to unite continents.

21 Mega Churches

One example of a church in the process of growing into a cell-style mega church is London City Church. Based at Kensington Temple, part of the Elim Pentecostal Churches of Great Britain, and a well-known church since the Jeffrey Brothers' days, Colin Dye has made it international and 'grows' it after the G12 model of César Castellanos, Colombia.

21.1   Colin Dye, 'Kensington Temple: London City Church', http://www.kt.org/g12/london.php (2004)

Our dream has always been to play our part in winning London and the world for Christ. That's our mission. We consider that the Lord has mandated us as a church of influence in London with an apostolic and prophetic call for Britain, Europe and the nations of the world. Where are we now in relation to this vision?

New Millennium strategy

For years we have been pioneering new ways of doing church in London. The London City Church vision is unique. From 1985 to 2000, we planted around 150 churches together with 450 other groups and ministries networked together in one fellowship, one church – LCC. This meant we had achieved 30 per cent of our total goals. We have never tried to become some mega church centred on one or two superstar preachers. Rather, we have always been about establishing the kingdom of God in people's hearts and discipling them into the body of Christ as active members.

The underachievement of our goals, however, meant we needed to find new ways of mobilising God's people. The goal is for every member of the KT/LCC network to be serving Jesus and fulfilling the vision of Christ – to make, mature and mobilise disciples of all nations. We fulfilled our vision for the 1990s: to become a fully functioning City Church. Now, the church is moving forward in the G12 Vision and continuing to win London for Christ and to reach out into the unevangelised nations of the world.

The focus is now on the cells as the principal means of becoming the church of influence, which Christ has called us to be. We want to become a very effective discipling force in London. Our Mission Statement is still 'London and the World for Christ'. The London City Church is now set to move forward in this mission.

Blessings from Bogotá

In the summer of 2000, Colin and Amanda Dye led a team of leaders to Bogotá, Colombia, in South America. They went to look at the ministry of Pastor César Castellanos. His church, The International Charismatic Mission had grown from 8 members to well over 120,000 in just 18 years. Most of this growth had occurred in the previous five or six years. What was the reason for this explosion? The Lord gave Pastor César a vision of the multitudes and a strategy to reach them. It is a cell church ministry based on groups of 12 (G12). Colin said that the G12 strategy was the best method of training, releasing and mobilising the body of Christ that he had ever seen. It was a God-given strategy for the Church of the end times. But he saw it was much, much more than a strategy or a method. It was a vision from the Lord. The team came back from Bogotá full of joy and ready for the public launch of KT's own G12 vision – Discipleship Cell Explosion.

Building bigger people

In line with the national vision of the Elim Church, Colin Dye emphasizes the growth of the church by discipleship. This was his motivation in moving to a cell church model.

The cell church transition

In September 2003, Kensington Temple, London City Church completed a three-year transition into the G12 model of cell church, having grown to 11,000 people in 1,800 cells. With now around 70 per cent of the church active in cells the leadership are well on their way to achieve their goal of maximum mobilization. Now, the main thrust of the life and ministry of the church is through the cells. These cells are considered tiny units of 'church' doing everything that 'church' should be doing. Cells are now where the evangelism, discipleship, pastoral care and prayer life of the Kensington Temple takes place.

The fruit of the cell vision

Kensington Temple has seen remarkable growth seeing a retention rate for new believers grow from under 10 per cent to over 60 per cent. New believers are being added to the cells every day and 1,700 new leaders have been raised over the last two years. The G12 strategy is also being adopted by churches all over Europe where there are early signs of fruit as some churches transitioning to G12 are reporting a doubling and trebling of their numbers. The strategy is proving to be adaptable to cultures outside Latin America.

Used by permission of Colin Dye, senior leader, London City Church. http://www.kt.org

Further Reading

Journals

Asian Journal of Pentecostal Studies, starts in 1998. http://www.apts.edu/ajps
Australasian Pentecostal Studies starts 1998
Cyberjournal For Pentecostal/Charismatic Research. http://www.pctii.org/cybertab.html
Journal of Asian Mission, starts 1999.
Journal of Pentecostal Theology (University of Sheffield Press), starts in 1992.
Journal of the European Pentecostal Theological Association (run by EPTA), starts *c.* 1981.
Pneuma, starts 1979, run by the Society for Pentecostal Studies, a scholarly society for looking at Pentecostal theology and history; originally North American but now wider.
The Spirit and the Church, starts 1999.

Out-of-print journals like *Confidence* or *Word and Witness* may be available from the research centres either directly on line or by purchasing a CD-ROM

Annotated suggestions for further reading

Allen, D. (1994), *The Unfailing Stream*, Tonbridge, Sovereign World. [Traces charismata through church history in a readable account.]
Anderson, A. (2004), *An Introduction to Pentecostalism: Global Charismatic Christianity*, Cambridge: Cambridge University Press.
Anderson A. and Tang, E. (eds) (2004), *Asian and Pentecostal: The Charismatic Face of Asian Christianity*, Oxford: Regnum.
Barrett, D. and Johnson, T. (2002), 'Global Statistics', in S. Burgess and E. Van der Maas (eds), *New International Dictionary of Pentecostal and Charismatic Movements*, 2nd edn, Grand Rapids, Mich.: Zondervan. [The best statistical data available on this subject.]
Barrett, D. B. and Johnson, T. M. (1998), 'Annual statistical table on global mission: 1998', *International Bulletin* 22.1, 26, 27.
Barron, B. (1987), *The Health and Wealth Gospel*, Downers Grove, Ill.: Inter-Varsity Press. [Critique of health and wealth: faith teaching, a relatively recent phenomenon.]
Bloch-Hoell, N. (1964), *The Pentecostal Movement*, London: Allen and Unwin. [Early classic.]

Blumhofer, E. W. (1985), *The Assemblies of God: A Popular History*, Springfield: Gospel Publishing House. [Paperback version of a 2-volume history by a Harvard-trained historian.]

Blumhofer, E. W. (1993), *Aimee Semple McPherson: Everybody's Sister*, Grand Rapids, Mich.: Eerdmans. [Edith Blumhofer looks at a key female evangelist and church founder.]

Boulton, E. C. W. (1928), *George Jeffreys: A Ministry of the Miraculous*, London: Elim Publishing House. [Early account of Jeffreys' ministry. Jeffreys founded Elim.]

Bundy, D., (1992), 'Thomas B. Barratt and Byposten: An Early European Pentecostal Leader and his Periodical', in J. A. B. Jongeneel, C. van der Laan, P. N. van der Laan, M. Robinson and P. Staples (eds), *Pentecost, Mission and Ecumenism: Essays on Intercultural Theology*, Berlin: Peter Lang.

Burgess, S. M. and van der Maas, E. (eds) (2002), *New International Dictionary of the Pentecostal and Charismatic Movements*, Grand Rapids, Mich.: Zondervan. [Promises to be *the* book to tell you everything; this edition is less North American in focus.]

Cartledge, M. J. (2002), *Charismatic Glossolalia*, Aldershot: Ashgate. [An interpretation of charismatic glossolalia using van der Ven's methods and approach.]

Cartwright, D. W. (1986), *The Great Evangelists*, Basingstoke: Marshall Pickering. [Detailed and factual account of Stephen and George Jeffreys.]

Cartwright, D. W. (2000), *The Real Wigglesworth*, Tonbridge: Sovereign World. [Accurate and stirring account of influential Pentecostal hero; probably the best of many.]

Coleman, S. (2000), *The Globalisation of Charismatic Christianity*, Cambridge: Cambridge University Press. [A Swedish charismatic church that embraces 'word of faith' teaching, written by an eloquent and neutral anthropologist.]

Conn, C. W. (1977), *Like a Mighty Army: A History of the Church of God 1886–1976*, Cleveland, Tenn.: Pathway Press. [Church of God history that reveals the pre-1900 precursors of Pentecostalism.]

Cox, H. (1996), *Fire from Heaven: The Rise of Pentecostal Spirituality and the Reshaping of Religion in the Twenty-first Century*, London: Cassell. [Popular study by non-Pentecostal.]

Daniels, D. D. (1999), '"Everybody Bids You Welcome": A Multicultural Approach to North American Pentecostalism', in M. W. Dempster, B. D. Klaus and D. Petersen (eds), *The Globalisation of Pentecostalism*, Oxford: Regnum. [Collection of chapters that addresses the global phenomenon of Pentecostalism from an academic perspective.]

Daniels, D. D. (2002), 'Charles Harrison Mason: The Interracial Impulse of

Early Pentecostalism', in J. R. Goff and Grant Wacker (eds), *Portraits of a Generation*, Fayetteville: University of Arkansas Press.

Dayton, D. W. (1987), *Theological Roots of Pentecostalism*, Peabody, Mass.: Hendrickson. [From Methodism to Pentecostalism–an excellent historico-theological study.]

Del Colle, R. (1997), 'Oneness and Trinity: A Preliminary Proposal for Dialogue with Oneness Pentecostalism', *Journal of Pentecostal Theology* 10, 85–110.

Dempster, M. W., Klaus, B. D. and Petersen, D. (eds) (1999), *The Globalisation of Pentecostalism*, Oxford: Regnum [Thoughtful set of essays by a range of Pentecostal scholars.]

Faupel, D. W. (1996), *The Everlasting Gospel: The Significance of Eschatology in the Development of Pentecostal Thought*, Sheffield: Sheffield Academic Press. [Excellent account dealing with the early years.]

Gee, G. (1967), *Wind and Flame*, Nottingham: Assemblies of God Publishing House. [Hard to obtain but written by a respected participator in the events; unreferenced, though.]

Hocken, P. (1994), *The Glory and the Shame*, Guildford: Eagle. [Leading Catholic charismatic scholar ponders the outpouring of the Spirit.]

Hocken, P. D. (1984), 'Baptised in the Spirit: The Origins and Early Development of the Charismatic Movement in Great Britain', doctoral dissertation, University of Birmingham.

Hollenweger, W. J. (1972), *The Pentecostals*, London: SCM Press [A huge German-language doctorate using multi-lingual resources that has been boiled down into a big book; Hollenweger became Professor of Mission at Birmingham after working for the World Council of Churches.]

Hollenweger, W. J. (1997), *Pentecostalism: Origins and Developments Worldwide*, Peabody, Mass.: Hendrickson. [Provocative but magisterial.]

Horton, H. (1946), *The Gifts of the Spirit*, 2nd edn, Luton: Redemption Tidings Bookroom. [Classic Pentecostal view, written first in the 1930s.]

Hunt, S., Hamilton, M. and Walter, T. (eds), (1997), *Charismatic Christianity: Sociological Perspectives*, Basingstoke: Macmillan. [Sociological perspectives; high quality chapters.]

Hwa Yung (2003), 'Endued with Power: The Pentecostal–Charismatic Renewal and the Asian Church of the Twenty-first Century', *Asian Journal of Pentecostal Studies* 6.1, 63–82.

Jeffreys, G. (1929), *The Miraculous Foursquare Gospel*, vol. 1, London: Elim Publishing Company. [Early account by Jeffreys himself.]

Jeffreys, G. (1932), *Healing Rays*, London: Elim Publishing Company. [Provides a dispensational doctrine of healing and questions and answers at the end.]

Jones, B. P. (1995), *An Instrument of Revival: The Complete Life of Evan Roberts 1878–1951*, South Plainfield, NJ.: Bridge Publishing. [A bit uncritical but you get an idea of Evan Roberts and his impact.]

Kay, W. K. (1990), *Inside Story*, Mattersey: LifeStream/Mattersey Hall Publishing. [Denominational history of British Assemblies of God.]

Kay, W. K. (1992), 'Three Generations On: The Methodology of Pentecostal Historiography', *EPTA Bulletin* 10.1–2, 58–70 (actually the 1990 issue published late). [Theoretical account of problems of writing history that includes miracles etc.]

Kay, W. K. (2000), *Pentecostals in Britain*, Carlisle: Paternoster. [Takes Assemblies of God, Elim, the Apostolics and the Church of God and tells four parallel histories as well as providing empirical data on ministerial beliefs and values.]

Kildahl, J. P. (1972), *The Psychology of Speaking in Tongues*, London: Hodder & Stoughton. [Outdated and hostile, but influential at one point in time.]

Land, S. J. (1993), *Pentecostal Spirituality: A Passion for the Kingdom*, Sheffield: Sheffield Academic Press. [Original and passionate; a good theological read.]

MacRobert, I. (1992), 'The Black Roots of Pentecostalism', in J. A. B. Jongeneel, C. van der Laan, P. N. Van der Laan, M. Robinson and P. Staples (eds), *Pentecost, Mission and Ecumenism: Essays on Intercultural Theology*, Berlin: Peter Lang. [Emphasizing black roots to Pentecostalism.]

Martin, D. (1996), *Forbidden Revolutions*, London: SPCK. [Looks at Pentecostalism comparing it with secular revolutionary forces.]

Martin, D. (2002), *Pentecostalism: The World is their Parish*, Oxford: Blackwell Publishers. [Great breadth and compression; why does Pentecostalism do better in S. America and Asia than Europe? Martin provides some ideas.]

McDonnell, K., and Montague, G. T. (1991), *Christian Initiation and Baptism in the Holy Spirit*, Collegeville, Minn.: Liturgical Press. [Roman Catholic charismatic scholars work with early texts; a sympathetic account.]

McGee, G. B. (ed.) (1991), *Initial Evidence: Historical and Biblical Perspectives on the Pentecostal Doctrine of Spirit Baptism*, Peabody, Mass.: Hendrickson. [The debate about speaking in tongues brought up to date.]

Poloma, M. M. (1989), *Assemblies of God at the Crossroads*, Knoxville, Tenn.: University of Tennessee Press. [Classic account of AG in the States; is the fire in danger of going out?]

Riss, Richard M. (1988), *A Survey of Twentieth Century Revival Movements in North America*, Peabody, Mass: Hendrickson.

Robeck, C. M. (2002), 'Azusa Street Revival', in S. Burgess and E. Van der Maas (eds), *New International Dictionary of Pentecostal and Charismatic Movements*, 2nd edn, Grand Rapids, Mich.: Zondervan.

Samarin, W. J. (1959), 'Glossolalia as Learned Behaviour', *Canadian Journal of Theology* 15, 60–4. [Classic but hostile account from a linguist about speaking in tongues.]

Springer, K. (ed.) (1987), *Riding the Third Wave*, Basingstoke: Marshall Pickering.

Strachan, G. (1973), *The Pentecostal Theology of Edward Irving*, London, Darton, Longman & Todd. [Excellent introductory account to the life and work of the great Edward Irving.]

Synan, V. (1997), *The Holiness–Pentecostal Tradition*, Grand Rapids: Eerdmans. [American viewpoint; first published in 1971 and now updated.]

Synan, V. (ed.) (2001), *The Century of the Holy Spirit*, Nashville: Thomas Nelson. [Good chapters on TV evangelists; a simple book to start with, but too North American.]

Taylor, M. J. (1994), 'Publish and Be Blessed: A Case Study in Early Pentecostal Publishing History, 1906–1926', unpublished PhD dissertation, University of Birmingham.

Turnbull, T. N. (1963), *Brothers in Arms*, Bradford: Puritan Press. [The Welsh Apostolics, told uncritically.]

Virgo, T. (1985), *Restoration in the Church*, Eastbourne: Kingsway. [House church theology.]

Virgo, T. (2001), *No Well-Worn Paths*, Eastbourne: Kingsway. [Leader of NFI tells his arresting story.]

Wakefield, G. (2001), *The First Pentecostal Anglican: The Life and Legacy of Alexander Boddy*, Grove Booklets. [Excellent short introduction to Boddy's life and work; see also the rest of the Grove renewal series.]

Walker, A. (1998), *Restoring the Kingdom*, Guildford: Eagle. [*The* book on the emergence of the new churches in Britain from the 1970s onwards.]

Warner, Rob, 'Ecstatic Spirituality and Entrepreneurial Revivalism: Reflections on the "Toronto Blessing"', in A. Walker and K. Aune (eds), *On Revival: A Critical Examination*, Carlisle: Paternoster. [Series of authoritative studies and reflections.]

Warrington, K. (ed.), *Pentecostal Perspectives*, Carlisle: Paternoster. [Contains interesting chapters on theology and history by British Pentecostals.]

Whittaker, C. (1983), *Seven Pentecostal Pioneers*, Basingstoke: Marshall Morgan & Scott.

Williams, C. G. (1981), *Tongues of the Spirit*, Cardiff: University of Wales Press. [Scholarly and sympathetic but ultimately inconclusive book on speaking in tongues.]

Wilson, B. R. (1961), *Sects and Society*, London: Heinnemann. [Classic sociological account dealing with Elim.]

Worsfold, J. E. (1991), *The Origins of the Apostolic Church in Great Britain*, Wellington, NZ: Julian Literature Trust. [Deals with the Apostolics.]

Glossary of terms

Words that have a particular technical meaning within the text are given a brief definition.

Anointed/anointing[s]	To be given particular empowering for a task by God through His Spirit. Particular times of endowment.
Baby-boomers	The generation born during the immediate post World War 2 years.
Cell groups/Cell Church	Small groups within a local church with particular emphasis on multiplying as do the body's cells: some church growth theories are based on these groups and presume that most of the main functions and sacraments of 'church' are carried out; celebrations are at congregational level. (See G12)
Cessationism	The view that spiritual gifts were restricted to the generation of the first Apostles and have since ceased.
Charismata	See spiritual gifts.
Community	Groups of Christians began to form communities by sharing lifestyles, homes and finance to enable a community to present a dynamic Christian witness to the world, mostly with a charismatic ethos.
Deliverance	A ministry whereby people are freed from evil spirits, from bondages and sicknesses in the name of Christ, by the power of Christ through the Holy Spirit.
Eschatology	Study of the last things in God's plan for the world and universe.
Evangelist	The gift of being able to equip the Church for evangelism; more often understood as the one who preaches for conversion of non-believers effectively.
Exorcism	The term for delivering someone oppressed/ possessed/demonized by evil spirits.
G12	A cell church growth system which focuses on each leader winning and training 12

	people who subsequently form their own groups of 12, created by Cesar Castellanos in Colombia. (See Cell Church)
Generation-X	The generation born between 1965 and 1985.
Gifts of the spirit/ charismata (See spiritual gifts)	Usually thought of as the 9 gifts of the Holy Spirit listed in 1 Cor. 11. C. P. Wagner, however, lists 27 such gifts.
Holiness/sanctification	A state of being acceptable – holy – before God whether considered a crisis or process in discipleship.
Holy Ghost baptism/ the baptism in or of the Spirit/Pentecostal baptism/Spirit-baptism	Outpouring, falling upon, infilling with the power of the Holy Spirit.
Initial evidence	Classical Pentecostals understand that speaking in unknown tongues is the first sign of being baptized in the Spirit. Charismatics (and ELIM) debate that position, claiming other gifts/signs are equally valid as initial evidence of the Baptism in the Holy Spirit.
Justification	A legal term for what takes place at conversion/regeneration/new birth, used by Paul (Rom. 3–8) for being freed from the punishment and guilt of sin by Christ's atoning death.
Latter Rain Movement	This movement, originating in Canada in late 1940s, used for its name the eschatological term for the last days; it is metaphorically based on the former and latter rainy seasons in Israel, the latter heavier than the former; they hoped for revival in the last days and adopted the Ephesians 4.11 ministry gifts for their leadership.
Laying on of hands	Following biblical patterns found, e.g. Acts 19.6, Heb. 6.2, Pentecostal and Charismatic people used this method of imparting the Holy Spirit to those desiring Spirit baptism, healing, releasing of giftings, etc.
Mega-church	A size of church with members numbered in the thousands.
Millennium	This term for 1000 years has become associated with a post-*parousia* stage in earth's history, when Christ will reign with his saints on earth in utopian peace. Pre, post and A-

millennial terms also form part of the eschatological debate. (NB in earthly time sense
20–21st centuries see 6.0, 19.1, 21.1.)

Ministry Gifts	Apostles, Prophets, Evangelists, Pastors, Teachers c.f. Ephesians 4.11. Gifts of Christ to the Church. Debate has been over function or office of these five.
Paraclete	A term for the Holy Spirit found in John's Gospel, meaning one who comes alongside implying to strengthen, counsel, comfort.
Parousia	Literally an 'appearance' or 'presence', it is an eschatological term for the Second Coming of Christ as Judge and King, as promised in Acts 1.11.
Pentecostal	An adjective for the term derived from the Feast of Pentecost, 50 days after Passover noted in Acts 2, it describes the experience of the disciples which is seen as duplicated in the experience of many believers during the 20th century, particularly triggered by events at Azusa St.
Pentecostalism	A term used by traditions outside the Pentecostal Movement.
Power encounter	A confrontation of the Holy Spirit through a Christian, with a non-Christian power, often in cross-cultural situations. It is hoped that these will stimulate conversions to Christ.
Prophecy	Words given by God's Spirit through a person so gifted/enabled at that time, to include forth-telling and fore-telling God's word, as instruction, guidance, comfort.
Prophesy/prophesying	Ability to give a vocal (occasionally written) message from God's Holy Spirit to the church/individual/even nation[s]. Spiritual gift see 1 Cor. 12–14.
Prophet	One who gives prophetic words through God's Spirit for the church; both forth-telling and fore-telling can be included.
Rapture	A stage in eschatological terms when Christ will catch up his people, resurrected and alive to be with him at his *parousia*, to reign with him. The debate is centred on when it will take place – pre/mid/post tribulation.

Renewal	A term mostly mainline denominational Charismatics use, hoping for renewal of spiritual life in their churches, often through small prayer groups where *charismata* can be used.
Restoration	An understanding of the Church being restored to New Testament principles, as part of an eschatological sign, with hope for world wide revival before Christ's *parousia*.
Sacrament / sacramental	A particular emphasis on Eucharist, baptism and other rituals as marks of the Church, which have more than symbolic meaning. An act or means of receiving grace.
Sanctification	A doctrinal stance on the means to holiness. (See holiness.)
Shepherding	A view of church leadership and pastoral care whereby church members submit themselves to be guided authoritatively by the leaders/ pastors on every issue of life.
Slain under the power/ fell under the hand of the Lord	Fallen prostrate, overcome by the Spirit.
Spiritual gifts	Usually thought of as the 9 gifts enabled by the Holy Spirit listed in 1 Cor. 11. C. P. Wagner, however, lists 27 possibilities. Spiritual warfare based on the Ephesians 6.10–18 metaphor of spiritual armour. There are various advocates of how to go about the battle with evil forces, through prayer, praise, research into spiritual use of physical territory/items, aiming to ease conversions.
Tele-evangelist	Evangelists have created, broadcast and sponsored television programmes for purposes of world evangelization, particularly from the USA since the 1950s, often with healing ministries involved, and as the means of sponsoring humanitarian aid.
The Fall	Augustinian and Reformation doctrine stressed the sinfulness of man is inherited from Adam who 'fell' from God's intended glory and grace for mankind through disobedience.
The New Churches	Churches considering themselves outside denominational lines; formed during the era after 1950/60; mostly 'charismatic'/Third Wave.

Third Wave	Churches with experience of charismata who do not count themselves as part of the First (Pentecostal) or Second (Charismatic) waves of the Holy Spirit's work in the 20th century.
Tongues	An ability/gift to speak in languages other than any learned intellectually: a spiritual gift, see 1 Cor. 12–14, Acts 2, 10, 19.
Tribulation	A stage in eschatological terms for a severe persecution of God's people. The debate is centred on when it will take place – pre/mid/post rapture/ millennium.

Time Line of Events of the Pentecostal and Charismatic Movements in Britain and the USA

UK	Influences from the rest of the world	USA

1860s onwards Holiness Movements used terminology, like Baptism in the Holy Ghost, later adopted with new meaning by the Pentecostal Movement. Various streams from these American or British Keswick Higher Life teachings (1875 onwards) were instrumental in building a platform for the Pentecostals.

1867 IPHC National Holiness Association formed in Vineland, NJ. (IPHC[1])

1887 Christian and Missionary Alliance founded by **A. B. Simpson** promoting the **'Fourfold Gospel', Jesus Saviour, Healer, Baptiser and Coming King**.

1879 Iowa Holiness Association formed.

1886 Barney Creek meetings became the proto-**Church of God**.[2]

1895–98 First Pentecostal Holiness congregation organized in Goldsboro, NC.

1899 Fire-Baptized Holiness Association (national) formed; B. H. Irwin elected general overseer.

UK	Influences from the rest of the world	USA
		1901 Charles Parham at Topeka, Kansas. **Agnes Ozman** received the gift of tongues and that began to become a sign of receiving the Baptism of the Holy Ghost.
		1902 first Church of God is formed.
	1904 The Welsh Revival became a catalyst for furthering hunger for God in Britain, India, France and California.	
		1905 W. J. Seymour accepts Parham's doctrine.
		1906–07 First General Assembly of the Church of God, Cleveland, Tennessee.
		1906–09 Azusa Street Revival, Los Angeles, became the centre of Pentecostal experience, with **W. J. Seymour** at the centre after events of 9 April 1906 at Bonnie Brae Street. Joseph Smale and Frank Bartleman became involved.

UK	Influences from the rest of the world	USA
		1906 T. B. Barratt visits Los Angeles, and returns to Norway to commence Pentecostal meetings there.
1907 T. B. Barratt visits Sunderland Parish Church.		
		1908 W. H. Durham visits Azusa Street from Chicago.
	1909 Willis C. Hoover founds **Pentecostal Methodist Church** of Chile.	
1909 Confidence Paper published in Sunderland.		
1909 Pentecostal Missionary Union formed through the auspices of Sunderland's Revd Alexander A. Boddy and Cecil Polhill. India and China form the initial destinations.		
1909 Apostolic Church UK formed by D. P. Williams as Apostle, and brother W. J. Williams as Prophet at Penygroes.		
		1910 David Wesley Myland wrote his book *The Latter Rain Covenant*.
		1911 Fire Baptized Holiness and Pentecostal Holiness Church mergedn Falcon, NC, and S. D. Page elected first general superintendent.

UK	Influences from the rest of the world	USA
		1910 W. H. Durham begins **Finished Work** movement in Chicago.
		1911 A second visit of W. H. Durham to Azusa Street led to Seymour expelling him for his teaching the Spirit's coming as a two-stage event, not three. Controversy ensued.
		1911 onwards 'Jesus only'/Oneness Doctrine controversy; rejected by 1915 by Assemblies of God, USA.
		1914 Assemblies of God USA formed in Hot Springs, Arkansas.
1915 Elim Pentecostal Churches UK formed by George Jeffreys in Ireland; spread to Britain especially over 1920s–30s with evangelistic campaigns planting new churches.		
1915 W. F. P. Burton forms the **Congo Evangelistic Mission**, which would accept Pentecostal workers from various Pentecostal denominations.		
1919–30s George and Stephen Jeffreys' campaigns in Britain create many Pentecostal churches.		

UK	Influences from the rest of the world	USA
1919 Hampstead Heath Bible School, London, formed with Howard Carter as Principal, continuing the PMU's training schemes.		
1922–24 Negotiations in Britain among Pentecostal Assemblies.		
1924 The Assemblies of God Great Britain and Northern Ireland formed, unrelated to the American one.		**Aimee Semple McPherson** began preaching in 1918, and in 1923 established the 5,300 seat Angelus Temple,[3] which became the centre of her revival, healing and benevolent ministries. She was the first woman to receive an FCC radio licence and was a pioneer religious broadcaster.
		1930 Kathryn Kuhlman gains recognition by opening Denver Revival Tabernacle.
	1939 European Pentecostal Conference in Stockholm, Sweden.	
	1939–45 World War II intervenes.	

UK	Influences from the rest of the world	USA
	1947 First World Pentecostal Conference. 1947–62 David du Plessis from South Africa became General Secretary for the World Pentecostal Conferences. Donald Gee became editor of the conference's paper, *Pentecost*, until he died.	
		1948 Latter Rain Movement[4] resurfaced in North Battleford Saskatchewan by Brother Hawtin and P. G. Hunt after meeting William Branham. **20 April 1949** Opposed by Assemblies of God USA.
		1948 onwards Healing Evangelists like T. L. Osborn, W. Branham, Oral Roberts, A. A. Allen, A. C. Valdez and Katherine Kuhlman roam the world. *Voice of Healing* promotes these from Gordon Lindsay's Christ for all Nations College, Texas. **1980s** Others like Benny Hinn and Marilyn Hickey follow suit.

UK	Influences from the rest of the world	USA
		1951 Full Gospel Business Men's Fellowship International started in California by Demos Shakarian,[5] now led by Richard Shakarian it is in 132 nations, reaching Businessmen for Christ from a 'lay' perspective.
		1953 Oral Roberts begins TV ministry.
1950s Early signs of the **Charismatic Movement** in Britain.		
1961 'Another Springtime' message from Donald Gee at AoG General Conference challenged the Pentecostals to new growth in their next generation. Leaders like Nelson Parr had big churches – Bethshan in Manchester – which declined after their deaths.		

UK	Influences from the rest of the world	USA
	1962 Ecumenical Moves by David du Plessis introducing teaching on Pentecostal themes to Roman Catholics after spiritual encounters at Notre Dame. du Plessis disfellowshipped from Assemblies of God USA for contact with World Council of Churches, despite Donald Gee's support for him.	
1964 The Fountain Trust established as an organ for Charismatic Renewal among mainline churches, especially Anglicans; Michael Harper became its Director.		
		1965 Oral Roberts University chartered. The **Jesus Movement** grew up in California and spread. Arthur Blessit walked with a cross around the world during the next decade.
1965 David Watson came to St Cuthbert's Church in York and filled St Michael le Belfry by 1973 (he died in 1984). Much Evangelism resulted from renewal at this church, continuing with John Wimber's ministry visits and continues until 2000s.		

UK	Influences from the rest of the world	USA
1966 Donald Gee died.		
		1967 Catholic Charismatic Renewal begins in Pittsburg, Pennsylvania. Communities like Mother of God, Gaithersburg, Maryland, began during the 1970s–90s
Later 1960s Selwyn Hughes (originally an AoG pastor) started writing **Every Day with Jesus** as daily devotional notes, which became very popular. His **Crusade for World Revival** also began taking courses on Dynamic Christian Living, counselling, etc.		
Early 1970s Terry Virgo begins New Frontiers International from Brighton, England, and subsequently hosts Charismatic Leaders meetings.		
1974 Icthus began under **Roger Forster** in Forest Hill, London, as a holistic evangelistic training ministry.		
1975 The Jesus Fellowship formed a community group with Charismatic characteristics, and evangelistic zeal. [6]		

UK	Influences from the rest of the world	USA

1975 Bryn Jones formed the Bradford Church from three congregations,[7] which became the Headquarters for **Restoration Harvest Time** network of churches mainly in the north of UK.

1975 *Charisma* magazine begins publication.

Mid 1970s Basingstoke community churches grew up under **Barney Coombs. Cornerstone**, now **c.net churches**, grew up around **Tony Morton** in Southampton area. Major Pentecostal churches continued to grow, e.g. **Nottingham's Talbot Street Christian Centre (AoG)** under the Shearman family leadership (to around 1000 members), **Kensington Temple (Elim)** under Wynn Lewis, while others decline.

1978 CBN University (now Regent University) founded by Pat Robertson.

Late 1970s Gerald Coates in Cobham, south of London, started **Kingdom Life**, and **John Noble led Team Spirit** based in Romford, Essex. This later became **Pioneer Network of churches**.

UK	Influences from the rest of the world	USA
1981 Ground Level network begins in Lincolnshire, UK, with **Stuart Bell** as leader. 'Grapevine' commenced as annual camp for all the churches' members.		
1981 Colin Urquhart, after Anglican Ministry at Luton, was based initially with Bethany Fellowship at The Hyde (late 1970s). He developed **Kingdom Faith Ministries** with annual 'Faith Camp' at Peterborough. In 1986 they moved to Roffey House, Horsham, Surrey, as the place for Kingdom Faith Revival College. They have influence worldwide.[8]		
		1981 A Third Wave begins at Fuller Theological Seminar in California under **John Wimber**, taken up by C. P. Wagner and others.
By mid 1980s **Wimber's** influence was felt in Britain in Anglican churches e.g. **St Michael's York** and **Holy Trinity Brompton**, London, and then **Restoration groups**, as in Bradford, and other		

UK	Influences from the rest of the world	USA

denominational churches like Ansdell Baptist on the Fylde, Lancashire. Emphases were on Power Evangelism and Healing.

Throughout the 1950s–90s Pentecostal Evangelists, mainly Americans, continued to hold campaigns across the world (Britain had some evangelists like Melvyn Banks).

1992 Colin Urquhart started **Kingdom Faith Church at the National Revival Centre,** Horsham, UK, finally buying the building in 2002. A network of connected churches has since developed.

1993–January 1994 Toronto Blessing begins in Toronto Vineyard, Canada, under John Arnott; visitors arrive from all over the world.[9]

1994/95 Sunderland Revival with Ken Gott (AoG) stirs controversy over Toronto issues in UK.

1995 Brownsville Assembly of God, Pastor John Kilpatrick and Evangelist Steve Hill, Pensacola Revival, Florida, USA.[10]

UK	Influences from the rest of the world	USA
	1990s Cell Church Movement gets underway in Singapore and spreads under Lawrence Kong, Ralph Neighbour and Lawrence Singlehurst (YWAM).	
	1991 onwards G12 system of Cell Church growth develops under **Cesar Castellanos**, Colombia.	
By 2000 Metro Church International (AoG), Sunderland. Under **Ken Gott** the church began to use G12 patterns for church growth.[11]		
2000 Kensington Temple (Elim Pentecostal origins) and its many satellite churches in London make the transition to G12 Cell Church under Colin Dye.[12] (17000 membership in 2003.)[13]		

Notes

[1] http://www.IPHC.org
[2] http://www.chofgod.org/history.cfm
[3] http://www.angelustemple.org/history1.shtml
[4] http://www.discernment.org/restorat.htm#The%20Early%20Roots%20of%20
Latter%20Rain%20Theology
[5] http://www.fgbmfi.org/
[6] http://www.jesus.org.uk/ja/ja_depth.shtml
[7] http://www.deemat.pwp.blueyonder.co.uk/news.htm

8 http://www.kingdomfaith.com
9 http://www.tacf.org/
10 http://www.brownsville-revival.org/
11 http://www.mci12.org.uk/
12 http://www.kt.org
13 http://www.elim.org.uk/

Sources and Acknowledgements

There are many sources for the texts contained in this book. Full bibliographic details may be found for each excerpt on its page. The authors acknowledge below all those who have kindly consented to their material being included. For these they are grateful. Excerpts not needing such permissions are not included. Every effort has been made to trace copyright ownership, if any copyright material is found to have been used here without permission the authors apologize and ask to be informed and necessary attribution will be included in future editions.

Dave Allen for [3.5] *The Millennium – An Embarrassment or a Fundamental of the Faith?* Published as an *EPTA Conference Paper Brussels 16/4/1987* (used by permission).
Assemblies of God Great Britain and Northern Ireland for:
    [4.3] H. Horton, *The Gifts of the Spirit*.
    [4.6] C. Parker, *Gifts of Healing*.
    [5.4] D. Gee, *The Initial Evidence of the Baptism of the Holy Spirit*.
    [7.5] *Preface of Redemption Hymnal*.
    [7.6] H. Tee and C. H. Morris, *Hymns from Redemption Hymnal*.
    [12.1] J. Roswell Flower, *The Present Position of Pentecost*.
    (Used by permission.)
Assemblies of God, Springfield, USA, for [7.2] D. Gee, *Upon all Flesh: A Pentecostal World Tour*. (Permission sought.)
and The Flower Pentecostal Heritage Centre, Springfield, USA, for older articles provided:
    [2.6] George R. Hawtin, Latter Rain Movement – Letter to Wayne Warner.
    [5.2] William H. Durham, *Pentecostal Testimony 1907*.
    [6.2] William H. Durham, *Pentecostal Testimony 1907*.
    [7.3] M. B. W. Etter, Sermon on Dancing.
    [7.4] Niels P. Thomsen, *A Broken Spirit the Key to Acceptable Worship*.
    [11.1] Arthur Sydney Booth-Clibborn, *Blood Against Blood*.
    [11.2] Minutes of the General Council of the Assemblies of God.
    [15.1] E. N. Bell, 'Women Elders'.
    [17.1] Statement of the Executive Presbytery of the General Council of the Assemblies of God, USA.
    (Used by permission.)
and The Gospel Publishing House, Springfield, USA, for [6.2] William H. Durham, *Pentecostal Testimony 1907*. (Used by permission.)

Augsburg Publishing, Minneapolis, USA, for:
  [8.3] L. Christenson, *The Church: An Ordered Body*.
  [8.7] L. Christenson, 'The Church: A Servant'.
  (Used by permission.)
Baker Book House, Grand Rapids, USA, for:
  [18.4] G. Otis Jr., 'Exorcism and Spiritual Warfare'.
  (Used by permission.)
Chris Bowater for [7.8] *Creative Worship: A Guide to Spirit-filled Worship*.
  (Used by permission.)
Central African Mission, (c/o Ivor Pepper, 355 Blackpool Road, Preston
  Lancs PR2 3AB, UK), for:
  [10.3] W. P. F. Burton, *A Luban Pentecost: Missionary Pioneering in Congo
    Forests*.
  [10.4] H. Womersley, *Wm F. P. Burton Pioneer*.
  (Used by permission.)
Chosen Books LLC, New York, USA, for [18.2] Don Basham, *Deliver Us
  From Evil*. (Used by permission.)
Mike Conway for [5.9] Peter Hocken, *The Glory and the Shame*.
CopyCare for [7.11b] John Wimber, 'Spirit Song' ©1979, Mercy/Vineyard
  Publishing. (Used by permission.)
Derek Prince Publications, Charlotte, USA, for [8.4] D. Prince, *Discipleship,
  Shepherding, Commitment*. (Used by permission.)
Eagle Publishing, Guildford, UK, for:
  [5.9] P. Hocken, *The Glory and the Shame*.
  [6.5] J. White, *Holiness: A Guide for Sinners*.
  (Used by permission.)
Elim Publishing House, London, UK, for [4.4] G. Jeffreys, *Healing Rays*.
  (Used by permission.)
Foursquare, Los Angeles, USA, for [3.4] Aimee Semple McPherson, *Pre-
  Millennial Signal Towers: Sermon delivered at the Angelus Temple 24 Aug
  1924*. (Used by permission.)
Michael Harper for [13.2] *Beauty or Ashes? The Ashe Lecture 1979*. (Used by
  permission.)
Harvard University Press, Boston MA, USA, for [6.3] G. Wacker, *Heaven
  Below: Early Pentecostals and American Culture*. (Used by permission.)
Hodder & Stoughton, UK, and Harper Collins, USA, for [9.6] D. Watson, *I
  Believe in Evangelism*. (Permission sought.)
Lois Hodges for [10.5] *A Theology of the Church and Its Mission: The Holy
  Spirit and the Church*. (Used by permission.)
International Pentecostal Holiness Church for [9.8] Vinson Synan, 'The
  Yoido Full Gospel Church'. (Permission granted by Society for
  Pentecostal Studies.)
Jesus Fellowship/New Creation Christian Community, Nether Heyford,

UK, for [21.1] Noel Stanton, http://www.jesus.org.uk/nccc/articles_-christiancommunity.shtml (used by permission.)

Kenneth Copeland Ministries Publications, Fort Worth, USA, for [14.1] Kenneth Copeland, *Dear Partner*. (Used by permission.)

Kingsway Publications, Eastbourne, UK, for:

[5.6] Dennis and Rita Bennett, *The Holy Spirit and You*.

[7.7] Joel Edwards, *Let's Praise Him Again*.

[7.9] Graham Kendrick, *Worship*.

[9.3] Reinhard Bonnke, *Evangelism by Fire*.

(Used by permission.)

Charles Kraft for [10.6] *What Kind of Encounters do We Need in Our Christian Witness?* (Used by permission.)

Robert Liardon Ministries Laguna Hills, USA, for [4.2] sermon excerpt by Smith Wigglesworth in R. Liardon, *Smith Wigglesworth: The Complete Collection of His Life Teachings*. (Used by permission.)

T. L. Osborn for [4.7] *Faith and Our Five Senses: Healing the Sick*. (Used by permission.)

Paternoster Press, Carlisle, UK, for:

[5.5] David Petts, *Baptism in the Holy Spirit: The Theological Distinctive*.

[9.2] Margaret Poloma, *A Reconfiguration of Pentecostalism*.

(Used by permission.)

The Presbyterian Church USA for [5.7] K. McDonnell, Report of the Presbyterian Church USA, 1971. (Used by permission.)

Regal Books for

[7.1] Jack Hayford, *Worship His Majesty*.

Wesley Richards for

[9.4] *Pentecost is Dynamite*. (Used by permission.)

SPCK, London, UK, for

[18.5] Andrew Walker, 'The Devil You Think You Know'. (Used by permission.)

Kevin Springer for:

[4.1] J. Wimber with K. Springer, *Power Healing*. (Permission sought.)

[9.7] J. Wimber with K. Springer, *Power Evangelism*. (Permission sought.)

Strang Communications, Lake Mary, USA, for:

[5.11] and [8.6] Mike Bickle with Michael Sullivant, *Growing in the Prophetic*.

[19.1] John Arnott, *The Father's Blessing*.

(Used by permission.)

Thomas Nelson Publishers, Nashville, USA, for:

[4.9] O. Roberts, *Expect a Miracle: My Life and Ministry. Oral Roberts an Autobiography*. (Used by permission.)

Colin Urquhart for [6.6] *Holy Fire*. (Used by permission.)

Zondervan, Grand Rapids, USA, for [3.6] J. Rodman Williams, *Renewal Theology: The Millennium.* (Used by permission.)

For the following excerpts, permission is under application:

[4.8] Kathleen Kuhlman, *I Believe in* Miracles.

[3.7] David Wilkerson, *The* Vision.

[9.8] Yoido Website, *Yoido Full Gospel* Church.

[16.1] David Wilkerson, *The Cross and the Switchblade.*

[18.1] David Du Plessis, *Simple and Profound.* (Permission sought but unobtainable from Paraclete Press or author.)

[18.3] Terry Law, *Principles of Praise.*

Excerpts 1.1, 2.1, 2.2, 2.3, 2.4, 2.5, 2.6, 3.2, 4.5, 5.2, 6.1, 7.1, 7.3, 7.4, 8.1, 8.2, 8.5, 9.5, 10.2, 11.1, 11.2, 13.1, 15.1, 15.2, 17.1 are out of copyright or were freely given by AOG Britain and America, and The Flower Pentecostal Heritage Centre, which are acknowledged in general with appreciation for their help.

Information

Research centres

The Flower Pentecostal Heritage Center, 1445 North Boonville Avenue, Springfield, Missouri 65802, USA
(417) 862-1447 ext 4400
http://agheritage.org/index.cfm

International Pentecostal Holiness Church Archives and Research Center, PO Box 12609, Oklahoma City, OK 73157, USA
http://www.pctii.org/

The Donald Gee Centre for Pentecostal and Charismatic Research, Mattersey Hall, Mattersey, Notts. DN10 5HD, UK
+44(0)1777 817663
office@matterseyhall.co.uk

Associations

Society for Pentecostal Studies, PO 3802, Cleveland, Tennessee, USA
http://sps-usa.org/

European Pentecostal Theological Association, Regents Theological College, London Road, Nantwich, Cheshire CW5 6LW, UK
+44(0)1270 615405

Index of Subjects and Names